A HISTORY OF
VENETIAN ARCHTECTURE

The history of Venetian architecture is
no less remarkable than the history of that
city itself, and Ennio Concina's compre-
hensive survey draws on extensive original
research on the city's cultural history
to offer fresh insights and an energetic
approach to the architecture. Beginning
with the traces of classical activity found
in the territory which was to become ducal
Venice, through its establishment as an
urba magna in the Byzantine age, and the
architectural glories of the Renaissance
and Baroque city, Concina discusses the
influence of Venice's extraordinary position
in history and geography on the architectural styles to be found there. Concina
overturns many long established theories
on the development of the lagoon city, and
discusses the work of many of history's
most famous architects – Sansovino,
Sanmicheli, Palladio, Longhena – and he
brings the story of the city up to date, with
his examination of the twentieth century's
attemptto expand the economy, and
preserve the city's heritage: to ensure
an 'untouched gem of ancient art, set in
the vibrant steel of modernity'.

ENNIO CONCINA

A HISTORY OF
VENETIAN
ARCHITECTURE

TRANSLATED BY JUDITH LANDRY

CAMBRIDGE
UNIVERSITY PRESS

PUBLISHED BY THE PRESS SYNDICATE OF THE UNIVERSITY OF CAMBRIDGE
The Pitt Building, Trumpington Street, Cambridge CB2 1RP, United Kingdom

CAMBRIDGE UNIVERSITY PRESS
The Edinburgh Building, Cambridge CB2 2RU, United Kingdom
40 West 20th Street, New York, NY 10011–4211, USA
10 Stamford Road, Oakleigh, Melbourne 3166, Australia

Originally Published in Italian as *Storia dell' architettura di Venezia*, by Electa, Milan, 1995 and © Electa 1995

English edition © Cambridge University Press 1998

First published in English by Cambridge University Press 1998 as
A history of Venetian architecture

Printed in Italy by Elemond Spa. Martellago (VE)

Typeset in Berthold Walbaum 8.5/13pt, in QuarkXPress™ [GC]

A catalogue record for this book is available from the British Library

ISBN 0 521 57338 6 hardback

Contents

NEPTUNE'S WALLS: THE MYTHS OF THE ORIGINS

ORIGO CIVITATUM ITALIAE SEU VENETIARUM

Antiquorum ystorias scire desider-
ans ipsarum principium oportet
conoscere

*Should you desire to know the affairs
of the ancients, it is well to know their
beginnings*

Toti isti antiquiores Veneti ... fecerunt
ecclesias pulchras et palati multa

*All these earliest Venetians ... built
beautiful churches and many palaces*

THE Venice of Renaissance myth deliberately built up an image of herself as a
miracolosissima city, born as though from
nothing – an independent shard of history,
coiled in self-defence – at the time of the
waning of the ancient world: the 'ark of
the seed' of the civilization of Republican
Rome.

Venice, it was claimed, was born as a
fully-formed and perfect fabrication, whose
true nature was in fact disclosed by history
rather than revealed by visual scrutiny,
however searching.

As her jurists wrote during the Renaissance, Venice was free and independent,
answerable to no superior authority:
she had her own law, determined by the
uniqueness of her origins. Venice was unlike
any other city – even Rome, the *sulcus prim-
igenius* of whose foundation had been dug
out by the plough, with the upturned clod
on the innermost side becoming the symbol
of the future walls, and the gates themselves
having been positioned in relation to the
plough ('porta a portando aratrum', called
'porta', 'gate' from the 'portege' lifting, of the
plough, to interrupt the furrow-boundary of
the walled city). Alone of all her kind, the
city of Venice had not been generated by the
earth, nor had she risen upon it.

Yet despite the visual evidence, and
various lightly made assertions, she was not
an island-city either, nor an archipelago-
city. We find categorical statements to the
effect that 'Venetiarum civitas non est insula',
Venice is not an island, because houses
built in the sea cannot correctly be defined
as islands; and Venice had been founded *in
alveo maris*, rising directly from the depths
of the sea, destined to remain unique and
inimitable throughout the course of history.[1]

It is such elaborations of the myth of the
city and her political peculiarities, and their
distant medieval precedents, that lie at the
root of the various interpretations of her
form as an 'elsewhere'.

Liutprand of Cremona's image of a
Venice whose inhabitants neither ploughed
nor sowed, nor harvested, although they
reaped; Salimbene de Adam's image of a
race of idolaters who worshipped Neptune;
the medieval definition of a *miraculosissima
civitas*, reworked in the sixteenth century
by Francesco Sansovino in praise of 'an
impossibility ... outside the order of all
other cities'; and the reinterpretation of the
city as a microcosm – 'an image of the earth
... in the midst of the ocean sea', locked in an
immutable balance 'between two elements
suspended': directly or indirectly, all these
strands lay at the root of the matter of modern and contemporary myths, as well as of
most of the codes established for the reading
of the urban space and its configuration.[2]

In the opinion of a protagonist of the
architectural Renaissance such as Michele
Sanmicheli, the lagoon space could not fail
to appear as a 'new world', between sky
and water, to the eyes of anyone who was
not native to it: 'men born on *terra firma*,
who have never been in these lagoons',
arriving there by chance, found the place
unexpected and disturbing. 'They shook
like leaves.'[3] Probably unconsciously, he

was returning to an earlier image: 'Alter Venetia mundus', 'Venice is another world', Petrarch had written around 1350. However, the explanations and resonance of the myths have been countered, in more recent research into the sources and the terrain, by a very different reconstruction of the historical dynamics of the city's origins: this research has linked archaic Venice to the early signs of organization and structure of the nearby coastal strip; to the economic and political dynamics of the classical age in the upper Adriatic, and to the widespread and persistent traces of late-Roman activity apparent throughout the territory which was subsequently to become that of ducal Venice.[4]

Furthermore, the earliest historical memory of the origins of Venice, to be found in the group of texts collected under the title *Origo civitatum Italiae seu Venetiarum*, presents complex and elaborate processes of interpretation at the dawn of relations between city and architecture.[5]

These are manuscripts of the utmost importance, because they are contemporary with both the city's becoming an *urbs magna*, and with the age of the Contarini San Marco, which Venice used to build up the kernel of her own history and artistic culture.

In point of fact, Venetian traditions concerning her origins, collected between the eleventh and twelfth centuries, and preserved through various thirteenth-century manuscripts, do not lay emphasis upon a landscape of treacherous still waters and virgin cane-brakes, a haven for groups of conquered exiles, like the one usually conjured up by various sixteenth-century sources, including Domenico Tintoretto in the *Dream of St Mark* painted for the upper room of the Scuola Grande of the same name.

Surprisingly enough, the search for Venetic memory opens with a reference – though a medievalized one – to one of the greatest and most significant of classical myths, that of Orpheus. In Venetic texts, the figure with the power to charm the elements and raw forces of nature is also the originator of the urban idea, the first builder of cities and walled villages. The divine and sanctifying power of musical harmony, which is Orpheus' prerogative, causes stone to rise upon stone, brings about the building of his city, the first in history; and causes a previously brutish humanity to acquire the habit of living together. Orpheus builds himself an *oraculum* there, which is the first piece of public architecture. The hero gives it the name of *Neptunia Menia*. In this way the city of Neptune's Walls, where the urban principle is associated with a maritime element, stood at the dawn of civilization for the builders of Venice.

In fact – somewhat uncertainly, and in an evident attempt to rescue the various explanatory fragments from obscurity – the walls put up by Orpheus were the walls of mighty Troy, the earliest centre of the West's stock of poetic images, a place of origins for rulers and peoples, cities and states.

Ancient lineages descended from the *magna civitas*: not just the generally better-known ones of Aeneas and Antenor, but also the fruit of obscurer workings of Venetian memory, and more deeply-rooted in her narrative logic. The lists of the ancient Veneti go right back to the Trojan *civitas* with a mythical family from the age of the tribunes, the Villiareni Mastalici, whose riches came from the Orient; they link this family to their own origins, identifying them as 'rulers' of a city, Verona, which was great and remarkable in its every ornament; as builders of *mirabilia edificia* including the church, the *castellum* and the bridge of Ammiana, set amidst the lagoons; and as being present among the notables consulted for the building of the *magnissima* 'torre Auria' (Auria tower).

In this way – for the culture of the great Venetic benefactors of the eleventh and twelfth centuries at least – those who commissioned the ducal chapel of San Marco, S. Fosca, the rebuilding of the episcopal cathedral of Torcello and the church of Santi Maria e Donato on Murano – one single unbroken thread linked the ancient civilizations of the Mediterranean to the first glories of the Venetic era.

As elaborated by the authors of the *Origo*, the Venetian version of the birth of Aquileia, capital of the Augustan tenth region, the Roman *Venetia*, confirms the importance of the ideas both of descent, and of foreshadowing.

Antenor arrived in Italy and founded Aquileia in approximately the same way as Aeneas reached the shores of Latium and gave rise to Rome; and their two histories

Domenico Tintoretto, *St. Mark blessing the islands of the lagoon and their earliest inhabitants.* Venice, Scuola Grande di San Marco.

ran on roughly in parallel, even if they were clearly not unrelated. From the medieval Venetian viewpoint, Aquileia – the acknowledged mother of Venice – was the *civitas prima Italiae*, a direct and autonomous transposition of the oldest urban model: 'Meanwhile Antenor entered with seven galleys' – the number is implicitly sacred, echoing that of the seven hills of Rome – 'and there he founded the city called Aquilegia, which means "girt by the waters" '.[6] In other words Aquileia, built by those who had been born within Orpheus' Neptune's Walls, was girt (*ligata*) by the waters in accordance with another deliberate anticipatory analogy with Venice herself, the seed of whose destiny Aquileia already bore.

The narrative structure of the derivation of the urban model has close analogies with the genealogical structure of the catalogues of families – civil and ecclesiastical, from the age of the tribunes and the empire – and with that of the *conditores* (founders) of Venetic churches to which the chronicles of the *Origo* give so much space and evident interest. Indeed, this first phase of urban descent, thus understood, ultimately and inevitably became intertwined with the pious and imperial myths of the founding of Constantinople and the Christian empire, a fantastical account of which, with its clear points of contact with the narratives of the Byzantine *patria*, is also given space, significantly enough, in these same sources. It was Constantine, *sanctissimus imperator*, who, inspired by this same story, was to raise Aquileia to the rank of metropolis, a

left, above and *below*
Aquileia, road and remains of dwellings from the
Roman period.

right
Roman mosaic flooring, detail.

5

rank which Venice was to claim for herself, quite literally, as her hereditary right. The time of Aquileia's downfall coincided with the legitimate coming of age – recognized and celebrated by early medieval accounts – of this *secunda Venecia*, the territory and city of the waters.

Here the local myths concerning the dawn of the ducal city subdivide and ramify, breaking up and regrouping into narrow imaginary strands and traditions – those of *Methamaucum*, Torcello and Grado – themselves further fuelled by any number of political, devotional and social forces.

But one point is clear: namely, that the building of the city of Grado – the first 'capital' of the Venetic lagoons – was seen as consciously deriving from the model of the abandoned metropolis: 'We must build (it) from the foundations . . . and they built every building in the image of the magnificent city of Aquileia, first among all others.'[7] For Johannes Diaconus – a chronicler who wrote between the end of the tenth and the beginning of the eleventh century – the reorganization of the *egregia* new imperial coastal province, which he referred to as *nova Venetia*, was to be seen as an out-and-out *recreatio*, that is, a reproduction and living restatement of the models preexisting in the great late-antique urban centres of the region laid low by the barbarian thrust.[8] This was a time of considerable building activity along the coast, leading to the founding of *munitissima castra et civitates* at the very time when the early medieval West was experiencing a decline

in city-building, and the partial reruralization of its former centres. For the writer of the *Origo*, the towers, the *palacium* and all the other splendid buildings of old Aquileia were taken as prototypes to be adopted in the building of the new city. Furthermore, the texts do not discuss only the nobler structures; they also mention canalizations, drainage systems and the sewage network. Around the year 1000, in the Venetian mind, 'founding a city'[9] implied an ideal derivation from the older model, several times removed but identical in principle both in its splendour, and in its material structure and technical expertise. Reference to such a model, almost with the value of a metaphor, resurfaces surprisingly in a passage from this same collection of chronicles, where there is an obvious allusion to Alexandrian mechanics: the account of the fabled baptismal font at San Giovanni Battista on Torcello, with water flowing out from the bronze jaws of figures of wild animals by means of hidden piping, has close parallels with Heron's devices, with the 'Leontarion' of Hagia Sopliia described by Byzantine Sources, and with fountains and contrivances described by medieval Arabic sources.[10]

In short, medieval Venetian sources confirm the original deeply urban nature of Venetic culture, and the equally deep sense of continuity with the culture of the Antique: at its roots lay *translatio* and *recreatio*, a transferring and reformulation which were not born of the territory itself, structured and partly settled as it already was at the decline of the ancient world,

but which were superimposed upon it, to give it form.

Following an archaeology of memory, we see that the apparently fragmentary and incoherent sources nonetheless yield up a coherent line: if the history of Venice has always been an urban history, this is because it was understood as a history of the transfer of ideal archetypes and physical models. It was therefore characterized from the start by the language and techniques of a deliberate continuity, a perfect narrative *raison d'être* for the Venetic reference to the myth of Orpheus, to the legend of Troy and to the myths of Antenor and Constantine in connection with Aquileia *aquils ligata*.

Only now, then, do we find the real appearance of the myth of the *mirabilis habitacio*, free and impregnable, of the first self-celebration of the uniqueness of the settlement, 'amongst watery marshes', later to be extended and amended. This myth, furthermore, seems directed at fostering an awareness of the two components present at the formation of the Venetic duchy: on the one hand, it might be presented as a renewal and perpetuation of Aquileia, which had welcomed Antenor and his civilization; on the other, it seems to harbour the memory of an older, and parallel, agrarian *felicitas*, subsequently largelydisavowed.[11]

Furthermore, the account which medieval Venice gave of herself, of the birth of her society and first institutions, was not limited to the fable of the journey and arrival of the urban idea in the northern lagoons

of the Adriatic, to become the cradle of the
second, glorious *Venetia*. As well as deriving
the forms of the lagoon cities from those of
the ancient metropolises, it also made reference, for symbolic purposes, to the memory
of three works of architecture of the earliest
times, dating from an age of turmoil, but
also of magnificence.

The first of these three was the work
of a patriarch of Grado, but founded on the
remains, and using the spoils, of an ancient
temple; the second was the work of one of
the great tribunes who had ruled the earliest Venetic society; the third was the work
of a patrician commander of the imperial
armies of Constantinople.

Thus we have a significant break-down
into components of those responsible for
the earliest buildings, pointing in all probability to indissoluble links with Roman
greatness – late-antique and Byzantine –
and confirming them by identifying the
paradigmatic stages of the cultural
translatio towards maritime Venice.

The first work of architecture considered
by the *Origo Civitatum* is a church built not
far from Aquileia by Elias, the patriarch of
Grado, a historical figure who, as we shall
see, commissioned various important
buildings in the second half of the sixth
century. One of these, according to the
chronicle, was a church dedicated to St.
Julian, built on the site and using the materials of a pagan temple destroyed by the
barbarians, but nonetheless a *mira res
edificii*, that is, a work of architecture

wonderful for its use of rare and costly
marbles.[12] The second architectural *exemplum* was the basilica of S. Maria on Torcello,
believed to be the work of the tribune Aurio:
the text describes it as 'gloriosissima', 'preciosa' and 'excelsa', with its polychrome
flooring, with a large and 'very beautifully
made' wheel-shaped motif in the centre.[13]

Johannes Diaconus, for his part, did not
limit himself to restating the excellence of
the *condecoratio variis marmoribus* of the
basilica at Torcello, of its columns and *tabulae*, the slabs of Grado stone; he also noted
a further enrichment of forms and materials
completely consistent with those which had
gone before, correctly dating them from his
own time, that of Pietro II Orseolo (991–1009):
this latter decoration – no longer only in
marble, but also, to his wonderment, in gold
– now covered the spaces of the new ducal
chapel; it did not clash with the earlier
work, but complemented it.

The overall interpretation poses no
problem. In the earliest historical memory
which Venice elaborated for herself, her
artistic roots in Aquileia and in the late-
antique and early Christian eras were
listed, and became intertwined. The art
of creating buildings and decoration of
the highest dignity, and emblematic of
continuity, was her very birthright. In
short, together with the urban idea and
model, archaic Venice laid claim to every
dedalicum instrumentum, that is, the very
means of art, using an image – itself of
venerable descent – belonging specifically to
the lexicon and culture of Venice between

the tenth and eleventh centuries.[14]

The archaic sources thus saw polychrome decoration and precious marble as constituting one of the main signs, in Venice's own tradition of continuity with the Antique. Moreover, the systematic and detailed mention, in these same Venetic chronicles, of the marbles used for the eastern imperial tombs in the church of the Holy Apostles in Constantinople, linked this elaborate use of coloured stone – the porphyries and marbles of Thessaly and the Proconnesus, the stones known as *iritione*, *litinio* and *ieraptide* – with the courtly splendours of Byzantium, itself the holder of the *imperii transmissio*, as stated in these same sources.[15]

In this way, the meaning and aesthetic value of this marble and mosaic facing, of the flooring in *opus sectile* and *tessellatum*, but more particularly the use of the remains of ancient buildings now in ruins – by no means purely for reasons of economy – were now sanctioned and made manifest.

The authors of these narratives were also perfectly aware of the importance of light. The architecture of S. Maria on Torcello, dating from the age of the tribunes, was 'gloriosissima' above all for its *prelucida claritas*, its dazzling, and admirable, lightness.[16]

Interest in the structure of the first great Venetic basilicas and contemporary civil buildings was actually thrust into the background by fascination with their effulgent luminosity. This light was not purely physical: it was a sign of splendour and nobility in itself. It was striven for by the architects of the early Christian tradition partly for its mystical and symbolic connotations, linked to the Old and New Testaments: in the book of Tobit, *claritas* is the splendour of Jerusalem.

Claritas was also the glory of God which lit up the city of the righteous, the New Jerusalem of the Apocalypse.

Here there is a close and far from random affinity between the Venetian and Ravennan sources. In the chronicle of Andrea Agnello (ninth century), the light in the chapel of S. Andrea is described as being born free, or reigning freely, in its architecture; it is a light which has escaped from Olympus – another classical reminiscence – produced by the purple reflections of the chapel's marble facing. The marble decoration of Sant'Apollinare, too, gleams by night as well as by day. These are expressions, and interpretations, which in their turn look back to the older texts of the *De Aedificiis* by Procopius, to his celebration of the architecture of Justinian, as part of an imperial universalistic programme, and to the enthusiastic description of Haghia Sophia by Paul the Silentiary.[17]

These, then, would seem to be the archetypes, the aesthetic conceptions accompanying the development of the art and architecture of the Venetian Middle Ages (indeed, in many ways the Venetic disavowal of the 'medieval'): *varietas colorum* and radiant *claritas* emerge as the preeminent rules for beauty and magnificence in works of architecture and, at the same time, witnesses to and symbols of continuity with the artistic culture of the waning classical world.

But at the same time, alongside the late-antique tradition of Aquileia, what might be defined as the more markedly philo-Byzantine strand of the early Venetian imagination also took into consideration a third early work of architecture, predating the first ducal chapel of San Marco and linked to imperial memories.

Yet another powerful and significant myth was interwoven with those already mentioned. This was the myth of Narses, a patrician and general from Constantinople, the promoter of the architecture which was regarded as first having characterized the place of power in the emergent city; the myth, in other words, of a Venice of the age of Justinian.[18] This Byzantine figure, who had fought in the ferocious campaigns against the Goths, had founded two churches in Venice: S. Teodoro, near which San Marco was subsequently to be built, and SS Geminiano e Mena, in front of it. In this way, according to sources going back at least to the year 1000, what was to become the space of piazza San Marco was already marked by the presence of architecture linked to the memory of Byzantium the golden. Narses actually lived in S. Teodoro, so it was claimed. Beside it, the sources added, stood the palace of the Venetic duke; they also described the splendid ceremonial put on for the arrival, from Ravenna, of the patrician and prefect Longinus. In short, claims were made for an extremely early nexus between the buildings of San

Marco and public ceremonies. It was also claimed that the nearby church of S. Moisè had been built by the Greek Chrystophoros, a relative both of Narses and of Longinus.

The texts say nothing more about the church of Sti Geminiano e Mena. S. Teodoro is described and celebrated for its sumptuous columns and ornamental marbles, but above all for its dome, the elaborately shaped *cuba depicta* with its crowning commemorative inscription.

By incorporating into its origins an architectural *exemplum* which somehow derived from Byzantine greatness, Venetian architecture was expressing its inclination to share Byzantium's interest in domed organisms and the symbolism connected to them.

Looked at more closely, these inclinations were highly significant: they implied a desire to proclaim that Venice's continuity with late Antiquity was nourished by her relation with the *urbs*, Constantinople, the only true capital of the medieval world, Constantinople with its 'thousand churches and thousand monasteries – all with four or five domes . . . (and) its two-storey houses with atriums in marble and gold', as an anonymous Byzantine lament was to remind Venice in an imaginary dialogue written as its history drew to a tragic close.[19]

In view of the extent of the art-historical literature on Venice, the main bibliographical references to the relevant subjects will not be mentioned in the notes to the various chapters; we refer the reader to the brief bibliography at the end of the volume, organized in order of subject.

The notes are therefore limited to the mention of sources, whether published or archival, which flesh out the bibliographical apparatus where necessary and, in some cases, provide historiographical bases for the claims and hypotheses formulated or recapitulated in the text.

1 M. A. Peregrino, *De privilegiis et iuribus fisci. Libri octo*, Vicenza 1626, pp. 358, 366.

2 Liutprandi, *Relatio de legatione Constantinopolitana*, in M.G.H., S.S., Hanover and Leipzig, 1909–1913, III, p. 359; Salimbene de Adam, *Chronica*, in M.G.H., S.S., *op. cit.*, XXXII, p. 565; F. Sansovino, *Delle cose notabili che sono in Venetia*, Venice 1565, *passim*; M. A. Sabellico, *Del sito di Venezia Città (1502)*, ed. G. Meneghetti, Venice 1985, *passim*.

3 22.2.1543, in A. Bertoldi, *Michele Sanmicheli al servizio della Repubblica Veneta*, Verona 1874, pp. 27–32.

4 Here we are referring in particular to the important works by W. Dorigo cited in the brief bibliography at the end of this volume.

5 *Origo Civitatum Italiae Seu Venetiarum. (Chronicon Altinate et Chronicon Gradense)*, ed. R. Cessi, Rome 1933.

6 'Anthenor autem in litore lacum intravit cum septem galeis, ibique civitatem Aquilegia nomine, idest aquis ligata, edificavit', *Origo Civitatum, op. cit.*, p. 7.

7 'A fundamentis . . . edificare debemus . . . et ita fecerunt et construxerunt pulcherrimam et preclaram civitatem usque ad culmen mellorum et a circuitu fecerunt turres. De intus autem edificaverunt pulcherrimum palacium, ut in omni parte meatos habens ad rigandum ab omni emundatione ediusdem palacii. Ab intus autem in omnique parte eiusdem civitatis cloacas fecerunt. Simile autem a parvitate de illa magnifica et precipua Aquilegia civitate ad eius similitudinem omneque edificium edificaverunt', *Origo Civitatum, op. cit.*, p. 161.

8 *La cronaca veneziana del diacono Giovanni*, in *Cronache veneziane antichissime*, I, ed. G. Monticolo, Rome 1890.

9 This phrase, dating from the sixteenth century, is taken from G. G. Leonardi, 'Il libro delle fortificazioni dei nostri tempi', ed. T. Scalesse, in *Quaderni dell'istituto di Storia dell'Architettura* (University of Rome), 1975.

10 *Origo Civitatum, op. cit.*, pp. 34, 63. See for example Al-Jazari, *The Book of Knowledge of Ingenious Mechanical Devices*, ed. D. Hill, Dordrecht and Boston 1979, and the animal-fountains in M. J. Rubiera y Mata, *L'immaginario e l'architettura della letteratura araba medievale*, ed. E. Concina, Genoa 1990, pp. 62–7.

11 *Origo Civitatum, op. cit.*, pp. 60–1.

12 *Ibid.*, p. 78.

13 *Ibid.*, pp. 31, 57.

14 *La cronaca veneziana, op. cit.*, p. 105.

15 *Origo Civitatum, op. cit.*, pp. 19–23.

16 *Ibid.*, p. 57.

17 *Il libro de Agnello Istorico*, ed. M. Pierpaoli, Ravenna 1988; Procopius, *De aedificiis*, in *Procopii Caesariensis opera*, III/2, Leipzig 1913; *Johannes von Gaza und Paulus Silentiarius*, ed. P. Friedlander, Leipzig and Berlin 1912.

18 *Origo Civitatum, op. cit.*, pp. 66–9, 71–3, 79–80, 132.

19 *La caduta di Costantinopoli. L'eco nel mondo*, ed. A Pertusi, Verona 1990, 2nd edn, p. 381.

BYZANTINE, DUCAL AND COMMUNAL VENICE

IN fact, from many points of view, the history of the origins of Venice is the history of one long formative process, of the organization of a territorial system and its settlements. After having been that of an imperial Roman region, the city's future name – as the annotators of its thirteenth-century statutes pointed out – was now applied to a small coastal region, a short strip of the northern Adriatic shoreline between Grado and Cavarzere, scrupulously defined at the beginning of the eighth century by a treaty drawn up between the military authorities of the Byzantine province and the Lombard Liutprand, and subsequently acknowledged by his successor Aistulf. In fact, the gradual concentrating of the original ducal territory which made Rialto – *corpus Veneciarum* – its capital city, indeed *Venecia*, the present-day Venice, was concluded only in the late thirteenth century.

In the early medieval coastal *Venetia*, forms and models of settlements deriving directly from late Antiquity were undoubtedly found alongside examples of urban innovation, giving rise to and reinforcing a specific architectural culture.

By the sixth century, the unity of the *Regio Decima*, Roman Venetia and Istria, was definitively shattered. For the new Venetia, the transfer of the episcopal see of Aquileia ushered in a new period of history.

Paul, the patriarch of Aquileia, left the old regional capital in 568 for Grado, a port-of-call on the lagoon.

While the new Lombard patriarchate of Aquileia was to be established on Friulian territory, the original patriarchal throne, which claimed traditional legitimacy for itself alone, thus found itself settled in a basically urban habitat marked by the influence of Rome, and situated at the eastern extremity of *Venetia maritima*.

During the fifth century the pre-existing centre had been extensively reorganized for defensive purposes. Enclosed by a rectangular circle of walls – which probably had a crucial effect on the alignment of the main buildings within the city, as the lie of the south-west side of the cathedral would imply – the *castrum* of Grado was transformed into one of the chief fortified junctions of the Byzantine north-Adriatic coastal region. Apart from recognizable stretches of the circle of walls, much of the tower of the Campiello still stands in partly legible form: polygonal in plan, it was one of the two towers which flanked the city gates, giving access to the fortified zone. Immediately after the death of Justinian, during the reign of Justin II (565–78), when this urban centre took on the explicit role of *Nova Aquileia*, as the religious centre of the Venetic province and adjacent Adriatic territories, it was to be the object of important alterations which, though partly respecting pre-existing religious buildings, nonetheless played a crucial role in creating the new architectural culture of coastal *Venetia*. These undertakings – the rebuilding of S. Eufemia and S. Maria – were probably part of a unitary programme promoted and implemented by Elias, a former Greek monk and subsequently patriarch, between 571 and

topped by relieving arches with deep lunettes, is articulated by pilaster strips, its upper section lightened by a three-light window and, above, by two semi-sunbursts of a kind known in the decorative repertoire of both Grado and Ravenna; the bare brickwork is thus treated with an evident concern for colouristic effect. At some point, this same concern was extended into the interior, and is visible both in the mosaic flooring and the traces of stuccoes still visible in the splayed window in the apse; but it is far more evident in the nearby patriarchal cathedral of S. Eufemia, the artistic heart of the oldest *Venetia maritima*. The ceremony of its consecration, on 3 November 579, occurred during the synod which declared Grado a *Nova Aquileia* and seat of the Metropolitan of Venetia and Istria, with an accompanying affirmation of continuity and renewal reminiscent of the narratives collected in the chronicles of the *Origo venetiarum*. Equally significantly, the *Chronicon* linked the bishop's declaration to the beginnings of ducal authority: the Veneto-Byzantine duke himself apparently went to Rome to seek its sanctioning.[1]

In this context, the basilica dedicated to the martyr and patron saint of the Council of Chalcedon represented an architectural act of open celebration, which associated the patriarch Elias, and his proud epigraphic self-description as *fundator*, with a named throng of patrons and donors. These included various *viri clarissimi*, imperial dignitaries one of whom is described as a palace official, together with lectors, notaries,

586, of the holy Church of Aquileia, as he tellingly signs himself. Not long before, the basilica at piazza della Vittoria, possibly the church of S. Giovanni Evangelista built by bishop Macedonio between 539 and 557, had also been rebuilt.

The rebuilding of the church of S. Maria reintroduced some of the features already documented in the architecture of Grado during the previous century, for instance in the first basilica on piazza della Vittoria. Both have a rectangular perimeter with an inscribed apse, and a *synthronon* and bishop's throne, flanked by pastophories, on a model which has similarities with the early Christian architecture of Syria, the Aegean and Anatolia. The baptistry of the basilica

on piazza della Vittoria, too, derived from the earlier local tradition: octagonal in plan with an east-facing apsidiole, it echoed the ground plan of the larger baptistry of S. Eufemia, still standing to the north side of the cathedral and generally dated from the second half of the fifth century.

While the structures of the basilica on piazza della Vittoria are known to us through archaeological excavations carried out some time ago, S. Maria delle Grazie still exists; together with the baptistry and S. Eufemia, it undoubtedly constitutes an important architectural complex from the Venetic period.

The facade, with its three architraved portals giving on to the nave and aisles,

above
Facade.

left
Grado, S. Maria delle Grazie, interior looking towards the 'pergula' and apse.

primicerions, deacons, soldiers and towns-people, members of an urban society of considerable social and cultural complexity.

Like the slightly earlier basilica of S. Euphrasia at Poreč in Istria, Elias' cathedral was actually an architectural complex: it was originally preceded by a four-sided portico with three arches on the facade, flanked to the south by a *diaconicon* and a rectangular hall, and to the north by a baptistry – all older – with the further addition of a *prothesis* extending into a triconch space probably built to house sacred relics.

Continuity with Aquileia is still clearly visible in the extensive mosaic flooring – despite a thorough-going restoration and 'completion' between 1939 and 1952 – and the arches of the double row of columns which divide the interior into a nave and two aisles. It is also evident in the clearly deliberate and symbolic *translatio* of reused polychrome marbles originally from Aquileia or the surrounding country-side – as attributed by the early Venetic chronicles to the mythicized figure of the patriarch Elias himself; in the columns in Greek marble, black marble flecked with white from Chios, cipolin, and granite; and in the capitals, which are almost all Roman (only seven date from the time of Elias).

Contrary to Ravennan practice, Elias made no use of wall mosaics in his church, nor do the arches stand on pulvins. However, those of the Corinthian capitals not taken from local ruins are reminiscent of the art of Ravenna; more particularly, the large apse with the patriarch's throne in its centre is Ravennan in type, semi-circular internally and polygonal externally. This solution is also found at an earlier date in the *castrum* of Grado (it had been used for the fifth-century restructuring of the very modest *basilicula* which had preceded S. Eufemia) but Elias' cathedral gave it unprecedented importance.

As Richard Krautheimer has noted, there is a marked contrast, in S. Eufemia, between the rough and ready execution of the structures, and the studied elegance of the decoration. In point of fact, in the dedicatory inscription Elias himself set out his rules for the building of *atria*, as Ovid had defined the abodes of the divine: namely, a *varius decor*, where *varietas* did not mean just variety of ornament, but also gradations of colour, those of the *pictum marmor*, contrasting with the rough bareness of the ground they cover and conceal, and which are suddenly revealed, in all their symbolism, to anyone crossing the threshold of the cathedral, beyond the grudging masonry shell on the outside.

Such a space needed light, and the architectural structure was adapted to this need: the apse is lit by three windows, three more open up in the facade – much larger than the three-light one in S. Maria – while others pierce the side walls, still with their original round-headed brick arches.

The sense of colour, rhythm and space of Elias' cathedral therefore reflects the aesthetic codes mentioned in the earliest Venetic texts; it was here that the main features of Venetian art and architecture had their roots.

Grado also transmitted the Aquileian tradition of the mosaic floor, and certain aspects of the arrangement of the liturgical space, to the architecture of the early medieval Venetic centres, including Rivoalto, the future Venice. The *pergula* of S. Maria, for example, was to be the model for several churches under Grado's jurisdiction.[2] But the Grado tradition was reflected above all in a local group of small basilicas with a nave and two aisles and inscribed apses: from S. Mauro at Jesolo, extremely similar to the old cathedral of S. Maria Assunta in its earliest version, to S. Leonardo at Fossa Mala and S. Marco on Torcello.[3] This influence is readily understandable in the light of Grado's metropolitan authority over the bishoprics of Caorle, *Equilium*, Heraclea, Olivolo, *Methamaucum* and Torcello. But closer and more specific relations were very soon established with the emergent city of Venice. The patriarch of Grado, who in the ninth century seems to have had a palace in Venice near S. Zulian, not far from San Marco, certainly exercised authority over the church of S. Silvestro di Rialto from the tenth century, and had a residence and *fondaco* (foreign merchants' warehouses) nearby. He also had direct authority over a group of Venetian parishes and monasteries. Furthermore, in 887 the atrium of S. Eufemia was to house the tomb of doge Pietro I Candiano; and between 993 and 995 Pietro II Orseolo promoted a general overhaul of the old Grado, with the restoration and partial rebuilding of the circle of walls and religious buildings, and the founding of a *palatium* near the tower. These events were registered by the chronicles, which further clarify the means and forms of a knowledge of early Christian Grado in the Venetian Middle Ages.[4] Moreover, the patriarchate of Grado, and its claims of continuity with Aquileia, were to merge, on 8 October 1451, in the episcopal see of Venice.

During the decades immediately after the reign of Justinian, the province of Venetia might therefore be seen as the northern margin of a cultural area extending from the Adriatic regions to the Mediterranean Levant and the Near East. Within it, the orientalisms of Grado, Aquileian in origin, are certainly to be linked with the influence of Alexandria, that is, with the eastern ties of the church of Aquileia, predating the formation of the legend of St. Mark. But the reminiscences of Ravenna undoubtedly present in the architectural vocabulary of the sixth century, however obvious and well-established, did not reflect any direct dependence upon that city, or any lack of autonomous expression. Real Byzantinisms were strictly limited. In architecture, the clearest mutual ties were therefore those found interwoven throughout the whole area of the northern Adriatic centres, from the territory of the Exarchate to Poreč and Salona.

The urban panorama of *Venetia maritima* was reinvigorated in the seventh century by the founding of another city, by the creation of a further group of episcopal sees – including that of Torcello – and, at its end, by the

'Spicatum' paving in the sandbanks near Tessera.

G. Casoni, ground plan of the 'small baptismal
church' near S. Pietro di Castello in Venice, 1810.
Venice, museo Correr.

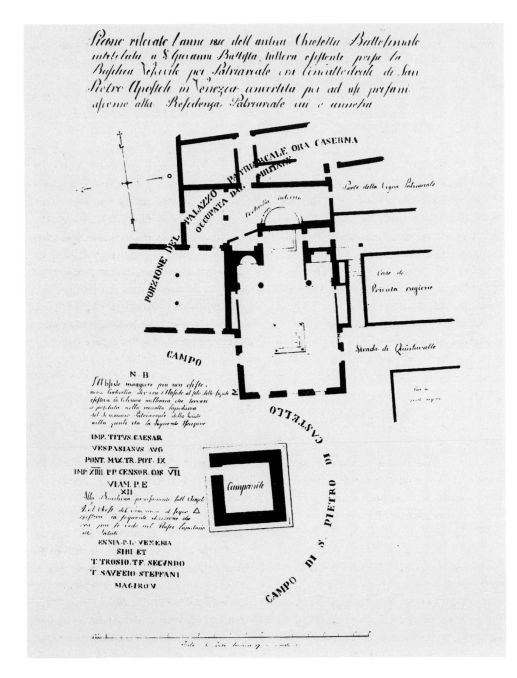

birth of the ducal authority, destined to endure for over ten centuries.

As a consequence of powerful Lombard pressure along the borders of the Adriatic province, and the fall of the fortress of *Opitergium*, a new city now arose at the mouth of the eastern-most branch of the Piave delta, not far from the via Annia and within what had been the *agrum centuriatum* of Altino: *magnopere constructa*, grandiosely built, as one of the oldest sources puts it, this was Cittanova, also known as *Heraclia* or *Civitas Heracliana*, which Constantine Porphyrogenitus was to know as *Neokastron*. The information given by the chronicles is meagre but significant: Cittanova was a fortified harbour settlement, the seat of a *magister militum* built in the context of a rigorous military reorganization of the territory subject to the exarchate of Ravenna, an episcopal see which now absorbed that of *Opitergium. Heraclia* was already de-populated by the Middle Ages, but its ruins, and the remains of its mosaics, were still visible in the fifteenth and sixteenth centuries. Little or nothing, however, remained of its architecture. The remnants of its cathedral, dedicated to St. Peter and rediscovered by chance, are damaged beyond recognition, as are those of a baptistry on a circular plan with a square piscina and an apsidiole, of which we have an extremely sketchy survey and a few photographic images; we shall therefore have to await the results of further research before we can ascertain their role in the Venetic culture of the early Middle Ages.

However, there is no doubting the meaning of the augural dedication to the emperor Heraclius (610–41), seen in connection with other traces of actions performed during his lifetime and under his authority. The eponymous emperor of the new *civitas* of *Venetia maritima* reappears as the donor, to the church of Grado, of the marble throne of Mark the evangelist (subsequently placed in the church of San Marco in Venice), a relic that legitimized Grado's descent from Aquileia. Furthermore, the medieval Venetian tradition, perpetuated in the Renaissance by the patrician Stefano Magno, was to be elaborated upon in a most significant fashion in this connection: St. Mark's throne from Alexandria was to be considered as a sign of imperial gratitude, sent to the patriarch of the Adriatic province in thanks for the part Venice played in Heraclius' defeat of Chosroes and in his glorious reconquest of Jerusalem.[5]

Also in the name of Heraclius, the building of the basilica of S. Maria *Dei Genitrix* on Torcello was begun in 639, on the lands ruled over by Maurice – *magister militum* and governor of the province – in memory of the credit due to this latter and to his army, by order of the exarch Isaac, whose sarcophagus is still to be seen in S. Vitale in Ravenna. The coastal Venetia of the seventh century was therefore the subject of intense building activity linked to imperial authority; its ties with the eastern empire became closer and more vital at the very time when Heraclius was bringing about crucial changes in the structure, society and culture of the empire, which was now ceasing to be Roman, and becoming truly Byzantine. It was at Venetic *Heraclia* – where finds such as the seal of the patrician Anastasius, with a Greek invocation to the *Theotokos*, confirm the influx of elements extraneous to the provincial social structure[6] – that the first duke – doge of the province was appointed, one Paulicius. All the main families who were to monopolize the ducal office from the mid-ninth century until the tenth – the Particiaci, the Candiani, the Orseoli – were also originally from *Heraclia*. It was the Heraclean families who moved to the territory of Rivoalto in the eighth century, identified by means of the typical medieval genealogical information, who were attributed by the sources with the role of the first great building patrons in Venetian history – 'they built many churches and fine palaces' – and who were associated with the founding of a large group of ecclesiastical buildings, including SS Sergio e Bacco at Olivolo and S. Giacomo di Rialto, the very heart of Venice.[7] Clearly, continuing the tradition of Aquileia and Grado, *Heraclia*, itself destined ultimately to merge with Venice and then disappear, was forging new and ever stronger Ravennan ties with distant Constantinople.

Here then, in the mid-seventh century, we find the origins of the long imperial thread which bound the history of Venice to that of the great capital of the East until, in the thirteenth century, she assumed ascendancy over the latter, and hence her role as *alterum Byzantium*. The better-known cases of Grado and *Heraclia* may serve to clarify others whose memory, at least for the present, is more confused and incomplete. They foreshadow and, in part, co-exist with a complex, segmented history of numerous settlements and building activities occurring in the same period throughout the province of Venetia. The military organization of the Byzantine-Lombard frontier entailed the building of defensive works in numerous other places. The ducal seat moved from *Heraclia* to *Methamaucum* for less than a century, directly affecting what was to become the urban space of Venice. Early historiographical tradition dates the origins of Rivoalto to the beginning of the fifth century, to the period of the Grado *castrum*. It provides information concerning a church dedicated to SS Sergio e Bacco (a cult peculiar to the Byzantine army) adjacent to the *castrum Helibolis*, the Castle of Olivolo whose memory is still present in the city's toponymy.

This tradition associates the earliest conformation of the area that was to become piazza San Marco with the memory of Narses and the sixth-century age of Justinian. Recent archaeological excavations basically confirm this general picture, together with an early dating for the settlement of Rivoalto, though not, of course, the chronological distortions, exaggerations or personal identifications proposed by the medieval political imagination. Surveys currently under way at Castello for example, at the extreme eastern end of the city, have led not only to the identification of certain partly datable artefacts – including a golden *tremissa* from the time of Heraclius and several Byzantine lead seals dating from the sixth and seventh centuries – but have also provided information concerning techniques for the reinforcement of the terrain which correspond perfectly to those referred to in Cassiodorus' famous letter to the tribunes.[8]

At all events, the last quarter of the eighth century and the beginning of the ninth were to be a crucial period for the development of the settlements of Olivolo and Rivoalto, with the institution, in 774-5, of the episcopal see of Olivolo at Castello (where it was to remain until 1807), at the orders of Maurice of Heraclia – *magister militum, consul et imperialis dux* – and the definitive transfer of the ducal seat to the area of Rivoalto, in 810.

The transfer of civil power and its assumption by the great dynasty of the Particiaci – also from Heraclia – was accompanied by intense building activity, which continued for several decades into the ninth century in the context of a clearly recognizable programme of urbanization. A family of tribunes with extensive and longstanding landed interests both inside and outside the province of Venetia, the Particiaci – possessors of the Byzantine dignity of *ypatoi* – seem to have had connections with Constantinople, since Justinian I Particiaco stayed there in 814 and Agnello II in 820, though they were also open to the stimuli coming from the Carolingian world.

Agnello I is acknowledged by the sources as the builder, on the probable site of a small Byzantine fortress controlling the waters in front of it, of the *palatium* mentioned as still standing in the eleventh century by Johannes Diaconus: this was the original nucleus of the Ducal palace, to which a chapel appears to have been annexed by the year 819. Also attributed with the building of the monastic complexes of S. Lorenzo and S. Severo, he therefore worked towards consolidating the neighbouring terrain, and that which lay in the direction of Olivolo; shortly afterwards, his son Justinian continued the process, endowing another large religious complex, the monastery of San Zaccaria, described by a later medieval forgery as having been funded and planned by Leo V the Armenian (813-20). Bearing in mind that the church of S. Teodoro – sketchily described by the sources and partly incorporated into the present-day San Marco – must already have been in existence, even if not for very long, together, in all probability, with the nearby S. Geminiano; and that the building of the first S. Zulian, by the father of Pietro the future patriarch of Grado, is also seen as dating from the time of Giovanni Particiaco, it is clear that by the first quarter of the ninth century the pivotal points of the area around San Marco were already in place. At the same time, the building of the basilica of S. Pietro di Castello, near the older, smaller church of Sti Sergio e Bacco, also provided a permanent home for the episcopal see of Olivolo; another monastic foundation, that of S. Ilario, the

burial place of the Particiaci, was now given political significance by the dukes of *Venetia maritima* as a statement of territorial sovereignty, directed at the neighbouring hinterland, which was now Carolingian. Occupying a key position in terms of agriculture and communications, the monastery soon embarked on various works of drainage and buttressing, together with the building of storerooms and hospices.[9]

Indeed, in the ninth century the ducal figure seems deliberately to have taken on the role of *fundator* (founder) and *fabricator* (maker), of *sanctarum ecclesiarum custos* (guardian of the holy church) as a renewer of a former greatness, and at the same time a faithful interpreter, within his own sphere, of one of the main functions of supreme imperial authority.[10]

Two further interlinked events that were to be decisive for the birth, identity, culture and architecture of the city now occurred within the context of this political activity: the translation of the body of St. Mark, accompanied by a positive national cult of the saint throughout the Venetic duchy, and the foundation of the first great ducal church.

In his will of 829, doge Justinian I laid the basis for the main Venetian church just one year after the remains of the evangelist had been snatched by the Venetians from Alexandria and brought to the lagoon. In this way, the emergent city was placed under the protection of the saint whom hagiographic tradition saw as the first evangelizer of the north-eastern region of Roman imperial Italy, with unambiguous

Large arch facing on to the piazzetta dei Leoncini in the north flank of the basilica of San Marco, probably originally part of the church of S. Teodoro.

political implications. In the eyes of the Christian Mediterranean, and of the West, the emergent centre of Rivoalto, the final resting-place of the body of the author of the second gospel, now had all the prestige of an apostolic shrine. The primacy of the maritime province and its church were hereby reaffirmed vis-à-vis the Carolingian hinterland; it now had a dignity all its own. Furthermore, these events occurred shortly after the synod of Mantua (827), which had actually reinstated the primacy of Aquileia over Grado; significantly, this was also the period of the rebuilding of the patriarchal basilica of Aquileia, carried out between 810 and 840 by Maxentius with staunch support from Charlemagne himself and intended to symbolize a *renovatio aquileiensis* proclaimed by the Frankish empire.

The political and religious implications of this undertaking must have been associated with the rise of ducal power and its seat, so recently redefined in the urban space of the developing city, following the Byzantine model of the close relationship between church and state, politics and religion, but also in connection with the Carolingian idea of the palatine chapel which had taken shape shortly beforehand at Aachen (796–805). Contrary to what might have been expected, on its arrival the body of St. Mark had not been taken either to the episcopal church of S. Pietro di Castello, nor to that of Grado, where Heraclius had sent the evangelist's throne and where, at least from the beginning of the ninth century, there was

a chapel dedicated to him, where the patriarch Giovanni had been buried (c. 802). The body of St. Mark was laid first in a votive chapel built 'at the corner of the . . . palace';[11] the Venetic *duces* thus made themselves the guardians of the sacred relics, combining their own authority with that of protectors of the apostolic site. The church envisaged by doge Giustiniano and built by his brother Giovanni (829–34) was therefore built as a *martyrium*, as the private property of the dukes and as a ducal chapel, documented as early as 982. The ninth-century building, which recent studies identify as partly surviving in the present-day crypt, seems deliberately to have been built on a Greek cross following a model derived, according to the sources, from the Holy Sepulchre in Jerusalem, that is, with a dome or *xilotroulos* at the crossing of the arms: it thus diverged from the basilican layout of the great episcopal churches of the lagoon, and was distinguished by a particular courtly sense of holiness. The plan certainly had links, on the one hand, with the northern Adriatic churches, though in a more monumental version, despite the fact that it must have been smaller than the one we know to-day; yet it also made use of an architectural symbol that was not only obvious and universal – that of the cross, 'fount of all blessing' – but also particularly suited to a place perpetuating the memory of one of the four first witnesses to its own meaning and triumph. Recent debate on the original San Marco has given rise to other more or less mutually exclusive interpretations:

from the one which regards the present crypt as that of the first church, contemporary with the one built during the ninth-century reconstruction of the basilica at Aquileia – a view which also tends to regard the plan of the old cathedral of Jesolo as deriving from the Particiaci basilica of San Marco – to positions which identify the remains of the original structure in other parts of the church, such as the chapels of S. Pietro and S. Clemente, and which lead to other hypotheses, for instance that the west atrium of the first ducal chapel was rebuilt as a large porticoed courtyard with fortified access.

This aside, the picture of ninth-century Venetic architecture is still unclear and hard to interpret. Work is still being carried out in connection with recent finds in the church of S. Lorenzo – on a basilican plan and also founded by the Particiaci – which may provide important clarifications in this context.[12] Here too, as in other more or less well documented cases, extensive use was made of reclaimed stone and brick (pedalis, sesquipedalis and 'altinelle' of half a Roman foot) and masonry techniques of the late-Roman period, a practice which long remained in use in Venetic architecture.

Little or nothing remains of the S. Zaccaria of the age of the Particiaci; but the low crypt with three small aisles still under the chapel of S. Tarasio, in the apse dating from the tenth century – semi-circular internally and pentagonal externally – is proof of some continuity with the architecture of the territory of the former Exarchate

of Ravenna, while its masonry structures, with their reuse of Roman brick, show continuity with the techniques of late Antiquity. The wave motif, formed of interlinked peltae, found in the small stretch of mosaic pavement discovered under the floor of this same chapel (now generally dated from the eleventh century) is highly reminiscent, as are other more or less contemporary examples, of the mosaic flooring of Grado cathedral, and more generally of early stylistic features found throughout the Adriatic region. Some of the ninth-century mosaic flooring of the original Benedictine church of S. Ilario was revealed by old excavations: here too the compositional schemes imply the influence of late Antiquity and the early Christian era, mainly local but also with near-eastern reminiscences, albeit weaker and less fluent than their models.

Such remains as we have of the sculpture which decorated the Venetic buildings of the eighth and ninth centuries extend and to some degree clarify this picture, even though many uncertainties persist. If what appear to be the earliest *plutei* are still clearly in the early Christian tradition, those datable from the tenth century combine the usual symbols with the type of ornament known as trelliswork, Carolingian in origin, evidence of the presence, within the duchy, of models and workforces from beyond its borders. Finally, in the late tenth century, we find signs of overt borrowings from the typically Byzantine repertoire.

The few capitals dating from the ninth and tenth centuries, too (*spolia* being

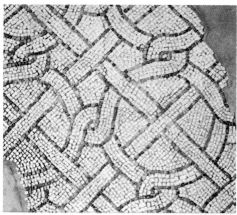

Fragments of mosaic flooring from the monastic church of S. Ilario, founded by the Particiaci, ninth century. Venice, museo Archeologico.

used for the most part, as was the custom throughout the Mediterranean during the early Middle Ages) reveal that the Venetic builders of the time of the Particiaci worked within the ambit of the Italic sculptural culture of Carolingian circles. In short, on the one hand it would seem clear that the works based on the early Christian tradition, and the use of salvaged material, expressed and fuelled early Venetic culture's sense of continuity with its origins, in architecture as elsewhere; and that, on the other, the adoption of certain features of the Italic version of the Carolingian *renovatio* might be interpreted as deriving from a sense of rivalry with Aquileia, possibly in relation to a parallel between the rebuilding of the patriarchal basilica and the building of the ducal basilica. Meanwhile, for the Rivoalto of the Particiaci, Byzantium was standing in the background, riven by the political, doctrinal and artistic crisis of iconoclasm, which ended shortly before the middle of the ninth century. At the end of the tenth century and during the first decades of the eleventh, the capitals once more confirm a return to a style more in line with tradition, with an awareness of what we might call the classical spirit of Ravenna. What seemed to be emerging, therefore, was a return to an Antiquity which had never been forgotten in the finest stone-cutters' workshops active on the territory of the earlier Exarchate; a return encouraged, in fact, by the Constantinople-inspired climate of the Macedonian Renaissance, the cultural backbone of the Middle Byzantine artistic

flowering, and which had parallels with aspects of the Ottonian Renaissance.

At the end of the tenth century, too, a sense of renewal was at work in the duchy, expressed both through the symbolic reinstatement of the earliest urban nexuses of *Venetia maritima*, and emblematic works of artistic redefinition in the *civitas* of Rivoalto itself (or Venice, as it was by now), together with a certain amount of reshuffling, by the chroniclers, of the historic memory of the Venetian duchy. Pietro II Orseolo – who had changed his own son Pietro's name in honour of the emperor of the West, Otto III, and had joined his other son Giovanni in marriage to a niece of Romanus II and Basil II, emperors of the East – now restored Grado, as we have said, building a *palatium* there; he built a second *palatium* and a completely new church in Heraclea, where his own family originally came from; he was also active on Torcello and in the Marcian complex in Venice. In talking of the *dedalico instrumento* (instruments of Daedalus) – that is, of the artistic means used for the building of the ducal chapel – Johannes Diaconus, Pietro's chaplain, clearly wished to point to the uniqueness conferred upon the work by recourse to an unaccustomed magnificence: the reign of his doge was characterized not merely by the use of precious marbles (which he commented upon at the relevant point in his chronicles), but also by that of the extraordinary, Byzantinizing use of ornament in gold.

Again through the testimony of Johannes Diaconus, it should be noted that the Venetic

courtly culture of the late tenth and early eleventh centuries now explicitly associated the figure of the doge with the idea of *triumphalis gloria*, a potential spur not only to prestigious undertakings, but also to the pursuit of overtly imperial artistic models.

The overall picture of medieval Venetian architecture, however, is hard to reconstruct before the tenth to eleventh centuries, even in highly legible buildings. At this point, though, its heart lay in the rebuilding of San Marco.

After restorations following the fire of 976, the ducal chapel was radically, and very finely rebuilt and enlarged, probably from 1063 onwards, but certainly during the dogeships of Domenico Contarini (1042–71) and Vitale Falier (1086–96). The conflicts between the patriarchal see of Aquileia and that of Venice-Grado reappear against this background of renewal, ending with the Roman synod of 1053. Once again, the magnificent rebuilding of his church by the patriarch Poppo (1019–42), during the years of its triumph and the humiliation of that of the Venetian duchy, was to be followed, in the years of Venice's own triumph, by the glorious rebirth of the 'apostolic' chapel of Mark the evangelist. If Poppo, otherwise known as Wolfgang of Treffen, was not simply the patriarch, but also the great feudatory of the Western empire and its Germanic dynasties, the doge, with the Venetian church at last victorious, was the custodian of public piety and of its outward and visible signs.

Ground plan of the basilica of San Marco, with the Ducal palace and Piazza, beginning of nineteenth century. Paris, Bibliothèque Nationale.

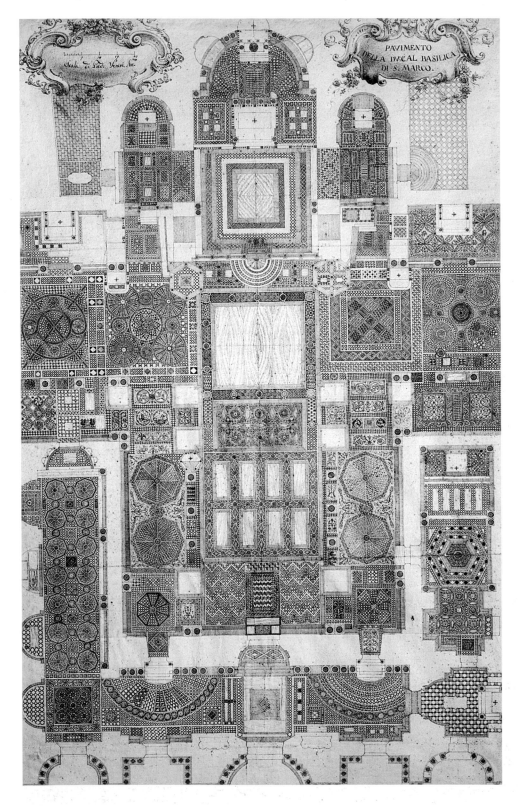

Antonio Visentini, flooring of the Ducal Basilica of San Marco, eighteenth century. Venice, Procuratoria di San Marco.

Thus the new San Marco, the one we see today, symbolized the proud celebration of the political, economic and military power of the Venetians: of a power legitimized and recognized – now as of old, in the time of the Particiaci – by the empire of the Romans with its seat in Constantinople; and which was now heaping the doge with increasingly lofty titles and dignities. The *dux* and *ypatos* of the one-time province was now being made *protospatharios*, *antypatos*, an imperial patrician, an imperial *magister*, *proto-proedros* and *protosebastos*: during the eleventh and early twelfth centuries, and in particular from the period of Pietro II Orseolo onwards, he was taking on the same titles as the governors of the great Byzantine 'themes' of Anatolia, Armenia and Thrace, dignities which made him the equivalent, in legal terms, of the members of the imperial family.[13] The frescoes in the apse of Poppo's Romanesque basilica at Aquileia included depictions of Conrad the Salic (1024–39), the empress Gisela and prince Henry among the saints and martyrs; Venice deliberately and promptly countered them with the magnificent and legitimizing symbol of the golden ducal basilica, based on models drawn from the sources of Constantinople's imperial tradition. It was from this, once and for all, that she derived the ideal centre of her own space – both urban and territorial – and of her history.

Equally significantly, around that same time, and also in association with the cult of St. Mark, Venice was further honoured by

Church of San Marco in the thirteenth-century mosaic depicting the finding of the body of the Saint. Venice, San Marco, right-hand arm of the transept.

Facade of San Marco.

the visit in 1095 of the emperor Henry IV, and by his praise of the site and the orderly beauty of the city, as recalled by Dandolo. The San Marco of the time of doge Domenico Contarini was also cruciform; but over the slightly elongated Greek cross, at the crossing of the arms and above each of them, stood five domes. The memory of the pre-existing *capella ducis* persisted, but reinterpreted and redefined in manifestly courtly forms, as duly noted by the chroniclers: 'it is built in a fashion similar to that of the complex work in honour of the XII Apostles in Constantinople'.[14] They also make mention of the summoning to Venice of certain 'leading' architects from the imperial capital, though elsewhere we find a fantastical attribution of the work to Joachim of Fiore ('and the master who created it was the abbot Joachim'), a statement inspired by a prophetic and eschatological interpretation of the church's iconographical programmes.[15]

The Marcian basilica thus derived from the prototype of the *Apostoleion*, dating from the time of Justinian, a building with five domes and an elongated western arm, itself also associated with Byzantine public court ceremonies, an apostolic shrine-church containing imperial tombs, as the Venetian chroniclers were well aware, since they include a long list of them, together with a description of the precious marbles of the sarcophagi. The Venetian use of the great domed basilicas which had given outward expression to the ceremonial requirements of the Byzantine state thus seems to have been deliberate. All the more so in

The domes of San Marco.

that, like the emperors in the *Apostoleion*, between 1070 and 1117 four doges – Domenico Selvo, Vitale Falier, Vitale I Michiel and Ordelaf Falier – were buried in the atrium of the Marcian basilica, whose interior was now being covered with its mosaic cycles.

This choice must have been influenced by the fact that this same domed cruciform plan had been used in a very similar way for the church of St. John at Ephesus, built by Justinian and Theodora over the tomb of the evangelist between 535 and 565. In the Middle Ages Ephesus, a centre on the Anatolian coast, had been an important place of pilgrimage for the entire Christian world, with fairs and markets and a harbour; visited by the Venetians during the eleventh century, it also featured amony the main places where they enjoyed special privileges, as listed in the famous chrysobul of Alexius I Comnenus (1081–1118).[16] By a process of evident analogy, the seat of Mark the Evangelist was thus made to derive from the same form, the same architectural mould, as those of the evangelists Luke – the *Apostoleion*[17] – and John. Meanwhile, the growth of Norman power, against which the Byzantine and Venetian forces were currently allied, was taking on physical form with the building of the cathedral of the coastal town of Salerno (1080), dedicated to the apostle and evangelist Matthew, as Dandolo's Venetian chronicle duly noted: a symbol of greatness commissioned by Robert Guiscard, *maximus triumphator* over the empire of Constantinople.[18]

Church of the Apostles (Apostoleion) in
Constantinople, illumination. Paris,
Bibliothèque Nationale.

The solemn spaces of San Marco, rigorously, learnedly, yet apparently effortlessly
structured, were thus a scrupulous evocation of the basic architectural concepts of
the Early Byzantine sixth century. Yet it
also had features that showed signs of
compromise: the church of the Apostles
at Constantinople was in fact known to the
architect of San Marco through a version
where the structure of the domes had been
altered, and in the Venetian church the
overall sensibility bears the mark of the
Middle Byzantine idiom. There are also
compromises with Western tradition, as well
as certain clearly Romanesque elements;
the masonry and stone-cutting techniques
were distinctly western in character.

At all events, the Byzantine magnificence
of the ducal San Marco was undoubtedly
a unique architectural phenomenon in
eleventh-century Venice, destined subsequently to exert considerable influence.

The clearest evidence in this direction is
provided by what we know of the features
of the Benedictine church of S. Nicolò del
Lido, also founded in the mid-eleventh
century by doge Domenico Contarini with
the probable aim of combining the maritime
cult of St. Nicholas, 'glorious over land and
sea', with that of St. Mark, in the context
of the political role which Venice was
already arrogating to herself throughout
the Mediterranean. Archaeological sources
and surveys have revealed that it was a
basilica with columns, without a transept
and ending in three semi-circular apses. Its
capitals looked back to prototypes from the

29

right
St. John at Ephesus, view of pillars
and columns separating the nave
from the left-hand aisle.

below
Ground plan (from *Ephesos*, 1951).

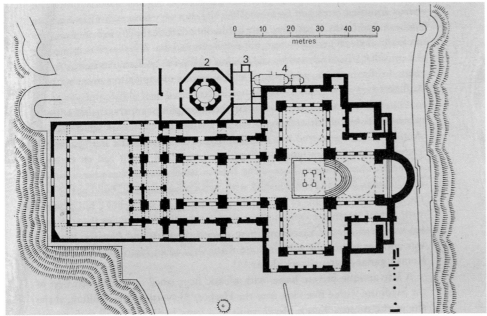

time of the Exarchate, and it had a mosaic floor similar to those of Aquileia and Pomposa, with elegantly intertwined geometrical and plant motifs which also look back to late Antiquity.

The early Christian tradition was also essentially adhered to in the great episcopal church at Torcello, whose surviving structures are those given to it by the great works of rebuilding done in the eleventh and twelfth centuries.

If the origins of the church of S. Maria can unhesitatingly be dated from the seventh century, as we have said, the reconstruction of its architectural and artistic history is more controversial. This church too is based on a basilican plan with a nave and two aisles ending in as many apses, with a pseudocrypt preceded by a portico and, originally, by a baptistry in front of the facade. After various modifications carried out as early as the end of the seventh and beginning of the eighth centuries, a further rebuilding at the wishes of bishop Deusdedit gave the facade its present form, with its three blind arches, and saw the positioning of the bases of the present-day columns, the laying of a first mosaic floor with two-coloured floral and geometrical motifs, and the sculptural decoration, of which the *plutei* and friezes, some still in the church itself, some in the neighbouring museum, were originally part. Its radical reconstruction, which may be safely attributed to Orso Orseolo, son of doge Pietro II and bishop of Torcello, is usually dated from the beginning of the eleventh century, when the

San Marco, south dome and masonry surfaces
without thirteenth-century marble cladding.

G. Canella, original appearance of south front of San Marco.

The *Kalenderhane Camii* (church of the Panaghia Kyriotissa?) at Constantinople, twelfth century, detail of the exterior.

colonnades and apses were rebuilt and the
pseudocrypt created (the latter is in fact an
ambulatory conceived in relation to the cult
of St. Heliodorus, bishop of Altinum, whose
body had been placed there in a third-
century Roman sarcophagus).

The stiff figures of the apostles in the
lower register of the apse, together with
the oldest part of the mosaic decoration of
the *diaconicon*, may date from this period,
which preceded the Contarini San Marco
by several decades. Lastly, work was
resumed on the fabric of S. Maria in the
twelfth century with the rebuilding of the
stilted arches of the colonnades, the laying
of the new flooring – now in *opus sectile*, its
motifs and coloured marbles distinguishing
the nave from the aisles and characterizing
the space of the chancel behind the holy
doorway of the iconostasis – and the new
mosaic cycles, with the hieratic image of
the *Theotokos* standing in lonely glory
amidst the motionless abstraction of a field
of gold, and the awesome yet triumphal
scene of the Last Judgment which occupies
the vast space of the west wall.

For purposes of general interpretation, it
is worth noting the intentional link between
the layout of the apses and the memory of
St. Heliodorus, mentioned by the medieval
Venetic chronicles as heading the list of
bishops of Altinum from which the episcopal
see of Torcello derived. Equally intentional
(particularly for the doge who had it rebuilt,
himself the son of the doge who had rebuilt
Grado) was S. Maria's continuity with early
Christian architecture: it looked back both

Marble flooring with 'sea wave' motif, eleventh century. Venice, S. Zaccaria.

to the Venetic tradition – in the *synthronon*, for example, in the iconostasis, and in the use of golden proportions as used in S. Eufemia in Grado – and to that of the art of the Exarchate, an influence particularly evident in the right-hand apsidiole, where angels are holding up a medallion clearly deriving from the art of Ravenna, even if through the probable intermediary of Greek mosaicists.

Thus various more strictly Byzantine features were grafted on to this system of deliberate cultural references, visible in the wall mosaics rather than in the architectural structures themselves (though the latter do make use of the stilted arch) and in the sculptural decoration, probably largely salvaged.

Similar components are found in the architectural culture which influenced the rebuilding of another episcopal church on Venetian territory, S. Stefano at Caorle, consecrated in 1038. Here, while the chancel shows a general affinity with the architecture of Grado, the apse and more especially the contemporary cylindrical campanile are reminiscent of models from Ravenna, while the lure of Byzantium is seen in the decorative reuse of two bas-reliefs with Saints Agathonicus and George to the sides of the portal. However, the use of a system of alternating supports – columns and pillars – for the arches which separate the nave from the aisles, implies a stylistic shift away from tradition which foreshadows later developments in Venetian architectural culture. The nielloed abacuses also

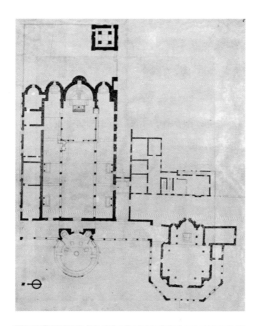

above
Torcello, ground plan of the complex of the
cathedral, baptistry and church of S. Fosca
(F. Forlati, 1940).

below
Ground plan of the cathedral (R. Cattaneo, 1896).

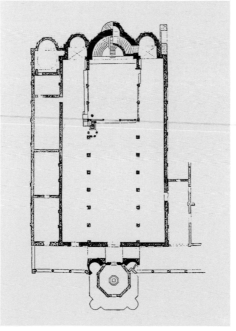

suggest links with the architectural decoration of San Marco.

Characteristics fairly similar to those of the basilica of Torcello were also to be seen in another cathedral on the lagoon, destroyed by fire in the seventeenth century: that of S. Maria at Chioggia, which had harboured the old episcopal see of *Methamaucum* at the beginning of the twelfth century. This too was a three-aisled basilica, with iconostasis, flooring in *opus sectile* and numerous columns of rare marble.

We know little about the seat of the bishop of Olivolo at Castello, rebuilt in the first half of the twelfth century, except that it too was a large basilican building; according to the sources, the rebuilding partly reused the earlier plan. Francesco Sansovino's claim that its architecture was 'derived from the Greek manner of building' should probably be interpreted in the sense already mentioned, that is, as having a basic continuity with the Venetic and exarchal traditions. Another Renaissance source, Marc' Antonio Sabellico, also suggests that its interior bore a close resemblance to that of S. Maria on Torcello: its floor was in *opus sectile*, it had a double colonnade of 'foreign marbles', and gold mosaic in the cove of the apse. All these features, as the author himself observed, were prevalent in Venetian religious architecture as he knew it at the end of the fifteenth century.[19] The church of S. Ilario too had a similar plan – three-aisled, with three semi-circular apses – and was renovated around the same period.

The architectural type of the basilica with columns, roofed with wooden trusses, was not used only for episcopal and monastic churches. It appears to have been very widespread in Venice for parish churches too, for instance S. Zan Degolà (S. Giovanni Decollato), which repeated the eleventh-century basilican model, divided into three aisles by a double series of eight columns of Greek marble.

But this was not the only plan found frequently during these centuries. Torcello itself, with the juxtaposition of the basilican S. Maria and the cruciform S. Fosca, points to the existence of a second large group of ecclesiastical forms where, stripped of their courtly Marcian language, architectural models of Byzantine origin revealed their rootedness in the Venetian Middle Ages.

S. Fosca is reliably documented at the beginnings of the second decade of the eleventh century, though its possible relations with a hypothetical pre-existing building are far from clear. A lucid sense of geometry, a scrupulous concern for symmetry and a skilful balance of volumes give this little church a calculated dignity of its own.

Its plan is organized around a perfect central square, three sides of which open into three arms roofed with barrel vaulting by large arches which emphasize the design of the Greek cross. The corners of the cross are roofed with lesser cross-vaulting, while the stilted arches – linked by wooden tie-beams as at S. Maria, and as was current practice in Venetian architecture – stand on

S. Maria, Torcello, view of the apses.

A capital from the portico.

Nave looking towards the internal facade, with the mosaic of the Last Judgment.

S. Stefano at Caorle, campanile.

identical Corinthian capitals, with red marble abacuses as in the nearby cathedral. The width of the smaller vaults at the four sides of the cross, which dictates the main dimensions of the building according to simple ratios, acts as a module for a well-proportioned space whose balance is thus made easily legible.

The fourth side of the square central space extends into a chancel divided into three small aisles with apses, the middle one of which is three times wider than the side ones and separated from them by a short sequence of two arches, a spatial expedient inspired by the basilican form which, among other things, adapts the apparently Greco-Byzantine model to the needs of the Latin liturgy. This same central square was originally roofed by a dome – which may have collapsed during an earthquake in 1117 – using an arrangement of double corner pendentives; the lowest fillets of this dome are still in place. Other interpretations have been put forward concerning the original roofing, including that of a *xilotroulos*. It currently has a low conical roof with a timber framework.

The structural system is therefore distinctly Byzantine, even if the basic measurements of S. Fosca were clearly calculated in Roman feet, and the use of brickwork of the Roman type has been detected in its masonry structures.

Externally, the cruciform structure emerges clearly in the simple clarity of the volumes, rising above the later portico on a semi-octagonal plan. The two side apses

are less protruding than the central one, which is pentagonal on the outside, with a double series of blind arches, framed by slender paired columns in the lower order and by shallow pilaster strips in the upper one; above them runs a frieze with hanging triangles and strips of dog-tooth. S. Fosca has long been seen as deriving from, or having some similarities with, the cathedral of khristianò at Trifillia, in Messenia, and with the Panagia Lykodemu in Athens, both built in the eleventh century. The apse decoration may clearly be seen as deriving from the repertoire current in Constantinople, and elsewhere in the Greek Levant, during the Comnene period. Thus if, as in San Marco, these features of S. Fosca appear as somewhat indirect translations, their links with Middle Byzantine architecture are still extremely clear.

S. Fosca is proof, in Venice, of the architectural type based on a central plan with an inscribed Greek cross. The free Greek cross plan, on the other hand, used for small ecclesiastical buildings, is found at S. Giacomo di Rialto, a church particularly closely bound up with the origins of the city and significantly attributed, by writings of the Renaissance period, to a mythical Greek architect from Crete, Entinopos of Candia. Although several sources talk of a rebuilding, and the addition of mosaics, by doge Domenico Selva (1071–84), and although traces of pavement have been found at considerable depths below the present level of the floor, the earliest reliable documentation concerning S. Giacomo dates from

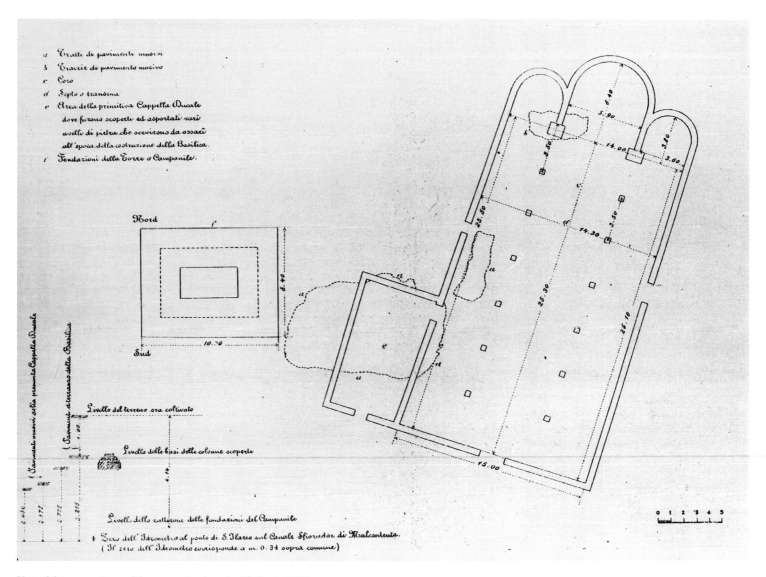

Plan of the excavations of the monastic church of S. Ilario, 1873.

S. Fosca, Torcello, facade.

above
Corner squinches.

left
S. Fosca, the apse.

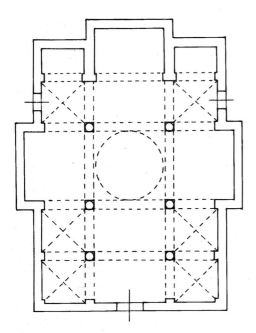

S. Giacomo di Rialto, ground plan.

1152. At all events, the basic architectural layout, still partly visible, is to be dated from the twelfth century. Beyond the Gothic portico, the main short arm of the cross, subdivided into three aisles by just two bays, leads into the barely protruding transept, with a dome, along whose base runs a cornice also datable from the twelfth century. Six reused columns in Greek marble divide the space up longitudinally and support the dome and vaulting; their capitals, with pulvins, are also in Greek marble, and two of them, larger than the rest, mark off the transept.

If we consider not just the existing structures, but also the descriptive and iconographical evidence and archaeo logical data, S. Fosca and S. Giacomo do not appear to be isolated cases. In all likelihood, there were a group of twenty or more religious buildings on a central Greek cross plan, whether inscribed or free, apparently more or less concentrated around the area of Rialto and San Marco, including several parish churches. This category included some of the oldest buildings of Venice, antedating or roughly contemporary with the first San Marco, such as S. Teodoro and S. Geminiano, both probably on an inscribed Greek cross, and others such as S. Maria Formosa, rebuilt between the eleventh and twelfth centuries, which evidence from the Renaissance period describes as having been built 'on the model of the central body of the church of S. Marco', that is, architecturally inspired by the Contarini ducal basilica.[20]

Another important example of twelfth-century Venetian architecture, the basilica of SS Maria e Donato on Murano, should be seen in this context. Although it reused part of the old sculptural ornament in various ways, the present-day basilica, completed around 1141, shows clear signs of independence from the building which pre-existed on the same site until a little after the end of the eleventh century. Its plan is of the widespread basilican type, with three aisles divided up by two rows of columns of Greek marble, and a main apse, semi-circular internally, flanked by two side ones. It has a definite transept, though it does not protrude on the plan; above the side aisles its arms rise transversally to the height of the nave, making the form of the cross clearly visible on the outside. As was customary in Venetian medieval architecture, the vast external brickwork surfaces are visually lightened by pilaster strips, blind arcades, and typically Veneto-Byzantine splayed windows (though these were probably created during the restoration of 1858–73). The spare, unfussy features of the facade, however, with its small double window, point towards early Christian origins.

A baptistry stood in front of it until the beginning of the eighteenth century, facing westwards, as in nearby Torcello. But there is a striking contrast between the simplicity of the facade and the ornate exterior of the apses facing the canal: here, the lower order of the main apse is treated as a false portico, articulated by seven deep niches between paired columns, as are the

Internal view of the dome.

Interior looking towards the apse.

above
S. Donato, Murano, south side with apse.

below
S. Donato, Murano, nave.

above
S. Donato, Murano, south side with apse.

below
S. Donato, Murano, nave.

straight end walls of the smaller apses. Above runs an airy gallery, with powerful arches also supported by paired columns, giving the structures a sense of lightness, as do the brickwork frieze, the deliberately ornamental texture of the masonry and the use and reuse of Veneto-Byzantine decorative sculptural elements.

The interior is equally dignified and coherent. Spaces and architectural elements are inter-related by a clearly perceptible system of ratios: the distance between one column and another is related to the width of the aisles, which in its turn is related to that of the nave, with the transept and radius of the main apse proportioned accordingly. The classicizing capitals, with their acanthus leaves, are extremely elegant, with their nielloed abacuses with palmettes standing on columns of Proconnesus marble. The spacious internal plan, with its lucid geometrical volumes, thus draws upon a highly sophisticated and self-aware building culture, as Ruskin had already sensed. The result is a skilful combination of a central plan, reflected in the arrangement of the choir and transept (so that one may even hypothesize that its piers might originally have been intended to support a dome), and a basilican layout with a particularly wide nave. The composition and details of the striking flooring in *opus sectile* and *opus tessellatum* once again include motifs characteristic of the early Christian tradition of Ravenna and Grado, with affinities with S. Eufemia in Grado, San Marco in Venice and S. Giovanni

Evangelista in Ravenna. As at Torcello, the nave of the basilica of SS Maria e Donato ends with an apsidal cove where the figure of the *Theotokos* stands in splendid isolation, following the Byzantine scheme.

All in all, it is clear that this is one of the most important of the many monuments variously and powerfully influenced by the Contarini San Marco, although here too there are signs of some knowledge of the Romanesque architecture of the Po area. Another large Venetian church, S. Salvador, rebuilt in the second half of the twelfth century, must have been very similar. Its main features are known to us from the bird's-eye view by Jacopo de' Barbari (1500) and an accurate drawing datable from the beginning of the sixteenth century. It was a basilican church with three aisles and three apses, semi-circular on the inside, with a wide domed transept which did not protrude on the plan but which, together with the nave, must have been higher than the aisles, so that a cross inscribed within the parallelogram of the plan must have been clearly legible. As in San Donato on Murano, the main apse was articulated externally by seven deep niches, clearly evident in the measured drawing now in the State Archives in Venice.

Recent excavations, together with iconographical and documentary evidence, reveal similarities between the main features of the church of S. Salvador and those of S. Lorenzo, which was also rebuilt in the twelfth century, even if we do not know how the outer walls of the apse were treated. The exterior of the main apse of the cathedral of S. Maria Assunta at *Equilum* also had a ground-level order of seven tall, deep niches. This church – whose ruins can be seen not far from present-day Jesolo – also dated from the twelfth century: on an elongated Greek cross plan noted by Cattaneo, it was very similar to the Contarini San Marco in layout, in that it too had lateral women's galleries, a crypt and niches on the interior of the apses, with three wide aisles separated by alternating pillars and columns.

The Venice of this period had forged herself by raising trade to the level of an affair of state; she had remodelled herself as a commune – with a doge still at its head, though his powers were limited by councils; she was striving to create her own 'stato da mar' by dominating the waters of the gulf, and by control or possession of a number of harbour-strongholds and crossing-points. A city in a state of flux, she was now also intent on renewing and reorganizing her urban configuration. From the middle of the twelfth century onwards, this was to occur by means of a series of architectural and urbanistic initiatives conceived and undertaken for the most part during the dogeship of Sebastiano Ziani (1172–8), and certainly from the impetus he set in train. He had particular significance as the first elected doge, following upon predecessors who had been largely autocratic; he was also fabulously rich, and he and his family were front-ranking figures among the great financiers of maritime trade.

It was now that the area of the Rialto market, which had been public property

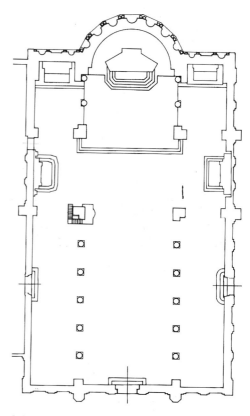

S. Donato, ground plan.

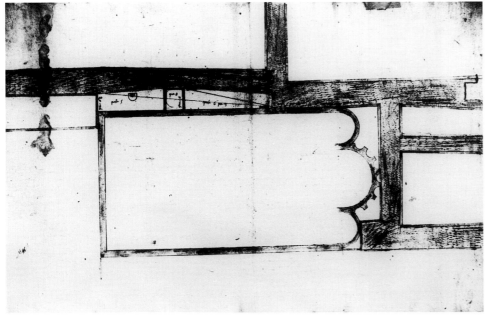

since the end of the eleventh century, began
to exert a crucial pull upon trade and building investment: it now had a bridge linking
it to the other bank of the Grand Canal, where
San Marco was, so that all the magistracies
and offices concerned with commercial life
now began to be concentrated in this district. It was during this same period that the
first Fontego (fondaco, foreign merchants'
centre) was built for German merchants in
the nearby district of S. Bortolomio: this
was a 'small but rich' building on two
floors, reliably documented from the first
decades of the thirteenth century, when we
also have information concerning a number of similar publicly-owned buildings.
Between the end of the twelfth century and
the beginning of the following, conditions
were also in place for the development of
the *Arsena Comunis*: as yet a relatively
small fortified complex, also documented
by early thirteenth-century sources (shortly
before the first information concerning the
Venetian *arsana* at Constantinople, dating
from 1231), it was to develop into the largest
late-medieval arsenal in the Mediterranean.
At this time there was still another public
arsenal at Terranova, not far from the ducal
castle-residence, a timber depot also serving
as a dockyard until the fourteenth century,
following an urban pattern widespread
in the Islamic area, and also known in
medieval Sicily.[21]

By the second half of the twelfth century,
the main operational mechanisms and
focal points of Venice, *urbs magna*,[22] were
thus already emerging.

During the dogeship of Sebastiano Ziani, particular attention was paid to the area of San Marco. The belltower overlooking the harbour mouths and the canal of San Marco had been completed during the dogeship of Domenico Morosini (1148–56); but from the time of Ziani onwards, what seems to have been a fully-fledged programme of renewal for the area and buildings immediately surrounding the ducal castle and nearby chapel began to be implemented. Briefly, its main preoccupations were the following:

– the adapting of the site of the old *castrum* to the new institutional requirements of the *Comunis Veneciarum,* with the building of a law court looking on to what was to become the Piazzetta, and of a *Palatium Communis* overlooking the waters of the basin, both with colonnades and loggias;

– alterations to the fabric of the Contarini San Marco;

– the building of a *molo*, or quay, a *litus marmoreum* (marble quay) – roughly corresponding to the site of the waterfront of the present-day Piazzetta, but protruding into the waters of the basin from the banks on either side – and the erecting of two large monolithic granite columns, from Greece or the Orient, described by the chroniclers as being the work of a Lombard *inzegnario* (engineer), Nicolò de' Baretteri;

– the extending of the *brolium* in front of the ducal basilica of San Marco with the filling in of the *rivus Batarius* which flowed through it, and the demolition of the old church dedicated to Saints Geminiano and Mena;

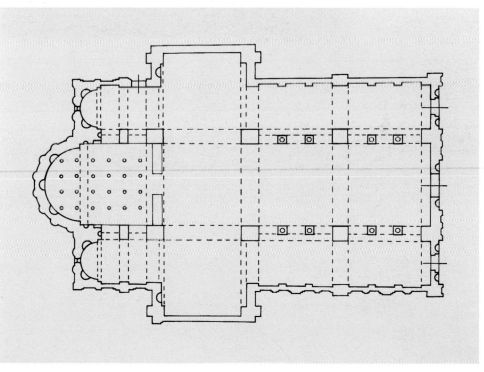

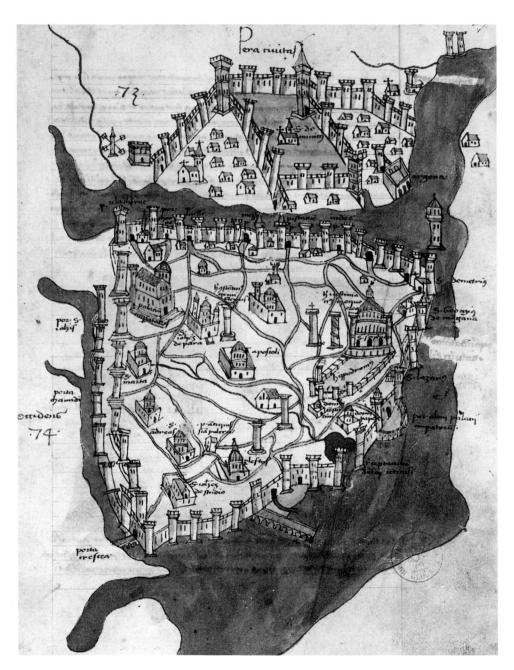

– the rebuilding of the latter at the new, and definitive, western limit of the *brolo* (1172–8); – the construction, along the north side of the *brolo*, of the long building of the Procuratie (c. 1178–1210), subsequently rebuilt in the early sixteenth century, but whose overall appearance is familiar to us from the famous *Procession in Piazza San Marco* by Gentile Bellini (1496), now in the Accademia.

It is therefore quite clear that the first configuration of the original *brolium* and the area around San Marco as a piazza, and the earliest attention paid to the deliberate defining of the city's maritime frontage, both date from the time of Ziani and Venice's earliest period as a commune. There is no doubt that the two columns, one bearing the lion of St. Mark and the other the statue of St. Theodore Stratelates, with their complex political symbolism, should be seen as powerful architectural emblems with implications for the whole city, combining connotations of both the celebratory imperial columns of Constantinople, still visible from the surrounding waters of the harbour, and the two columns which signalled the arrival of the via Appia at Brindisi. These emblems acted as guardians of a hallowed point of entry – the city's harbour – and as the triumphal conclusion of the *iter maritimum veneticorum* (sea route of the Venetii). The idea behind the erecting of these columns undoubtedly had its parallel both in the attribution of *triumphalia insignia* to doge Ziani (1177), and in the insistence with which the

chronicles date the elaboration of the political rite of the *desponsatio maris* (marriage with the sea) from the years of his dogeship, that is, the ritual accompanying the doge's annual trip to the harbour mouth at S. Nicolò for the symbolic wedding between Venice and the waters of the Adriatic gulf 'as a sign of perpetual dominion', which may also have suggested the aulic idea of the colonnaded pier from which it embarked.

The further definition of the piazza and fabric of the basilica of San Marco continued to be the focus of building work in thirteenth-century Venice, immediately after the taking of Constantinople and the setting up of a Latin empire in the East whose rule was basically secured by Venice, together with direct control of its maritime area.

We have already referred to the modifications to the Contarini San Marco which occurred during the twelfth century. The sources date certain embellishments to the city's main buildings from as early as 1159. But the most significant of the numerous works of architecture, sculpture and mosaic dated from the beginning of the thirteenth century. The outline of the domes now changed: with the probable use of techniques already known to Islamic architecture, two tall timber extradoses, covered with layers of lead and topped by lanterns with small domes, were superimposed upon the original masonry calottes. The resulting structures were now more commanding, visible from all around – from the extended space of the *brolium*, now the Piazza, and from the waters of the canal of San Marco in front of it – giving visual emphasis to the symbols at the hallowed centre of the city-state. Meanwhile, the wall surfaces of the Contarini period, with their niches and decorative brickwork motifs – deriving from models widespread in the Middle Byzantine period – disappeared from view. The narthex was extended to the two sides of the western arm of the church, and the outer walls, like the inner ones, were now clad with slabs of precious marble, mosaics, bas-reliefs and panels, together with columns over two orders framing the deeply splayed portals. The outer central portal and the 'porta da mar', which opened to the south, were given bronze leaves in *opus clatratum* dating from the age of Justinian and brought from Constantinople, while the four horses taken from the Hippodrome in the same city after the Latin conquest were placed above it. The sculptured porphyry group of the Tetrarchs – the four sons of Constantine, locked in a symbolic embrace demonstrating political harmony – which had decorated the square of the *Philadelphion* at the bifurcation of the main central street in imperial Byzantium, the *Mesè*,[23] was placed at the corner between the palazzo and the ducal chapel, near the south door. The two decorated pillars, possibly originally from the ciborium in the church of St. Polyeuktos in Constantinople, were placed a few feet away, giving added grandeur to the gilded, domed basilica.

These actions naturally represented much more than the mere transport and relocating of plunder from a conquered city. By 1207, the doge of the Venetians (of those who lived in the *urbs magna* of the lagoons, and also of the thousands who lived in Constantinople) had assumed the princely dignity of *dominator* of three quarters of the Roman Empire. A Venetian nobleman, Tommaso Morosini – a descendant of doge Domenico (1148–56) and uncle of doge Marino (1249–53) – was solemnly elected patriarch of Constantinople in Hagia Sophia: and if the tradition according to which there had been talk of moving the seat of Venetian government to Byzantium in the early thirteenth century is purely legendary, the fact remains that a Venetian government of the East had indeed been formed there, headed by a *despotes et dominator* who had robed himself in the imperial colours, just as the doge decked himself out in Byzantine imperial rayment at this period.[24]

The renovation of the basilica and the laying out of the adjacent areas should therefore be understood literally as the city's donning of *regalia insignia*. They should be interpreted as her express identification with the Byzantium in whose memory, sovereign magnificence and splendid many-coloured emblems she was now triumphantly clothing herself. San Marco, embellished with the *quadriga* and other works of Byzantine art, together with the square in front of it, was consciously imitating Hagia Sophia and the Hippodrome, as may also be seen from the close resemblance between the general reorganization of the Venetian Piazza and the representation of the equivalent centre in Constantinople shown in the earliest cartography of the Byzantine capital.

Other traditions, undoubtedly medieval in origin even if they were collected and transcribed during the Renaissance, confirm the purport of these undertakings, though they provide a different version of the origin of the great bronze statues. The manuscripts of Stefano Magno – who also mentioned San Marco as deriving from the model of the *Apostoleion* – gives a version of the transfer of the four bronze horses which is of considerable importance: according to him, the statues were ancient works of art, made in Asia, taken to Rome as plunder to be placed – as on the facade of San Marco – on four columns 'as a sign of great triumph'. It was the emperor Constantine who took them to Constantinople and raised them, again on four columns, as symbols of *translatio imperii* (transfer of power). However, here the four horses were not said to have come directly from the Hippodrome, but 'from a place known as the Holy Cross, and it was from here that the doge took them'. This detail is of some significance: the place of the Holy Cross is recognizable in the topography of Constantinople as the square of Stavrion, connected with the Hippodrome and closed in by porticoes, as was the thirteenth-century Piazza San Marco. In fact, together with the Forum of Constantine and the square of the Philadelphion, Stavrion was a symbolic space for the imperial capital, one of the three places where Constantine the Great was vouchsafed his vision of victory by the divine will. The

place of the Cross was given the name *Nika*:
'thou shalt conquer'.[25] In the same context
we also find a brief reference which links
the pillars placed at the corner of the south
side of the church of San Marco not with
St. Jean d'Acre, but as follows: 'The square
pillars near the door of the palace come from
a door in Alexandria', the first patriarchal
see of St. Mark, and hence as key elements
in the system of outward signs which proclaimed the ties between Venice and history
in the heart of the city.[26]

The variously-coloured marble facing
of the basilica was also attributed with a
symbolic provenance: it was claimed to
have come from Aquileia, Ravenna and
Byzantium, that is, from the three metropolises which summed up the history and
greatness of the imperial idea, and of the
origins of Venice.[27]

From the thirteenth century, with its
external array of marbles, decorative reliefs
and mosaic cycles anticipating the internal
iconographical system, the facade of San
Marco no longer appeared as a dividing
screen, or barrier: multi-coloured and
light-filled, it could now be interpreted as a
surface communicating between the piazza
and the sacred and liturgical recesses
within the basilica. Through the stories of
the translation of the body of the evangelist
saint, the facade took on the functions of a
vast and elaborate iconostasis in relation
to the open spaces of the *platea*, a positive
ceremonial nave. But the precious plunder
incorporated into San Marco inspired other
interpretations, complex symbolic analogies

Columns on the Piazzetta and the basin of San Marco, detail from Battista d'Agnolo del Moro, *St. Mark watching over the Provveditori all'armar.* Venice, museo Navale (on loan from the galleries of the Accademia).

which were to be unhesitatingly accepted and reworked by the Renaissance literature of the myth of Venice. A group of columns in the narthex were identified as the splendid remains of the temple of Solomon itself, removed from Jerusalem to Byzantium and thence to Venice, symbols of the transfer, to the ducal city, of the memory of the sacred place *par excellence* of the Old Testament.[28] The ritual of the unveiling of the *pala d'oro* and the exposition, on the high altar, of the church plate from the treasure of San Marco beneath the newly erected ciborium (c. 1209),

were further declarations of this link. The treasure of San Marco, made up for the most part of ancient and Byzantine items, now appeared as a replica of the Jerusalem treasure kept in the temple of Solomon, and made up of the booty taken by David when he triumphed over the Arameans, Moabites, Ammonites, Philistines and Amalekites, a treasure compared by Byzantine sources to that with which Justinian had endowed Hagia Sophia. This yearning for symbolic analogies persisted down the ages: as late as 1519 there were those who, with Tschudi,

The thirteenth-century Procuratie, detail from
Gentile Bellini, *Procession in Piazza S. Marco.*
Venice, Accademia.

would claim that the decoration of San Marco in Venice bore a similarity to that of the temple of Solomon, the Dome of the Rock, and the church of the Nativity at Bethlehem.[29]

Then, as a crowning glory, the hieratical icon of the *Nicopeia* arrived in San Marco. No mere figured panel but, it was claimed, a holy painting which had occupied a central place in imperial liturgy, it portrayed the Virgin as patron saint of the Romans and the 'leader of legions'; it was originally kept in a chapel in the palace and depicted on the city gates of the former capital of the Bosphorus, the royal city of the *Theotokos*. So that 'with the passing of that image from the Greek camp to the Latin, the protection and support of the Great Mother of God was likewise transferred from them to us'.[30] By shaping the very core of her public urban space in this way, early thirteenth-century Venice was thus inventing herself as an imperial city and another Constantinople.

The parallel development of her civil buildings, however, remains more obscure and less amenable to interpretation. Almost nothing remains of the buildings of piazza San Marco at the time of Sebastiano Ziani, apart from documentary and iconographical evidence, and a few traces and stone artefacts. From such evidence as we have, the church of S. Geminiano seems to have been rebuilt on a central Greek cross plan with a dome, and thus fits unproblematically into the series of works deriving from Byzantine-Marcian inspiration. But a different tendency seemed to be emerging in the large adjacent and basically

53

G. Casoni, arch with jambs in red Verona marble,
discovered during nineteenth-century work at
the Arsenal. Venice, museo Correr.

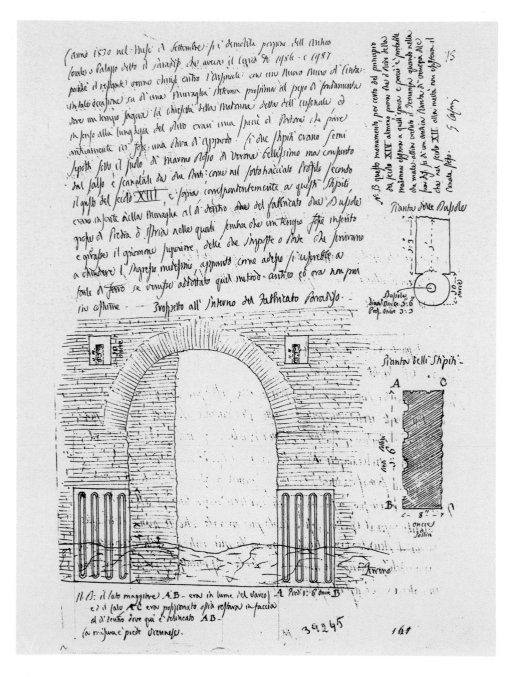

contemporary building of the Procuratie.
From the depictions known to us, its facade
seems to have consisted of a long ground-
floor portico, a series of over forty round-
headed arches standing on bevelled
cube-shaped capitals, with a loggia above,
with slighter columns and capitals, sur-
mounted by a coping of dense crenellations.
One of the capitals came to light during
excavations carried out around the campanile of San Marco, revealing it to have
been basically Romanesque in form, while
Bellini's view of this same portico ties in
with what we know about a small group of
partly extant contemporary structures: the
traces – a column and pillar – of the palace
of the patriarch of Grado at S. Silvestro,
near the Rialto; the arcading of Corte del
Fontego at Santa Margherita, of Calle del
Remedio at Castello and of Corte del Teatro
Vecchio at S. Cassiano, and the portico now
in the interior of a building on Rio Terà
Santi Apostoli, which Renaissance traditions
were to identify as belonging to an old
tribune's palazzo from the period of the
Particiaci.[31] It thus seems certain that in the
first layout of her own Piazza, communal
Venice looked towards the culture of the Po
hinterland from which she had drawn the
forms of her new institutions. But the fact
remains that the Romanesque vocabulary,
probably from the territory of Verona (like
the marbles which were then beginning
o be imported from the same city), with a
certain admixture of Veneto-Byzantine
components, was organized in a completely
individual and autonomous way. The

Arcaded well-head from Murano, twelfth
century. Venice, Fondaco dei Turchi.

long celebratory sequence of arcades of
the portico and loggia of Sebastiano Ziani's
Procuratie virtually obscured the wall of
the frontage on to the Piazza, becoming the
first real evidence of that specific character
of Venetian civil architecture between the
Middle Ages and the Renaissance which
Sebastiano Serlio was to sum up as 'the
copious presence of lights'.[32]

Thus there were a number of stylistic
instruments and combinations available for
use in Venice between the twelfth and thirteenth centuries. This was also the time
when pacts and agreements were being
made with the sultans of Aleppo and Egypt,
and with the king of Tunis; now Venice's
physical presence in the Near East was
being organized and strengthened, for
instance by new commercial and religious
installations in the Venetian quarter of
St. Jean d'Acre (now Akko, Israel). Venice
duly registered her progress eastwards by
recourse to probable quotations of elaborate Islamic motifs, possibly Fatimid in origin, for some of the arches of the basilica,
both internal and external (particularly the
one in the north portal). But the question of
the relations between medieval Venice and
Islamic architecture remains elusive and
insufficiently explored: specific parallels
are hard to pin down, and are best considered against the general background of the
complex circulation of forms and models
around the Mediterranean as a whole.

During this same period, when the
civil architecture of medieval Venice was
emerging from the shadows, and relations

right
Arch with archivolt decorated in
bas-relief, corte del Milion, twelfth
century.

below
Arcading in courtyard at the
Fontego at S. Margherita, twelfth
century.

with the Levant were becoming more intense and complex, we also have documentation concerning the configuration of the Venetian '*casa-fondaco*' (or rather, perhaps, of the 'casa da statio con magazeni', the aristocratic residence with storerooms).

A passage from the Renaissance writer Francesco Sansovino already draws attention to its essential features and functional aspects: 'Some of their facades have ground floor porticoes with columns and arches, but aligned with the rest of the facade. This had been done in the earliest times, for the reason that, when they brought goods here, they unloaded them in the porticoes, at whose sides stood the storerooms to put them in.'[33] The purpose of the long ground-floor portico, overlooking the waters of the Grand Canal (then fully navigable) or other main canals, is made very clear: it served as a landing stage for merchandise. We are also enlightened as to the crucial part played in the formal definition of the facade by the series of arches. In point of fact, a fairly extensive group of noble Venetian palazzi, mostly datable from the thirteenth century but with definite precedents in at least the eleventh, have characteristics similar to those mentioned by Francesco: lengthy buildings along the waterfront, with a ground plan based on a broad through corridor and opening on to the frontage with a space parallel to the loggia (Ca' Farsetti), sometimes flanked to the sides by two lesser spaces (corresponding to the tripartite division of the facade as in Ca' Loredan, or to the side blocks *a torreselle* (with small

56

towers) as in palazzo Palmieri da Pesaro, later Fontego dei Turchi).

The nature of the ground, and of the sites, necessitated the use of structural techniques and solutions which would lighten the actual fabric: this implied an absence of vaults, walls of limited thickness and the widespread use of brick. The shortage of building space and the resulting pressure upon it led to both a system of dwelling spaces clustered behind the main house, often arranged around a family courtyard, and the speedy formation of a continuous urban fabric. Both these phenomena were in evidence at the end of the twelfth and beginning of the thirteenth centuries, when the housing shortage was already reflected in the earliest Venetian statutes.[34]

The fact that, in medieval Venice, the system of waterways had priority over the street system, and the particular commercial and mostly private use of the ground-floor porticoes overlooking the waterways, explains why no network of porticoed streets developed in Venice, in contrast, as Francesco Sansovino had already observed, with the main feature of some of the large communal cities of the Venetian hinterland and nearby Po plain, such as Padua and Bologna.

From this general situation it follows, among other things, that in the Venetian *casa-fondaco* only the facade was designed with any particular attention to its architectural form. As we see, it was characterized throughout its length by the superimposition of long porticoes and corresponding

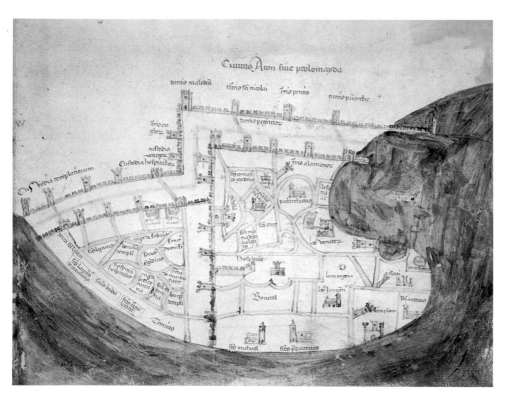

upper rows of windows; it was framed at the sides by two 'towers', as in Ca' Pesaro among other buildings mentioned in the sources, or punctuated by two pillars between columns, by a double pair of twinned columns or sometimes simply by capitals of a different shape from the others in the series, so as to suggest a tripartite scheme in which the middle section had more arches than the two outer ones. The rhythm of such ground-floor porticoes, for example at Ca' Dandolo-Farsetti on the Grand Canal, at the so-called Fontego dei Foscolo on rio di Ca' Foscari or at Ca' da

Mosto, was sometimes interrupted by the presence of a wider, celebrative arch. The tendency towards continuity – longitudinal, uniform and compositionally open – shown by the porticoes and loggias of the great Venetian palazzi datable prior to the fourteenth century, and the prevalence of openings in their walls, are consistent with the features known to us of the Procuratie built by Sebastiano Ziani: indeed the work under way around the Piazza could not fail to have influenced contemporary private building. But the origin of the Venetian palazzo of the pre-Gothic period should not be seen

as deriving purely from that particular example of public architecture, significant though it was. There is a tendency nowadays to see the medieval Venetian facade with its portico and loggia as deriving from the late-classical type of the porticoed villa with projecting side blocks, also documented iconographically over the area of the Veneto by an early Christian mosaic at *Opitergium* (Oderzo).[35] According to this view, the two avant-corps of the classical villa would have developed into *torreselle*, small towers, as in Ca' Pesaro (later Fondaco dei Turchi), or into the side sections of porticoes and rows of windows treated as mentioned above. In other cases (for example palazzo Falier at the Sti Apostoli, casa Bragadin on the Grand Canal, palazzo Vitturi at S. Maria Formosa) they were treated as solid areas of masonry flanking voids consisting of multi-light windows with fewer arches. The similarities with manuscript representations of Byzantine palazzi, or with archaeological remains of buildings at Constantinople such as the palace of Romanus I Lecapenus (920–44) might be explained on the basis of a single late-antique original. Nevertheless, some scholars claim a Middle Byzantine origin at least for the Venetian type with a ground plan based on the through passageway with the lesser rooms aligned along it, widespread in the late Middle Ages and probably related to the ground plans of princely Bulgarian and Armenian residences. Other similarities are discernible between the development – from the late-Gothic period onwards – of

Venetian ambassadors at the gate of Damascus,
end of fifteenth – beginning of sixteenth century.
Paris, Louvre.

Late-antique villa with loggia and towers, Tunis, Bardo museum.

the facade of the Venetian house in the direction of a tripartite scheme with a central four- or three-light window, and the widespread if later popularity around the Mediterranean of facades with airy three-light windows, found from Anatolia to the coasts of the Near East. But this problem is as yet unsolved, and will remain so until we have a better knowledge of the private residences of Byzantium and other Greco-Byzantine centres, and until the course taken by early medieval Venetian palazzo architecture has been more fully charted, also from an archaeological point of view.[36]

In fact, the *casa-fondaco* might also take other forms: Ca' Lion at S. Giovanni Crisostomo, for example, is set well back from the bank of the Grand Canal, leaving a wide empty area in front of it with a well-head – a sort of courtyard on the water – from which the *piano nobile* above the big storerooms was reached by an outside staircase up against the facade.

What is fairly clear, however, is that a degree of Byzantine influence, particularly in the decoration of the facades, made itself felt in the architecture of the Venetian *casa-fondaco* between the twelfth and thirteenth centuries as a result of the combined effect of the capture of Constantinople and the resumption of building work in the Marcian area. The fascination exerted by Byzantine palace architecture transpires clearly from the western sources concerning the conquest: they repeatedly extol the beauties of the palace of the emperor Alexius at Chalcedon – 'one of the most

left
Palazzo Dandolo-Farsetti, Grand Canal.

below
Palazzo Pesaro (Fontego dei Turchi), before
the nineteenth-century restorations.

Ca' Loredan, riva del Carbon.

beautiful and . . . delightful that the human eye had ever looked upon, with all the enchantments that men desire, and which should be present in the house of a prince' – of the palace of the Blanchernae and the many rich, tall, solid palaces of the nobility.[37]

Equally frequent was praise of the palace in Constantinople – 'one of the most beautiful in the world' – where the Venetian doge, Andrea Dandolo, took up residence.[38] Significantly enough, it was this building which, through an act of ducal patronage, the Venetian chroniclers saw as leading to the prototype, the exemplary blueprint, of thirteenth-century palace architecture, Ca' Dandolo on the Grand Canal. In fact it was from Constantinople that 'Messer lo Doxe' (His Honour the Doge), who was to be buried in Hagia Sophia, wrote 'to his son concerning the building of a palace at S. Luca on the Grand Canal, dispatching thither suitable stones, and thus was built a very seemly building, according to the fashions of the time'. The precious marbles of the façade were thus a symbol, for Venetian historical memory, of her longstanding triumphs in the Levant.[39]

Byzantine influence found expression in the widespread use of facings of precious marble (around this same time Istrian stone also began to be introduced, replacing the Aurisina stone which had been used from the ninth to the thirteenth centuries); of stilted arches, also found in the additions to the narthex of San Marco; and of string-courses decorated with acanthus leaves with their tips touching the wall, alternating

left
Ca' Foscolo, rio di Ca' Foscari.

below left
Palazzo Businello, Grand Canal.

Ca' da Mosto, Grand Canal.

Ca' Lion at S. Giovanni Crisostomo.

65

left
Ca' Falier at Sti Apostoli, multi-light windows.

below
Palazzo Priuli Bon at S. Stae.

with others pointing outwards, also found in the ducal basilica and probably on the facade of the Procuratie. Palazzo da Mosto, built after the middle of the thirteenth century, perfectly epitomizes the use of this set of characteristics. At the same time, with its decorative array of paterae, marble slabs, crosses and floral friezes above the great six-light window in the *piano nobile*, and a whole complex bestiary, originally polychrome, to the two sides of an enthroned Christ raising his hand in blessing, it also documents further tendencies towards a sumptuously self-celebrating ornamentation, equally in evidence in the arches with cusped extradoses, outlined by a rich dentilled cornice.

With certain exceptions, then, overall, Venetian architecture remained aloof from that of the West. It was this same aloofness – as the distinctive features of the myth of Venice and her self-aware uniqueness were becoming established – which not also distanced her from a hostile hinterland, which was elaborating its own brand of anti-Venetianism, directed against a race of proud and superstitious misers, haughty oppressors of the world at large, a people sufficient unto themselves, a 'quintessence' recognizing neither God, nor church, nor emperor, nor sea, nor land, except as far as they were so minded.[40] It was true that, around the middle of the thirteenth century, some of the ties with Byzantine models were slackening; overt anti-Venetian feeling was now emerging in the East, its literary roots already discernible in the twelfth century in the historical works of John Cinnamus, and later in those of Maximos Planoudes, Demetrios Kydones and Sylvester Syropoulos. Yet even in fourteenth-century Venice, when the shift to the Gothic was already imminent, the image of Constantinople as the measure of all magnificence was very much alive: even in the 1350s, in the view of Andrea Dandolo, procurator of San Marco and later doge (1343–54), whose chronicles nevertheless also perpetuated the historical memory of medieval Venice, Hagia Sophia – *Agiosophia*, as he called it – built on the model shown by the Angel to Justinian,[41] quite simply outshone any work of architecture ever built.

1 *Origo Civitatum, op. cit.*, p. 28.
2 P. L. Zovatto, *Mosaici paleocristiane delle Venezie*, Udine 1963, p. 158.
3 W. Dorigo, *Venezia origine. Fondamenti, ipotesi, metodi*, Milan 1983, p. 630.
4 *Origo Civitatum, op. cit., passim.*
5 Biblioteca nazionale marciana, Venice (hereafter B.N.M.V.), mss. it. cl. VII, 517 (=7883), f. 18.
6 A. Carile and G. Fedalto, *Le origine di Venezia*, Bologna 1978, pp. 207, 221, plate V.
7 *Origo Civitatum, op. cit., passim.*
8 S. Tuzzato, 'Le strutture lignee altomedievalli a Olivolo (S. Pietro di Castello – Venezia)', in *Studi di archeologia della X Regio in ricordo di Michele Tombolani*, ed. B. M. Scarfi, Rome 1994, pp. 479–88.
9 *SS. Ilario e Benedetto* and *S. Gregorio*, ed. L. Lanfranchi and B. Strina, Venice 1965.
10 *La cronaca veneziana, op. cit., passim.*
11 *Ibid.*, p. 110.
12 M. De Min, 'Lo scavo archeologico nella chiesa di S. Lorenzo di Castello a Venezia', in *Studi di archeologia, op. cit.*, pp. 495–518. These excavations are still under way.
13 A. Perusi, '*Quaedam regalia insignia*'. 'Ricerche sulle insegne del potere ducale a Venezia durante il medioevo', in *Studi Veneziani*, vol. 7, 1965, p. 77.
14 Biblioteca del civico museo Correr, Venice (hereafter B.M.C.V.), *Annales Mundi*, mss Cicogna 3530, f. 113v.
15 B.N.M.V., mss. it. cl. VII, 518 (=7884), f. 36v.
16 C. Foss, *Ephesus after Antiquity: A Late Antique, Byzantine and Turkish City*, Cambridge 1979, with extensive bibliography.
17 The miraculous finding and presence in the *Apostoleion* of the body of the evangelist Luke, together with those of saints Andrew and Timothy, is mentioned with particular insistence by Procopius in his *De aedificiis*.
18 A. Dandolo, *Chronicon Venetum*, ed. E. Pastorello, Bologna 1938, p. 213;

M. D'Onofrio, *La Campania*, vol. IV of *Italia romanica*, Milan 1981, pp. 238–50; *I Normanni*, ed. M. D'Onofrio, exhibition catalogue, Venice 1994, pp. 199–207.
19 F. Sansovino and G. Martinioni, *Venetia città nobilissima et singolare*, Venice 1663 (The work was reprinted both in 1604 with additions by Giovanni Sringa, canon of San Marco, and in 1663 with additions by Martinioni), p. 6; M. A. Sabellico, *Del sito, op. cit.*, pp. 26, 32.
20 F. Sansovino and G. Martinioni, *Venetia, op. cit.*, p. 39.
21 P. Corrao, *Arsenali, costruzioni navali e attrezzature portuali in Sicilia (secoli X–XV)*, in *Arsenali e città nell'Occidente europeo*. For the Venetian *arsana* at Constantinople, see the 1231 treaty between Jacopo Tiepolo and the Western emperor in G. L. Fr. Tafel and G. M. Thomas, *Urkunden zur Älteren Handels- und Staatsgeschichte der Republik Venedig*, Vienna 1856, II, p. 289, ed. E. Concina, Rome 1987, pp. 35–50.
22 G. Cracco, *Società e stato nel medioevo veneziano (secoli XII–XIV)*, Florence 1967, p. 14.
23 C. Mango, *Le Développment urbain de Constantinople (IVe–VIIe siècles)*, Paris 1990, p. 29.
24 G. Fasoli, 'Liturgia e cerimoniale ducale', in *Venezia e il Levante fino al secolo XV*, ed. A. Pertusi, Florence 1973, pp. 261–93.
25 B.N.M.V., mss. it. cl. VII, 517 (=7883), f. 68v; G. Dragon, *Constantinople imaginaire. Etudes sur le recueil des 'Patria'*, Paris 1984, pp. 165, 183.
26 B.N.M.V., mss. it. cl. VII, 518 (=7884), f. 36v.
27 *Ibid.*
28 F. Sansovino and G. Martinioni, *Venetia, op. cit.*, p. 96; F. Corner, *Notizie storiche delle chiese e monasteri di Venezia e di Torcello*, Padua 1758, p. 191.
29 G. Dragon, *Constantinople, op. cit.*, pp. 296–8; Tschudi is mentioned by K. A. C. Creswell,

L'architettura islamica delle origini, Milan 1966, p. 43.
30 The image of Constantinople as the city of the Mother of God goes back to Theodore Syncellus; for the Nicopeia: G. Tiepolo, *Trattato dell'immagine della Gloriosa Vergine dipinta da San Luca, conservata già da molti secoli nella ducal chiesa di San Marco*, Venice 1618, p. 20.
31 N. Zeno, *Dell'origine de'barbari che distrussero per tutto 'l mondo l'imperio di Roma, onde hebbe principio la città di Venetia*, Venice 1550 (2nd edn revised by the author), p. 29.
32 A. K. Placzek, J. S. Ackerman and M. N. Rosenfeld, *Sebastiano Serlio on Domestic Architecture. The Sixteenth-century Manuscript of Book VI in the Avery Library of Columbia University*, Cambridge, Mass. and London, p. lv.
33 F. Sansovino and G. Martinioni, *Venetia, op. cit.*, p. 384.
34 See G. Cracco, *Società, op. cit.*, p. 36.
35 P. L. Zovatto, *Mosaici, op. cit.*, pp. 18–19.
36 See the positions summarised by R. Krautheimer, *Early Christian and Byzantine architecture*, Harmonsworth 1965, pp. 286 ff.
37 G. Villehardouin, *La conquista di Costantinopoli*, Milan 1988, pp. 44, 59, 71–4.
38 *Ibid.*, p. 79.
39 B.N.M.V., mss. it. cl. VII, 517 (=7883), f. 56.
40 See G. Cracco, *Società, op. cit.*, pp. 223–4.
41 A. Dandolo, *Chronicon, op. cit.*, p. 68. With the exception of the 'examplar sibi ab angelo ostensum', Dandolo's judgment ('que cuncta edificia ita excelit, ut simile usque in odiernum reperiri non possit') is very similar to that of Paulus Diaconus, *Historia Longobardorum*, I.25 ('cuius opus adeo cuncta aedificia excellit, ut in totis terrarum spatiis huic simile non possit inveniri'): Andrea Dandolo's updating in time is however extremely significant.

VENICE AND THE GOTHIC

A̲ᴛ the end of the thirteenth century, Venice's acceptance and subsequent autonomous elaboration of the Gothic style occurred in the peculiar circumstances that characterized her cultural and social context as a whole: with many reservations, compromises and stylistic blendings, and with inevitable accommodations to a setting that was itself extremely dynamic and complex. After Martino da Canal had celebrated the city and its history in his famous chronicle in the French language, and after another member of her mercantile aristocracy, Bartolomeo Zorzi, had written his verses in Provençal, Venice turned to the *opus francigenum*: at a time, namely, that roughly coincided with the end of any aspirations for the Venetian dialect to become a literary language, and with the rapid and early spread, in Venice, of Tuscan poetry.

Here an important part was played by the Serenissima's dawning interest in the hinterland, particularly with the acquisition of Treviso and its territory (1339). But a balanced historical view would also have to bear in mind the widespread popularity of late-Romanesque and Gothic forms throughout the Mediterranean Levant, which partly preceded and partly accompanied the new period of Venetian architecture. These forms took root in the territories of the kingdom of Jerusalem, and in Cyprus and Rhodes. They circulated in the Western colonies of Greece and Asia Minor before finally taking root in Byzantine architecture itself, at least in terms of the adoption of stylistic elements.

At the end of the seventeenth century, Gravier d'Ortières executed a remarkable view of St. Jean d'Acre, on what is now the coast of Israel (Akko); here, in the twelfth and thirteenth centuries, the Venetians had had their own quarter, their own 'fondaco', a church dedicated to St. Mark and various fortified structures. In Gravier d'Ortières's view it still appears as dominated by the spectacular Gothic ruins of the Eglise Sainct André, with its tall pointed trefoil windows, with a quatrefoil oculus above, similar to those of the church of St. John and the gaunt and massive bulk of the Palace of the Grand Master which the Venetian merchants had seen and frequented until 1291.[1]

Gothic architecture entered Venice along with a whole series of 'great transformations', as Giovanni Villani put it: in navigational techniques, in the organization of maritime trade, in social and institutional structures; and in parallel with a spurt in urban development which, at the beginning of the fourteenth century, took the population of the city to almost 115,000 inhabitants.

If the inroads made by lexical elements of the Gothic can already be sensed in the thirteenth century, its mature acceptance in Venice – always with certain reservations – did not occur before the first half of the fourteenth century, when it was quickened on the one hand by the great surge of convent building, and on the other by the series of major public enterprises embarked upon shortly afterwards around the area of the

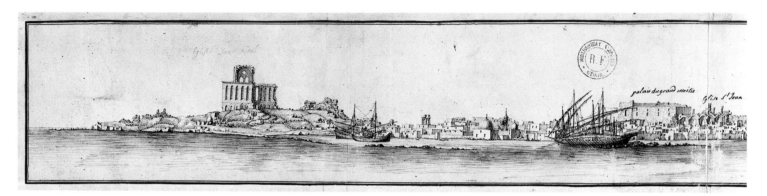

above
St. Jean d'Acre with ruins of the Gothic
churches of St. Andrew and St. John,
bird's-eye view, seventeenth century.
Paris, Bibliothèque Nationale.

right
Plan of Venice from the fourteenth-
century manuscript of the *Chronologia
magna*, Venice, Biblioteca nazionale
marciana.

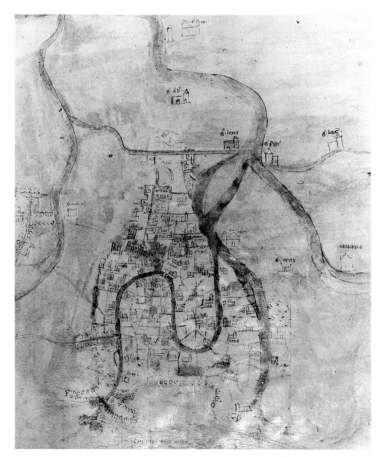

basin of San Marco, from the Arsenal to the confluence of the Grand Canal and that of the Giudecca.

Between the thirteenth and fourteenth centuries, therefore, Venice was growing particularly rapidly: by the mid-thirteenth century she had assumed the role of unchallenged capital of the territory around the lagoon, whose centres she now controlled through her own officials.

In the city, while certain 'industrial' activities were now being driven out of the urban areas, building land was being extended into the lagoon shallows, often partly through the random undertakings of private individuals, as graphically documented by the jagged outline of the northern perimeter as seen in the famous map in the *Chronologia Magna*, pre-dating 1325 at least.[2] Craftsmen now began to move to these expanding areas, where the expectations and social tensions inherent in thirteenth-century Venice were at their most heated, as were renewed outbursts of religious fervour. Here, too, the mendicant orders and several new monastic foundations put up a number of buildings which came to constitute so many points of reference for the transformations under way.

Nor was it any coincidence that, while it was doge Marino Morosini (1249–53) – the nephew of the first Western patriarch of Constantinople, and closely linked to members of the thirteenth-century Venetian aristocracy – who commissioned important mosaic decorations for the central church of S. Salvador, it was doge Jacopo

SS Giovanni e Paolo, facade and South flank.

Anon., plan of the complex of SS Giovanni e
Paolo. Venice, museo Correr.

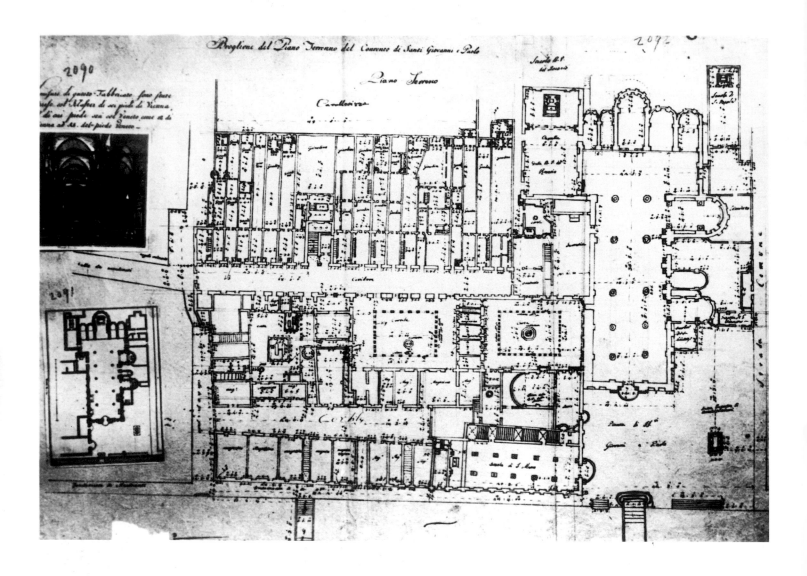

Tiepolo (1229–49), politically very mindful of popular opinion,[3] who encouraged the building of the Dominican and Franciscan complexes of SS Giovanni e Paolo and S. Maria Gloriosa dei Frari in the developing outer suburbs.

We cannot state with any certainty, however, that the almost certain Byzantinism of the mosaics was in intentional contrast with the definite westernizing tendency in architectural culture of the convent buildings, though this is not unlikely. The latter were radically rebuilt from the early fourteenth century, by which time they had come to embody two of the main routes for Gothic architecture's definitive entry into the city.

Even if it is difficult to establish either a precise chronology for the rebuilding of the church and convent of SS Giovanni e Paolo, founded in 1234, or the exact relationship between the thirteenth-century buildings and the fourteenth-century one, work on this latter must have begun around 1315, when a proposed extension of the existing religious building was announced. We have evidence of intense activity during the 1330s and 40s, for instance concerning the use of stone discarded from the worksite of the Ducal palace, implying some contact between the two sites. Work slowed down towards the middle of the century, with the great plague of 1348–9, to be resumed with greater momentum and regularity above all between 1373 and 1385. But in 1395 the main body of the building had still not been completed: it was consecrated only in 1430,

Church of SS Giovanni e Paolo in the Venetian townscape.

and the dome was not put into position until the middle of the fifteenth century. The main portal, on which Bartolomeo Bon seems to have worked and which already shows elements of a shift towards an early Renaissance style, was not in place until 1458–60, while the facade was left unfinished. The Dominican church of SS Giovanni e Paolo thus had a long-drawn-out and complex history, experiencing difficulties and disruptions similar to those of various other important contemporary buildings. But it was still one of the main Gothic buildings in Venice, and recognized as such by Renaissance art historical literature: 'A most vast work, whose too great height causes its summit to be wreathed in mist, and quite enormous in size', an unmistakable landmark in the urban landscape of the city-state, according to Sabellico: a noble structure 'for its great size and the beauty of its paintings, statues and other notable features, although the manner of its architecture be German' according to Francesco Sansovino.[4]

SS Giovanni e Paolo gives the impression of having been carefully planned, despite the time-lag between the body of the building and the area of the apses, and despite certain evident irregularities of execution. Its ground plan is closely related to those of other contemporary churches, including S. Maria Novella in Florence – also a Dominican church – which also has a series of high, deep recesses on the facade, intended for tombs, as do the Eremitani at Padua and S. Lorenzo at Vicenza. The plan of SS Giovanni e Paolo is a Latin cross with a clearly projecting transept: a considerable novelty in relation to local medieval traditions, with their propensity for basilican or centralized plans. Its nave is made up of five almost square bays, flanked by two aisles whose width is half that of the nave. The transept – along which the main chapel, with a polygonal apse, and four lesser apses are aligned – is lit to the south by a large tracery window, unusual in Venetian religious architecture (although bearing some similarity with the Gothic rose-window in the end wall of the right-hand arm of the transept of San Marco).

The main body of the church is governed by a precise and lucid system of proportions: the height of the nave is equal to one hundred Venetian feet, that is, two and a half times its width; the width of the transept (and the internal height of the dome) is three times that of the nave, and so on. But the architectural system as a whole has none of the rigorous, strained and almost formulaic feeling typical of the northern Gothic. Respectful of traditional technical experience and adapting to the needs of a site described by thirteenth-century deeds of gift as a muddy lagoon bank, the structure was lightened and simplified accordingly. The rhythm of the arches is broad and airy; they are slightly more closely set in the bays of the main body of the church, and more widely in the area of the choir, transept and chancel, where they rise on a square of forty Venetian feet per side. The role of light is paramount in conferring unity upon the space so created; its task is made easier by the cylindrical shape of the pillars, which are unfluted, and therefore unscalloped by lines which might cause tense shadow, with the light pouring triumphantly into the chancel through the extraordinary apsidal tracery with three orders of openings, showing the influence of northern prototypes, possibly via the church of S. Nicolò in nearby Treviso.

The last bay of the nave is distinguished by two clustered pillars, trilobed in section, with rich capitals with flattened foliage: they designate the boundary of the marble partition of the monks' choir, which was demolished in 1692. The original presence of this choir also helps clarify the implications of the dome, built as a modification of the earlier design. Within the Latin cross of the ground plan as a whole, the enclosure made by the last bay of the nave, the transept, and the large apsidal chapel inscribed the Greek cross of a space of greater liturgical importance, enhanced by the celebratory and sanctifying form of the dome: a scheme undoubtedly conceived as a gesture in the direction of Veneto-Byzantine architecture.

The Franciscan church of S. Maria dei Frari was built during the fourth decade of the thirteenth century, not very far from the commercial district of Rialto, but in an area which was still secluded, semi-rural and partly marshy, which the activity of the Friars Minor had helped to bring definitively into the city fabric between the thirteenth and fourteenth centuries. The

S. Maria Gloriosa dei Frari, facade.

S. Maria Gloriosa dei Frari, interior.

first stone of the new building, dedicated to S. Maria Gloriosa (the Virgin enthroned in Glory), was laid in 1250, but the Franciscan ethos and the Minorite presence did not really gain a hold upon the city until the third rebuilding of the church, which began around 1330 and was concluded only in the following century, as with SS Giovanni e Paolo. The Frari entered the city toponymy with the name 'Ca' Granda' (literally 'big house'), testifying to the impression its vast size made upon the collective imagination of late-medieval Venice, and to the profoundly changed relations that now obtained between the religious order and the city.

The Gothic building was not only far larger than the medieval church, but its original orientation was also reversed. The apses of the fourteenth-fifteenth century church now stood on the site of the campo that had been in front of the facade of the second S. Maria at the beginning of the fourteenth century: the change had meant abandoning the traditional liturgical orientation (the apses now faced south-west) in favour of siting the new facade towards the canal, the bridge (built in 1428) and the streets of artisans' workshops which led towards S. Polo and the commercial area of Rialto.

The architecture of S. Maria dei Frari – based on a Latin cross plan with a double series of apsidal chapels to each side of the main one – has evident parallels with the central Italian models typical of the Franciscan order. But it also bears a fairly close resemblance to the contemporary

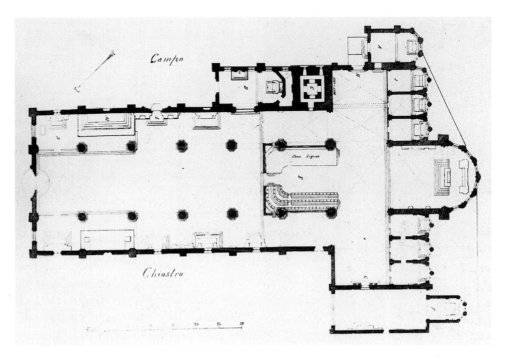

S. Maria Gloriosa dei Frari, ground plan (from Cicognara-Diedo-Selva, 1838-40).

Dominican church of SS Giovanni e Paolo, sharing its concern for the lightening of its structure and for the creation of an internal space which would be unitary, measured and serene. It also has several typically Venetian features, such as the use of wooden tie-beams, as at SS Giovanni e Paolo, linking the tall pillars, and arches with cusped extradoses framing the lower order of the windows of the main apse.

But Ca' Granda also has several important features not shared by SS Giovanni e Paolo. Not only does it have no dome over the crossing, but its facade is far more sober, and was never intended to have the arcaded gallery, with its tall, deep, blind niches, found on the lower part of the facade of Giovanni e Paolo. Its main portal is much less self-important; the swaying upper outline of the facade is entirely in brick, rather than stone.

Brick is also used for the prominent crowning cornices – which run along the sides – for the geometrical, star-shaped motifs of the moulded cornices of the windows, and for the ornament on the apse; it is used again in the interior for the minute designs on the windows in the main chapel. The Frari therefore seems to stand in deliberate contrast to the Dominican church by virtue of a marked sobriety of forms, and an avoidance of costly materials where not strictly necessary or required by some particular function. Such choices reflected not just the order's general attitude but, more specifically, the ideals of poverty which were emerging in Franciscan centres in

and around Venice at the end of the thirteenth century and during the first half of the fourteenth.[5] The Frari is also unique among Venetian churches in that its choir is still in the original fifteenth-century position: the intended sense of internal space is thus perfectly legible, with its clear-cut division between the nave and aisles, for the ordinary congregation, and the complex of the choir-transept-apsidal chapels, whose liturgical role was clarified and underscored accordingly.

The third main example of Gothic monastic architecture in Venice, which has now almost completely vanished, was the church of S. Maria dei Servi, founded in 1318 but consecrated only in 1491, 'of such a size that it has twenty-two altars', a 'magnificent' piece of architecture endowed with two 'majestic' chapels.[6]

Of its two remaining portals, the main one, overlooking the canal, has various interesting features, particularly the use of alternating ashlar quoins in white Istrian stone and 'broccatello' marble from Verona in the taller ogival arch, and the reuse, beneath it, of a Veneto-Byzantine round-headed arch in Greek marble decorated with plant volutes, standing on an architrave and jambs with differently-shaped outlines, also pre-Gothic. Far from being a random or approximate combination, it has all the hallmarks of something carefully planned, an episode of stylistic blending achieved through the use of salvaged material comparable to the use of Veneto-Byzantine capitals and columns in

the aedicules crowning the Frari, and to
other similar cases to be found in contemporary civil architecture.

With the three monastic complexes,
areas that had previously been more or less
marginal now became fully defined parts of
the urban landscape. Stretches of medieval
outskirts now took on the form of piazzas,
'most noble *campi* . . . almost at the city's
heart'.[7] As the bird's-eye view by Jacopo de'
Barbari was to demonstrate so clearly, the
main Venetian Gothic churches extended
the area of urban splendour and left a
strongly assertive mark on the city's profile,
as Erhard Reeuwich had already perceived
as early as 1486.[8]

These buildings were extraordinary
architectural testimonies to piety in late-
Gothic Venice, the building of which had
numerous social implications and repercussions: above all, they were associated
with the last phases of what has been called
the 'establishing' of the Venetian church.
The great religious spaces of the three late-
Gothic monastic churches thus also
became the appointed settings, and instruments, for the celebration of the great men
who stood at the pinnacle of the triumphant
holy republic of Mark the evangelist. From
the middle of the fourteenth century, the
doges' tombs ceased to be placed in the
basilica of San Marco, and tended to be
clustered in the Frari, the Servi and above
all SS Giovanni e Paolo; so that these
churches too began to register emergent
late-Gothic tendencies in the architecture
and decoration of their tombs.

View through the arches of the 'squeri' of the darsena dell'Arsenale Vecchio (dockyard of the Old Arsenal).

Palazzo dei Patroni at the Arsenal, known as 'Purgatorio'.

During the first half of the fourteenth century, around the same time as the great Gothic monastic churches were being built, work also started on a group of publicly-commissioned buildings which were to be of crucial significance for the history of the urban structure and artistic culture of Venice, namely, the reorganization of her harbour installations and, more particularly, the redevelopment of urban areas overlooking the basin of San Marco, which had begun in the last quarter of the thirteenth century and which were now given new momentum.

The most important was that of the Arsenal, the earliest purpose-built and spatially defined waterfront site of the *civitas* of Rialto. Between the end of the thirteenth century and the first decades of the fourteenth, work centred around the rebuilding of the *Arsena Vetus* (old Arsenal), the building of the new communal Arsenal, the *domus canipi Communis* (Rope-factory of the Tana) and the new granaries of S. Biagio, documented from 1324.

Apart from serving for the seasonal maintenance and repair of ships, at an early stage the old Arsenal also seems to have been used as a depot for siege machinery. In 1265 a permanent depot was built there, or an existing one enlarged, for storing timber for the building of galleys and, a little later (1278), an *armamentarium* (ordnance depot). The first building housing the Corderie della Tana (Rope-factories) for the storing and working of hemp dates from (1291–1323) taking its place in the roll-call

of the Serenissima's architectural peculiarities as early as the fifteenth century: 'The longest and widest house that ever I saw, or anyone else, I do believe', as a Frenchman noted.[9]

Meanwhile, in February 1302, a decree had been passed forbidding the fitting out of communal galleys anywhere except in the Arsenal, already paving the way for the building of the new one, fron 1326 onwards, in an area 'all marsh and waters'.[10]

The expansion of Venice's dockyard installations was characterized by innovation rather than by mere quantitative growth; on the distributive level, the organization of the relevant space was conceived in terms of a speedy and intensive fitting out of their main 'product', the galley. The Arsenal was now not used just as an ordnance depot, and for maintenance, but also, and primarily, for shipbuilding. It also served as base for a small fleet, and guaranteed the safety of the harbour. From the fourteenth century onwards it produced side-arms and firearms, and was capable of providing the main centres of the Venetian 'stato da mar' with an impressive flow of supplies. As a public body, it played an important logistical role in the reorganizing of maritime power, and gave constant backing to the city's great public undertakings from an early date.

But its dawning relationship with the city was not purely functional. The great fourteenth-century building of the Arsenal seemed to generate tendencies for the

establishing, or refining, of new nexuses within the urban structure as a whole.

Around this same period, when work on the adjacent rope factory had probably already been completed, the old *salaria* (salt states) of S. Biagio, near the public dockyards, were being radically restructured and turned into granaries (1322–3). In the nearby districts of S. Martino and S. Biagio the first nuclei of the 'Case di San Marco' were also coming into being (1330–1409), free housing for the *proti* (foremen) and workers in the Arsenal. The creation of the new *granaria* (granaries) of S. Biagio marked the beginning of a further expansion outwards. At about the same time as they were being restructured, work was beginning both on new salt depots on the site of the future Dogana 'da mar' (maritime customs house), and on the other public granaries of Terranova, near San Marco, replacing one of the old areas of communal dockyards outside the Arsenal. Clearly, a wholesale process of replacement and redistribution was now occurring in spaces and functions throughout the harbour area.

From 1340 onwards, the ducal *palatium* too was being restructured in the forms we see today. After initial work in the late thirteenth century, from 1324 onwards the bank of the lagoon between San Marco and Castello was paved, as was its extension westwards, the 'fondamenta' of the Molo; and a linked series of stone bridges was built between 1333 and 1360, that of San Marco being still partly intact. The *ripa*

Sancti Marci was now taking shape:
already referred to among the Venetian
sites celebrated by Petrarch, and later
referred to by Sanudo as one of the
mirabilia urbis, it was unfailingly picked
out by cartographers of the early sixteenth
century as one of the city's distinctive
landmarks.

But these were no longer mere works of
substitution or functional redistribution:
they emerge as part of a general programme for the defining and characterizing of the whole harbour area 'on the
Basin, which is our port'.[11] This cluster
of undertakings ultimately gave rise to
the fully-fledged basin of San Marco, the
meeting-point of the navigable canals
flowing in from the sea as seen in the map
in the *Chronologia magna*, the 'place of
Neptune' in the bird's-eye view by de'
Barbari, and the centre of the lagoon microcosm in the view by Benedetto Bordone: it
was consistently identified as the centre of
a city which, as a whole, struck Petrarch
as resembling a 'public harbour for the
human race'.[12] Seen in this context, we
may understand the meaning of the
modifications now made to the columns on
the Piazzetta, with the addition of the statue
of Venice's protector, St. Theodore (1329),
fashioned out of an imperial Roman torso
and a Greek head. But the aspirations to a
new grandeur clearly ran much deeper.

The reasoning behind these important
revisions had largely been utilitarian, fed
by a desire to revitalize and boost the city's
economic role in Europe and the

Mediterranean. But their outward configurations were also bound up with a concern for display which emerged quite clearly between the end of the thirteenth century and the first half of the fourteenth.

Venice's ruling class and constitutional bodies also took on definitive shape during the period between 1310 and 1338: the *civitatis forma* was fixed and codified, as was the legal system in whose connection Andrea Dandolo (1343–54) talked of *reformare deformata* (the reforming of that which had become deformed). In parallel with the physical ordering of the city as a whole, the magistrature *super publicis* now came into being (1282), the body responsible for defining relations between public and private landowners as the city expanded. The fourteenth-century manuscript of the *Chronologia Magna*, the earliest known map of the city, confirmed that it was now possible to take in its overall form, together with that of its waterways and connections with the sea.[13]

It also becomes clear that the second, but by no means secondary, purpose underlying the fourteenth-century operations around the 'Canal of San Marco' was to reassert the *honor civitatis*, a phrase and concept explicitly used in connection with the layout of the *riva marciana* (embankment of San Marco).

Venice was elaborating this self-image precisely when she was being perceived as a negative place, an object of widespread and persistent hostility, in need of vindication; when anti-Venetian feeling was

above
Ducal Palace, facade on to the lagoon.

left
So-called palace of Constantine Porphyrogenitus (Tekfur Sarayi), Istanbul.

painting the Venetians as a grasping people, rapacious wolves, faithless men, without any integrity or values, as already mentioned.

It is not difficult to see the fourteenth-century decisions which gave meaningful shape to the port-canal of San Marco[14] – pivotal as it was to the space of the city – as preparation for a new *splendor civitatis*, pursued on two levels: an internal one, directed at the people of this *civitas*, and an external one, directed at the western world of trade and passing traffic. For the first, the siting of the granaries of Terranova on an axis with the Piazza and palace of San Marco had its own significance: the granaries were the physical symbol of good government within the city and of an *abundantia rerum* (abundance of goods) generated by the *nova instituta* (new institutions), which in their turn gave rise to the second, namely the palace, reflecting the new social order following the political triumph of the great Venetian traders.

But all in all – bearing in mind that it was the monopoly of grain and salt which lay at the root of the city's fourteenth-century success in trade and also, largely, of the hostility of the Po area towards Venice – the relocating of *granaria* and *salaria* in the new buildings on the San Marco basin could also be seen as a symbolic statement, a stubborn response to any number of accusations and threats, and a challenge calling for emulation. It was here, significantly enough, between Terranova and the Ducal palace, that the Gothic style was raised to the level of a public language, that the new symbols proclaiming Venice's power and mercantile nature came into being through an international style, an architectural *langue* 'qui cort parmi le mond' (which is current throughout the world).[15]

The granaries of Terranova were the first civil public building in Venice to have features that were recognizably Gothic. Though it was demolished in the early nineteenth century, the building is known to us through a number of graphic sources and *vedute* which show it to have been a large complex of one hundred Venetian feet in depth, by three hundred and thirty-three in length (equivalent to about 115 metres), consisting of four four-storey blocks, separated by *calli* to be used in case of fire, lit and ventilated by a large number of windows, and reachable from the 'Piazza della Pescaria' in front of it for the periodic maintenance of its storerooms. The blocks were linked by tall pointed arches over the *calli*, the central one of which had a large bas-relief with the lion of St. Mark; the facade was given a sense of unity by a continuous cornice crowned by slender crenellations on small hanging arches, with alternating triangular elements and delicate pinnacles, not unlike the later one crowning the Ducal palace.

The decision to build a large new assembly hall for the Maggior Consiglio, which then led to the general rebuilding of the Ducal palace, was taken on 28 December 1340. It is possible that a unitary idea for the general restructuring of the ducal and council buildings dated from 1341. But there is no doubt that the New palace completed in the first years of the fifteenth century corresponds to the south front of the palace as we know it today, a longitudinal block whose facade, over the *riva* and basin of San Marco, opened on to the latter with seventeen arches; in depth it extended into the Piazzetta with just the seven southern bays. The facade consisted of a double order of arches, in the Venetian palazzo tradition, above which stretched a vast flat wall surface without any sculptural ornament, but polychrome, in white and red marble, crowned by elegant slender crenellations and pierced by wide ogival windows; the capitals of the ground-floor colonnade had exuberant sculptural decorations with a range of iconographical themes. It bore a close resemblance to the now vanished Ca' Barozzi, on a *castrum*-type plan, which originally overlooked the Grand Canal at S. Moisè, and which appears meticulously depicted in the bird's-eye view plan by Jacopo de' Barbari.

In addition to these, Lombard influence, and more remote western influences in general, were also visible in the fourteenth-century architecture of the Ducal palace. Yet it appeared unique and sophisticated, a highly original synthesis of the basic features of Venetian experience: its delicate use of colour, with the juxtaposing of white Istrian stone and red Verona marble, seems to hark back to the imperial colours of Constantinople and the similarly elaborate use of two colours and decorative geometrical

Balcony overlooking the Piazzetta.

Balcony of the Sala del Maggior Consiglio, Ducal palace.

motifs found in contemporary Byzantine architecture such as the palace of Constantine Porphyrogenitus (Tekfur Sarayi). The comparisons formerly suggested with the decorative brickwork found in Seljuk architecture and the Mongolian architecture of northern Iran,[16] however, now seem somewhat far-fetched. Oddly enough, the palazzo was to be regarded by Vincenzo Scamozzi as having been built using Greek materials, while his classicizing outlook caused him to judge it extremely negatively: 'nothing more than one great block supported by the puniest shafts of columns',[17] in a significant reversal of the Renaissance interpretation of the structure, regarded as a 'formidable and sensational' technical feat according to the Venetian tradition documented by Pietro Contarini (1542).

The first half of the fourteenth century was thus a period of great vitality for Venice: the public worksites were now highly organized, and the respective fields of architects and 'inzegnarii' (engineers) were becoming more clearly defined.

After having given legal status to the building guilds, Venice now reorganized and regulated the brick industry with the introduction of uniform dimensions and standards of quality. The use of new types of brick (medieval 'altinelle' – small red bricks – or bricks *ad mensuram parvam*), is documented from the twelfth century; in the fourteenth, important innovations were made with the introduction of large 'Gothic' bricks. These were probably produced by the brickyards set up by the commune with

Piazza San Marco in a late-fifteenth-century illumination. Chantilly, musée Condé.

a decree dated March 1326, near the church of S. Biagio, and elsewhere shortly afterwards, to supply the worksite of the Arsenal and other public buildings; bricks continued to be imported from the region around Treviso, and the nobility invested in local production, which still proved insufficient for the needs of the time. A specific engineering culture also seems to have developed, with masters such as Silvestro, Andrea and Marco; and the *bonus ingeniator* who worked at the Arsenal in 1330 alongside the *protomagister* Marco; active there from 1331; and Francesco dalle Barche, who designed mechanisms for dredging mud from the canals, and who worked on the installations of the port of Candia (Heraklion) and its arsenal. Outstanding and influential figures now emerge from the shadows, though they cannot be related to any specific work, at least as research currently stands: they include 'maestro' Paganino, active around the first decade of the fourteenth century, who must have played a key role in the great building projects of the Gothic period, if it can be claimed that all Venice was in his hands.[18]

This was the background – energetic, technically dynamic and receptive to experiences from all around the Mediterranean – for such somewhat unclear information as we have concerning the attribution of the fabric of the new Ducal palace: during the early years it certainly seems to have involved Pietro Baseggio – *magister prothus Palatii nostri novi* – who died before 1351, to be followed immediately afterwards by

87

top right
Passageway between the Porta della Carta and the internal courtyard of the Ducal palace.

below right
Loggia Foscara.

below
Porta della Carta.

above
External staircase in the courtyard at Ca' Centani at S. Toma (Goldoni's house).

below
External staircase in the smaller courtyard in palazzo Sanudo van Axel.

'maestro' Enrico (1351–6). The group of masters working on the New palace probably also included Filippo Calendario, a stonemason from the district of S. Samuele, an entrepreneur and executor of Baseggio's will, renowned in Venetian chronicles for his involvement in the conspiracy of Marino Falier and his subsequent beheading. There is no direct contemporary evidence for the fourteenth-century tradition which attributes him with a first unitary plan for the architecture of the palace, though this view has recently been partially accepted by certain art historians.[19]

Work on the New palace extended over many decades, partly as a result of the terrible plague that occurred in the middle of the fourteenth century, and partly because of the Genoese conquest of Chioggia, which brought the enemy virtually to the city 'gates'. Work on the facade overlooking the lagoon was not complete until the beginning of the fifteenth century.

Further concern for the reputation of the state, and of the city, led to the deliberations of 22 July 1400 in connection with the execution of the project, already in existence on a sheet of parchment, for the monumental balcony of the Sala del Maggior Consiglio. Here, after framing the existing broad ogival window with a double pair of small twinned columns, Pierpaolo di Jacobello delle Masegne added two slender tall outer pillars, with aedicules containing statues of vices and virtues, rising above the coping of the facade. In the wall above the oculus he placed the image of the doge,

kneeling before the lion of St. Mark, crowning the composition with a tall stone canopy whose niches house St. Mark, protector of the city, and Saints Peter and Paul, respectively the cornerstone and codifier of Christianity.

The graceful, strongly three-dimensional figures, created with great attention to their context, reveal a broad knowledge of the latest developments: they bear the mark of Florentine, Milanese and Mantuan experience, brought together here in a serene and solemn embodiment of the values of the Serenissima.

The saints to either side of the broad balcony, in red Verona marble, are George and Theodore, Byzantine warrior saints; always very popular in Venice, they were to be venerated with new devotion during the fifteenth century. The figures of the cardinal and theological virtues are those which should accompany the government of a prince, in particular that of Antonio Venier – doge from 1382 until a few months after the final decision concerning the Ducal palace, and looked to as an *exemplum iustitiae* (example of justice) for the merciless severity with which he treated his own son.

The doge was portrayed on his knees before the symbol of the state, the lion of St. Mark, signalling his submission to the higher authority of laws and statutes. This emblematic allusion to the state, and its head, is figuratively crowned, that is, both empowered and protected, by the sanctifying apostolic trio.

The iconographical programme of the 'great gilded window' – looking towards the sea, as emphasized by the contract for its execution – is therefore easily interpreted: it is the faithful transcription, in figurative terms, of the celebration of the idea of the Venetian state as it emerged in the roughly contemporary writings of Rafain de Caresinis and Lorenzo de Monacis, that is, as the barque of St. Peter, as the barque of St. Mark approaching safe harbour; Venice as a 'quintessence' standing apart from the four natural elements, a bastion of faith against the Turk and other infidels; Venice where the law is king, where true *politia* is at work, and where that which is not good is not *politicum*.[20]

This symbolic message is reinforced by the pair of tall pinnacles framing the cere- monial window of the Sala del Maggior Consiglio (the council which, in the Serenissima's constitution, was to be *in similitudinem populi* in the likeness of the people). They are of the same type as those framing the two tabernacles to the sides of the chancel which houses the Blessed Sacrament in the adjacent basilica. The bal- dachin which crowns the composition acts as a further symbol of authority, regality and sovereign power.

Nor was it by mere chance that the pre- cious polychrome decor of the balcony should overlook the waters of the basin: its message of authority and piety was addressed to the city's piazza 'da mar' ('seaside' piazza), as it were, to the basin where the columns of Mark and Theodore proclaimed the arrival point of the *iter maritimum*, the reaching of the city triumphant. It was to the sea that evangelist, apostles, virtues and warrior saints addressed themselves during those years of the conquest of Nauplia and Argos, Shkodër and Durrës, and the retaking of Corfu.

The sculptures of the palace were to be interpreted by the Venetian collective imagination as prophecies and predictions. Jacopo Bellini studied and reproduced the glorious architecture of the balcony, making no secret of the fascination it exerted upon him. Pierpaolo's Gothic balcony was already ushering in the long succession of works of architecture celebrating the myth of Venice.

Significantly enough, despite its predominantly Gothic forms, Giovanni Bembo in his chronicles interpreted the balcony as a *maenianum*, that is, as deriving from the balcony or outer gallery of classical tradition, *in forma ianuae*, like a triumphal doorway.[21]

This interpretation was overtly echoed during the dogeship of Andrea Gritti (1523–38), when the great fifteenth-century window came to be repeated on the facade of the palace overlooking the piazzetta: its forms and meanings were now faithfully repeated for the benefit of the sixteenth-century observer with the incorporation of two winged victories at the sides of the ogee of the arch, transforming the tops of the pillars into eloquent obelisks suggesting perpetuity, and replacing the warrior saints with the likenesses of Mars and Neptune.

With the building of the great staircase, by the beginning of the fifteenth century the southern front of the New palace was complete.

A new cycle of extremely important public works, undertaken in the meantime, was further to delay completion of the palace. Between the end of the fourteenth century and the beginning of the fifteenth, a new group of works of military architecture gave the lagoon defences a distinctly Gothic appearance, while a series of planning acts laid down the basis for the rebuilding and repopulation of Chioggia. The building of the castle of la Lova (1384–5) was followed by that of Mestre and Motta di Livenza; Michele Steno (1401–13) rebuilt the tower of S. Nicolo del Lido, and erected the new *castrum* of S. Andrea on a harbour bar, giving rise to the complex of the Due Castelli, an extremely sensitive focal point in Venetian harbour space. Bearing in mind that the squat and sturdy rectangular tower at the end of the new 'dogana da mar' (maritime customs house) was built in 1414, to defend its warehouses and to act as an observation point at the confluence between the Grand Canal and that of the Giudecca, it may be said that the Venetian system of defence was basically in place by the first decades of the fifteenth century. In the meanwhile, the rebuilding of Chioggia had led to the creation of a real late-Gothic new town in the southern lagoon, financed by a carefully planned combination of private capital and public funding, as outlined by Pietro Emo in

his special additions to the city statutes (1392–3).[22]

Only in the 1420s was public attention refocused on Venice herself, with the resumption of work on the *platea* of San Marco and the great complex of the Ducal palace; it was then that doge Tommaso Mocenigo made the dramatic gesture, on 27 September 1422, of drawing a thousand ducats from his own personal funds, in order to reopen discussion of the extension of the building, previously expressly forbidden because of the parlous state of the city's finances.

At stake here was nothing less than the demolition of the old Veneto-Romanesque *Palatium ad jus reddendum* (law courts) founded by Sebastiano Ziani (1172–8), now in a precarious state of repair, and the building of a new wing in a form *decora et convenienti* (decorous fitting), in keeping with the august origins – the words occur in the decision taken by the Maggior Consiglio – of the New palace.

It is not impossible that this important undertaking might have derived from an initial overall project dating back to 1341. At all events, there is no doubt that once demolition had been completed, by 1424, the building on the piazzetta was a complete and faithful imitation of the south wing of the building, both in terms of architecture – here too consisting of a double row of arches beneath a vast wall surface, unarticulated but polychrome, crowned by elegant slender crenellations and pierced by large pointed windows – and of the

sculptural decoration of the capitals of the ground-floor arches. These latter – bringing together apparently purely narrative subjects with personifications of vices and virtues, by various different Tuscan stone-carvers – are not only directly derived from the fourteenth-century series of the *riva*, but in some cases are actually copies of them.

Now that the ducal residence and the older annexes had been brought together into one imposing four-sided complex, not dissimilar in layout, as had already been observed, to that of a princely castle with a central courtyard, and that its decoration had been stylistically regularized, the palace became an even more assertive formal image of the Venetian state as embodied by the seat of its main institutions.

The immediate purpose of this costly and magnificent architectural undertaking, with its use of the international and 'courtly' late-Gothic language, was the celebration of Venice's new-found greatness: the greatness bestowed upon her, during the dogeship of Tommaso Mocenigo (1414–33) by the formation of the 'stato da terra' (mainland possessions) and by the capitulation of her former mother, Aquileia (5 August 1420); by her expansion in Dalmatia, with the taking of imperial Split, with its memories of Diocletian; and by the surrender, albeit temporary, of Thessalonica, the second city of the eastern Roman empire (24 September 1423). During this same period Venice's uniqueness as an apostolic shrine was crowned by what the

above
Palazzo Soranzo at S. Polo.

right
Ca' Magno, well-head.

sources present as a positive 'reunion': the arrival, in the ducal basilica, of what was regarded as the autograph gospel of St. Mark. The elaborate forms and declaration of architectural 'decorum' promoted by Mocenigo, even if realized by his successor, could not but appear as the symbol and foreshadowing of that glorious age which the doge's own political legacy foretold to the Venetians, should they follow the course he had outlined: 'You shall be lords of gold.'[23]

Work on the new wing thus also afforded the perfect opportunity for the elaboration of an iconography interpreting the public myths now taking on conclusive shape.

At the point of juncture between the earlier part of the palazzo and the new building, marked by a ground-floor column with a wider diameter than the others, and by a clustered column on the floor above, the series of lobed oculi of the tracery of the loggia is interrupted by a roundel representing Justice. Clearly intended as a reference to the earlier site of the palace *ad jus reddendum* (law courts), it was placed above the long series of portrayals of virtues and vices.

But the accompanying inscription makes the nature of the subject even plainer: this was Venice herself in the form of Justice, implying a complete identification between the republic and the most frequently invoked of political virtues.

The north-west corner of the new wing reinforced the iconographic message: in a sculptural group executed by Bartolomeo

Bon around 1435, Solomon, in a serene attitude inspired by his God-given wisdom, passes judgment on the true and false mothers, while the executioner is about to smite the infant. The Dominante (ruler), triumphant and aristocratic (the year 1423 had seen the suppression of the *concio* (popular assembly), the last vestige of any political role for the ordinary people) hereby offered reassurance to the various earthly powers that she would not wage any 'unjust war' against them, and promised her own states and subjects that the *politicum* would always tally with the *bonum* (public good), at the very time when she was proving her own liberality through her works of architecture. Directly beneath the group of the judgment of Solomon, the so-called Capital of Justice depicts Moses, Scipio and Trajan together with Numa Pompilius, the builder king, 'raiser of temples and churches'.

As we have already stressed, the fifteenth-century wing of the Ducal palace remained staunchly faithful to the model of the previous century. As a result, while Brunelleschi was already engaged in his most innovative work in Florence, the architectural style selected for the Ducal palace fully endorsed the implications of the late-Gothic in its Venetian variant, as a conveyer of courtly meanings. Tommaso Mocenigo had decreed that the new wing on to the piazzetta *correspondeat solemnissimo principio nostri Palacii* (should be in keeping with the very august origin of our Palace). The architectural image of the

Dominante, too, would necessarily be fashioned by its essential respect for continuity with tradition as a vital component of stability and greatness.

His successor, Francesco Foscari (1423–57) inevitably found himself complying with this approach, demonstrating that he intended to remain faithful to the codified system of public magnificence despite the diversity of his own political line.

He proceeded in a similar way with the architectural concept for the new ceremonial entrance, the Porta Grande or Porta della Carta, for which the *provveditori al Sal* drew up a contract with Giovanni and Bartolomeo Bon on 10 November 1438.

The doorway is flanked by tall pillars, which also frame a large tracery window, as in the balcony of the Sala del Maggior Consiglio (Hall of the Great Council). It is crowned by a mixtilinear arch, which repeats a motif used a few years earlier in San Marco for the altar of the Mascoli chapel, also commissioned by Francesco Foscari. The doge, kneeling before the lion, the symbol of St. Mark and of the city-state, forms the iconographical focus of the sculptural decoration, articulated as four virtues in niches – Temperance, Charity, Fortitude and Prudence – with the bust of St. Mark supported by an angelic host and, above, another personification of Justice seated in majesty on the top of the arch, which originally stood out against the sky rather than against the wall, which was put up later. From heaven, righteousness turns her

93

Palazzetto Dandolo on the Grand Canal.

Palazzo Priuli at S. Severo.

gaze upon the earth, as in Psalm 85. The polychrome marbles were originally heightened by rich touches of gold and ultramarine, colours which had their own heraldic symbolism.

The doorway leads into a porticoed *androne* (hallway), a sequence of six bays roofed with cross-vaulting, with the figures of the four evangelists depicted on the keystones, which in its turn leads into the arco Foscari. Built in stages between 1450 and 1480, this structure is a triumph of the late-Gothic, though far from typical in terms of volume; it also uses elements inspired by the classical lexicon. This entry to the palace – which also served as backdrop for the doge's ceremonial exits for his periodical 'triumphal turns' about the city, and which Bartolomeo Bon signed proudly and ostentatiously upon the architrave – was also linked, for the purposes of ceremonial functions, to the space in front of the main staircase.

The triumph, and impending crisis, of the Venetian Gothic are therefore fully in evidence in the sequence of works of architecture which characterize the interim space between the Piazza and the courtyard of the Ducal palace. But here we also sense the tenacious hold exerted, for almost half a century, by the 'gentle' style, the *sermo ducalis* (ducal language) which, in the meantime, had become the collective language of aristocratic self-celebration.

Private patrons, who had been responsible for intense building activity during the fourteenth century, were now beginning to update the architecture of their great family dwellings, and to invest in the works of popular building which were now starting to define and stitch together whole stretches of the urban fabric, filling in such gaps as still remained. Basically, the most significant and legible examples of this large-scale fourteenth-century private building followed the distributive features of the Veneto-Byzantine house, mainly in its most widespread 'L-type plan'. But the so-called 'C-type' also rapidly became widespread, as did interest in the repeated combining of the two.

We now see the virtually systematic adoption of a distributive layout incorporating a courtyard enclosed by the building on three of its sides (the so-called C-type), at a tangent to the 'portego' (large central hall). In this way, the rooms were better lit and the courtyard's role as a focus for the everyday running of domestic life was reinforced. This increasing interest in light was also prompted by a concern for hygiene, documented at length in sixteenth-century discussion of wells placed in the centre of courtyards, in the light and open air, which stressed the purifying virtues of the sun's rays.[24] The Gothic courtyard also had features which made it a distinctively 'da terra' (landside) component, enclosed within the family residential complex, its entrance marked by heraldic bas-reliefs of an almost feudal nature, as was the case with the doorway to Corte Morosina at S. Giovanni Crisostomo, which gave access to the

Portal of palazzo Sanudo van Axel at the Miracoli.

right
Palazzo Arian, view of the facade.

below
Palazzo Arian, six-light window.

'case da stazio' (aristocratic dwellings) renovated during the second half of the fourteenth century by Marino Morosini. Somewhat later, the ground-floor portal was often ostentatiously adorned with polychrome marbles, as in palazzo Venier Sanudo van Axel (1473–9), with visible traces of the older pre-existing Veneto-Byzantine fabric, or was sometimes incorporated into crenellated boundary walls, another element which late-Gothic culture was to adopt and popularize (see the brick crenellations at Ca' Amadi at the Miracoli, or the crenellations with quatrefoil roundels at Ca' Contarini at S. Canciano). The importance of the courtyard in the late-Gothic Venetian palazzo was also often underlined by the corresponding importance given to the external staircase, giving rise, in the fifteenth century, to a series of monumental examples, from Ca' d'Oro, whose courtyard was overlooked by what amounts to a second facade, to palazzo Venier Sanudo van Axel at the Miracoli, Ca' Cappello at S. Giovanni in Laterano, Ca' Centani at S. Tomà, Ca' Priuli at S. Severo and Ca' Grifalconi on calle della Testa at SS Giovanni e Paolo, a building with a distinctly 'transitional' feel, its balustrade decorated with late-Gothic fleurons alternating with *all'antica* heads crowned with laurel.

The role of the courtyard was often given added importance by the presence of particularly fine well-heads, in Istrian stone or, more rarely, in Verona marble, often exuberantly and powerfully carved.

In the late-Gothic Venetian palazzo, the importance of the great through-room running the depth of the building, and forming the distributive and formal axis of the *piano nobile*, not only persisted, but became entrenched and systematized; and since the facade was normally arranged so as to correspond to the internal layout, from the fourteenth century onwards the tripartite pattern became firmly established, with the 'portego', or large central hall, making its presence felt through elaborate and imposing multi-light windows. There might also be two rows of such windows, reflecting the presence of two *piani nobili* in the same 'casa da stazio', occupying the central section of the facade and acting as a formal and compositional fulcrum.

The outstanding new feature of fourteenth-century Venetian aristocratic architecture was the decorative use of the pointed trefoil arch, giving a new 'international' splendour to rich and unitary facades. The multi-light windows of palazzetto Dandolo on the Grand Canal, at Riva del Carbon, or of palazzo Priuli at S. Severo, show this particularly clearly.

Another important example is the complex of palazzo Soranzo at S. Polo: or rather, the two 'case da stazio', the 'old' and the 'new' – the former dating from roughly the middle of the fourteenth century – which stand side by side, with some degree of architectural unity, on the campo, originally a market place. Their facade, slightly but noticeably concave, actually follows the lie of a canal which originally separated it

left
Ca' d'Oro.

below
Five-light window at palazzo Agnusdio.

from the open space in front, and which is thus an early and authoritative precedent for other important examples of architecture adapting to its site, found even at the height of the Renaissance. The facades follow the canonic pattern just described, as do both of their ground plans (of the C-type); the design of the arches of the single and multi-light windows belong to what Ruskin classified as the fourth order of the Venetian Gothic. The multi-light windows are set beneath generous borders with dentilled cornices, faced with Greek marble and decorated with polychrome marble roundels and paterae with zoomorphic motifs – eagles, griffins and paired doves – and by a tondo depicting Hercules and the Nemean lion, drawn from the repertoire of classical myth. There are evident similarities with the decoration of palazzo Loredan at Rialto, and with Ca' da Mosto at the Sti Apostoli. But they are all the more significant if we bear in mind that the marble panels on the 'old' palazzo Soranzo, while deriving from thirteenth-century culture, were carved specially for the building around the middle of the fourteenth century.[25]

The emergent forms, the sense of the new, thus still went hand in hand with a deliberate loyalty to Veneto-Byzantine taste, as we see from many examples of aristocratic city buildings, with their systematic reuse of earlier bas-reliefs and frequent use of facing in polychrome marble: from palazzo Priuli on rio dell'Osmarin to the five-light window in casa Viaro Zane at S. Maria Mater Domini, which has thirteenth-century paterae set into the top of the arches; from Ca' Loredan de Gheltoff at S. Girolamo, to the late fourteenth-century portal of Ca' Contarini dalla porta di Ferro in Salizada S. Francesco della Vigna, and the tall and elaborate five-light window at Palazzo Gritti at S. Giovanni in Bragora, framed in Proconnesus marble beneath trefoil tracery in polychrome marble, with the family coat-of-arms and a peacock, a symbol of immortality, dating from the beginning of the twelfth century.

Yet here again we find confirmation of the penchant, among the Venetian aristocracy and in Venetian culture in general, for keeping faith with their own past. But alongside this fondness for stability and the defining of structural and decorative canons, during the fourteenth century the leeway for autonomy in individual cases remained considerable. We see this clearly in the fourteenth-century five-light window of palazzo Agnusdio – with its reliefs of the Annunciation and winged emblems of the evangelists, and its two slightly larger, more prominent inflected side arches – and the famous traceried facade, also fourteenth-century, of palazzo Arian, whose six-light window, with its double row of superimposed quatrefoils, is reminiscent of examples from north-west Europe. But this was a very special case, and its strongly individual style might have been related to the disdainful isolation – and the parallel desire for social reinforcement – in which the family who had commissioned it locked themselves after their expulsion from the patriciate for bankruptcy in the mid-fourteenth century.[26]

Work on the building of Ca' d'Oro began in the 1420s and continued into the early 1430s, making it almost exactly contemporary with the new work on the Ducal place; yet despite the exceptional nature of certain of its features, it too included many of the canonic elements of late-Gothic civil architecture in Venice. This famous 'casa da stazio' was commissioned by Marino Contarini: he first employed the services of Matteo Raverti, who had been working on Milan cathedral, and who was to gather a large group of assistants around him; he in his turn was soon joined by members of a local workshop headed by Giovanni Bon, together with his son Bartolomeo and two garzoni (1423). Some parts of the building were executed by the two workshops jointly; elsewhere, one or other group was responsible for a whole section of the structure and its sumptuous decoration. Giovanni Bon pledged himself not to take on other work while he was active at Ca' d'Oro; Bartolomeo was taken to task by his client for neglecting the work agreed upon to the advantage of other commissions accepted in the meantime. Although Contarini's meticulous book-keeping tells us something about the individual contributions and responsibilities, the general picture is far from uncontroversial; but the attribution to Raverti of an overall plan for the facade finds no support in these documents, and the architectural interpretation of Ca' d'Oro is somewhat complex.

First and foremost, it was not built on an empty lot: it occupied the area of the pre-existing Ca' Zeno, making extensive reuse of the earlier capitals on the ground floor and other thirteenth-century decorative elements. It adopted a ground plan that was widespread in the fourteenth century, a conservative type organized on the axis of the deep ground-floor entrance hall and on the courtyard adjacent to the side calle, on to which the landside door opens. This entrance hall in its turn leads to a spacious five-arched loggia, opening directly on to the Grand Canal. The central arch – which is round headed – is wider and more imposing than the others, as in a thirteenth-century Veneto-Byzantine palazzo such as Ca' Farsetti or Ca' Loredan or – an even closer analogy – the nearby Ca' da Mosto.

Situated almost opposite the Rialto market, Ca' d'Oro is a virtually paradigmatic example of the casa-fondaco, the house of a great merchant of the late Middle Ages.

In its arrangement of voids and solids, despite their lack of symmetry, there is no doubt that Ca' d'Oro too should be ascribed to the type known as the 'casa con torreselle' (house with small towers).

The design of the facade, meticulously divided up horizontally and framed at the corners between twinned twisted colonnettes, is resolved through a play of contrasts between the chiaroscuro of the superimposed multi-light windows on the loggia, and the mainly solid masonry mass

of the right-hand section; between the airy interaction of the balconies and tracery and the measured, balanced pauses of the marble walls.

The idea of the open loggia on the *piano nobile* at Ca' d'Oro came from the Ducal palace; in the exuberant decoration of its multi-light window, Raverti developed this idea using the basic lexicon of the Flamboyant Gothic which he had brought with him from Milan cathedral, but which was essentially European in origin and tone. Thus in Ca' d'Oro a lingering respect for tradition was moving towards some degree of stylistic updating, using the forms of public grandeur associated with the city-state, executed with all the sustained energy a private individual could muster.

Here, the typical thirteenth- and fourteenth-century use of rare marbles to frame and enhance the multi-light windows, or to face broader strips of masonry, was extended to the entire available wall surface of the facade: the massive brick structures simply melted away, clad as they were with what early medieval sources were already terming the 'light' of the precious marbles.

The symbolic function of this 'light', was further intensified by the polychrome decoration commissioned in 1481 from Giovanni di Francia, Niccolò di Giovanni and others. The elegant decoration from the old Ca' Zeno, the delicate moulded cornices and the spandrels between the arches of the portico, to name but a few, were heightened by gold, ultramarine and red, the noblest

heraldic metals and enamels; the decoration on the coping of the facade was picked out in gold, blue and black.

In this way, Marino Contarini was deliberately making his house part of the series of fifteenth-century Venetian works of 'gilded architecture', as we might call them: the great 'gilded window' of the Maggior Consiglio in the Ducal palace, the 'golden doorway', another name for the Porta della Carta; the 'golden basilica' of San Marco itself, and the 'golden coffer', the Fondaco dei Tedeschi of the time, with its 'rooms of gold', which was being restructured around 1423. The gold of Ca' d'Oro, like that of the public buildings, was not just a dazzling display of wealth: together with the polychrome decoration, it was part of an emblematic language, an allusion to the myths which celebrated the city and its image.

It undoubtedly referred to the 'signoria dell'oro', the command of gold which Tommaso Mocenigo set forth as his city's goal, provided it upheld peace and equity; it also spoke of Venice's incorruptibility over time. In the city of Justice, this was the pure gold which covered the temple of Solomon, the transmuted matter which would stand the test of fire on the day of Judgment.[27] It was the building material used for the celestial city in the vision of the Apocalypse, foreshadowed by the city of St. Mark. Gold made manifest the solar nature of the Dominante: also in the fifteenth century, Marcanova's collection of epigraphs depicted the greatness of Venice, *Regina*

Palazzo Pisani Moretta, Grand Canal.

Orbis, (Queen of the World) in the form of the resplendent sun and crown.[28]

In this context, the gilded crenellations of the crowning of the facade took on particular significance: they looked back to a number of precedents, including the Ducal palace; but they may also have borne in mind the use of gold as marking out an exceptional space, as used to crown the walls of the paradisal *hortus conclusus* where the Virgin sits enthroned in the triptych for the Scuola Grande della Carità by Antonio Vivarini and Giovanni d'Alemagna, now in the Accademia (1446).

The decorative exuberance and resplendence of Ca' d'Oro should therefore not be seen as an isolated or extreme case in fifteenth-century Venice, though it is certainly a particularly striking one. These features were among the most immediate and significant precedents which, reinterpreted and further legitimized, were to underlie the vision of the early Venetian Renaissance. Ca' d'Oro and its like preceded and indeed foreshadowed the Venice of Marc'Antonio Sabellico, where 'there is no house but has its gilded rooms', where 'the houses would be entirely clad in gold, did not the laws prohibit such extravagance'.[29]

This sensational episode aside, for privately-commissioned late-Gothic civil architecture the fifteenth century was a time of codification and stabilization, but also of renewal. The decades immediately before the middle of the century witnessed both a final phase in the re-elaboration of the *casa-fondaco*, and the first signs of the abandonment of some of its earliest features.

The two-light corner window now made its appearance, for instance on palazzo Priuli at S. Severo, at palazzo Gritti at Bragora, at Ca' Mastelli at Madonna dell'Orto and at palazzo Zacco on rio di S. Marina. This was a feature also found throughout Venetian Istria, and which was to reappear in Ottoman architecture.

This same phase saw the broadly definitive emergence of those general characteristics of the Venetian house which Francesco Sansovino was to sum up so effectively and accurately as a result of his conversations with his father: 'In earlier times, the rooms were made in the shape of a crutch, that is, T-shaped, and the buildings were ungainly as a result. But as this custom fell away, the rooms ran straight from one facade of the dwelling to the other, and the openings of their windows corresponded from floor to floor. The same happened with the doors and windows of the rooms on either side, so that, each opening being in good proportion, apart from the generally pleasing appearance, the eye may run freely along the whole, and the rooms are very light and full of sun.'[30] This was tantamount to saying that the window system had now become the main instrument for stylistic codification.

Shortly before the middle of the fifteenth century, the elegant device of the multi-light window topped by quatrefoil tracery spread rapidly for the facades of the great 'case da stazio' (mainly, but not exclusively, aristocratic): sometimes such windows might be superimposed, in which case one of them, that of the *piano nobile*, might be more ornate. They were found in new buildings, but sometimes also served to give a sense of modernity to older ones (as for instance with the incorporation of a multi-light window of this type into the facade of palazzo Sagredo at S. Sofia).

This was the solution adopted around this same period by a large group of palazzi, including palazzo Dandolo on the riva degli Schiavoni, palazzo Corner Contarini dei Cavalli near Rialto, palazzo Contarini Corfu, palazzo Erizzo in the *contrada* of S. Maria Maddalena, palazzo Loredan dell'Ambasciatore, palazzo Morosini Brandolin, palazzo Pisani Moretta, Ca' Giustinian at S. Barnaba and the adjacent Ca' Foscari, all patrician residences. A vernacular version of this same solution also inspired the more modest Ca' Mastelli del Cammello, near the Scuola dei Mercanti at Madonna dell'Orto, which took its name from the remarkable bas-relief of a dromedary and its driver, a tribute to Venetian trade in the Levant, and of the spice trade in particular. Such multi-light windows with quatrefoil tracery had their immediate precedent in the loggia on the *piano nobile* at Ca' d'Oro, closely followed by Ca' Barbaro at S. Stefano; but this whole group of palazzi was also using them deliberately to declare their kinship with the Ducal palace.

In late-Gothic Venice, therefore, private commissioners of buildings were devising an eloquent updating of their image, a sort of architectural metaphor for the congruence and co-inciding of private fortunes and public greatness responsive to the subtle international elegance of the final flowering of the Gothic, by means of which aristocratic patrons affiliated themselves with the triumph of the Serenissima.

But a closer look at the more significant episodes reveals other tendencies, which must be taken into account for any general definition of the Gothic decades of the fifteenth century.

Various points of asymmetry on palazzo Bernardo at S. Polo, for example – one of the earliest palazzi ascribable to the group under discussion – should probably be seen as deriving from the dictates of the pre-existing building, rather than from any lack of concern for symmetry on the part of an architect interested only in decoration. Quite the reverse was true of the great builders of important 'case da stazio' of the time. The facade of palazzo Loredan dell'Ambasciatore is meticulously distributed horizontally by two powerfully moulded string-courses, and framed at the corners by quoins in Istrian stone and slender twisted colonnettes. It is also rigorously symmetrical, as is palazzo Pisani Moretta, where the *proto*'s careful study of the various possible schemes for the multi-light windows emerges clearly in the elegant and innovative pattern of the intersecting semi-circumferences of the upper series. The same might be said of the double Giustiniani palazzo at S. Barnaba –

Ca' Foscari, facade.

Palazzo Contarini Fasan.

nicknamed 'Buelle d'oro', golden entrails, with its addition of two large centrally-placed traceried windows, with quatrefoil motifs and small pensile arches reminiscent of those of the Porta della Carta.

All these tendencies were magisterially epitomized in the impressive bulk of Ca' Foscari, the noble dwelling-place of a doge who harboured imperial ambitions.

In 1452 Francesco Foscari acquired a towered and crenellated fourteenth-century building which he demolished, to move his family residence 'from the place where the courtyard now stands, to the corner of the *rio* off the Grand Canal which goes to S. Pantalon, where the house is now seen, leaving the courtyard behind it where that house originally stood', as Priuli tells us.[31]

The result was a building of the greatest importance, remarkable for its compositional rigour and blatant self-proclamation as a blueprint for late-Gothic Venetian architecture on a site that was of paramount significance for the creation of the urban image, namely, the 'Volta de Canal', the great bend in the canal on which it was built. Sansovino grasped its implications with great acumen: 'because it is placed on the corner of Rio di S. Pantalone, it has views all along the Grand Canal, from the left as far as Rialto and from the right as far as the Carità, not so far from San Marco, a fact which makes it most singular', as was after to be confirmed by the paintings of the vedutisti.[32]

Ca' Foscari stands above the waters of the Grand Canal on a tall Istrian stone base, its facade solidly framed at the corners by stone quoins and colonnettes, with a strongly projecting cornice and string-courses, its central section occupied by two traceried eight-light windows and a four-light one above.

While not gainsaying the language of tradition – its various links with Ca' d'Oro are clear, as is the desire to oust it as a touchstone of civic splendour – Ca' Foscari was essentially an updated, but also more powerful and severe, version of it. It should not be forgotten that Ca' Foscari was built after the middle of the fifteenth century, that is, after Michelozzo had already visited the city and designed the library for the monastery of S. Giorgio Maggiore. This 'most excellent of dwellings . . . which had belonged to our Most Serene Prince'[33] – a palazzo created for himself by a builder-doge, who had been responsible for the loggia Foscara, the arco Foscari and the Mascoli chapel in San Marco – represented a firm point of reference for the Venetian architectural culture of the time, not only setting forth the formal rules of its new magnificence, but also ensuring their continuity and vitality through its own endorsement of them. In short, through its own originality and coherence, the solemn architecture of the Foscari family palazzo was clearly aiming to underscore the proud autonomy of Venetian culture.

As we have said, the new building was deliberately moved forward towards the bank of the canal: indeed, during the late-Gothic period the fabric of the city was

right
Gothic house on calle dell'Oca.

below
Biscuit bakehouses on the *riva* near the mouth of
the rio dell'Arsenale.

beginning to achieve a formal sense of continuity and rhythm, first and foremost along
the Grand Canal, where the houses 'are
very much in demand, and worth more
than the others'.[34]

Thus after the mid-fifteenth century
the Grand Canal became one of the main
phenomena singled out for praise in
celebrations of the city. 'La rue la mieux
maisonnée qui soit en tout le monde' ('no
street in the world is better furnished
with houses'), as Philippe de Commines
recalled, in perfect agreement with the
Senate during this same period, which
defined it as 'the main ornament of this city
of ours.'[35] Marco Cornaro too recorded the
intense building activity along its banks,
the 'many who are building upon the said
canal', their technical feats and vast
expenses incurred. A touch contentiously,
he also mentions the harm done to the
canal bed by these great architectural
undertakings, including that of 'Francesco
Foscari of happy memory, who worked
upon the foundations of his house in over
seven feet of water . . . as did miser Marco
Corner el Cavalier, who shut off the foundations in order to build.'[36]

This barbed comment was not
unfounded: the filling in of the canal bed
did indeed cause problems for the circulation of the water. Solutions were sought
through works of excavation, including the
use of four large devices mounted on a
barge, built in 1469 on the model of an
earlier version designed by 'maestro'
Antonio, a French 'inzegnario' (engineer).

Small Gothic two-light window with brickwork arches at S. Giustina.

As early as 1462 a series of restrictions on maritime and other activity along the canal were passed: for example, stonecutters were to work at least four paces from loading and unloading points. The State, the owners of houses on the canal, the areas looking on to it, and the boats and barges for transport were all taxed 'for the digging out of the Grand Canal'.[37]

Although it was the main one in the city, the fact that the Grand Canal was now referred to as a *rue*, a *strada*, a street, was in some way a pointer to the decline of its old harbour functions. Together with other contemporary buildings, Ca' Foscari now had one significant point of difference with Ca' d'Oro, some twenty years its senior: its ground floor no longer opened on to the canal with a waterside portico. Despite many obvious references to tradition, and late-Gothic though it still was, the mid-fifteenth century brought about the almost definitive disappearance of one of the main features of the Venetian *casa-fondaco*.

Paradoxically, while Ca' Foscari was emerging as a key element in the continuous fabric of aristocratic palazzi on the Grand Canal, it was also the first one openly to violate it, constituting a first example of excess which, at the height of the Renaissance, was to be pointed to as legitimizing all those which followed, from Codussi's Ca' Loredan to Ca' Dolfin and Ca' Corner by Sansovino, and Ca' Grimani by Sanmicheli: 'By virtue of its site and size, it outdid all these', and every other contemporary structure too.[38] Deep and unmistakable

changes were therefore taking place within the apparent stability of such self-celebratory forms. After Ca' Foscari, the path of Venetian architectural culture bifurcated, or perhaps rather ramified.

While it laid down rules for itself, and followed them, for over two decades after the middle of the century, this culture now found itself facing new uncertainties; at the same time, it ceased to be impervious to the outside world.

The influence of classical antiquity now made an appearance 'at the bend in the Canal', in the bas-relief strip above the second-floor multi-light window at Ca' Foscari, with *putti* supporting the armorial bearings. One of the possible architectural options shortly after the middle of the fifteenth century was the one sometimes referred to as 'transitional', namely, an attempt to graft a free and 'courtly' version of the quest for antiquity – seen as a realm of the symbolic imagination, with highly elusive margins – on to the specific language being perfected in the great contemporary worksites.

This tendency may be seen in works such as the arco Foscari in the Ducal palace (which was not built until the dogeship of Cristoforo Moro, 1462–71), intentionally reminiscent of a triumphal arch, the product of a composite and inventive culture, but also mindful of the forms and ornaments of the ducal basilica of San Marco. Another transitional work, reliably datable between 1459 and 1460, is the stately, elegant portal of SS Giovanni e Paolo, with

delicate plant volutes running along its frieze, and twinned columns of Greek marble, from Torcello. Lovely clinging garlands surround the family emblems on the old doorway of the Bakeries of S. Biagio, near the Arsenal: a publicly commissioned late-Gothic work flanked by crenellations decorated with quatrefoil roundels, it was built at some point after 1473, and faced directly on to the Riva.

At the same time, various noblemen continued to commission family houses with unimpeachable late-Gothic facades, notable for their rigorous and lucid distribution and appropriate and meticulous sculptural decoration. One of these, in all likelihood, was the so-called house of Desdemona, the small palazzetto Contarini Fasan on the Grand Canal, which, at the beginning of the sixteenth century, belonged to Tommaso Contarini, the son of Zorzi il Cavaliere, count of Zaffo:[39] its carefully proportioned and symmetrical facade has balustrades with tracery with wheel motifs, a sophisticated interpretation of the Venetian late-Gothic decorative repertoire using elements from north-west Europe, possibly here too through the intermediary of Milan cathedral. But the general mood was one of great vitality: during these same years, as we shall see, certain patrician circles, attracted by humanistic culture, were already beginning to discuss the 'genuine' characteristics of classical grandeur.

Another long and complementary process seems to have reached a crucial phase during the Gothic period: that of the definition of the popular repeated building type which probably originated in the *rugae domorum* (row of houses) and the small terraced houses grouped around the master's courtyard which are already documented between the eleventh and thirteenth centuries. As we have seen, the fourteenth-century parchment map in the *Chronologia magna* gives a picture of a growing city, which exerted a powerful pressure on its outlying districts as early as the late thirteenth and early fourteenth centuries, and which indeed crept forward over the shallows in an attempt to solve its housing shortage. Very shortly afterwards, this same expansion saw the widespread use of serial architecture, made practicable by means of carefully planned operations with the repetition of modular units of identical forms and dimensions. One relatively early case was the complex one called Zotti at S. Sofia, a series of terraced Gothic houses based on the combination of two principles: that of the systematic clustering of single modules, and a second – socially extremely significant – being characterized by the mutual independence of the dwelling units (each with its 'own front door'). The end house of the series – which overlooked the narrow calle del Pistor, formerly part of a long commercial route running through the *sestiere* of Cannaregio parallel to the Grand Canal – was a typical example of house and workshop combined, found particularly in the central districts of the city. The following houses were exclusively residential; like the former, they had pointed windows on the first floor, grouped at regular intervals so as to form little three-light windows lighting a small 'portego' (central hall). This distributive plan, which is also legible on the facade, is thus tantamount to a scaled-down version of the layout of the aristocratic 'casa da stazio'.

Nor was the design of the popular houses on calle Zotti purely functional: some of the remaining three-light windows, with stone uprights and slender columns with chalice-like capitals, some decorated at the corners with simple leaves and very slight relief, still have their original pointed arches with decoration in moulded brick, whose component parts were mass-produced: these included small intersecting trefoil arches in a dentilled cornice, mouldings surrounded by a similar cornice, lozenges containing a rosette, or decoration with friezes of vine tendrils and bunches of grapes. Low-cost decoration was therefore used for serial building, mass-produced by the city's kilns and those of the surrounding areas. That such 'minor Gothic' was widely used for the modest decoration of popular fifteenth-century housing is confirmed by other very similar cases. The houses on Corte Contarina at Castello – a short double terrace of rented houses behind a block overlooking the canal, opposite the Corderie (Rope factories) of the Arsenal – have three variants of pointed arches of the type described: bordered with dentilled cornices, where the intersecting sequence of small lobed arches reappears, together with a motif with vine-shoots with corollas and rosettes, and a third version with soft foliage. Simplified versions appear on an important building overlooking calle delle Cappuccine, near the eastern end of Barbaria delle Tole. Here, in the district originally occupied by the timber yards which required labour from the mainland, a long building still retains the dimensions of the fifteenth-century terrace of ground-floor units with one single upper floor. The eastern end of this building still has many of the original features: once again, the small pointed two-light window, which implied the internal presence of the small 'portego', with a brick arch with an archivolt framed by a dentilled cornice, and by a second one with diamond points like that of the nearby one-light window.

At all events, around the middle of the fifteenth century serial building seems to have engaged the attention of both those who commissioned it and those who built it, encouraging the development and consolidation of existing types which closely paralleled those of the 'casa da stazio', with procedures for low-cost decoration and the elaboration of various distributive models. Soon after the middle of the century, Costantino and Bartolomeo da Brolo, members of a local merchant family, built the Ghetto Nuovo – well before its transformation into a Jewish quarter, which was to occur in 1516; this was a typical example of investment in serial building for rent, organized around a huge inner courtyard (the present-day campo). Redeveloped

Madonna dell'Orto, facade.

with debris from the nearby public copper foundries and other backfill, sold by auction in 1433, the new block of the 'terren del Geto' (foundry area) was purchased by the da Brolos in 1455. Building proceeded immediately, and fast, beginning in 1458 and probably already concluded between 1459 and 1465. The new buildings were put up around a roughly pentagonal area (the campo) where the da Brolos also seem to have intended to build an oratory. They were certainly responsible for digging the three wells, and organizing the system of communications with the surrounding areas. De' Barbari's bird's-eye view meticulously reproduces the appearance of the linear agglomerations of these buildings, registering the rhythmic sequence of the two-light windows, sometimes extended to three-light ones, which indicate the main rooms of the dwellings. There are marked similarities with numerous terraced complexes, for example at calle Zotti, Salizada S. Lio, S. Giustina and elsewhere, as we see from two brick-framed pointed windows, whose moulded brickwork uses the same late-Gothic foliage as that on the houses in Corte Contarina.

In the meantime, a parallel but independent course was being taken by the last works of late-Gothic religious architecture in the city, derived and re-elaborated from the main buildings begun in the previous century and still under construction during much of the first half of the fifteenth.

The Gothic religious architecture of this latter period showed a general preference for structural and stylistic solutions that were typically Venetian. S. Maria dell'Orto, for example, which was being rebuilt from the last quarter of the fourteenth century, returned to a triple-aisled basilican plan, without a transept, with a main pentagonal apse flanked by smaller flat-headed apsidioles. The nature of the terrain, but also a deliberate sobriety dictated by the ideals of the Umiliati to whom it belonged, suggested light, simple roofing with wooden trusses. The spans dividing the nave from the aisles were broadened to a distance of two Venetian passi (paces) (equivalent to a third of the length of the building), accentuating the flow of light and slowing down the rhythm of the arches. The use of uniform capitals for the columns of the nave confirms this desire for ordered clarity, as do the building's basic proportions and the correlation between the division of the interior and the scheme of the facade: this latter is divided into three by pilaster strips, with a central section corresponding to the nave, and two lower side sections also framed by pilaster strips on the outside, corresponding to the aisles, their sloping roofs crowned by arcading with statues of the twelve apostles.

Though simplified and reworked through Lombard reminiscences, the facade repeats the model of SS Giovanni e Paolo, which was also the model for the Augustinian church of S. Stefano, rebuilt between the fourteenth and fifteenth centuries on a basilican plan without a transept. The surprising addition of the presbytery was made possible only by a peculiarly Venetian feat of engineering: it was built over an actual bridge, put up over the waters of the canal which still flows under it. The age-old distrust of vaulting was here solved in a way that was technically and aesthetically more sophisticated than trusses: the nave has a ship's-keel ceiling, carved and polychrome, of the kind Venetian sources refer to as 'in forma di galea' (in the form of a galley). This solution, similar to others found elsewhere in the Veneto – at S. Zeno at Verona, for example – made use less of shipbuilding techniques as such, than the experience of the master-carpenters often active both inside and outside the Arsenal, an expertise somewhere between building and shipbuilding.

Work began on numerous other buildings during the first decades of the fifteenth century: on S. Alvise – St. Louis of Toulouse – not far from S. Cristoforo and S. Maria dell'Orto, for which pope Martin V granted indulgences in 1420 and which was still partly unfinished around 1440; and on S. Elena, given over to the Olivetans at the beginning of the century and immediately rebuilt, partly with funds from a bequest from Tommaso Talenti (d. 1403). Over the course of the century, two floors in Hispano-Moorish majolica were laid in the Borromeo and Giustinian chapels, confirming a taste for *mudejar* art which was by no means exceptional in fifteenth-century Venice, as we see for example in palazzo Mula on Murano.[40] Work was also

beginning on S. Andrea della Zirada, funded by the public coffers with a decree of 1475, where Bartolomeo Bon seems to have worked; on S. Giobbe (from c. 1450); on the rebuilding, from 1441 onwards, of the church of the Carità, and S. Gregorio. Models and techniques plainly circulated from one site to another, sometimes directly documented. The apse of S. Gregorio, for example, was undoubtedly based on that of the Frari, and the architect of the windows on the facade was expressly required to follow the design of those of the church of the Carità, where Bartolomeo Bon is documented as having been active.

S. Stefano, wooden roof 'in the form of a galley'.

The tendency towards the lightening and simplifying of the Gothic structure, and its replacement by local variants, were now further confirmed and reinforced: the Venetian late-Gothic churches built or rebuilt in the fifteenth century show a preference for roofing with wooden trusses rather than rib vaulting. A feeling for space deriving from the basilica, therefore, seems to have re-emerged in the first half of the fifteenth century, precisely when the broad Gothic naves of the Dominican and Franciscan churches were being completed; essentially, these latter thus remained major but exceptional episodes. In several cases, the buildings seem deliberately to abjure all forms of structural complexity, rejecting the internal division into nave and aisles in favour of a single space, while sometimes retaining the three-apsed chancel, as at S. Gregorio. The tripartite scheme of the facades of the two main monastic Gothic churches was widely adopted, sometimes with extreme sobriety, even where there was no correlation between the external sections of the facade and the composition of the inner spaces. This layout inspired much of fifteenth-century religious architecture, though with a variety of solutions for the upper part of the facade. The triple ogee crowning of the Carità was unusual, though it was imitated in S. Gregorio. But fifteenth-century Venetian Gothic religious architecture was more concerned with variations on the theme of the multi-lobed, mixtilinear pediment. The facade of the Frari was com-

pleted only at the beginning of the fifteenth
century, but the design for its upper section
was already moving away from that of
other similar examples: its central section
is of the type referred to above, but linked to
two lower side sections by a lobed motif.
Similar elements – elaborations of the
trilobe scheme with a central mixtilinear
arch – appear as crownings for the facades
of the parish churches of S. Aponal and
S. Giovanni in Bragora, not unlike that of
S. Andrea della Zirada.

Such designs probably derived from
combining memories of the facade of the
cathedral of Mantua (1396–1401), by the
Dalle Masegne, with decorative schemes
widely used by painters and stonemasons,
for instance on the funerary monument to
Agnese and Orsola Venier at Sti Giovanni e
Paolo (1411), or the sculpted polyptych in
the Mascoli chapel at San Marco (1430). At
all events, this type of facade and crowning
was popular and longlasting: in the first
half of the century it inspired the facade of
the old Scuola della Misericordia, reappear-
ing with variants on the mainland and in
Istria (in the parish church of Lupia in the
Vicenza area, and in the church at Muggia,
1467). Possibly together with Byzantine-
Balkan allusions (from Arta to Mistra,
Gračanica, Lagosta and elsewhere), it was
also a significant precedent for comparable Renaissance solutions of which we
shall say more later. Its popularity was also
confirmed by Jacopo Bellini, who presented
three facades of this kind in three drawings
in his notebooks; the real subject of one of

S. Giovanni in Bragora, facade.

them is indeed a religious building with a crowning whose lines are similar to those of S. Aponal.[41]

Significantly enough, this long series of religious buildings coincided not only with the increasingly firm and widespread control exerted by the Serenissima over its churches, but also with a crucial phase in the reorganizing of the ecclesiastical geography and jurisdiction of the Veneto: on 8 October 1451 Nicholas V abolished the episcopal see of Castello and the patriarchal see of Grado, replacing them with the new patriarchal see of Venice, occupied by Lorenzo Giustinian, bishop of Castello until 1433 and subsequently canonized. This event did not give rise to any important act of architectural patronage. Yet in all probability it was not without consequences for the history of the see of Venice, since the new line taken by the Venetian patriarchate lay at the root of the prevailing severity of subsequent Venetian Gothic religious architecture, as seen in the stark brick facades of convent buildings and parish churches. The first patriarch's stated opposition to *ampla aedificia*, to spacious rooms and over-comfortable cells in religious houses, and his austere stance and staunch loyalty to previous habits of worship – he himself had led the life of a virtual hermit in a bleak cell of mud and branches at the priory of Sti Fermo e Rustico on the hill of Lonigo – undoubtedly go some way towards explaining the reasons for the persistent formal poverty of the late-Gothic buildings in his patriarchate.[42]

1 Bibliothèque Nationale, Paris (hereafter B.N.P.), Départment des Cartes et Plans.

2 B.N.M.V., mss. lat. Z 2399 (=1610).

3 G. Cracco, *Società, op. cit.*

4 M. A. Sabellico, *Del sito, op. cit.*, p. 24; F. Sansovino and G. Martinioni, *Venetia, op. cit.*, p. 56.

5 P. Marangon, *Il pensiero ereticale nella Marca Trevigiana e a Venezia dal 1200 al 1350*, Abano Terme 1985.

6 M. A. Sabellico, *Del sito, op. cit.*, p. 22; *Il Forestiere illuminato intorno le cose più rare e curiose, antiche e moderne*, Venice 1745, p. 224.

7 F. Sansovino and G. Martinioni, *Venetia, op. cit.*, p. 56.

8 In the view published in B. Breydenbach, *Sanctarum peregrinationum . . . opusculum*, Mainz 1486.

9 Jean de Chambes (1459) in Ph. De Commines, *Mémoires*, Paris 1924-5, p. 408.

10 B.N.M.V., mss. it. cl. VII, 37 (=8222), f. 47r.

11 M. Sanudo, *De origine, situ et magistratibus urbis Venetae*, ed. A. Caracciolo Aricò, Milan 1980, p. 24.

12 Quoted in L. Lazzarini, 'Francesco Petrarca e il primo umanesimo a Venezia', in *Umanesimo europeo e umanesimo veneziano*, ed. V. Branca, Florence 1963, p. 71.

13 See note 2 above.

14 M. Sanudo, *De origine, op. cit.*, p. 24.

15 The phrase in inverted commas, referring to the *langue d'oïl*, is from M. Da Canal, *Les Estoires de Venise*, ed. A. Limentani, Florence 1972.

16 See the works by E. Grube and D. Howard listed in the brief bibliography at the end of this volume.

17 V. Scamozzi, *Dell'idea dell'architettura universale*, Venice 1615, part I, p. 58.

18 'Tota Venecia est in manibus eius', 22.7.1309, document quoted in B. Cecchetti, 'La vita dei veneziani nel 1300', in *Archivio Veneto*, vol. 29, 1885, p. 331.

19 W. Wolters, *La scultura veneziana gotica*, Venice 1976, pp. 40-8; see V. Lazzarini, *Marino Faliero*, Florence 1963, pp. 159-60, 308-14.

20 L. De Monacis, *Chronicon de rebus Venetis*, Venice 1758, pp. 276-7; R. De Caresinis, *Chronica*, ed. E. Pastorello, in R.I.S., vol. XII, 2, Bologna 1922, pp. 30-1.

21 P. Contarini, *Argo vulgar*, Venice 1542, p. a iiii: 'a palace standing upon many columns, whose topmost parts have been carved with many prophets who have foreseen the future'. Dandolo, *Chronica, op. cit.*, pp. 399-405.

22 B.N.M.V., *Statuta et leges. Novem Statuta Petri Emo Potestatis Clugiae (correctiones Petri Aymi)*, mss. V, 69 (=2966).

23 G. Luzzatto, *Storia economica di Venezia dall'XI al XVI secolo*, Venice 1961, pp. 165-8.

24 F. Sansovino and G. Martinioni, *Venetia, op. cit.*, p. 384.

25 A. Rizzi, *Scultura esterna a Venezia*, Venice 1987, pp. 31-377 [recte 31-7?].

26 A. Zorzi and P. Marton, *I palazzi veneziani*, Udine 1984, p. 122.

27 I Kings, 20-30; St Paul's First Letter to the Corinthians, 3, 12.

28 Biblioteca Civica, Modena, ms. L 992 d L 5.15, f. 177r.

29 M. A. Sabellico, *Del sito, op. cit.*, p. 32.

30 F. Sansovino and G. Martinioni, *Venetia, op. cit.*, pp. 384-5.

31 Quoted by E. Arslan, *Venezia gotica. L'architettura civile gotica veneziana*, Venice 1970, pp. 245-6.

32 F. Sansovino and G. Martinioni, *Venetia, op. cit.*, p. 388.

33 M. Sanudo, *De origine, op. cit.*, p. 21.

34 *Ibid.*

35 Decree of 20.3.1462, published in M. Cornaro, *Scritture sulla laguna*, ed. G. Pavanello, Venice 1919, pp. 154-6.

36 *Ibid.*, p. 151.

37 1463: D. Malipiero, 'Annali', in *Archivio Storico Italiano*, vol. 12, part II, 1844, p. 654.

38 F. Sansovino and G. Martinioni, *Venetia, op. cit.*, p. 388.

39 Archivio di stato, Venice (hereafter A.S.V.), Savi alle Decime, 1537, b. 83, cond. 527; *ibid.*, M. Barbaro, *Arbori de' Patritii*, misc. codd. St. Ven. 18.

40 *Azulejos* in the Museo della Floridiana, Naples, from the Palazzo Da Mula: G. Morazzoni, *La maiolica antica veneta*, Milan 1955, plate 10.

41 V. Golubew, *Les Dessins de Jacopo Bellini au Louvre et au British Museum*, vol. I, *British Museum*; vol. II, *Louvre*, Brussels 1908-12; B. Degenhart and A. Schmitt, *Corpus des italienischen Zeichnungen 1300-1450*, tome II, *Venedig*, vols. V-VIII, Berlin 1990.

42 B. Giustinian, *Vita Beati Larentii Iustiniani Venetiarum Proto Patriarchae*, Rome 1962, p. 96.

RENOVATIO MARCIANA: THE EARLY RENAISSANCE

As we have said, it is possible to date the earliest important Venetian debate on the architecture of classical antiquity with some precision, namely, from some time before 1454, since Flavio Biondo gives an account of it in the proem to the ninth book of his *Roma Trionfante*, mentioning the great Francesco Barbaro as a fellow-debater.[1]

Over the course of lengthy disquisitions on the topography of Republican Rome, Biondo tells us, 'many days were spent debating this subject of buildings', whose size and magnificence had no parallel in those of the capitals of fifteenth-century Italy. If any process of renewal were to occur, it would inevitably have to be 'triumphant', like Rome itself; of extraordinary richness, unaccustomed splendour, rare refinement. Such convictions, coming after the attitudes of late-Gothic patronage, could not fail to leave their mark on new developments in Venetian architecture during the second half of the fifteenth century.

The set of circumstances that acted as backdrop to these debates and reconstructions was particularly significant. The funeral encomium for Francesco Foscari, written by Bernardo Giustinian in 1457, uses the terms of classical rhetoric to extol the imperial idea of Venice as it was emerging at the time: this was a Venice whose empire would eclipse that of Athens by sea, that of Sparta by land, and that of Rome in its Republican institutions.[2] On 9 May 1462, in fact, Venice ceased to refer to herself with the medieval title of 'commune', and adopted that of 'dominio' (dominion).

Now the Serenissima was preparing to rewrite her own history, to re-elaborate her relations with the past and the ancient world. The years 1459–60 saw plans for an official historiography of the republic, based on Graeco-Roman models. The setting up of the second chair of *studia humanitatis* (for the study of oratory and, more significantly, of history) at the Scuola della Cancelleria of San Marco[3] dated from 1460.

The end of the 1460s thus witnessed the deliberate creation of a new cultural framework for the 'moderate and holy republic' by a group of thinkers many of whom were also engaged in the 'concrete' reconstruction of an image of Rome as the city whose last legitimate heir Venice was ever more openly and assuredly proclaiming herself.

The main graphic interpretation of the dialogues between Barbaro, Biondo and their circles – and proof that these discussions were less narrow than might have been imagined – was given by the notebooks of Jacopo Bellini. Here the classical world was evoked with all the power it clearly exerted upon contemporary Venetian culture, and expressed architecturally through the triumphal dimensions of the great Roman arch, with its twinned columns, winged victories and torch-bearing *putti*.[4]

In actual fact, in Jacopo's imaginary city settings, late-Gothic forms and structures co-exist with what in many cases seems to be uncertain, hypothetical transcriptions of their move towards ideas for a new architecture: for example, the dominant scheme of the facades of the aristocratic

Jacopo Bellini, 'Large arch with twinned columns'.

Jacopo Bellini, 'Triumphal arch', detail of the *Annunciation*.
Paris, Louvre, Cabinet des dessins.

The 'magna porta' (great doorway) from the
Hypnerotomachia Poliphili, Venice, 1499.

houses of the middle of the century – the multi-light window with trefoil tracery – is given a sense of modernity by redesigning the ogee arches as round-headed ones, or by similar treatment of the corner two-light windows (as was indeed to occur in certain built examples).

Progress towards the early Renaissance was encouraged not only by literary culture and its graphic interpretation, but also by visits to classical sites in the eastern Mediterranean, by the study of the Antique in Venice itself, and by the antiquarian collecting stemming from it.

The quintessence of Venetian humanism was indeed the journey to the Levant, whether for reasons of diplomacy, trade or war: the east was now seen with a new visual and intellectual readiness to look afresh at the spiritual landscape of classical poetry, now visual as the setting for the great events whose memory had been perpetuated by Graeco-Roman historiography. A new-found interest in identifying the sites of such events, and in rediscovering their visual traces, was by no means restricted to scholarly circles alone.

Even before the fall of Constantinople, the 'stato da mar' had offered the possibility of an intellectual return to the classical world. The anonymous Venetian who left the Latin account of a journey to the Black Sea, made between 1404 and 1407, was one of the first to reinterpret the eastern Mediterranean, the Aeolian islands and the Aegean sea through the mythical lens of Virgil's Aeneid. He seems already to have

known of the so-called temple of Venus at Cerigo (Kythera), whose remains were still clearly visible at the time; of the ruins of Tenedos and above all of the signs of the greatness of Teucris, the Homeric region of Troas. He wandered through what were then believed to be the ruined buildings of the city of Priam, 'with its vestiges of vast walls, where a large part of the royal hall is to be seen, not yet destroyed to its very foundations . . . marble girders . . . admirable sculpted figures'.[5]

The 1472 naval campaign headed by Pietro Mocenigo, who was soon to become doge – and whose imposing classicizing monument by Pietro Lombardo is on the west wall of SS Giovanni e Paolo – and the taking of Smyrna, led to what were regarded as discoveries of exceptional importance: Homer's tomb, first and foremost; and the bleached ruins of Delos and its temple of Apollo. 'Many vestiges of the temple and amphitheatre may still be seen . . . in the whitest and finest marble; several very beautiful columns and a great number of statues in ancient marble, and a colossus fifteen cubits in height.'[6]

Until the first decades of the sixteenth century, this was the background to the Venetians' extensive surveys of the monuments of Constantinople, to their visits to the hill of Mycenae, not far from Navplion, to Kythera and Delos and the supposed site of Troy; and to Alexandria and north Africa, where a thorough survey of the site of Carthage was carried out.[7]

Figured capital. Corinth, agora.

This was the background not only to the development of collecting in Venice, but also to the activities of Nicolò Corner as an early recreator and restorer of classical settings, recorded in the early fifteenth century by the Florentine Buondelmonti.

In one of his possessions on the island of Crete, at the site known as *ston Platano* not far from Thrapsanò, Corner laid out a garden *all'antica*, 'a viridarium . . . (which) he adorned and set about with very ancient marble statues. A living spring gushes forth from the marble mouth of a male figure. To right and left his forebears had placed a bust of Mark Antony and another of Pompey. There I saw fine marbles transported from other buildings', in all likelihood from the nearby ruins of Lyktos, also owned by the Corner family.[8]

It was no mere rhetorical flight of fancy, therefore, that led Raffaello Zovenzoni, who also knew the collections of the Bellini and admired one classical statue of Venus in particular, to compose an *epenodia* in praise of doge Andrea Vendramin (1476–8), with its Hellenized portrait of Venice, describing the ducal basilica as 'gleaming in Parian marble' and over-flowing with works of art comparable with those of Scopas, the great Zeuxis and Polycletus.[9]

Moreover, a type of Venetian Ionic capital quite frequently found during the early Renaissance bore a marked resemblance to examples found in Constantinople in the area of the imperial palaces (where we know that Venetians purchased antiquities), while other figured pseudocorinthian capitals seem to be reminiscent of certain capitals from the agora in Corinth.

More relevantly, perhaps, it was from this particular strand of early Renaissance Venetian culture – and indeed through identifiable channels – that Sebastiano Serlio derived his reconstruction of a work of Greek architecture with one hundred columns and, more generally, his strong sense of the architectural primacy of Hellas, formulated so powerfully and passionately in the third book of his treatise.

Signs of the classical past, or what were thought of as such, were also visible in other parts of the Serenissima: apart from the antiquities of Verona, those of Pola (Istria) were also particularly important for the history of Venetian architecture, as we shall see; they are already mentioned in the early fifteenth-century writing referred to above, and also, in the second half of the century, by Marin Sanudo, who describes not only the amphitheatre, but other works of architecture, in his *Itinerarium cum syndicis Terrae firmae* of 1483.

Porta Rata, the arch of the Sergii at Pola – 'regalis filia Romae'[10] – was known not only to Ciriaco d'Ancona, Felice Feliciano and Giovanni Marcanova, but seems to have been one of the monuments that were most studied and drawn during the Renaissance: by fra' Giocondo, Falconetto, Serlio, Palladio and Giovanni Battista and Bastiano da Sangallo. During this period, too, the Istrian stone quarries were being intensively exploited to satisfy the needs of Venetian Renaissance architecture.[11]

Two other centres of antiquity played an important part in the elaboration of early Renaissance architectural culture in Venice: Aquileia, which became a permanent part of the 'stato da terra' from 1420, and Ravenna, which belonged to the Serenissima throughout the second half of the fifteenth century.

Signs of classical greatness continued to come to light in the countryside around Aquileia, as Giovanni Candido tells us at the beginning of the sixteenth century: in particular, *marmorea pavimenta et emblemata vermiculata*, that is, paving in *opus sectile* in precious marbles, and exquisite figured mosaic fragments which, as we infer from key passages in the medieval chronicles already mentioned, supplied the humanists with their ideas as to the essence of the magnificence of the mother of *Venetia*. Their impact must have been considerable, if we bear in mind that Aquileia had been the see of Mark the evangelist, its *primus antistes* (first bishop) on the throne subsequently transferred to the ducal basilica in the middle of the fifteenth century, together with the supposedly autograph gospel and the rank of patriarchate. Not was it any coincidence that in this work, printed in Venice in 1521, Candido addressed himself to Domenico Grimani, cardinal and patriarch of the capital of *Venetia prima*, urging him to spearhead a movement of cultural renewal from the region under his care, a *renovatio Aquileiensis*: from the fifteenth century onwards the memory of Aquileia was to be used by Domenico, Marino, Marco and

Giovanni Grimani, for the sanctioning and guiding of the Roman-oriented tendencies of the culture and architecture of the Venetian Renaissance.[12]

Meanwhile, however, while not engaging with the monuments of Rome itself, fifteenth-century scholarship was becoming broader and deeper. The site of Spina was now identified in the marshes around Ferrara, and traces of classical remains were found at Primaro, at the mouth of the Po. Above all, the scholars of the time were interested in Ravenna, whose port – from which 'all the Orient (could) pass into the bowels of the West, with all their foreigners and precious merchandise' – was seen as foreshadowing the wealthy port of Venice.[13]

In his eulogy of Foscari, Bernardo Giustinian was already describing Ravenna as *vetustissima praeclarissimaque civitas, regum imperatorumque sedes* ('very ancient and famous city, seat of Kings and emperors'). In 1489 Antonio Marcello, a Venetian patrician, was to be the dedicatee of Desiderio Spreti's *De amplitudine, de vastatione et instauratione urbis Ravennae* (Of the greatness, downfall and rebirth of the city of Ravenna) (and here the *instauratio* was in fact that of Venice itself), which gave an erudite and impassioned interpretation of the architectural glories of the city. It drew attention to the *spetiosum* (splendid) mausoleum of Galla Placidia, to S. Vitale, 'built in the likeness of the temple of Hagia Sofia at Constantinople', with its bas-relief with dancing *putti*, which Spreti attributed unhesitatingly to Polycletus and which was

to end up in Venice, first on the exterior of a house near San Marco, then at S. Maria dei Miracoli, where it was to be seen by Titian and Sansovino, and finally in the archaeological Museum. Among the ancient buildings which spoke of Ravenna's imperial magnificence, he included S. Apollinare in Classe (where Codussi worked in 1477–8), the glorious church whose foundation was attributed to Narses. Lastly – and this is important for our line of argument – he stressed that *varium marmorum ornamentum*, polychrome marble decoration, was typical of the art and architecture of Ravenna.[14]

The reference to Narses is also highly significant, since the late fifteenth-century re-elaboration of the myth of Justinian's general as a builder of Venetian churches was now being used to reinforce the theory that the earliest architecture of Venice derived from that of Ravenna, as noted by Sanudo.[15]

An increasingly broad range of symbols and models was thus now being identified, and with growing accuracy. Research and investigations were under way within Venice itself. On the one hand, Roman inscriptions were being discovered and transcribed everywhere, with Venice as *regina orbis*, as Giovanni Marcanova defined her; they acted as powerful spurs to humanistic culture.[16] On the other, the ruins of the ancient lagoon cities of *Heraclia* and *Equilium* were being identified, cities whose greatness was still recognizable 'from the ornaments of the temples, from the ports, the height of the

towers and the vastness of the places laid out for all manner of uses. So that it is no wonder, when those had been destroyed, that Rialto should have grown up with all the amplitude we see today.'[17]

The origins of the duchy were thus clearly seen by the humanistic culture of the fifteenth century as rooted in an ancient splendour, which acted as an intermediary, a point of liaison, between the culture of Roman Aquileia and that of Venetian Rivoalto.

This splendour was still to be found within the city itself: in a number of 'very ancient' buildings which many fifteenth-century scholars regarded as earlier ducal seats antedating the palace (though interpreted in a more sophisticated manner in the late sixteenth century). It was reflected in the 'antiquity of certain houses', deserving of honour 'and almost reverence', a *pietas* in connection with the monumental past of the earliest ducal Venice which could not fail to make its mark on the thinking (and traditionalism) of Venetian architectural humanism.[18]

There was clearly no shortage of interest, knowledge and research underlying the culture of the *de re aedificatoria* of the early Venetian Renaissance. It was further underpinned by the proud assertion of the primacy of its own building techniques as formulated in the second half of the century, in connection specifically with the great undertakings along the Grand Canal and elsewhere in the city from the late-Gothic period onwards.[19]

It is therefore hardly surprising that the message of the Florentine Renaissance made little impact on fifteenth-century Venice, nor that the great Tuscans who spent time there – from Alberti to Paolo Uccello, from Andrea del Castagno to Michelozzo and, later, Leonardo da Vinci – should have made so little impression on the city.

In the *miraculosissima civitas* of Venice, Vitruvian *firmitas* (and Bernardo Giustinian, to name but one, knew and quoted Vitruvius) was subject to its own peculiar rules. In relation to the buildings of the noble merchants, *utilitas* was of the kind dictated by the mechanisms and living conditions of a maritime trading city founded on water traffic, and hence subject to rules of its own.

As far as the language of architectural forms was concerned, the Florentine version – whose roots were so closely inter-twined with the Medici – was bound to seem in many ways unsuited to the needs of Venice; furthermore, anti-Venetian feeling was rife in Florentine circles from around the middle of the century, after the break-up of the friendship between the two cities, and it was only logical that Venice should eschew any overt 'Tuscanization'.[20]

Naturally, Venice was not without elements acting as mediators between the two cultures. But when the time came to revitalize her architecture, fifteenth-century Venice was to choose a path of her own, largely based on the cultural considerations briefly alluded to above.

In fact, it was the entrance of Mahomet II into the old capital of the eastern Roman

empire, and Ottoman expansion in Greece and the Balkans, which brought about a turning-point in Venice's international role, precipitating her search for new architectural and artistic forms the better to embody her new-found role.

Spiritually and culturally at least, Venice embraced the legacy of the 'new Rome' on the Bosphorus by looking back to the original values of the earlier Rome. It can be no coincidence that the earliest thoroughly humanist fifteenth-century Venetian architecture was built at the Arsenal, to frame the entrance to the republic's great complex for the building and fitting out of ships. It was equally inevitable that it should have had certain peculiar features, explicable only within the Mediterranean context referred to above. After a series of decisions taken between 1458 and 1459, in the spring of 1460 work began on the building of a great gateway, the Porta Magna, conceived as a monumental triumphal arch crowned by an attic storey with a pediment, deriving essentially from one of the most famous classical relics: the arch of the Sergii at Pola, the *porta aurata* of the Istrian Roman city bordering the Balkan areas of Ottoman expansion by land.

While basically repeating the classical pattern – altered on the basis of hypothetical reconstructions similar to those made in Tuscan artistic culture at more or less the same time – the gateway's twinned columns reused medieval shafts of Greek marble and 'exarchate' capitals, following a longstanding Venetian tradition taking as its starting point the solemn portals of San Marco, at once ducal and 'Byzantine'.

The Arsenal gateway was therefore another example of stylistic contamination; but that it was deliberate, reflecting a shift in meaning, is implied by the direct or indirect involvement of a number of humanist noblemen in the events leading up to its construction, including Zaccaria Trevisan, Paolo Barbo, Lodovico Foscarini, Gerolamo Barbarigo and Candian Bollani.

The 'Roman' architectural 'text' underlying the Arsenal gateway, and the Veneto-Byzantine quotations within it, should be interpreted as intentional allusions to the role which Venice was ascribing to herself in the above context. In commissioning her first work inspired by the Antique, a strongly self-celebratory work, the Serenissima wanted to emphasize its implications of continuity, its value as a twofold reference to imperial symbols. The architecture of the Porta Magna is therefore to be understood as proclaiming an ambitious programme in the very citadel of the city's maritime greatness: it evoked the idea of Venice as the true heir to Rome, but also as *alterum Byzantium* (a new Byzantium) a position which contemporary political myth-making was striving to establish for the city-republic.

Moreover, it is perfectly clear that the design for the Arsenal gateway was conceived with a full awareness of the main principles of Renaissance art as practised in the chief artistic centres of the time.

Despite some aberrations in execution, and later tamperings – mainly during the sixteenth century – this awareness is evident in the ratios that recur throughout the building. The lower part of the facade, up to the level of the support of the architrave, is inscribed in a square measuring four Venetian *passi* per side, a lucid geometrical figure giving rise to an immediately perceptible system of simple relationships, generating the layout of the structure by means of a compositional procedure *ad quadratum*, implying knowledge of the basic principle of *finitio*.

Since sixteenth-century iconography documents the existence of marble spheres placed like acroteria on the pediment, the overall height of the original facade must have been double that of its base: so that the Porta Magna would have been perfectly inscribed in two superimposed squares. The height of the entablature and the design of the upper masonry elevation, too, seem broadly generated by the same system of ratios. If the gateway thus seems clearly to have marked a turning-point in Venetian architecture by the year 1460, its authorship is less clear-cut. While the earlier attribution to Antonio Gambello is problematical and unjustified for obvious stylistic reasons, it is not improbable that suggestions concerning the approach to be adopted might have reached the circle of doge Pasquale Malipiero – who was in close contact with Lombardy – from Antonio Averlino, il Filarete, who visited the city several times during this period and who had already tackled the theme of the arch in 1454 for the celebration of the peace of Lodi at Cremona.

S. Zaccaria, interior.

S. Zaccaria, facade.

At all events, the architectural novelty of the gateway was registered as highly significant, and indeed it soon triggered off changes in the city fabric immediately around it. In the years 1467–8 measures were taken for the purchase and demolition of a group of houses in front of the gateway in order to open up a *via lata et pulchra* (wide & beautiful street).

The *dignitas operis* (dignity of the building) – the architectural implications of the gateway *perpulchram et honorificum* (splendid and honorific) – demanded that it be placed *in pulcherrimo . . . prospectu* (in a most beautiful prospect), with a fine outlook, an unencumbered line of vision created by incorporating the space previously occupied by the demolished buildings into that of a small pre-existing *fondamenta* (embankment).[21]

This space was also conceived in terms of a specific piece of state ritual: the regular visits paid to the Arsenal by the doge, together with the representatives of foreign powers. The ceremonial cortèges would therefore process along the first real *via triumphalis* of early Renaissance Venice.

Between 1456 and 1458, work began at the new Benedictine monastery of S. Zaccaria, one of the oldest churches in the city (where Andrea del Castagno had recently been working on the frescoes in the chapel of S. Tarasio): the considerable financial backing granted by the Senate was seen as justified by the site's importance *in centro et oculis urbis nostre* (in the centre and under the gaze of our city), and by its

historical position as the first building to be placed under ducal authority at the beginning of the ninth century.

The interpretation of the *marmorea aedes* (marble buildings) of S. Zaccaria – a composite work with various exceptional features and complex symbolic allusions – has been confused by the superimposed work of various architects and a group of very disparate sculptors.

At first, its construction was assigned to Antonio Gambello, who must essentially have completed the unfaced facade, the lower order of its elaborate architectural ornament, part of the colonnading of the nave and aisles and part of the interior of the apse between 1458 and 1481. Between 1481 and the first half of 1483 work proceeded rather slackly under the direction of two master masons. Then, when the church had almost reached completion, Mauro Codussi was called in as the new *proto*.

In fact, S. Zaccaria had numerous features that were previously unknown in Venice, and Gambello's contribution moved, from a context still strongly coloured by the Gothic, towards a freely imaginative interpretation of the Antique.

The main body of the church is clearly and rationally informed by simple and obvious ratios. The floor level of the choir is two steps higher than the rest of the building, and here both forms and spaces become unexpected, and strongly articulated. Beyond the last bay of the nave, the high altar is set within a double order of superimposed arches on a semi-octagonal

ground plan, with the half-cove of the apse above. Sixteenth-century sources dwell on the richness of the precious marbles on the high altar, including a great porphyry slab reminiscent of eastern imperial sarcophagi; indeed the general impression is similar to the Holy Sepulchre as represented in typical Renaissance iconography. An ambulatory the width of the aisles runs around the central space of the choir, with four radial chapels opening off it (the fifth, envisaged in the original scheme, was never built, so as not to occupy part of the apse of the earlier church, preserved alongside the new one).

Such a solution is rare in Italy, and hitherto completely unknown in this form in Venice. It intrigued Jacopo Bellini, who used it as a source of inspiration in the notebook now in the British Museum; if anywhere, a geographically close precedent might be found in Sant'Antonio in Padua. But in view of the traditional deeply-felt devotion to a 'monument after the fashion of that of Our Lord' recorded in the medieval sources in the apsidal area of the old building, we cannot be certain that the fifteenth-century choir was not indeed intended as a reminiscence of the Holy Sepulchre in Jerusalem – well-known to the Venetians, who were currently involved in organizing the international pilgrim traffic to the Holy Land – which has pronounced similarities with it, above all in its eastern section. The two tall columns at its threshold have sculpted images of seraphim, iconographically associated with the throne of God.

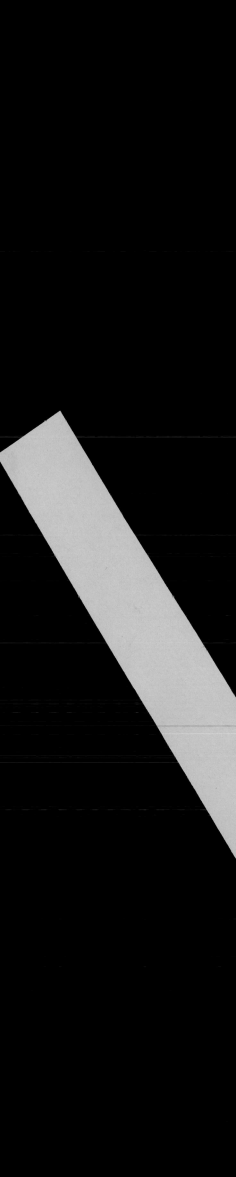

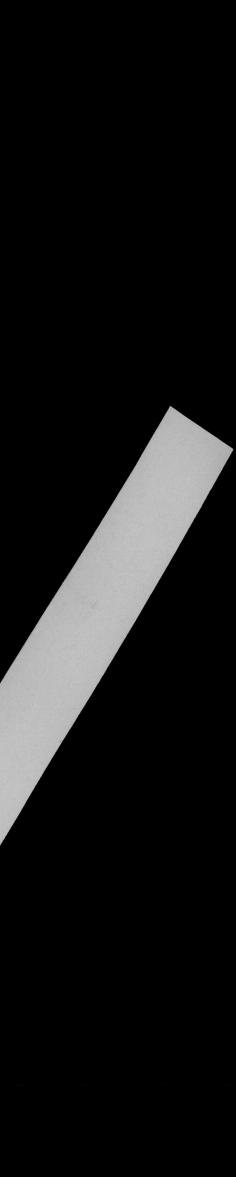

At all events, the choir of S. Zaccaria has a distinctly ceremonial character, conceived for collective worship, as emphasized by the dome above the last bay of the nave, and by the cluster of five small domes which roof the ambulatory, corresponding to the radial chapels. They may have been built by Mauro Codussi to an earlier plan by Gambello and are certainly in keeping with the Venetian fondness for domed spaces, Byzantine in origin but recently confirmed at SS Giovanni e Paolo and S. Maria dei Servi.

In S. Zaccaria, as we see, transitional features are particularly in evidence. In the choir, the upper traceried Gothic two-light windows open above round-headed arches on reused columns whose capitals, similar to those of S. Michele in Isola, are clearly attempts, albeit extremely free ones, at an ull'antica tone. Broad round-headed arches divide the space of the nave from the aisles, while these latter have their own pointed arches. The supports of the nave, in particular, are imaginative classicizing inventions: powerful columns with figured capitals with eagles in majesty and classical festoons, set on octagonal bases which in their turn stand on great plinths. Here, overlapping motifs (similar to some found in the Hellenistic era in Asia Minor but also in other works of fifteenth-century Venetian architecture), fluting, bean motifs and other classical reminiscences are combined with medieval brackets interpreted as double 'Renaissance' scrolls. In one case only, this latter element is replaced by powerful marble 'handles', similar to those on late-antique and early Byzantine sarcophagi.

The architectural ideas described above may be ascribed to Gambello, assisted by a host of collaborators including Giovanni Buora; Mauro Codussi was probably responsible for the entire upper part of the building. The ground storey of the facade is also by Gambello, treated as fasciae and panels, with a lively polychrome interplay of red and white marble, like the facades of the Ducal palace and the Porta della Carta.

But Gambello was certainly not responsible for the portal, on which Giovanni Buora and Domenico Duca were working in 1483: with its curved pediment and jambs decorated with candelabra supporting a phoenix and an eagle in majesty (both symbols of rebirth through faith), it undoubtedly derived from the repertoire of the Lombardo family. The attribution of the second order of the facade, with its series of blind arches decorated with elegant shells, is also still controversial; this interesting motif, which had already been used by Brunelleschi, is here highly reminiscent of the shell-capped niches found in the Ravennan art of the fifth to sixth centuries, as well as in the basilica of San Marco (and also in the repertoire of the Bellini). Codussi was now to take over and redesign the median and top sections of the facade, using horizontal strips with pronounced string-courses, dividing it up vertically and framing it with twinned columns and pilasters. This median section, linked to the two side parts by curved buttresses, now rose above them in an order punctuated

with pairs of columns, and crowned by a large stately semi-circular pediment. The surfaces are visually lightened and quickened by means of a meticulous distribution of openings from the third register to the tympanum, ranging from a broad three-light window to two two-light ones and culminating in the deep single oculus of the pediment; thus the upper part of the facade is vigorously structured and lucidly organized, in contrast with the rich colourism which characterized Gambello's somewhat hesitant approach.

The overall result, at all events, was extremely significant: a solemn architectural structure, whose internal magnificence fully reflected the contemporary debates mentioned above, and with all the trappings of a building of some official standing, an aspect which explains the frequent references, both architectural and decorative, to the nearby basilica of San Marco.

In fact, S. Zaccaria was conceived as a ceremonial structure closely associated with the ducal court and its public rituals, and sources dating from the time of its rebuilding emphasize the link between the church and the *honores et triumphi ducatus*.[22] This also explains the imperial symbols of the great eagles with their outstretched wings on the capitals of the nave, which was where the doge's procession ended.

Furthermore, the fifteenth-century capitals clearly repeat the model of Byzantine or Veneto-Byzantine precedents,[23] of which we have direct records, once again in

S. Giobbe, dome over the chancel.   View of the chancel.

relation to the myths of ancient ties between imperial Constantinople and the emergent ducal Venice, between the architectural expertise of the eastern empire and Venice's earliest splendours; while monastic sources contemporary with the rebuilding of the church attempted to prove a connection between the 'holy empire of Rome' and the origins of the monastery, between Giustiniano Particiaco, 'loyal to the empire and doge of Venice', and Leo V, the emperor of Byzantium who 'dispatched masters', that is, who is said to have sent architects to Venice from Constantinople.[24]

The second great period of Venetian architecture, too, thus loudly proclaimed its links with the imperial triumphs and the idea of *alterum Byzantium*.

Public financing for S. Zaccaria had been organized towards the end of the dogeship of Pasquale Malipiero, with the support of the humanist Zaccaria Trevisan the Doctor, while the monastery's representative was Candian Bollani, who had intervened in 1460 to speed up work on the gateway of the Arsenal. A programme based on well-defined cultural attitudes was now beginning to take shape, to be continued by the doge who followed Malipiero, Cristoforo Moro (1462–71).

The chief architectural event of Moro's dogeship was the building, in an outlying district, of the Franciscan church of S. Giobbe, documented as being in many ways paradigmatic of an architectural renaissance *more veneto* ('in the Venetian fashion').

Although the overall scheme of the portal in particular, with its curved pediment, looked to Florentine models, it reinterpreted them with an airy sensibility and a feeling for classical motifs treated with exquisite lucidity and lightness of touch. Here, Pietro Lombardo's version of the Renaissance already emerged as an elaborate vision rather than as a return to a lost grammar. A similar approach is found again in the chancel, heightened in tone and scale, and deriving from an even more subtle formal thinking. The solemn space of the main chapel opens up beyond a great arch with a frieze with the armorial bearings of the doge *imperator optimus*; on a square plan and roofed with a dome, it was to be imitated shortly afterwards by Cima in his altarpiece with the Virgin and saints in the cathedral at Conegliano (1492–3).[25]

The four roundels with the evangelists in the pendentives are clearly Tuscan in tone, reminiscent in some ways of Brunelleschi. But the hemispherical form of the dome, with the eight windows piercing the base of the ring so that the light is concentrated upon the high altar and on the very simple ground-level tomb of Cristoforo Moro, is much closer to the kind typical of Byzantine architecture in the version given of it at San Marco.

One iconographical clue to the interpretation of the work is to be found in the bas-relief roundels of the pillars of the arch leading into the chancel, with the two evangelists Mark and Luke. The church had recently been the centre of an important devotional episode: Moro had arranged for the body of a saint from Bosnia, currently being invaded by the Ottomans, to be placed there, and cardinal Bessarion – a central figure in relations between Byzantium and humanism – had unhesitatingly identified it as that of the evangelist Luke. In this political context – a clash between East and West – the presence in the city of these venerable remains was a powerful boost to the prestige of the republic and its importance as a shrine, particularly since the very popular *Legenda Aurea* by Jacopo da Varagine told of the protection granted by the saint to Antioch when besieged by the Turks, and since the original placing of his body in the church of the Twelve Apostles, the Byzantine model for San Marco, was well-known in Venice.[26]

As it happened, a papal judgment issued by Paul II had refuted Bessarion's original opinion, and subsequently the body was identified as that of St. Luke of Stiris. Nonetheless, until the eighteenth century, both convent and city chose to persist in their belief that the identity proposed by the eminent cardinal of Graeco-Byzantine origins was valid.

It therefore seems clear that Pietro Lombardo's 'Marcian' dome was intended as a public devotional space for the cult of the second evangelist to arrive in Venice after the Turks began to gain ground in the Levant, a space conceived in imitation of the one dedicated to the first evangelist-protector of the republic, both of which shared the iconography of the triumphal arch. S. Giobbe was therefore yet another architectural evocation of the ducal basilica, associated with the times, the men, and the political and celebrative themes of the myth of Venice as a second Byzantium. In 1501, together with San Marco and S. Francesco della Vigna, it was to issue indulgences to finance Venetian opposition to Turkish expansion.[27]

Another interesting feature of S. Giobbe is the series of chapels aligned along the north side of the main space, raised above the level of the nave by two steps. One of these is the highly distinctive Martini chapel, a rare point of direct and early contact between the Venetian and Tuscan Renaissances. Built by a wealthy family of silk-merchants originally from Lucca, it is a sedate cubic space completely independent of the main body of the church, opening off it through a large arch decorated with bunches of fruit and leaves supported by fluted Corinthian pillars and roofed with a pendentive dome faced with glazed terracotta tiles made by the Della Robbia Workshop, a literal quotation of Florentine spaces such as the chapel of the cardinal of Portugal in S. Miniato.

Although the Florentinism of the Martini chapel did exert some influence on the nearby and much later chapel of Pietro Grimani, a procurator of San Marco, it did not really amount to much more than a brief side-step from the main course being followed by Venetian architecture at the time, and was explicable in terms of the specific circumstances of its commission.

This course continued to be prevalently that of Pietro Lombardo and his assistants, as exemplified in S. Maria dei Miracoli, which had its origins in the popular cult of a sacred image placed, at the beginning of the fifteenth century, outside the nearby houses belonging to Angelo Amadi.

The first stone was laid in 1480; the cult of the miraculous image continued to be celebrated in a temporary timber chapel put up in the spring of the following year; all the Scuole Grandi took part in this solemn ritual at the express orders of the Council of Ten. This was therefore to be a building of the utmost importance for the life of the city, an example of the architectural expression of public piety. When the project had possibly already been drafted, there was talk of the future building taking the form of a *sacellum*: and indeed the little church of S. Maria dei Miracoli was conceived as a votive oratory, probably over two stages, as suggested, among other things, by the difference in proportion between the nave and the domed apse. It is a single space roofed with wooden barrel vaulting, running from the west end, with its hanging choir, up to a stately chancel reached by a tall flight of steps, and flanked by two side tribunes with ambos, very similar to the *tribuna magna* of the cathedral of Aquileia.

The chancel, built above a pseudocrypt used as a sacristy, ends in an apsidal space roofed by a dome with a double calotte, like that of San Marco, on a drum pierced by seven windows and crowned by another smaller dome. Externally, the walls are punctuated by the pilaster strips of a lower Corinthian order with architrave, and by those of a superimposed Ionic order with arches; a large semi-circular pediment crowns the facade. The plinths of the pedestals on which the pilasters on the canalside stand, are supported in their turn by powerful Ionic corbels suspended over the water, which laps right up against them, often actually submerging them at high tide.

The cultural roots of this work are undoubtedly complex, but marvellously illuminating. Florentine allusions can be sensed in the references to the rhythm of the first and second order of the Baptistry, similarly sheathed in marble, though the latter makes use of the typically Tuscan two-tone scheme – as well as in the sober treatment of the external pilaster strips. The influence of Alberti has been suggested for the wooden ceiling of the marble-encrusted interior, derived from an unrealized idea for the tempio Malatestiano at Rimini.

Nor should such reminiscences seem surprising: the Amadi, who supervised the drawing up of the plan, and the execution of the work, were in fact the son and nephew of a Tuscan merchant, formerly the administrator of the Scuola dei Lucchesi in Venice.

But this undoubted interest in the Florentine Renaissance was combined with two other important components: namely, an exuberant, highly sophisticated use of forms and idioms deriving from the Antique, and blatant quotations from the basilica of San Marco.

The artists working on S. Maria dei Miracoli used classical antiquity in a very selective way: they paid scant attention to classical grammar in the use of the orders, with the Ionic for example being supported by the Corinthian. Interest was concentrated rather on deploying a rich and elegant repertoire of ornament, with a series of displays of antiquarian erudition, sometimes with close analogies to roughly contemporary graphic sources such as the Rothschild notebook, the illustrations to the *Hypnerotomachia Poliphili* published by Manuzio, or the iconographical stock-in-trade of illuminators active in Venice in the second half of the fifteenth century. The series of facing griffins on the frieze of the facade – shown in a very similar way on the Scuola Grande di San Marco – is a free rendering of the frieze of the Roman temple of Antoninus and Faustina, used at more or less the same time on the doorway to palazzo Sacrati-Prosperi at Ferrara, and in the brick cornice of the Monghini houses in Ravenna (now at the entrance to S. Vitale), but also possibly derived from sculptural fragments which may have been part of antiquarian collections.

Here and there there are quotations of decorative motifs from the late-antique and early Christian era (for instance overlapping motifs and sea creatures with tridents on the altar screen, and the cross in the apsidal frieze).

Even more intriguing is the unusual overall appearance of the main body of the church, often compared to a jewel box or reliquary, and which has a remarkable affinity with the structures of an important

S. Maria dei Miracoli, facade.

group of early Christian sarcophagi of Ravennan origin: these are typically shaped like small buildings roofed with barrel vaulting on columns, with decorated ends, their sides sometimes articulated with an order of small Corinthian arches, and they were undoubtedly taken as sources of information concerning classical architecture during the early Renaissance. This is proved conclusively by the drawings in the Modena manuscript of Marcanova which attempt an imaginary reconstruction of Roman antiquities. One of them, for example, reuses the barrel vaulting of a large sarcophagus placed over the imaginary tomb of Romulus to roof the *aula* of the Therma Diocletiani and the palace of Cicero, not without similarities to the building of the Miracoli.

There are also certain other revealing circumstances in play here: the activity in Ravenna of both Pietro Lombardo (1483) and Mauro Codussi (1477–8), and the late fifteenth-century reworking in Ravennan myth, documented by Sanudo, of Narses as founder of the first Venetian churches, that is, of the transference of architectural models from Ravenna to emergent Venice.[28] At S. Maria dei Miracoli, therefore, the overall forms of classical antiquity seem to have been reconstructed according to a process that was basically antiquarian, drawing yet again upon the repertoire found within the territories of the Marcian republic and upon its 'golden' ducal architecture.

Equally significantly, S. Maria dei Miracoli may be regarded as at once the

S. Maria dei Miracoli, base of the right-hand pilaster of the triumphal arch.

S. Maria dei Miracoli, interior.

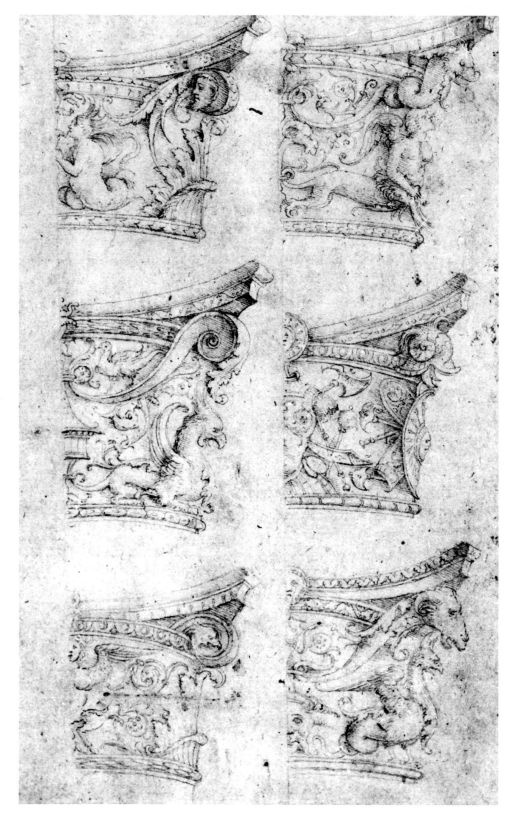

Figured capitals. Paris, Louvre, Cabinet des dessins, Rothschild notebook.

prototype, and the most striking example, of the brilliant and elaborate use of polychrome marble so typical of the early Venetian Renaissance: a tendency which has led some scholars to talk of a decorative preciosity lacking any real relationship with the return to classical Antiquity.

The church has a sumptuous polychrome facing, 'of the finest marble, and within likewise, on the floor and elsewhere',[29] with a lavish display of bejewelled crosses and of roundels in serpentine and Parian, Carrara and Verona marble, with hardwearing Istrian stone being used for structural purposes or those intended to appear as such.

In fact, classicizing reminiscences and elaborate polychrome decoration need not be seen as contradictory. Indeed, the line of research opened up by the discussions between Francesco Barbaro and Flavio Biondo, whose tenor is partly reflected in the pages of Biondo's *Roma trionfante*, provides the key to the problem. Here, such classical magnificence is seen as indeed consisting largely in the use of precious materials, in the splendour of colour introduced through a 'change in building', an architectural turning-point reached in the age of Augustus after the severity of earlier times, illustrated at length by Biondo with a wealth of examples.[30] Such classical magnificence and splendour, rooted in earliest historical memory, re-emerging from the grassy ground of Aquileia and clearly visible in Venetian Ravenna, were deliberately recreated in Lombardo's

S. Maria dei Miracoli and in much of the Venetian architecture of the early Renaissance. Overall, for Venice, the church seemed to symbolize a move towards the reconstruction of the classical architectural tradition which was absent from the space of the city as a whole.

But this decorative use of marble patently also belonged to the second group of references, namely those to San Marco. Soon after it was finished, S. Maria dei Miracoli was considered as second only to the ducal basilica, and as 'exceeding all others . . . for workmanship and materials'[31] by these same circles of Venetian humanists; as an artistic achievement which was crucial for the creation of the new Renaissance image of the city.

The facade of the Scuola Grande di San Marco, too, was largely to follow the line of interpretation taken by the nearby S. Maria dei Miracoli, as we shall see.

However, the most important privately commissioned work of civil architecture to make use of this polychrome magnificence as reinterpreted by Biondo, and realized anew by Pietro Lombardo, was undoubtedly the palazzetto of Ca' Dario on the Grand Canal, with its lavish parade of elaborate marble devices, its discs, wheels and intertwining motifs, signifying at once the noble rebirth of 'Roman' greatness, and continuity with the more recent Veneto-Byzantine past, in part also Gothic and late-Gothic, which had never completely ceased using *crustae* of Greek marble and roundels in other rare marbles.[32] In many ways the

palazzetto is unique, an extreme example of decorative display. Yet in fact it too should be regarded as the source for the frequent penchant of many private patrons, between the late fifteenth century and the beginning of the following, for chromatic refinements which were nonetheless believed to be signs of a classical language, the one also used, among others, for the noble imaginary architecture of the dream of Polifilo (1499).

Thus during these first decades, the Venetian Renaissance followed a line that was distinctly *more veneto* (in the Venetian fashion): apart from looking to Tuscan and Lombard achievements, it also paid particular attention to the traces left by classical art in the states of the Serenissima itself, with a variety of quotations and allusions which found favour with local aristocratic patrons. Here reminiscences of the ducal basilica of San Marco and, to a lesser degree, of other works of Veneto-Byzantine origin, were already a powerful component.

These tendencies were already broadly understood by sixteenth-century writers on art, as we see in particular from certain pages of Francesco Sansovino's *Venetia città nobilissima*, which bring together opinions and interpretations that had been circulating in the city for some time. Interestingly enough, this work also attempts to trace some thread of continuity between the oldest and most revered works of architecture in the city-state. If the 'composition of the *testudo* (roofing), of the church of S. Giacomo, 'so well held in place and kept together by the vaults which support the

arches that it is a marvel to behold . . . might be said to be the model for the church of San Marco', and if it was dated from 421, that is, from a late period but one that preceded the definitive collapse of the Roman empire, and if the architecture of San Marco was a model for other works such as S. Maria Formosa and S. Maria Mater Domini as early as the Middle Ages, it is clear that at least one venerable relic of classical architecture, part of the very origins of the city's magnificence, was regarded as having been situated in Venice herself: a relic which, moreover, still acted as a valid source of inspiration.[33]

Even Vasari, despite his academic and pro-Tuscan reservations concerning the architecture of San Marco – which he discussed at some length, regarding it as the work of several masters, all Graeco-Byzantine – puts it on a par with the SS Apostoli in Florence, 'built by Charlemagne', but which Filippo Brunelleschi had nonetheless deigned to use for the design of S. Spirito and S. Lorenzo.[34]

Such attitudes were implicitly confirmed by the works of art represented in the great Venetian paintings of the time: we see the influence of San Marco in the cove of the apse with the five motionless seraphim in the gilded mosaic of Giovanni Bellini's altarpiece originally at S. Giobbe; in the resplendent gilded mosaic cladding of the space where the Virgin is seated in the triptych of the Pesaro chapel in the Frari; in the cove of the apse in the altarpiece at S. Zaccaria, and in the great arch with Greek

Trebizond (Trabzon), polychrome marble cladding of the apse of the church of Panaghia Chrisokephalos (now Fatih Camii).

Ca' Dario, facade overlooking the Grand Canal.

Cima da Conegliano, *Virgin with Child and Saints*. Berlin, Staatliche Museen. The mosaics are based closely on those in the first dome with scenes from the life of Joseph in the narthex of San Marco.

inscriptions in the altarpiece at S. Giovanni Crisostomo, all by Bellini. On several occasions Cima da Conegliano gave his sacred subjects architectural backgrounds in the form of a domed organism very similar to those being built at the time. Such works were undoubtedly pictorial distillations of discussions which actually occurred in Venetian art circles, and, as such, are a helpful source of complementary information concerning them. The *Virgin enthroned with Child and saints* in Conegliano cathedral, for example, painted between 1492 and 1493, provides a number of highly detailed pieces of information. The cubic space, roofed by a dome on pendentives, looks less to pictorial prototypes than to built architecture, in particular to the chancel of S. Giobbe. The roundels in the pendentives of the dome are based on those in San Marco. Closely related architectural ideas were elaborated by Cima on several other occasions: in the *Virgin with Child and saints* now in Berlin (1495–7), originally from the sacristy of S. Michele in Isola, the mosaic depicted is a faithful replica of the one with the stories of Joseph in the narthex of San Marco. Cima's interest in domed organisms takes on added meaning in the *St. John* in the Madonna dell'Orto, a canvas set in a marble cornice similar in style to those of Pietro Lombardo. 'St. John the Baptist' – as Ridolfi says – is 'standing under a classical tribune, where the flecks of marble and the chips caused by time are imitated with great accuracy': here, a 'Marcian' interpretation of such structures appears

perfectly compatible with a 'classicizing' reading of them, as demonstrated by the 'pagan' iconography of the decoration Cima has invented for them. Examination of other pictorial works would prove similarly informative.[35]

Here mention should be made of another phenomenon of particular importance for an understanding of the Marcian model in late fifteenth-century Venice: during this same period, the generally accepted prototype for San Marco, the church of the Apostoleion, built in the time of Justinian, vanished for ever from the urban landscape of Constantinople. Between 1463 and 1471 its place was taken on the fourth hill of the Eastern capital by the Fatih Mehmed Camii, the mosque of Mahomet II the Conqueror, which immediately became the architectural symbol of the fraught shift towards an Islamic Istanbul, and of the imperial order which the Ottoman dynasty was imposing upon the territories it was conquering. This event cannot have escaped the notice of the Venetian patriciate and the highly cultured Greek community in the city, enhancing the value and meaning of the golden Venetian basilica accordingly,[36] especially since the second half of the fifteenth century saw the beginning of a series of Venetian eye-witness accounts of the new imperial Ottoman architecture: the five-domed church, such as the Apostoleion, the very emblem of the magnificence of Byzantium in Graeco-Byzantine works such as the anonymous *Lament of Constantinople*, now took on great symbolic significance in

artistic culture immediately after the Paleologue period known to Venetian circles, as documented for example by the Cretan icon in S. Giorgio dei Greci, where it was associated with Demetrius, a warrior saint.

However, this does not mean that there was no connection between what was happening in Venice, and other Renaissance architectural research into domed organisms, which was wide-spread and certainly not peculiarly Venetian; what it does mean is that such knowledge was perceived and adopted as a public language only in so far as it could be read as the reformulation of an *all'antica* style in keeping with the origins of the city, where it had never completely died out, indeed where it was proclaimed in all its potential splendour in San Marco. In fact, between the end of the fifteenth century and the beginning of the sixteenth, variations on the theme of San Marco and the Veneto-Byzantine were also to be found in built architecture, combined and intertwined in any number of ways and degrees; in all probability, moreover, this same period saw the Venetian Renaissance predilection for the Corinthian order, noted at length by Sebastiano Serlio.[37]

The work of Mauro Codussi, the great stonemason and architect born near Bergamo, was in some ways a continuation of these basic tendencies. But he was also to propose a new version of the *renovatio more veneto* (renewal in the Venetian fashion) based both on a greater knowledge and understanding of the principles of

Tuscan architecture, and on an idea of the Antique which was different from and more mature than that of Pietro Lombardo, and which inevitably left its own mark on his public and private works.

S. Michele in Isola (mostly built between 1468–9 and 1477) made a deep impression on contemporary Venetian architectural culture. Indeed, it seemed to suggest open competition with the Madonna dei Miracoli, in the sense that, like this latter, it was declared second only to San Marco, the pride and jewel of the whole city.

The highly erudite circle of Camaldolesians, and the humanist patriciate associated with it, were quick to sense how closely their own intellectual and aesthetic aspirations tallied with the resources and coherent style of the young Codussi, described by the sources as *cupidissimus*, consumed by a desire to conclude the work assigned to him.

His skills are immediately apparent in the spatial organization of the interior, a basilican space divided into a nave and two aisles and roofed with a flat coffered ceiling like that of Brunelleschi's S. Lorenzo in Florence. This leads into a chancel with two side chapels flanking the main one, entered through a large arch, with a dome with pendentives, ending in the curved apse (whereas the chapel of the Holy Cross, commissioned from him by Pietro Priuli as a space adjoining the church, combines a Tuscanizing entrance portal with an apse that is polygonal on the outside, following the northern Adriatic type found throughout the former territories of the exarchate).

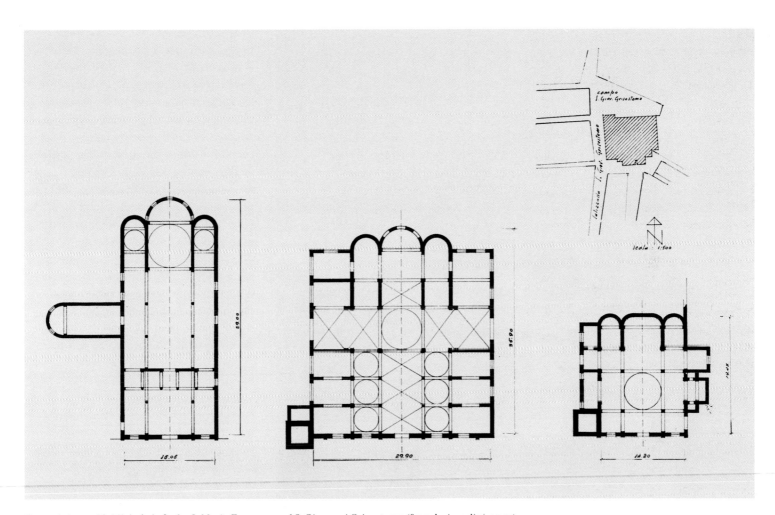

Ground plans of S. Michele in Isola, S. Maria Formosa and S. Giovanni Crisostomo (from L. Angelini, 1945).

But the truly innovative feature, the one most clearly indicative of Codussi's inventiveness, is the restrained and learned facade, almost entirely autograph with the exception of the portal with its triangular pediment. Despite the obvious similarities with the tripartite scheme crowned by a semi-circle so frequently found in fifteenth-century churches in Venice and the Veneto (and despite certain formal similarities with the facade of San Marco that have long been noted), Mauro Codussi's project seems to derive directly from Leon Battista Alberti's plan for the tempio Malatestiano at Rimini, known through the famous medal by Matteo de' Pasti. A complete novelty for a Venetian religious building was the smooth rustication of the whole of the lower portion of the facade up to the architrave, divided up by pilaster strips which are also rusticated, and pierced by two tall single-light windows.

The texture of the wall, with its narrow clear-cut ashlar quoins and regular joins, was certainly an *all'antica* idea derived from classical examples and works of the Tuscan Renaissance. Here Codussi generally rejected the simple sense of refinement given by polychrome marble, or used it extremely sparingly (the monks' gallery across the nave, with its rich cladding in rare coloured stones, executed after 1480, is not by him). Instead, he made maximum use of the linear purity of the white surfaces of Istrian stone, offset by the slight play of shadow given by the rustication, and the stronger design of the cornices, contrasting with the deep shade of the openings. This

Mauro Codussi, S. Maria Formosa, view of the
nave looking towards the chancel.

View of the left-hand side chapels.

was the whiteness of eternal splendour: as classical and imperial for the ancient world as it was Biblical and apostolic for the Christian one. The glorificatory motif of the fluted shells in the tympana of the circular quadrants echoes and underlines that of the marble shell inscribed in the pediment. Here, a possible memory of Tuscan decorative themes is associated with that of the great triumphal shells in the Ravenna mosaics and the arcaded sixth- and seventh-century sarcophagi which Codussi certainly knew, having worked for the Camaldolesians on S. Apollinare in Classe.

Nitet venustate, glittering with beauty, is how S. Michele in Isola was described even while it was being built: the shell motif used so conspicuously on the facade, speaking so blatantly of the surrounding sea, here seems evocative of virginal purity, of Aphrodite rising from the watery spaces of the lagoon above which the building offers itself so 'jubilantly' to the eye, as another source puts it,[38] an embodiment of their hallowed nature as it was being formulated in the great contemporary public myths of humanist rhetoric at this same time.

S. Maria Formosa, on the other hand, which had been radically rebuilt since 1491, had been an example of the medieval imitation of the 'central core' of the basilica of San Marco, as Francesco Sansovino notes. Here, Codussi was more obviously attracted by Byzantine-Marcian schemes. As a result, his new church was based on a plan in which what was clearly a Greek cross was adapted to a Latin one, retaining the overall

features of the earlier design and then being inscribed, together with the adjoining spaces, in an almost perfect square. A dome was placed over the crossing between nave and transept (it collapsed and was rebuilt after an earthquake in 1688), while a double series of small domes emphasized the three square bays of the aisles, forming a complex and highly allusive organism. Furthermore, most unusually, two of the side bays on each side lead into deep chapels, which are also lit through two-light windows opening in the dividing walls. Here the problem which seems most to have interested the architect was the recreation of inter-connected spaces deriving from the idea of the old pre-existing building. S. Maria Formosa was another religious building to which the doge paid an annual ceremonial visit, and this may help to explain the elaborate hierarchy of the spaces, ending in a deep three-apsed chancel. Yet the interior as a whole is extremely spare, with no concessions to decorative refinement, either sculptural or chromatic. Furthermore, Codussi's project, and the worksite as a whole, seem to have been rigorously supervised and subject to a strict code of practice: a fact which may also have had polemical implications, bearing in mind that Lombardo's church of the Miracoli had just been completed in the immediate vicinity.

Codussi was facing similar problems in his rebuilding of the church of S. Giovanni Crisostomo after it had been seriously damaged by fire. During this period (from 1480 to 1516), the local parish priest was

Alvise di Zaccaria Talenti,[39] who was also a notary and ducal canon, and the descendent of a well-known Florentine family which had taken Venetian citizenship at the end of the fourteenth century.

Commissioned to rebuild S. Giovanni Crisostomo in 1497, Codussi made use of the Greek cross plan inscribed in a square – clearly visible from its external play of volumes – with a dome over the crossing, and a facade with a trilobed pediment. Here a central plan was adopted as particularly suited to the collective worship of a small parish, numbering under a thousand souls at the period in question. The tetrastyle layout on a Greek cross must have been deliberately derived from that of the earlier building, possibly together with its dimensions, which are based on a square of fifty Roman feet per side. Codussi's solution was therefore linked to the variant with an inscribed cross of a Byzantine kind, of which medieval Venice had at least a dozen examples, including the two famous churches associated with the myth of Narses, S. Teodoro and S. Geminiano. The devotional and symbolic reasons for this choice are clear, deriving specifically from the Byzantinizing components of the official culture of the Serenissima. The 'most sacred' memory of the relics of the doctor of the church (the patriarch of Constantinople and primate of the Eastern church), and of the place in Asia minor where they lay, had already been mentioned by a learned anonymous traveller of the early fifteenth century.[40] In particular, it should be remembered that 'the book written by San Zuan Boccadoro' (St. John Chrysostom), an iconographical motif in the altarpiece on the high altar of the church by Sebastiano del Piombo, was part of the group of holy relics in the ducal basilica which constituted evidence of the *translatio imperii* from the capital of the vanished Byzantine empire to the strong and powerful Venice.[41] S. Giovanni Crisostomo has various conspicuous Byzantinisms, from the Greek letters of the book depicted in this same altarpiece, and the symbolism associated with them, to the Greek verses from psalm 14 in the altarpiece with saints Jerome, Louis and Christopher signed by Giovanni Bellini in 1513.

But here too, even in this mature work, Codussi's interpretation of a Veneto-Byzantine architecture of the kind described still tended to reinstate an 'original' severity of form through what he must have believed to be an indirect model, rethinking it along Albertian lines and, ultimately, through his own desire for structural clarity.

Moreover, in its turn, S. Giovanni Crisostomo inaugurated an early Renaissance type of its own: many other churches were to be built in imitation of it until the early 1530s, such as the parish church of S. Felice, begun in 1529 by Giovanni Antonio da Carona.[42]

Giorgio Spavento, active between the late fifteenth century and 1509, followed a similar line of research. In 1486 he had been made *proto* of the Procuratoria of San Marco, that is, superintendent of the fabric

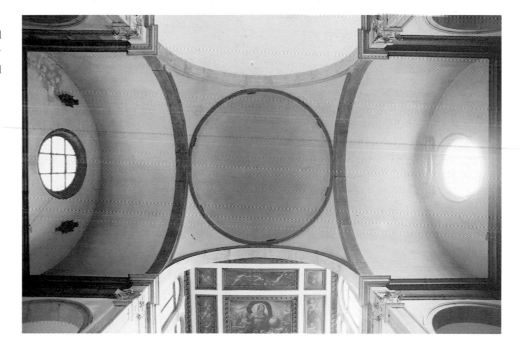

left
Mauro Codussi, S. Giovanni Crisostomo, interior.

below
S. Giovanni Crisostomo, the dome.

above
S. Geminiano, ground plan before demolition,
early nineteenth century.

below
Cross section of S. Geminiano. Paris,
Bibliothèque Nationale.

of the ducal basilica. That same year had
seen work begin on the little church of
S. Teodoro, behind San Marco, in honour
of the first Byzantine protector of the city
whose cult was the outcome not of some
random decision, as has been claimed, but
of a rekindling of public devotion which
began in the mid-fifteenth century and
grew during the early years of the sixteenth.
Spavento had already drawn inspiration
from the apses of San Marco for this small
building, on a semi-circular plan articulated
by five deep niches. But the experience he
gained along these same lines at S. Salvador,
completed by Tullio Lombardo, was far
more important. In part repeating the ground
plan of the pre-existing building, and more
particularly the main features of the architectural organism of San Marco, the new
Renaissance church took the form of a
cruciform basilica with domes, ending in
three semi-circular apses; it was conceived
in terms of the overlapping of two cubes
topped by a dome over the median one, the
measurement of whose side was the twelve
Venetian feet fixed in the agreements of 8
August 1506 with the building's backer, the
prior and subsequent patriarch of Venice,
Antonio Contarini. The main body of the
building then expanded by one quarter of
a side, corresponding to the ends of the
transept and the apse. Since the module that
had generated it in terms of volume had
been a domed organism characterized by
one main dome and four smaller ones
arranged in a quincunx, this church too
adopted the 'model . . . imitated from the

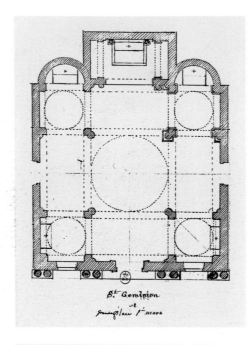

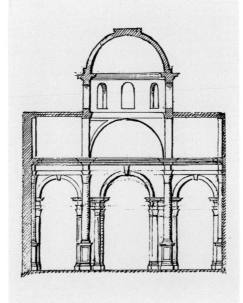

central core of the church of San Marco.'[43]
A variety of symbolic allusions – trinitarian,
christological and redemptive – had also
been incorporated into the structure and
decoration at Contarini's request: trinitarian in the number of apses, domes and
windows; christological in the cruciform
plan, in the number of lesser domes and in
the iconography of the figured Corinthian
columns of the nave. Here, the standard-
bearing lamb alludes to the resurrection;
the phoenix consumed by flames in its nest
is an image of Christ consumed by the fire
of the Passion at Jerusalem; the pelican
alludes to the Saviour and, indirectly, to
redemption and charity. Tullio Lombardo's
later continuation of Spavento's original
layout ensured a coherent use of the *all'
antica* language, albeit somewhat stiffly
and with some archaisms. As *proto* of the
work on the Zen chapel in San Marco from
1512, Tullio Lombardo had already demonstrated his learned detachment from the
family enterprise, as well as a receptiveness
to the classical novelties which constituted
a key moment of transition between the
experience of Codussi and Sansovino's
work of renewal.

The city centre, the 'navel' of 'this city
blessed by God, steeped in the blood of
Christ from its very origins, and fed and led
to greatness by it', in the words of Antonio
Contarini himself,[44] now had its own
'Marcian', cruciform church. This act of
reconsecration of the urban space was
further emphasized by the symbolic choice
of date for the laying of the first stone, 25

March 1507: 'On the day that, in 421, the city of Rivoalto was begun . . . on the day the world was made' and, lastly, 'Lord Jesus Christ was crucified, according to St. Augustine . . . on this day the first stone of the church of S. Salvador was laid, and its rebuilding begun . . . so that this is a day much celebrated.'[45] As early as 1507 S. Fantin, begun on a model by Sebastiano da Lugano, had used a simplified version of the scheme of S. Salvador, now influenced by other concomitant publicly-commissioned works including the rebuilding of the church of Sti Geminiano e Mena at the end of the Piazza, opposite the basilica of San Marco. In 1505, Leonardo Loredan had ordered its reconstruction on a ground plan – attributed to Cristoforo dal Legname – which, to judge from such surveys as remain, had borne a very close resemblance to that of S. Salvador. S. Geminiano too was a domed organism on an inscribed cross, roofed by a main dome and four smaller ones arranged in a quincunx, whose ground plan used the same ratios as those identifiable in S. Salvador. Now a whole cluster of vitally important sites were given formal unity and coherence in accordance with a scheme affecting all the central spaces of the city: S. Giacomo, the 'place of origins' par excellence, regarded as 'antique' and a model for San Marco; S. Geminiano, marking the earliest memories of relations between Venice and Justinian's Roman empire; S. Salvador, the focal point of the city, founded by the will of Christ himself and site of the body of the city's first protector; and the sacred building with

Giorgio Spavento and Tullio Lombardo, S. Salvador, ground plan (eighteenth century). Venice, Archivio di stato.

Giorgio Spavento and Tullio Lombardo, S. Salvador, interior looking towards the apse.

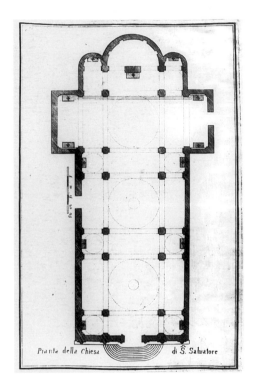

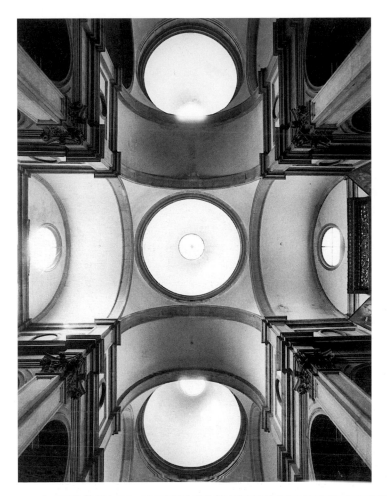

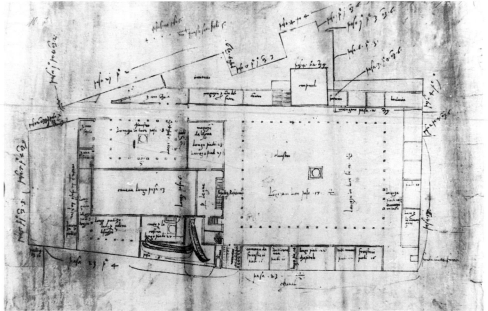

above, left
Giorgio Spavento and Tullio Lombardo,
S. Salvador, interior view of the domes.

above, right
Sante Lombardo, S. Giorgio dei Greci, facade.

left
Anon., sketch for the ground plan of the convent
of S. Salvador.

Anon., 'Arsenal for eighty galleys'. Design
for the extension of the Venice Arsenal, end
of fifteenth century. Venice, Archivio di stato.

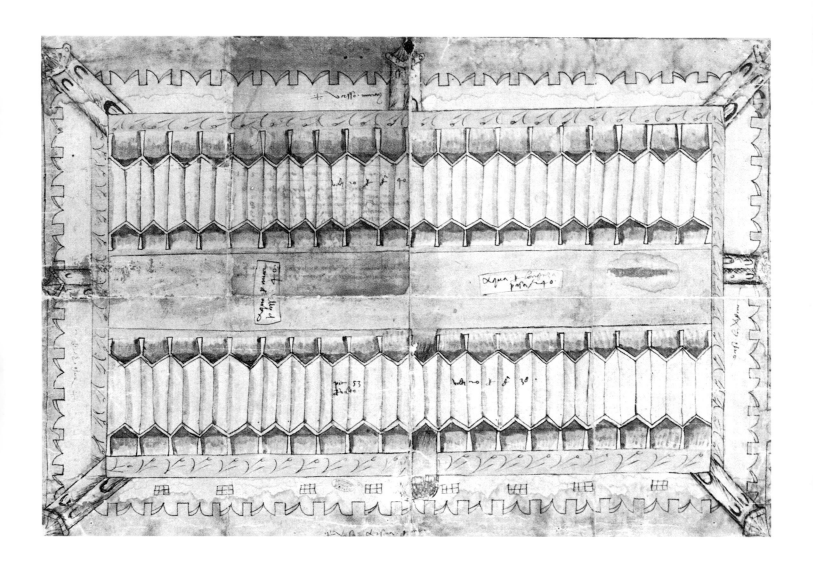

which the republic identified so strongly, San Marco.

This tendency was to be confirmed with the rebuilding of the Rialto churches by Scarpagnino, with domed crosses inscribed in a square at S. Giovanni Elemosinario and S. Matteo. But the time of what we might define as the *renovatio marciana*, of architectural Byzantinisms and Veneto-Byzantinisms, was now drawing to a close.

The next stage in this process, at the end of the 1530s, was significant but essentially conclusive: namely, the building of the only church in Venice actually to use the Byzantine rite, and whose long-drawn-out and by no means linear progress was, for a time, to set the Hellenic community against the Serenissima. This was S. Giorgio dei Greci, by Sante Lombardo, a building with a single nave whose interior is divided by a rich *templon* leading into a chancel, in accordance with the Byzantine liturgy. Its barrel-vaulted interior has a dome on a drum, giving the space a firmly-centred feeling. The unusual and elaborate facade is arranged on a two-level scheme, divided vertically into three and capped by an attic order flanked by scrolls.

The stone surfaces to the sides of the portal and the large central circular window are articulated by niches, and five other aedicules succeed one another along the upper order of the sides, while a sort of *serliana* – also with niches – is inscribed in the attic storey. The overall architectural idea has affinities with a reconstruction of a classical temple by Cesariano; with the

facade of a church from Serlio's treatise; and with a facade conceived for S. Francesco della Vigna depicted in a medal of 1534, with a three-light window in the attic storey among other things. The repeated use of aedicule-niches is most unusual for a Venetian church; Sante Lombardo drew it from his own repertoire, but gave it particular importance in S. Giorgio dei Greci. The dome and apses, and perhaps also the *serliana*, have Byzantine reminiscences, probably suggested by his patrons. The Greek community's desire for selfhood thus appears to have been thoroughly heeded and interpreted by Lombardo in a project which is in many ways a work of mediation between the Graeco-Byzantine legacy and the Renaissance forms which now also prevailed.

Meanwhile, during the last two decades of the fifteenth century, both as a result of disastrous fires, and of a specific policy of architectural renewal, work began on a long and important series of works of public rebuilding: first and foremost, that of the Ducal palace, as a result of the serious fire of September 1483.

One highly innovative proposal, which would have entailed the acquisition of all the buildings situated behind the ducal complex, beyond rio di Palazzo, and the creation of a completely new building, was shelved, then reconsidered by Andrea Gritti (1523–38), only then to be definitively abandoned.[46]

The project as ultimately built was entrusted to Antonio Rizzo, who supervised the work for many years, until, at the end of

the century, it emerged that he had been guilty of embezzlement. He then fled the city and died in exile. He is described by some sources as *architector palatii*, and is generally regarded as responsible for the rebuilding project in general, despite recent hypotheses suggesting the involvement of Mauro Codussi.[47]

The problem of attribution apart, the work has certain highly distinctive features, as well as others in common with various contemporary works of architecture, including some by Codussi. In point of fact, not only was the new building conditioned to a large extent by the pre-existing one; it also lacked all sense of architectural unity, since somewhat different solutions were used for the facade overlooking the courtyard and the one on the narrow rio di Palazzo. The internal facade is divided into two longitudinal sections: the lower one consists of a long arcade on round-headed arches, on octagonal pillars, topped by oculi and a loggia with pointed arches, on engaged pilasters and columns with medievalizing bases. In accordance with Gothic practice, the loggia is reached by means of a highly elaborate marble staircase, later to be known as the Scala dei Giganti. The upper order has two storeys with high entablatures, distinguished by the differing design of their windows, topped on the second storey by curved pediments projecting over a frieze; the wall surfaces between the windows are treated as deeply-carved panels. The striking asymmetry also reflects the distribution of

Drawing of the facade of the torre dell'Orologio (from L. Angelini, 1945).

bases, standing on consoles decorated with Ionic volutes.

The facade overlooking the canal is completely different; while not exactly unassuming, it is less excessive, less declamatory in tone. Here too, the long wall surface on to the *rio* is divided up horizontally by high strongly projecting architraves, incorporating both a sequence of roundels in precious marbles, and pediments over stilted arches. The motif of the false windows, derived from funerary monuments, was taken from the repertoire of notebooks of drawings from the Antique; together with other devices, and the meticulous manipulation of horizontal and vertical elements, it acts as a visual curb to the asymmetries and irregularities arising from the reuse of the medieval structures. The high base plinth with its diamond-faceted rustication, alternately protruding and re-entrant, is reminiscent of the unfinished Ca' del Duca on the Grand Canal, and serves to give the inert masonry mass a sense of power. Here too numerous devices are deployed to give the vast surface a feeling of movement: the slight projection outwards of the exterior of the watergates, the decreasing protrusion of the powerful cornices, and the diminishing formal importance, from bottom to top, of the windows of the three main floors above the ground floor and mezzanine. Here, great care and coherence have clearly gone into the making of a work of singular splendour, conceived by means of a process of allusion, with fragmentary 'finds' being skilfully manipulated so as to reinstate a

solemnity whose origins are plainly sensed, even though its precise rules are not yet fully understood.

The lavish expending of public resources on the great site of the Ducal palace was not an isolated case in early Renaissance Venice. This same period saw the building of the nearby torre delle Ore, by Mauro Codussi (1496–9). Designed as a tower over a high passageway situated at the entrance to the Mercerie, its purpose was to house the machinery which set off the movements of the angel and three kings as they saluted the Virgin; above these were the winged lion with doge Agostino Barbarigo in an act of homage, and, above them again, the two 'moors' who struck the bronze bell to inform the city of the passing hours. The facade of the tower towards the Piazza is governed by a lucid sense of proportion; the ground-floor arch – with columns placed up against pillars – has ornamental *crustae* and marble roundels, and the upper orders gradually decrease in height. The work has numerous symbolic allusions: from the Piazza, it clearly appears as a metaphor celebrating the policy inaugurated by the Serenissima in 1474 with the decree establishing public ownership of all 'ingenious devices', which encouraged all manner of new techniques and inventions.[48] At the same time, Codussi's architecture, serving as threshold, 'at the mouth of the Mercerie', to the commercial 'bowels' of the city, also promised other marvels, those displayed along the Mercerie a proof of the all-embracing nature of Venetian trade. The arch of the

Jacopo de' Barbari, bird's-eye view of Venice, 1500.

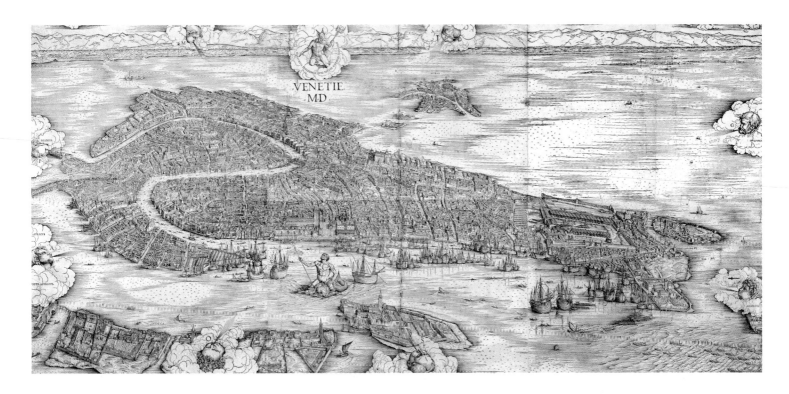

torre delle Ore led into a commercial street which tended to parade its wares in a profuse and ostentatious ritual, proclaiming the city's opulence ('great is the power of her trade', as Bernardo Giustinian had written during those same years, 'everything to be found the world over is hers').[49]

For these reasons – despite the economic effort required to sustain the war with Naples, and although work on the east wing of the Ducal palace had slowed down – the decision was taken to proceed with the tower: 'This work has been begun in order that it should not appear that our land is quite without financial resources.'[50]

International acclaim and *forma urbis* proceeded *pari passu*: this same context also explains why Jacopo de' Barbari now began work on his bird's-eye view of Venice (1498–1500), and why an appropriate updating of its main urban features was now seen as fundamental, and legitimate, by the city-state as it reworked its own identity. In 1512, another fire was to precipitate the process of renewal around Piazza San Marco. In 1514 work began on the 'Case nuove della Procuratia' (new houses of the Procuratia), now known as the 'Procuratie Vecchie', to be definitively completed only in 1532.

With their long ground-floor sequence of arcaded shops, and their two upper floors of apartments, the Procuratie now tended to define the way the adjacent *calli* and canals related to piazza San Marco, concluding and shaping the central pattern of commercial areas and street systems as they emerged on to the piazza. Fifty ground-floor arches on square piers, their surfaces treated as recessed panels, with extremely simple mouldings, support two long, unbroken superimposed series of windows, framed by fluted columns with Corinthian capitals and separated by two entablatures with tall plain friezes; the top storey has a third

149

above
The Procuratie Vecchie, detail.

below
Drawing of part of the facade of the Procuratie
Vecchie (from L. Angelini, 1945).

frieze pierced with simple circular oculi.
The facade is topped by a long crenellation
in Istrian stone, alternating with classicizing stone vases, a typical medieval feature
of Venetian civil architecture. In fact, the
early sixteenth-century building remained
faithful to the Romanesque version of the
Procuratie built by Sebastiano Ziani (1172–8),
whose appearance is known to us from the
Procession of the Relic of the true Cross by
Gentile Bellini (1496). With the exception of
an additional storey, the early Renaissance
Procuratie are quite simply a transcription,
or updating, of the medieval model. In short,
here too we have a key example of what we
might call a *renovatio more veneto*, of an ever
more intensive sanctifying of the forms of
the past, implying a deliberate pursuit of
changelessness for the *species urbis* (image
of the city); and, in parallel, of the limits
being imposed upon the *res aedificatoria* at
the very moment when its political function
was being enshrined, when *fidelitas* was
specifically being required of it.

Meanwhile, between 1505 and 1508,
rebuilding was also under way – once again
as a result of a random event – at the very
hub of Venice's commercial system, namely,
that of the Fontego dei Tedeschi, the most
important of the structures serving the
needs of the Serenissima's international
trade, both for the storing of merchandise
and as accommodation for merchants, their
deals and administrative activities. Situated
just off Rialto, the city's commercial heart,
and efficiently incorporated into the distributive network through the series of

ground-floor shops running along the two
adjacent *calli*, the Fontego was also well
served vis-à-vis water traffic by its tall, deep,
five-arch ground-floor portico giving on to
the Grand Canal, used for the loading and
unloading of men and merchandise. The
two side blocks project slightly from the
rest of the facade, and the entire building is
crowned by a long crenellation. Basically,
therefore, it had all the essential features of
the facade of a medieval *casa-fondaco*, even
down to the number of arches of the portico, also found in that of the nearby Ca' da
Mosto and Ca' d'Oro. However, the internal
organization of the spaces precluded the
presence of the peculiarly Venetian multi-
light window on the facade: the architect
simply divided it up with string-courses,
pairing the windows to break up the
monotony of the masonry surface, diversify-
ing their appearance and having them
diminish in importance from the first floor
to the third. Giorgione's frescos further
lightened the facade, which would otherwise
have been out of keeping with the colourful
light-filled *continuum* of frontages overlooking the Grand Canal into which it had
been incorporated; the iconographical programme, with its central figures of Peace
and Justice, was completed by Titian on the
landside facades. Inside, a square courtyard
with a central well was surrounded by porticoes beneath three orders of meticulously
calibrated loggias. It is possible that these
porticoes repeated certain of the features
of the pre-existing building, for example
the loggia which can just be seen in the

western courtyard of the Fontego in de' Barbari's bird's-eye view. At all events, there were undoubtedly many analogies between the form and functions of this building and certain types of commercial buildings, for example city *khan* and *fundug*, which often also had shops clustering along their exteriors. This architectural type was well-known in the Venice of the time. An important Venetian source from the second half of the fifteenth century actually makes the connection between such buildings and the Fontego: 'You should know that in the city of Constantinople there is a place called *bexestan* (bedestan), similar to the Fontico dei Tedeschi in Venice.'[51]

The authorship of the lucid, severe forms of the Fontego is by no means certain. In all likelihood, Gerolamo Tedesco (whose model was approved with a decree of 19 June 1505) should be regarded as the author of its functional and distributive scheme; Giorgio Spavento, *proto* of the procurators of San Marco, probably executed his plan, which had been elaborated under the supervision of the German trading community; while Scarpagnino, *proto* of the *provveditori al Sal*, was the author of the landside portal and, more importantly, the general overseer of the site. The involvement of fra' Giovanni Giocondo, though suggested by a contemporary, is not impossible, even though it is not directly documented.[52] The rebuilding of the Fontego also marked a turning-point in the general attitude to public architectural magnificence. A few years earlier, Domenico Morosini had maintained that

Rialto. Ruga degli Oresi with the buildings by Scarpagnino.

such magnificence was appropriate throughout the city; but the period preceding the crisis of Agnadello was beset with doubts and reflections, and circumstances were changing. The moralizing tendencies which were to characterize the long dogeship of Leonardo Loredan (1501–21) were now emerging. The architectural language of the Fontego dei Tedeschi was suitably spare and severe: with the exception of the eastern portal, with its Corinthian order (justified by the repeated allusions to the state in the form of Marcian lions), even the most minimal suggestion of the use of the orders and usual forms of decoration was now studiously avoided.

In fact, this austerity was the result neither of chance, nor of an independent decision on the part of the architect. It had been expressly required by the Senate (1505), which forbad all use of precious marble and carving. Here the architect was specifically asked to use a style commensurate with the 'dignity' of the site, articulating it in terms of the useful and the appropriate, combining the sobriety befitting a centre of trade, the ornate appearance suited to a key public place, and the stately deployment of forms acknowledged as necessary for palazzi housing the city's foremost institutions.

Here then, at the beginning of the sixteenth century, state patronage was already beginning to adopt the attitude which was to inform all subsequent public building during the Renaissance period, and which was to be formulated theoretically in the commentary on Vitruvius by Daniele

Barbaro (1556). In all probability, however, decisions concerning the Fontego dei Tedeschi taken by the public bodies commissioning it also bore witness to a new desire for a *renovatio more veneto* whose mood seems to have been embodied by Dolce (1557), in which great painting would proclaim its primacy over structural and architectural decoration: '. . . since, without the ornament of any painting, buildings both public and private . . . are greatly diminished in grace and beauty. And the exterior of houses and palaces painted by the hand of a skilled master delight the eye far more greatly than any encrustation of white marble, porphyry or serpentine embellished with gold. The same may be said of churches and cloisters . . .'[53]

The evident severity underlying the Fontego dei Tedeschi was duly to set the tone for the general rebuilding of Rialto, commissioned from Antonio Abbondi, 'lo Scarpagnino', after another fire in 1514. The new buildings, laid out as shops, warehouses and offices, were based on the simplest of schemes, giving the market area a business-like air of unity and uniformity. They took the form of long buildings on arcades of Istrian stone, standing on completely plain, rectangular, unpanelled piers. The two upper storeys, with their high entablatures, had plastered brick walls with extremely simple rectangular windows: this was a parsimonious, utilitarian architecture, designed for spaces to be occupied by shops, a symbolic endorsement of the prudent management of public

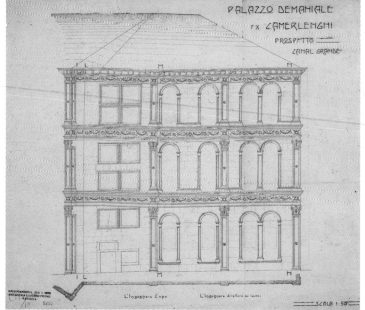

above
Rialto, palazzo dei Camerlenghi, general view.

left
Drawing of the facade over the Grand Canal, 1931. Venice, Soprintendenza ai BB.AA.AA.

expenditure, where the rules of art were asserted with virtuous restraint, untouched by the ornate style of the Ancients. The one exception, in this context, was the palazzo dei Camerlenghi, datable from between 1525 and 1528, with its display of ornament, use of precious marbles and opulent cladding in Istrian stone. Rather than a radical rebuilding, this was a skilful transformation into a unitary block of three preexisting ones, albeit on a very irregular plan. The external decorative apparatus, and the marble revetment of the facade, served to give stylistic unity to the structures and, above all, to give them the required sense of public dignity. Somewhat awkwardly, the *proto* therefore tried to give a traditional feeling to the facade overlooking the Grand Canal and the Ruga degli Oresi, opening up three-light windows, using richly figured capitals and framing the landside entrance with a Corinthian portal very similar to the one in the nearby Fontego dei Tedeschi, though with a more elaborate marble inlay. He divided the building up horizontally with the usual high entablatures, with friezes decorated with roundels interlinked by the classical theme of the festoon. As other details prove, the palazzo dei Camerlenghi is a free and less courtly version of aspects taken from the east wing of the Ducal palace. In both its general uniformity, and in the particularity of its one exception, the architecture of the Rialto proclaims its official endorsement of established tradition: not surprisingly, Vasari subjected it to critical, not to say sarcastic, attention.[54]

Here too, during these same years, Vitruvian culture had met with a rebuff. Numerous other architects apart from Scarpagnino had worked on the problem of the rebuilding of Rialto, including Giovanni Celestro, Alessandro Leopardi and above all fra' Giovanni Giocondo. Fra' Giocondo's project – rejected, according to Sanudo, because 'he did not understand the site'[55] – had represented the culmination of a high-minded and innovative mood. As Vasari tells us, this Dominican architect and theoretician had planned a radical rebuilding with strictly regular forms, severe and stately: a thoroughly unitary piece of town-planning, which would have totally renewed the heart of the Mediterranean capital, *alterum Byzantium*, just as the transformation of Constantinople into the Ottoman Istanbul had entailed the shift of the trading centre of the Eastern capital to the immediate vicinity of the old *Forum Tauri*. It would have been a 'perfect square', according to Vasari: for fra' Giocondo, Rialto would have taken the form of a *forum quadratum et columnis ornatum more graeco* (a square forum in the Greek manner, decorated with columns), of an agora, on a square plan bounded by huge double porticoes with closely-set columns and marble architraves, in accordance with Vitruvius' description.[56] Had it been built, Venice's commercial centre would therefore have been the site of the first architectural revival of classical Greece. At all events, this was a momentous plan.

Another project, formulated in 1515, although not built until later, should be seen in this same context: that of the building, on the Piazza – 'in foro Divi Marci' – of the public library made up mainly of the Greek manuscripts belonging to Bessarion, a casket for the 'secrets of venerable antiquity' handed down to the Venetians, 'terrae Graeciae Domini', lords of the land of Greece after the fall of imperial Constantinople. Moreover, in 1513 the gilded angel had been placed on the campanile of San Marco – 'the shining tower of our protector' – similar to the 'statue set upon a very tall tower in Athens which, as it turns, tells of the nature of the winds', a similarity strikingly borne out by fra' Giocondo's reconstruction of it in his 1511 edition of Vitruvius. The Rialto project thus seems to represent the synthesis, culmination and decline of that particular aristocratic Hellenizing version of the Renaissance which had characterized the Venetian return to classical antiquity since its start.

In point of fact, research into the architectural forms of the classical tradition had taken several directions in humanist circles. In 1511, a booklet by a member of Manutius' circle, *De comoedia libellus* by Vettor Fausto – who was professor of Greek literature at San Marco and was very knowledgeable about architecture – suggested a reconstruction of the *scaenae frons* based on the *Onomastikon* of Giulio Polluce. This in turn made possible the reconstruction of the porticoed stage documented by the Venetian Plautus of 1518 and, soon afterwards, the building of the five imposing arches, known to have been used as a theatrical space, of the loggia Cornaro at Padua by Giovan Maria Falconetto in 1524, the year after the reprinting of Vettor's booklet.[57]

The centres of the Venetian Scuole Grandi (religious and welfare confraternities) describe a broad semi-circle in the city space, running from the south-west to the north-east, with the Scuola Grande di San Marco, situated at the boundary between the *sestieri* of Castello and Cannaregio. Almost all established in their definitive positions by the end of the Middle Ages, they were situated over an arc of sites 'away from the piazze',[58] topographically intermediate, constituting crossing points, thresholds between the 'body' and the 'margins', the periphery of the city. In the context of relations between city and architecture emerging in the early Renaissance, their charitable functions and roles as upholders of the social order under the rule of the Council of Ten necessarily caused them to become centres of collective and public magnificence, calculated visually to convince visitors of the efficacy, stability and harmony of the model underpinning the Serenissima's political image. This was achieved, between the late fifteenth century and the first decades of the sixteenth, by means of the extensive works of modernization carried out on the Scuole Grandi of S. Giovanni Evangelista, S. Marco, S. Rocco and the Misericordia, bringing their architecture fully in line with the new forms advocated by humanist culture. The sixteenth-century observer could not fail to note the proudly-asserted uniqueness of

each confraternity, as well as the sense of belonging, of group identity which each aroused and fostered, to the point that every member felt 'almost as though in a Republic of his own', each with its own 'particular beauties', and the preferred artists who created them.[59]

The series of architectural restructurings began at the Scuola Grande of S. Giovanni Evangelista, where the most recent work had ended around 1456 with the building of the facade on to the *campiello*, with its five lovely Flamboyant Gothic windows. During the second half of the fourteenth century its importance as a place of pious pilgrimage had grown as a result of the cult of a relic of the True Cross, originally from Constantinople, and the ceremonies associated with it: here the courtyard played an important part, receiving a processional cortège of faithful from neighbouring districts, as we see in the *teler* by Lazzaro Bastiani now in the Accademia. Its position, and the ritual functions performed in it, explain the decision – taken between 1478 and 1479 – to create a space 'inside the courtyard or within the gates', as the medieval documents put it,[60] which would add lustre to the Scuola's standing. This latter now took a completely novel form: the space was divided up transversally by a marble-clad screen, in the centre of which was a doorway framed by fluted Corinthian pillars, topped by a semi-circular pediment on a highly-decorated entablature. Here, an architectural diaphragm was used as a substitute for a new facade, underlining

the ritual import-ance of the space. The *all'antica* frame-work of this screen was extended along the side walls of the *campiello*, punctuating them with three equidistant pilasters per side, supporting an entablature continuing that of the dividing screen in what amounted to a highly intelligent solution for a medieval courtyard space that had previously lacked any particular character. Its layout, formal sensibility, antiquarian culture and exquisite execution mark it out as linked to the Lombardo circle, though its attribution is uncertain. In all probability, however, it should largely be ascribed to Pietro Lombardo and his collaborators, although the latter were not necessarily responsible for the classicizing organization of the external space, which was interpreted by contemporary artistic literature on several occasions as an atrium rather than a piazzetta. It does indeed bear a close resemblance to one of the earliest literary reconstructions of the atrium and vestibule of the classical house, namely the one by Flavio Biondo who, as we have already seen, had connections with Venetian circles.[61]

At the end of the fifteenth century, this Scuola embarked on another important new work with the building of a double-branched ceremonial staircase 'for the ornament and convenience of the Scuola . . . and in honour and glory of the Most Holy Cross'. Mauro Codussi's double-ramp staircase, built to give monumental access to the upper hall and Sala della Croce, was to become something of a paradigm by

right
Scuola Grande di S. Giovanni Evangelista,
courtyard screen.

below
Facade and ground plan of the Scuola Grande
di San Marco and adjacent buildings, eighteenth
century. Venice, Archivio di stato.

right
Scuola Grande di S. Giovanni Evangelista,
courtyard screen.

below
Facade and ground plan of the Scuola Grande
di San Marco and adjacent buildings, eighteenth
century. Venice, Archivio di stato.

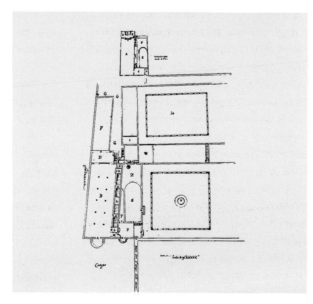

virtue of the architect's extensive and differentiated use of vaulting both to support and to roof the structure, a feature which was unusual in current Venetian architectural practice. Its perfectly judged formal treatment was especially striking: two symmetrical ramps, suitably shallow for the majestic ceremonial procession, lead upwards from the lower landings – two small spaces roofed with little domes on pendentives – to meet at the top on the wider floor leading into the main hall. This upper landing, stately and reverential, is a beautifully co-ordinated space, roofed with a solemn dome, leading into the main hall through a large triumphal arch on twinned columns flanked by pilasters, its fourth side taking the form of a typical Codussian airy two-light window with an oculus. A fitting culmination to the staircase, it leads triumphantly through into the room where the relics are housed, and is given added emphasis by the richness of its highly symbolic decoration, unusual for Codussi.[62]

The Scuola Grande di S. Marco, which took up permanent residence near the convent of Sti Giovanni e Paolo in 1437, was the object of a protracted series of building and rebuilding work between the late-Gothic period and the early Renaissance. Stefano and Matteo Bon had already finished work on the first new building by 1438, and Giovanni and Bartolomeo Bon, together with Antonio Rizzo, were working on extensions in 1476. Further rebuilding – redefining the Scuola in the form we know today – began about a decade later, once again as a result of one of the great fires (1485) which devastated the city with surprising frequency between the second half of the fifteenth and the first decades of the sixteenth century. Pietro Lombardo and Giovanni Buora, together with the stonemason Bartolomeo di Domenico Duca as *proto*, are documented as having been called to the site at the end of May 1489, and work then proceeded in accordance with a project which had certainly been elaborated some time earlier. Responsibility for the over-seeing of the site at the Scuola di S. Marco thus lacked continuity; finally, in 1490, it was assigned to Mauro Codussi, who left in 1495, by which time the only workers still employed there were those involved in the decoration.

The Scuola's striving for self-celebration reached its peak with the extraordinarily rich and elaborate facade. In reality, the front overlooking the campo is made up of two adjoining facades: the western one, tripartite in layout, taller and more elaborate, corresponding to the ground-floor *salone*, itself divided into three aisles by a double series of columns on tall pedestals, and to the chapter-house; and the eastern one, also triple-aisled, which gives unity and dignity to a somewhat complex site. The upper storey, the result of successive modifications, corresponds to the large 'sala dell'albergo' (hostel hall) which originally housed the cycle of the stories of St. Mark and the famous canvas by Palma il Vecchio and Paris Bordone depicting the doge receiving the ring (1534). The two

architectural sections of the facade therefore respect the hierarchy of the functions of the internal space, and are distinguished by the use of different structural and decorative schemes: the pilaster strips which divide each into three are differentl spaced, there are no griffins on the bas-reliefs of the eastern section of the frieze of the first entablature, and no columns in the eastern section of the long facade; lastly, the relief scenes in perspective on the marble surfaces of the lower order are seen from different viewpoints.

Careful examination of the western section – which we might describe as the main facade – reveals the complex origins of its compositional scheme. Several of its elements, however, point to an outright evocation of, rather than mere reference to, the facade of San Marco: the curved pediments, the repeated use of columns, probably largely antique, their particular grouping as support for the Marcian emblem on the attic storey, the resplendent cladding in rare marbles, and the original gilding and polychromy. This resemblance is further reinforced by the two warrior saints in niches in the side pediments, a direct echo of the two slabs with Sts George and Demetrius to the sides of the top of the great archway of the main portal of San Marco.

There is also a close resemblance between the layout of the facade of the Scuola Grande and the tripartite facade, crowned by its semi-circular pediments, of the church in the background of the *Preaching of St. Mark in Alexandria*, painted by Gentile

Bellini between 1504 and 1507 as a start to the renewal of the decoration of the Scuola of which he himself was a member. Nor is this a mere *a posteriori* reading of the architectural apparatus of the Scuola Grande on Gentile's part: in all probability, it suggests that its facade should be interpreted as a restatement of the greatness of the episcopal seat of this same patron saint in Alexandria, the capital of Christian Hellenism. This is proved in particular by one important iconographical element: the perspectives for the marble reliefs of Tullio Lombardo's ground-floor order – the long trabeated porticoes roofed with barrel vaulting and coffering, and those with arches with richly adorned flat roofs with the evangelist's lions and episodes from his life – are none other than the porticoes of Alexandria. This is further borne out by the use of the Corinthian order on the facade, in keeping with the late-antique tradition of the territories of the exarchate and Byzantium. Here, then, we have a reminder and public celebration of the evangelist, the bishop of Alexandria and first bishop of Roman *Venetia*, which may explain the exceptional use of free-standing columns in antique marble – *spolia* which signify a return, *restitutio*, rebirth – flanked by free-standing pilasters in niches, set forward triumphally from the threshold of the great ground-floor portal.

This main portal, by Giovanni Buora (though he reused a bas-relief from the pre-existing building by Bartolomeo Bon in the lunette) is a focal element in this grandiose

left-hand side. On the facade overlooking the campo, he repeated the Codussian theme of the two-light window with an oculus, combining it with the traditional multi-coloured decoration which gave visual emphasis to the main portal. When Bon was fired, he was succeeded as first *proto* by Sante Lombardo, with orders to do nothing without consulting with the officials of the Scuola. He organized the upper order of the back facade over the canal in three sections above a deep, broad portico, opening the side sections with large two-light windows, topped, unusually, by triangular pediments, as though in competition with Codussi's two-light windows, and framing the central one with an aedicule with a deep niche. This too was an original invention, with a classical sense of three-dimensionality, but also a reworking of the articulation and colour of San Marco, from which the powerful cornice also derives, a reinterpretation of similar protruding ones with acanthus leaves found throughout San Marco and other Veneto-Byzantine buildings. From 1527 onwards, Scarpagnino intensified the *all'antica* aspect of the facade with the elaborate two-light windows of the upper order. More importantly, he solved the problem of the 'different beauty' of the Scuola by means of the colonnade on to the campo with two superimposed orders of single Corinthian columns, a distant echo of the more archaic and triumphal use of columns on the Scuola Grande di San Marco. Scarpagnino's version, however, was more emphatic, an independent elaboration of designs for imaginary

classical works like certain of those in the Rothschild notebook already mentioned, both free reconstructions of triumphal arches, and related ideas for grandiose and ornate facades (as the *confratelli* had explicitly requested on several occasions).

It is possible that Scarpagnino might have taken suggestions concerning antique models from Sansovino, who was called to the Scuola della Misericordia in 1532.[64] But it is clear that, while Scarpagnino – as *proto al Sal* and to the Scuola di S. Rocco – was still attempting one last *renovatio more veneto*, Sansovino – *proto* of San Marco and the Scuola della Misericordia – was moving towards a Vitruvian 'discipline' which the commissioning Scuola was unlikely willingly to accept.

The turning-point, the rift with Venetian early Renaissance attitudes, had evidently now reached the Scuole Grandi. Yet if the building of the Misericordia, unfinished though it was, was to be entrusted to Sansovino, the differences and internal conflicts, the hesitations, changes of directions and lulls in activity which were to accompany its planning and implementation demonstrated all too clearly that innovation in Venetian architecture during the early sixteenth century proceeded in a far from straightforward fashion.

As we have said, a desire for self-celebration within the glorious and splendid context of the city-state had characterized the private, mainly aristocratic patronage of the late-Gothic period, and the early Renaissance had reinforced this tendency.

During the fifteenth century, the penchant of such patrons for the lavish and the exuberant when refashioning the image of their aristocratic family residences, legitimized by Biondo's reconstructions, did not yet incur the general public opprobrium it was to earn from the mid-sixteenth century onwards. The Venetian nobility therefore continued with their pursuit of opulence until the sudden, although not universal, change of mood that occurred in the second quarter of the sixteenth century.

Built not by a patrician, but by an ordinary citizen with various delicate diplomatic responsibilities in the negotiations with the Ottomans shortly after the fall of Constantinople, Ca' Dario was the clearest example, in private architecture, of a version of the Renaissance 'alla veneta', Venetian style, interpreted according to the elaborate and sumptuous Lombardesque vision of the classical Plinian *varietas marmorum et colorum*. The architect may also have had descriptions of Byzantine palaces in mind, such as the Comnene palace at Trebizond, which the Venetians had visited until very recent times, and which cardinal Bessarion himself had mentioned in his writings, praising its white marble floors, ceilings ablaze with colour and gold, the colonnades and frescos.[65] Moreover, Ca' Dario was dedicated *genio urbis*, to the genius of the city: the inscription on the facade associated this idea of magnificence with the presiding deity or tutelary principle of the city, with that entity which had determined her origins and her very nature. Strangely enough

above
Scuola Grande di S. Rocco, rear facade.

left
Scuola Grande di S. Rocco, facade.

– and possibly not by chance – this same dedication, *genio urbis augusto*, was to reappear in the mid-sixteenth century on the rigorously classical ground-floor portal of palazzo Grimani at S. Maria Formosa, establishing a radically different and contrasting understanding of the Venetian architectural Renaissance, the Rome-oriented vision of Giovanni Grimani, patriarch of Aquileia.

Ca' Dario had been an extreme case of the architecture of the 'casa da stazio' of the second half of the fifteenth century. In the meantime, however, a line of research had been taking root whose aim was to reconcile the recently codified features of the aristocratic Venetian palazzo with the antiquarian, if largely decorative, culture of the early Renaissance.

Palazzo Contarini at S. Vio, of uncertain authorship but datable around the last fifteen years of the fifteenth century, is a typical example of this tendency, with its rigorous observance of the traditional tripartite division of the facade, achieved here with an *all'antica* framework of pilaster strips and entablatures; but even more so for the typical marble cladding, roundels and shield-shaped ornaments in precious marble on the two *piani nobili*, as well as other references to antiquity: a triumphal watergate, a frieze on the base of the first *piano nobile* which makes great play of its Roman iconography with imperial eagles with spread wings, acroteria in the form of chalice-shaped vases on the first *piano nobile* and palmettes on the second. Thus it

is quite clearly an attempt at an iconographical reinstatement of the clas-sical style, grandiose and celebratory.

Ca' Gussoni, at S. Lio, overlooking the rio della Fava, aims at a similar effect; its attribution is equally controversial, though it was certainly by a member of the Lombardo circle active in the great Venetian worksites, and dates from around the time of palazzo Contarini at S. Vio. Here too a sense of magnificence was achieved by combining the classicizing iconography of the elaborate bas-reliefs with the classically-inspired marble facing. Particular attention had evidently been paid to the base plinth in Istrian stone, often hidden beneath the water line, reminiscent of the treatment of the Ionic consoles on the canalside facade of the nearby Miracoli: a long stone frieze, with panels containing large-petalled roses, supports a second decorative strip with circular motifs, which supports yet a third one with bean-shaped motifs. The visible upper level of the foundations is given special importance by hinting at the astounding Venetian skill in building right 'in the sea', and emphasized by a long strip of red Verona marble supporting the base order of the facade, itself in Istrian stone.

The direction taken by palazzo Contarini at S. Vio was continued some ten years later at palazzo Grimani-Marcello at S. Polo. Here, the search for distinctive forms that were more modern, yet still compatible with the canonic features of the Venetian 'casa da stazio', was achieved more soberly, despite the figured capitals, through a

lucidly designed facade with two superimposed three-light windows; the repertoire of aggrandizing symbols was extended by adding pediments in triangular tympana to the four-light windows on the ground floor.

Antiquarian allusions and quotations might vary to some degree, as might the scale of symbols and range of materials used to express magnificence, but always within well-tried limits. We see this for example in palazzo Trevisan-Cappello in Canonica, where the Ionic order makes an appearance. Here the wide multi-light window corresponds to an unusually wide 'portego', and hence to a particular desire for self-aggrandizement on the part of the clients, also evident in the nielli, coloured marbles and bas-reliefs. Once again, the marble facing, both in the panels and in the decorative inlaywork, was inspired by nearby San Marco; the ornamental apparatus of the facade was further enriched by the Cappello family with the two large slabs with the 'shield-bearers', actually two archangels (the one to the left is Michael, weigher of souls), brandishing helmets with *tricipitium* crests on their spears.

The decorative medallions on the upper frieze on palazzo Malipiero-Trevisan (c. 1510), overlooking the spacious campo of S. Maria Formosa, with their eight 'Roman' portraits, owe more to classical sculpture than to contemporary medal-making, being based on the great Roman bronzes and popular collections of engraved gems. Palazzo Malipiero, with its elaborate Corinthian order, also repeats the triangular pediments

above
Palazzo Gussoni at S. Lio, facade.

left
Palazzo Contarini at S. Vio, facade.

already found at Ca' Grimani at S. Polo, setting them over tall deep niches in the form of aedicules, which bite into the Istrian stone facing of the *piano nobile*; it also has tracery with coloured inlaywork, of vaguely early-Christian and medieval inspiration, in the two balconies of the multi-light windows.

Under construction from 1504, palazzo Contarini dalle Figure on the Grand Canal, which showed signs of the influence of Codussi, included another innovation alongside the repetition of the window-aedicules and exquisitely executed high-relief decoration: the Corinthian four-light window with fluted columns on the *piano nobile* is topped and emphasized by a somewhat elongated triangular pediment, a surprising feature which is also hard to date. However, this was not a complete novelty: the two-light windows designed by Scarpagnino for the upper storey of the facade of the Scuola di S. Rocco come to mind. But clearly a considerable semantic shift had occurred here, with imperial implications, as further proclaimed by the two-headed eagles standing on suits of armour placed to either side, between the window-aedicules on the *piano nobile*.

But the return to antiquity, and the pursuit of classical grandeur, remained largely formal and figurative, restricted to the sphere of the *venustas sermonis* rather than extending to the architecture of the aristocratic *domus* as a whole. Some of the examples considered, for instance palazzo Contarini at S. Vio and palazzo Malipiero Trevisan, had simply adapted a pre-existing Gothic

above
Palazzo Contarini dalle Figure on the Grand Canal, facade.

below
Palazzo Malipiero Trevisan at S. Maria Formosa, facade over the campo.

organism. Others had basically retained the traditional distributive pattern for their internal spaces (Grimani at S. Polo, Contarini dalle Figure). Palazzo Trevisan-Cappello, while it too reused masonry structures dating from the Gothic period and possibly earlier – although we cannot yet be sure to what extent – provided an updated solution for the old problem of unifying the facade of two independent residences. The particular solution adopted at Ca' Gussoni at S. Lio was undoubtedly dictated by its site: here an almost square block was organized around a courtyard, with one wing extending to the *rio*, with a long L-shaped *salone* with three lesser rooms aligned along its north side. Apart from episodes arising from specific circumstances, the characteristics assumed by the aristocratic 'casa da stazio' therefore seem to have remained static for much of the early Renaissance.

Yet the picture was not entirely unchanged, nor circumscribed within these terms. On occasions, the early Renaissance *all'antica* house in Venice might also take on features other than those briefly mentioned above. Somewhat different tendencies can be seen for example in Ca' del Duca, unfinished though it is, conceived as a vast and impressive building typical of the period of transition, not far from Ca' Foscari on the opposite bank of the Grand Canal. It was begun in 1457 to a commission by Andrea Corner, and sold to the duke of Milan. But work had ceased definitively by 1466, too soon for much to have been completed other than the massive foundations,

while work on the ground floor had hardly begun. Andrea Corner had turned to Bartolomeo Bon for the design; the duke of Milan had sent for Benedetto Ferrini, then Filarete, to revise and oversee the work, and indeed Filarete seems to have repeated its general idea in his famous design for a building on a marshy site. Assorted evidence shows that the palazzo was to have overlooked the Grand Canal with a long, deep gallery (that is, in imitation of the Veneto-Byzantine *casa-fondaco* with small towers, probably reworking it virtually as a fortified castle), while the deep main body of the building was to have been organized around two large court-yards, with a ground plan unprecedented in Venetian architectural culture. What remains of it is no more than an isolated fragment, but even as such it made a remarkable break with local custom: the basement level, in Istrian stone, is treated as smooth rustication, with square blocks alternating with rectangular ones (like the base of a towered 'castello da mar' or 'harbour castle'), while the built part of the ground floor, with its extraordinary corner column, has a surface of oblong diamond-point faceted blocks, a solution which was later to inspire the canalside facade of the Ducal palace.

In short, even in fifteenth-century Venice, a range of tendencies and, to some degree, of formal studies, diverging from the more widely accepted ones, might find a place in privately commissioned architec-ture; and it was this experimental path that

was to be followed by Mauro Codussi in
such architecture.

In effect, he approached the problem of
the Venetian patrician residence from a different viewpoint in each of the three palazzi
attributed to him. The earliest of the three is
now generally agreed to be palazzo Zorzi at
S. Severo, and Codussi was called to work
on it around 1480. Once again, this did not
entail the creation of a completely new
building, but the unifying of several pre-
existing ones. This was achieved using a
series of measures similar in some way to
those adopted for the rebuilding of the
Ducal palace on rio del Palazzo, where
earlier masonry features and asymmetries
were masked by manipulating the architectural layout in ways that were sometimes
quite surprising. Divided horizontally into a
ground-floor order (opening on to the canal
with three watergates), a *piano nobile* and
a mezzanine under the roof, the facade is
organized vertically on the *piano nobile* as
two wings with rectangular windows
beneath oculi framed by the usual discs of
polychrome marble, and a central section
with nine windows. Codussi's idea was to
respect the original tripartite plan – probably in a thirteenth-century prototype,
given the number of windows – by placing
two double pairs of two-light windows,
with capitals with pulvins, on either side of
an unusual central one-light one. Various
elements imply that the concept of this
multi-light window was conditioned by the
pre-existing masonry, but its unifying function is obvious, and is further emphasized

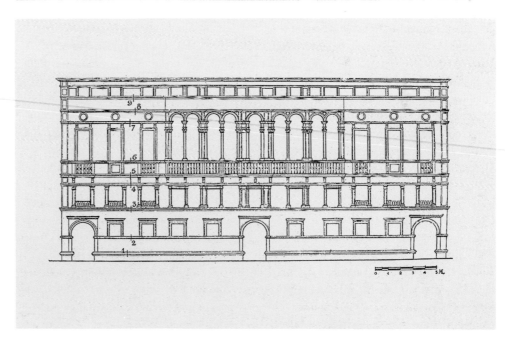

by the long balcony, which juts out briefly in front of the central single-light window. The same scheme is continued on the eastern side towards the *calle* (in open brick-work, not clad in Istrian stone), with a three-light window directly over the entrance portal leading to the porticoed courtyard. Palazzo Zorzi has rightly been seen as being in some respects a Codussian reinterpretation of the Romanesque build-ing of the Procuratie, and other medieval Venetian architecture. He could not there-fore be said to have rejected the idea of a *renovatio more veneto*; but at the same time Codussi's approach was completely per-sonal, with the use of rare marbles kept to the merest colourist touches. The bas-relief decoration too is sparingly used: adherence to tradition was thus combined with a grandeur that was quite without ostenta-tion, and such restraint was undoubtedly intended to prove a point.

Some ten years later, Codussi began work on palazzo Lando Corner Spinelli, where he used a classical framework – pilasters to the sides of the facade, and a crowning frieze with festoons and roundels – to delimit a three-storey facade in Istrian stone, with a ground floor with a mezzanine and two *piani nobili*. This too featured a number of innovations: first and foremost the surface of the lower order, entirely clad in smooth rustication, undoubtedly influenced by the nearby Ca' del Duca. But a knowledge of works such as palazzo Rucellai in Florence, or palazzo Piccolomini at Pienza, must have played their part, together with the earlier

smooth rustication used by Codussi himself for the facade of S. Michele in Isola. The ori-gins of this solution – which was to persist throughout the sixteenth century– were therefore far from simple, and took on par-ticular significance when it was adopted at Ca' Lando. If, as we have seen, the late-Gothic civil architecture of the time of Francesco Foscari had abandoned the waterside portico for the *casa-fondaco*, at the end of the century the rusticated wall of Codussi's new palazzo was tantamount to an obdurate confirmation of the turning-point made many years before: through the idea of impenetrability suggested by rusti-cation, the open form of the merchant's house had clearly been transmuted into the inaccessibility of the noble dwelling.

But not all features of the old architec-tural culture had been abandoned here either. As always, the facade remained tripartite in layout. The central multi-light windows became two juxtaposed two-light openings, though these were quite unlike those designed for Ca' Zorzi. Now the typi-cal Codussian two-light window beneath an oculus, inscribed in a large round-headed arch, makes its appearance. This was a new element, also with a complicated history: indeed in this first version the oculi are not perfectly circular, but tear-shaped, forming a countercurve as they come to rest upon the small round-headed arches below. Vaguely similar solutions had also evolved in Byzantine architecture; it is also worth noting that the intervening period between medieval tradition and Codussi's

research had been represented in Venice by numerous drawings by Jacopo Bellini (1398–c.1470–1). But a knowledge of Tuscan precedents – those of Alberti and Rossellino – must also have been decisive; indeed they had already been adopted for the two-light windows of an important building in Ravenna, the small palazzo on Piazza del Popolo, completed in 1463, and commissioned by none other than the Venetian *podestà* Vitale Lando.[66] So that Renaissance innovation and tradition continued to be interwoven not so much because of any indecision on the part of the architect, or the client's wishes, but rather because Codussi was apparently convinced of a compatibility between the two which did not derive exclusively from the elo-quent iconography of the sculptural decora-tion; in Ca' Lando Corner Spinelli too this remained modest and restrained.

Codussi's research into the 'casa da stazio' thus covered a range of possibilities. His most sensational venture in this field was for the Loredan, during his last active years at the beginning of the sixteenth century. Architecturally speaking, their palazzo at S. Marcuola was conceived as a 'theatre of magnificence': the facade, although related functionally to the struc-tural organism, is actually wider than the rest of the building behind it, like a *frons scaenae*. Compositionally, it is dominated by a framework formed of pilaster strips and Corinthian columns, a basement in Istrian stone and entablatures, the upper one of which has a figured frieze, with the use, for the first time in the private architecture of the early Renaissance, of double pilaster strips and columns. The hierarchy between the floors was achieved by combining the use of different materials – Istrian stone for the ground floor and marble cladding for the upper ones – but also by the nature and form of the supports: pilaster strips on the ground floor, fluted columns on the first *piano nobile*, and smooth-shafted columns for the upper one. Again, the use of the characteristic two-light opening (already seen in Ca' Lando, but here in a more refined version, because now the oculus is perfectly circular) for all the windows on the facade, made it possible to solve the problem of continuity in relation to the customary scheme: the broad central multi-light windows have been recreated by juxtaposing three large biforate windows per floor and separating them off from the side wings by doubling the columns. At the same time, Codussi made sober use of powerful ornamental motifs in the form of reliefs, roundels and stone plaques.

Unexpectedly, however, here he reworked the problem of the ground-floor entrance hall and its frontage on to the water: while not returning to the old solution of the portico, he once again opened it up and lit it generously by flanking the watergate – a triumphal feature, as the two imperial profiles make plain – with two other large two-light windows which thus bring the tripartition of the upper floors down to the ground floor as well. But the long broad space which runs from the canal to the garden behind completely loses its main original function as a landing-place for the bales of merchandise to be stored in the warehouses lined up on either side: decorated with Giorgione's frescos, with their allegories of Diligence and Prudence, it now became a Venetian version of the classical atrium. Indeed, towards the end of the Renaissance, Francesco Sansovino was to recognize it as the earliest of the 'principal' Venetian palazzi: the only one before Ca' Dolfin and Ca' Corner at S. Maurizio by Sansovino, and Ca' Grimani at S. Luca by Sanmicheli, to be built 'in our times and according to the doctrine of the ancient Vitruvius'.[67] Although not strictly true, this statement is evidence of the standing later to be accorded to the building, namely as a forerunner of a fully-fledged magnificence 'alla romana'. Yet it exerted no immediate influence; at most, some aspects of its brand of stateliness were looked to in publicly commissioned works such as the Scuola Grande di S. Rocco.

The crisis of the wars of the League of Cambrai and the Holy League, the fervent moralism of the long dogeship of Leonardo Loredan, and the change in social attitudes after the first decade of the sixteenth century, led to a rethinking of the question of private magnificence, while the functional relations between the 'casa da stazio' and the exercise of trade grew closer in parallel.

These new developments were clearly exemplified in Ca' Querini Stampalia, the residence of a noble family which still owned feudal possessions in the eastern Mediterranean at the time. The palazzo on S. Maria Formosa, originally commissioned by Nicolo Querini, is a pointer to the attitudes of an aristocratic family which played an important role in public life between 1513 and 1523, a decade which was crucial for the cultural changes under way.

Despite the 'many expenses incurred in the making of the great house',[68] it is clear that the client did not intend to create a work of self-celebration: he simply wanted to give his residence a fittingly 'decorous' form, sober, relatively up-to-date yet not too advanced architecturally.

The tripartite facade on the *campiello*, with two superimposed four-light windows, is treated with simple traditional tact, and based on a module of four Venetian feet, slightly contracted in the wall surfaces between the multi-light window and the single ones immediately next to them. Despite the use of 'marbles of various sorts' for the decorative roundels, and the documented acquisition of 'roundels of serpentine, some quite large',[69] unlike that of the neighbouring palazzo Malipiero Trevisan, the facade made no use of marble cladding or ornament. The main facade of Ca' Querini is comparable in tone with that of the sides of Ca' Loredan Vendramin Calergi: extremely sober, therefore, when viewed in context, despite the social standing of its owners and the events that took place there, which included the performance of the *Commedia Orba* by Cherea, and the meetings of the Compagnia dei Cortesi.

above
Mauro Codussi, palazzo Corner Spinelli, facade.

above, right
Mauro Codussi, palazzo Loredan
Vendramin Calergi.

right
Palazzo Querini at S. Maria Formosa, facade.

Ca' Querini's account books, too, are illuminating: by giving 1537 as the precise date for the conversion to other uses of the 'mezado da basso' (lower mezzanine) which Nicolò had originally intended as a storeroom for merchandise, they provide us with a symbolic conclusion to the string of changes that had occurred in the functions and distribution of the 'casa da stazio' from Marin Contarini's Ca' d'Oro down to this present example.

1 F. Biondo, *Roma trionfante . . . tradotta pur hora per Lucio Fauno*, Venice 1542, Book IX, pp. 303v–305r.

2 *Orazioni, elogi e vite scritte da letterati veneti patrizi in lode di Dogi ed altri illustri soggetti*, Venice 1798, p. 23.

3 B. Nardi, 'La scuola di Rialto e l'umanesimo veneziano', in *Umanesimo europeo e umanesimo veneziano, op. cit.*, pp. 93–140; Nardi, 'Letteratura e culture veneziana del Quattrocento', in *Storia della civiltà veneziana*, ed. V. Branca, vol. II, Florence 1979, pp. 181–204.

4 R. Pallucchini, 'L'arte a Venezia nel Quattrocento', in *Storia della civiltà veneziana, op. cit.*, p. 211; B. Degenhart and A. Schmitt, 'Ein Musterblatt des Jacopo Bellini mit Zeichnungen nach der Antike', in *Festschrift Luitpold Dusler*, Munich and Berlin 1972, pp. 139–68.

5 N. Jorga, 'Un viaggio da Venezia alla Tana', in *Nuovo Archivio Veneto*, vol. 11, 6, 1896, Part I, pp. 5–14.

6 D. Malipiero, 'Annali', *op. cit.*, pp. 73, 78.

7 J. Morelli, *Viaggiatori eruditi veneziani*, Venice 1808; E. Concina, *Dall'arabico a Venezia tra Rinascimento e Oriente*, Venice 1994, pp. 33–5.

8 C. Buondelmonti, *Descriptio insule Crete et Liber Insularum*, ed. M. A. Spitael, Heraklion 1981, pp. 277–8.

9 British Museum Library, London, ms.

10 B.N.M.V., mss. it. cl. IV, 68 (=4735), ff. 46r–47r.

11 G. Traversari, *L'Arco dei Sergi*, Padua 1971.

12 M. Sanudo, *Itinerario per la Terraferma veneziana*, Padua 1847, pp. 143–6; G. Candido, *Commentariorum Aquileiensium libri octo*, Venice 1521, dedication to Domenico Grimani and Book I: *Antiquitas, situs et mores Aquileiae*

ac res in ea praecipue memorandae usque ad Christi adventum.

13 B. Giustinian, *Historia . . . dell'origine di Venetia*, translated by L. Domenichi, Venice 1608, p. 68.

14 D. Spreti, *De amplitudine, de vastatione et de instauratione urbis Ravennae*, Venice 1489.

15 M. Sanudo, *De origine, op. cit.*, p. 14.

16 Biblioteca Civica, Modena, ms. L 992 d L 5.15, ff. 177r–179r.

17 For the myth of Rialto, see D. Calabi and P. Morachiello, *Rialto. Le fabbriche e il ponte*, Turin 1987, p. 11. The quotation from B. Giustinian is from *Historia, op. cit.*, p. 442.

18 *Ibid.*; see also N. Zeno, *Dell'origine, op. cit.*, p. 29.

19 B. Giustinian, *Historia, op. cit.*, p. 24.

20 The term *toscanizar* (to 'Tuscanize') appears in G. B. Maganza, *Herculana in lingua venetiana*, Venice 1571, f. A2.

21 A.S.V., Senato Terra, reg. 5, f. 175r, 18.1.1466.

22 F. Sansovino, *Delle cose notabili che sono in Venetia, op. cit.*, p. 496; A.S.V., San Zaccaria, b. 1 (parchments).

23 See F. W. Deichmann, *Corpus des Kapitelle der Kirche von San Marco zu Venedig*, Wiesbaden 1981, *passim*. Examples from Constantinople may be seen in the Archaeological Museum, Istanbul.

24 F. Sansovino, *Delle cose notabili che sono in Venetia, op. cit.*, p. 82; A.S.V., San Zaccaria, b. 1 (parchments); G. L. Fr. Tafel and G. M. Thomas, *Urkunden, op. cit.*, I, pp. 1–3.

25 See also G. Pillinini, 'Bollani, Candiano', in *Dizionario Biografico degli Italiani*, XI, Rome 1969, pp. 287–8, and the eulogy of Moro in *Orazioni, elogi e vite, op. cit.*, p. 70.

26 B.N.M.V., mss. lat. cl. XIV, 244 (=4681), ff. 139–41. On San Giobbe see also M. Ceriana,

'Due esercizi di lettura: la cappella Moro in S. Giobbe e le fabbriche dei Gussori a Venezia', in *Annuali de Achitettura*, 1993, pp. 22–41.

27 M. A. Sabellico, *Del sito, op. cit.*, p. 21. For events in 1501, see G. Priuli, *I diarii*, II, Bologna 1937, p. 121.

28 Biblioteca Civica, Modena, ms. L 992 d L 5.15. E. Mattaliano, 'La scultura a Ravenna nei luoghi e negli edifici pubblici fra Quattrocento e Cinquecento', in *Ravenna in età veneziana*, ed. D. Bolognesi, Ravenna 1986, pp. 321–66; V. Fontana, 'De instauratione urbis Ravennae. Architettura e urbanistica durante la dominazione veneziana', *ibid.*, pp. 295–304.

29 F. Sansovino and G. Martinioni, *Venetia, op. cit.*, p. 179.

30 F. Biondo, *Roma, op. cit.*, pp. 316–18, 320. On the Venetian use of marble, see L. Lazzarini, 'I materiali lapidei nell' edilizia storica veneziana', in *Restauro e città*, 1986, vol. 2, nos. 3/4, pp. 84–100.

31 M. A. Sabellico, *Del sito, op. cit.*, p. 23.

32 For the personality of the man who commissioned it, see G. Dario, *22 dispacci da Costantinopoli al doge G. Mocenigo*, ed. G. Calò, Venice 1992.

33 F. Sansovino and G. Martinioni, *Venetia, op. cit.*, pp. 4–5.

34 G. Vasari, *Le vite*, I, pp. 235–6.

35 On this subject see P. Humfrey, *Cima da Conegliano*, Cambridge 1983; M. Lucco, 'Venezia', in *La pittura nel Veneto. Il Quattrocento*, Milan 1989–90, p. 499; R. Goffen, *Giovanni Bellini*, Milan 1990.

36 See the *Echtesis chronica* dating from the sixteenth century, quoted by C. Mango, *Le Développement, op. cit.*, p. 27.

37 S. Serlio, *Tutte l'opere d'architettura et prospettiva*, Venice 1619, Book IV (Venice 1537), pp. 177–8.

38 M. A. Sabellico, *Del sito, op. cit.*, p. 39.

39 Talenti's activity as a notary is documented in A.S.V., Notarile, sez. Testamenti, b. 955.

40 N. Jorga, 'Un viaggio', *op. cit.*, p. 11.

41 M. Sanudo, *De origine, op. cit.*, p. 161.

42 A.S.V., Giudici del Piovego, b. 42/2, ff. 14v–15, 9.9.1529.

43 F. Sansovino and G. Martinioni, *Venetia, op. cit.*, p. 121.

44 Letter of 26.3.1515, published in B. Cecchetti, *La Repubblica di Venezia e la corte di Roma nei rapporti della religione*, vol. II, Venice 1874, pp. 349–50.

45 M. Sanudo, *I diarii*, LIII, col. 72.

46 D. Malipiero, 'Annali', *op. cit.*, p. 674.

47 T. Hirthe, 'Mauro Codussi als Architekt des Dogen-Palastes', in *Arte Veneta*, vol. 36, 1982, pp. 31–44.

48 19.3.1474, A.S.V., Senato Terra, reg. 7, f. 32r.

49 B. Giustinian, *Historia, op. cit.*, p. 68.

50 D. Malipiero, 'Annali', *op. cit.*, p. 699.

51 See K. Wultzinger and C. Watzinger, *Damaskus. Die Islamische Stadt*, Berlin 1924; J. Sauvaget, *Alep*, Paris 1941; P. Cuneo, *Storia dell'urbanistica. Il mondo islamico*, Rome and Bari 1986; G. Mandel, *I caravanserragli turchi*, Bergamo 1988; *Caravanserails*, exhibition catalogue, Paris 1990. The quotation is from G. M. Angiolello, *Viaggio di Negroponte. 1468*, Vicenza 1881, p. 27.

52 P. Contarini, *Argo vulgar, op. cit.*, p. a iiii.

53 Quoted in *Pittura murale esterna nel Veneto. Venezia e provincia*, Bassano 1991, p. 27.

54 G. Vasari, *Le vite, op. cit.*, V, p. 271.

55 M. Sanudo, *I diarii, op. cit.*, XVIII, col. 401.

56 *M. Vitruvius per Iocundum castigatior factus*, Venice 1511, Book V, pp. 9, 45.

57 V. Fausto, *De comoedia libellus*, Venice 1511.

58 The expression derives from M. Sanudo's reading of the urban space, *De origine, op. cit.*, p. 21.

59 F. Sansovino and G. Martinioni, *Venetia, op. cit.*, p. 282.

60 A.S.V., Avogaria di Comun, Processi per nobiltà, b. 485 (Enrico Badoer), deposition of 2.4.1346.

61 F. Biondo, *Roma, op. cit.*, p. 317v; in the Latin edition, Venice 1503, f. clvi *recto*: 'Qui domos amplas faciebant, locum ante ianuam relinquebant quel inter fores domus et viam relictus esset . . . et neque in via stabant, neque intra aedes.'

62 On the staircase in the mystical writings of Old and New Testaments, see for example Jacob's vision of 'a staircase placed upon the earth, whose summit reaches heaven (translatable, in architectural terms, as the dome), and the widespread patristic interpretation which saw it as the foreshadowing of Christ's cross'. GEN 28: 12.

63 See E. Merkel, 'Sala dell'Albergo', in *La memoria della salute. Venezia e il suo ospedale dal XVI al XX secolo*, Venice 1985, p. 38; R. Polacco, *San Marco. La basilica d'oro*, Modena 1991, p. 318.

64 M. Tafuri, *Venice and the Renaissance*, Cambridge, Mass. and London 1989, p. 87.

65 See C. Mango, *The Art of the Byzantine Empire 312–1453*, Toronto 1986, pp. 252–3, 'Bessarion. Encomium of Trebizond'.

66 V. Fontana, 'De instauratione urbis Ravennae', *op. cit.*, pp. 247–98.

67 F. Sansovino and G. Martinioni, *Venetia, op. cit.*, p. 387.

68 Archivio Querini Stampalia – Fondazione Querini Stampalia, Venice, account books of Francesco Querini, f. 13r (1523).

69 *Ibid.*

THE NEW MAGNIFICENCE:
THE CINQUECENTO

THE great programmes for cultural renewal in architecture, and the relationship between architecture and city, which were to be formulated from the second quarter of the sixteenth century, and which were profoundly to alter the image and urban landscape of the Serenissima, were in fact preceded by a new sense of self-awareness and self-knowledge which gained ground between the last decades of the fifteenth century and the first of the sixteenth. New magistracies, set up alongside others dating from medieval times, were giving rise to new forms of information concerning landed property and the revenue deriving from it. The built urban space could now be known and interpreted in terms of values and investment.

The expanses of water were now regarded, and managed, as the objects of the permanent attention of public bodies with specific technical expertise, rather than as symbolic areas in the imagination of the *miraculosissima civitas*. Such bodies now took on responsibility for the defensive reorganization of the lagoon, and of the Serenissima's land and sea possessions, as well as for the agrarian transformation of the mainland. The instruments for overall self-knowledge and the management of the city and her territory which Venice had forged herself by the mid-sixteenth century, and the complex interaction between them, should undoubtedly be seen as one of the main factors for change in the Renaissance city.

This can be sensed particularly clearly if we bear in mind that the institutions being established around this period (in particular the *magistrati alle Decime, alle Acque, ai Beni Inculti, alle Fortezze*) were coming into being alongside other, older ones (the *giudici del Piovego* and the *provveditori di Comun,* in particular), which had long been active in controlling building expansion, the public street system and so on. As we have said, the unrivalled bird's-eye view of the city which Jacopo de' Barbari published in 1500 seems closely linked to the developments briefly outlined above: indeed it appears as a fundamental statement, necessary for the development of a further overall knowledge which was also proof of the possibility of control and action within the urban space.

De' Barbari's was a quantitative representation of the city's built-up space (which was being assessed in economic terms at this same time through the city-wide descriptive registering of landed property), but it was also a celebratory representation of the symbolic and formal qualities of the city's focal points: a spur to and prefiguration of operations aimed both at the reorganization of spaces and functions, and at the completing of the *forma urbis*. The economic and social 'body' and 'bowels' of the city and the sites of her institutions and trading centre were now being recognized – or, more probably, better understood – as lying around the 'piazze' of Rialto and San Marco. The contradictory qualities, in their regard, of the outlying areas – whose

Anon., 'The Piazzetta with the new buildings by
Sansovino', sixteenth century, Venice, museo Correr.

physical borders on the lagoon sometimes still lay uncertainly between land and water – were also being acknowledged.

However, self-celebratory rhetoric and its artistic embodiments apart, the real gain in awareness made during the first half of the sixteenth century was that of the incompleteness of the structure and functional mechanisms of the city, as well as of its form.

It is therefore no coincidence that one of the most significant acts of artistic patronage promoted by doge Andrea Gritti (1523–38) – himself one of the chief forgers of the policies of renewal for sixteenth-century Venice – should have been for a tapestry depicting an extremely detailed bird's-eye view of the city: the age of knowledge and the age of great projects and new magnificence thus coincided.[1]

Furthermore, during the first decades of the sixteenth century some of the requirements, and hence the basic terms, of the myth and image of the Serenissima changed radically, as did her way of approaching the culture of the Antique. These changes occurred in tandem with shifts in the balance of power, the conflicts, and the interlocutors, between the Mediterranean and Europe on the international front. Early sixteenth-century Venice was a city seized with alarm at the Turkish conquest of Methone and Korone (1500). But more importantly, she was an Italian power which had been put on her guard by the dramatic clash with the papacy and empire; which had discovered, to her surprise, the hostility and pro-imperial attitude of much

View of the Piazzetta with the Mint and Marcian Library.

of the nobility of her 'stato da terra' (mainland possessions), while she herself deeply distrusted, indeed positively feared, the Habsburgs' imperial designs.

At the end of the 1520s, the momentum for Venice's renewed image of greatness was linked less to the once vigorous myth of *alterum Byzantium* than to the resumption and strengthening of her self-celebration as the new Rome, as sole heir to the *sancta* republic and its liberty and civic values.

The whole question of the shift from the architectural *renovatio more veneto* (renewal in the Venetian fashion) typical of the early Renaissance, to the solemn 'Roman style' as introduced into the city by Sansovino, should be seen as deriving from the political problems mentioned above, which were particularly pressing around the years 1529–30, with Charles V's descent into Italy and his coronation as *imperator*, namely, the 'return of Astraea'.[2]

The entire geographical, political and intellectual space of the European and Mediterranean world of the sixteenth century was a hotbed of clashes, confrontations and collisions between ideas of descendence from, or *restitutio* (re-establishment) of, the ancient empires; of conflicting birthright claims of all kinds, between self-proclaimed, reinvented and 'authentic' Romes which could not but be rivals, given the ideal oneness of the *Urbs*. It was a breeding-ground of competition between political entities large and small, each of which laid claim to this political identity and strove for a fitting imitation of it through the various instru-

ments of *ars suadendi* (art of persuasion) at their disposal. Armed engagements and diplomatic skirmishes and approaches proceeded *pari passu* with those between 'fictional underpinnings' and formal programmes. But Venice in particular, whose 'states' extended from the north of Italy to the eastern Mediterranean, herself *altera Roma* (a new Rome), was caught between two great 'returns', the rise of two empires: that of Charles V, *dominus mundi*, who restricted his claims to the *translatio imperii* (transfer of power) of the West, and even went so far as to have himself portrayed by Titian in the attitude of the equestrian statue of Marcus Aurelius; and that of Suleiman the Magnificent, who laid claim to the *translatio imperii* of the East, asserting himself as a new Alexander the Great and proclaiming himself successor to Constantine. Thus the Marcian republic had no choice but to represent herself in terms that were universally applicable: that is, by adopting Roman forms as a new language for the establishing of her sovereign magnificence, the only one consonant with her renewed and spirited claim to be the last legitimate descendant of ancient Rome, 'A second, rejuvenated Rome, a common fatherland on the model of the Urbs'; a position deriving from the absolute freedom accorded her – as the interested jurists maintained – by the partition of the Roman empire between Nicephorus I and Charlemagne, from which she alone had remained aloof. 'Decus ac splendor libertatis Italiae' (the glory and splendour of the

freedom of Italy), the Venetian republic did not recognize the imperial authority, and indeed her prince – so the theory ran – was heir to the imperial rights in her own dominions.[3]

Thus it could be no coincidence that the years of the imperial idea's triumphal return to Italy were also those which saw Jacopo Sansovino's appointment as *proto* of the procurators of San Marco – that is, as public architect of the basilica of San Marco and the surrounding piazza, the seat and centre of political institutions. It was therefore a Tuscan architect, who had spent years in Rome before settling in Venice, a well-versed and skilful interpreter of the 'rules of the ancients', who was now to be called upon to bring about such a renewal in the architectural language of Venice, the *altera* (second) and *novior* (new) Rome.

In the eyes of Vasari it was only then, and thanks to the efforts of Sansovino, that conditions were in place for a genuine rebirth of the *res aedificatoria* in Venice. It was Sansovino, with his 'new designs' who gave her magnificent public and private buildings the order and classical discipline of Vitruvius. This same position was forcefully expressed in the funerary inscription in the church of S. Geminiano composed by his son: Jacopo had restored a vanished honour to the architecture of Venice.[4]

In fact, if the Marcian Library was deliberately representative of the architecture of the great Venetian *renovatio urbis et magnificentiae*, and immediately acknowledged as such by his contemporaries, the first years of Sansovino's activity after 1527, when he settled permanently in Venice, were something of a trial period for his relations with a public and private clientele which was unadventurous, largely unprepared and indeed reluctant to accept radically innovative choices. The start of work on the church of S. Francesco della Vigna (from 1530), on the Scuola Grande della Misericordia (from 1535) and on palazzo Corner at S. Maurizio, was counterbalanced by the setback met with by the project for the palazzo 'alla romana' for Vettor Grimani; and Sansovino's early period in Venice was marked by an implicit but persistent flaunting of his technical 'expertise' and 'judgment' in planning – to use the terms formulated by Vasari on the basis of their friendly relations.

According to Vasari, Jacopo first proved that he could solve the problems of structural *firmitas* by working on the restoration of the domes of San Marco; he then demonstrated that he held the principle of *utilitas* in due regard, both as overseer of the basilica worksite and by proposing a series of projects for the rationalizing of spaces and functions around San Marco and the areas immediately adjacent to it, which also happened to swell the public coffers. Lastly, the new *proto* of the Procuratoria was to be faced with the problems of *decor* and *venustas* connected to public buildings.

In short, according to Vasari's revealingly structured account, the course taken by Sansovino's early activity emerges as not just attuned to the astute mercantile attitudes of the republican authorities, but also as an out-and-out demonstration of the roundedness, in the Vitruvian sense, of his figure as an architect, before he tackled the more demanding challenge of the great works on the Piazza.

In point of fact, Sansovino had been studying the area since 1529; the outburst of contemporary interest aroused by his successful bid for the removal of the butchers' stalls and wooden 'casotti' (booths) situated between the columns of Saints Mark and Theodore – highly symbolic places, as Francesco Sansovino himself made abundantly clear – was neither coincidental nor merely rhetorical. By restoring these public places to their original standing, by sweeping them clear of activities incompatible with the importance of the site, and by the removal of teetering amorphous constructions – deliberately re-establishing the view from the Piazza over the canal di San Marco, and from its waters to the city – and giving new shape to the 'main entrance',[5] namely her seaward access, punctuated as it was with portentous symbols, Sansovino was working out an explicit model, and calling for a coherent policy for the urban image, based on the resources of architecture. Despite the inevitable resistance, such a policy was indeed subsequently adopted in this instance, but also, and more importantly, as a general plan of action by the government of the city-state, as declared in the foreword to the text of 1535 which set up the public commission of *savi al comodo e all'ornato* (advisers concerned with the serviceable and the beautiful). Venice's international role and cultural ascendancy were thus explicitly associated with her urban form and image, with the perfection of her space and architecture, with her churches, private buildings and 'broad squares', and with the 'beauty and convenience' of the city at large, acknowledged as a universal attraction, a factor in the transformation of the original mythical island refuge into a capital and metropolis 'where people from all parts gather, drawn by the beauty and commodiousness of the . . . city'.[6]

In 1535, a turning-point occurred that had long been in the making. The whole urban scene was now subject to pressure in just such a direction: almost contemporaneously, the Senate set up the abovementioned commission to act upon 'the many unsightly built-up districts which detract from the splendour of the . . . city' (2 September 1535); and the Council of Ten commissioned Michele Sanmicheli to draw up an overall plan for the defence of Venice and her lagoon, preparing the first projects in this connection around January – July 1535. Following a decree by this same Council (4 December 1535), Jacopo Sansovino now began planning his first piece of great public architecture, the Mint, the design for which was approved on 23 March of the following year. His contribution to the 'spacious square of the rich Lion' (P. Contarini, 1542) had begun.

In existence since the thirteenth century, the Mint had originally been a central workshop employing a relatively large

above
Detail of the facade.

left
Jacopo Sansovino, the Mint, facade.

Courtyard of the Mint, now reading-room in the Biblioteca nazionale marciana.

Jacopo Sansovino, Marcian Library.

number of craftsmen engaged in a whole range of activities connected with coining: the assay of gold and silver, refining, founding and the cutting of the unworked pieces for the minting die; it also housed the public treasury, and offices for administration and inspection. 'Because it is in grave danger both from fire, and robbery',[7] the building naturally had to be extremely secure; fires were still frequent in sixteenth-century Venice, and one had recently broken out. But another problem to be considered was that of the site's proximity to a group of publicly-owned shops. Sansovino solved the distributive problem by articulating the space of the new building as two sections separated by a 'large loggia' or 'sotto-portego', a long corridor running from the Piazzetta to the canal behind it. The ground floor overlooking the *riva* was to accommodate offices and silver foundries, store-rooms for precious metals and premises for the *provveditori* and clerks; the northern section, organized around a large rectangular courtyard, housed a series of workshops for minting, storerooms for coal and so on. The distribution of functions was similar on the upper floor, where the 'ufficio dell'oro' (gold office) and the gold foundries were grouped alongside spaces for numerous other activities, including those of the striking of the coinage.

The whole ground-floor frontage of the building, completely separate from the adjacent premises, was given over not to the Mint, but to the series of shops of the Procuratoria of San Marco, set in tall

arches. Contemporary commentators regarded it as a work of exemplary service-ability, the finest Renaissance example of a purpose-built work. Approval was also unanimous as to its structural aspects: vaulting, rarely found in Venetian architecture, together with stone- and brick-work, 'with not so much as a palm of wood', virtually eliminated the risk of fire.[8] Its stylistic features, too, were a definitive novelty. Sansovino's building stood on the same site as the Mint which had been restructured in the fourteenth century, but the medieval commune's 'place of the coinage' was now to be reinterpreted *all'antica*, probably on advice from one of the humanists of Sansovino's circle, as the *aerarium reipublicae* (Treasury of the Republic), the equivalent of the *aerarium populi romani* housed in premises in the tall basement storey of the temple of Saturn, in the area of the forums, behind the basilica Giulia, and near the Curia, the seat of the Senate. The implications of its position in ancient Rome, clear also to Palladio, are confirmed by Daniele Barbaro's commentary on Vitruvius (1556). Sansovino therefore devised a suitably grandiose and austere language for his structure 'all in iron and stone'.

The nine rusticated arches of the ground floor support ten powerful rusticated Doric columns, framing tall windows with heavy architraves and severely unadorned entablatures where triglyphs alternate with metopes. The more restrained second floor was built only later (1558), with a rusticated Ionic order, and windows with triangular

Marcian Library, view along the portico.

Jacopo Sansovino, Library staircase.

Salone (great hall) of the Library.

pediments. Originally, a statue of Apollo holding golden ingots, by Danese Cattaneo, stood on an octagonal well in the courtyard with the silversmiths' workshops: a symbolic allusion to the origin of gold, created in the bowels of the earth by the remote heat of the sun, it served to emphasize the classical mood evoked by the expressive roughness of the rustication, previously known in the city in far less 'Roman' versions. Vasari speaks of it as a key moment in the dawning mood of innovation currently under way in Venetian architecture, and contemporaries too saw it as such: 'A worthy prison for that most precious gold . . . where the rustication so perfectly accords with the quality of the building', as Francesco Sansovino commented during his father's lifetime. Using an aptly mythological image, another contemporary saw it as 'the house of Vulcan'.[9]

Shortly after work had started on the Mint, Jacopo was commissioned to build the Marcian Library, the most prestigious and challenging of his works as architect to the republic. Its *raison d'être*, the main nucleus of its contents, was of particular cultural importance: the famous bequest of Bessarion's manuscripts was a conscious symbol of the *traditio* (handing down) of the great classical and Byzantine culture from imperial Constantinople to Venice as *alterum Byzantium*. Humanist circles contemporary with Sansovino had stressed the role of treasury of the 'secret of venerable antiquity' entrusted to the Serenissima, as befitted her image as a latterday Rome

above
Jacopo Sansovino, Library.

left
Jacopo Sansovino, Loggetta.

('Venice ... alone has remained as an example of the grandeur and magnificence of the Romans', as Palladio was to write), but also as a new Alexandria, heir to the Hellenistic capital of learning, as these same circles had been maintaining since the early sixteenth century.[10] The decision to house the collection in a building on the Piazza dated back to 1515, but it was only now, after further deliberations, that work actually began (1537), to be completed by Vincenzo Scamozzi only after the death of the architect, between 1583 and 1588. This too was above all an act which reinstated the dignity of the site: the new building was to occupy the spaces previously filled by shops and taverns, known to us from both iconographical and documentary evidence. In other words, Sansovino was to sweep away the humdrum with a work which spoke of the abiding nature of memory. The new building was to stand directly in front of the Ducal palace's facade on to the Piazzetta; in other words, the wisdom of the Venetian institutions would be reflected anew, through the use of a deliberate architectural metaphor, in the seat of ancient learning now to be erected directly in front of the older building, and at its wise behest.

Sansovino treated the facade as a long succession of two orders of superimposed arcades, Doric on the ground floor and Ionic on the one above; the obelisks placed at either end alluded to undying glory with a series of twenty-five statues of gods and heroes. The stately ground-floor Doric order was derived from the classical model of the theatre of Marcellus, also considered for the facade of a palazzo in the fourth book of Serlio's treatise, published in Venice in 1537;[11] the Ionic might have some link with the Roman arch at Aquinum. Overall, the work was conceived, presented and understood as a paradigm of the authority and expressive virtues of the laws of Antiquity: as a statement of the return, by the last heir of Republican Rome, to the original discipline of Vitruvius. Significantly enough, sixteenth-century commentators were particularly insistent in their praise of the manner in which the connecting angle towards the bakers' stalls had been solved. Here, the challenge had been to provide a correct interpretation for an unclear passage in Vitruvius which talked of a corner semi-metope in the Doric temple – a problem of the adherence to and historically accurate reinstatement of the rules, in which cardinal Bembo himself took a close interest: here Sansovino had to reinvent a 'correct' solution of his own for the connecting angle 'which would safeguard the proportion'. This was understood by the majority as a proof of Sansovino's capacity appropriately to apply the norms of art (despite the liberties he allowed himself in various details of the Library); by certain others it was regarded as 'a device never thought up by the ancients', that is, as a sign – in keeping with Venetian myth – not just of the renewal, but of the actual transcending of antiquity by the *res aedificatoria* that had been given new life by the Serenissima.[12]

The facade of the Library, however, was more than a display of architectural erudition. The sculptural decoration too was favourably received by contemporary assessments: the Library was 'the richest and most ornate building possibly ever created from Ancient times to our own', as Andrea Palladio put it.[13] In point of fact, this decoration verges on the excessive; powerful male figures – sea, river and earth gods – flanking the arches of the Ionic order on the ground floor, and winged victories on the upper one, transform each span into a triumphal arch, with male, female and leonine telamones as the keystones.

Marcian emblems alternate with trophies of arms and paterae on the metopes of the Doric frieze. The bas-reliefs on the intradoses recount the classical myths, and the highly elaborate Ionic frieze has jubilant *putti* holding heavy garlands, inspired by those that were in the Miracoli at the time, attributed to Praxiteles. Clearly, here Sansovino was deploying a decorative apparatus which would function as an external allusion to everything which the priceless Bessarion manuscripts[14] had handed down to modern memory, housed as they now were in what was indisputably one of the sacred places of humanism; at the same time, he was giving outward magnificence to the republic which was their jealous guardian. In their direct relation with the loggia of the palazzo opposite – the place of the wise institutions – the series of sculptural divinities now came to denote the presence of *Dei consentes* and

Jacopo Sansovino, Fabbriche
Nuove at Rialto, general view
of the facade.

Eglise de S. Jeminien. Chiesa di S. Geminiano.

Jacopo Sansovino, facade of
S. Geminiano in an eighteenth-
century engraving. Paris,
Bibliothèque Nationale.

right
Jacopo Sansovino, view of
the 'formidable and marvellous'
facade of the Misericordia in
the general townscape.

below
Side view of the Misericordia
overlooking the canal.

complices, divine advisers and companions: the very ones whom Republican Rome had placed over the portico of the same name in the Forum. Furthermore, the Roman quotation from the theatre of Marcellus may in fact derive from a deliberately learned reference which might well have been suggested by a man of letters such as Bembo, the Serenissima's historiographer and librarian at the Library from 1530: it could therefore be an ideal reminiscence of the *porticus et bibliothecae Octavianae* founded by Augustus in 721 in Rome, and mentioned by Ovid, adjacent to the theatre and associated by Plutarch with the name of Marcellus.

The *all'antica* reinterpretation of piazza San Marco which was being juxtaposed with, and in part superimposed upon, the Byzantine features that had been given to the area between the eleventh and thirteenth centuries, was continued with the small building of the Loggetta at the foot of the campanile, opposite the Porta della Carta, or main entrance to the Ducal palace, in a place of particular importance for state ceremonies. With its polychrome marbles, this elaborate little work (1538) established a precise – and, for Sansovino, unusual – symmetry with the fifteenth-century portal opposite. But the 'pyramid shape' and carved moral allegories of the Porta della Carta were deliberately countered by Sansovino's eloquent use of the scheme of the triumphal arch with three openings, between pairs of composite columns, in their turn framing niches with statues, crowned by an attic storey divided into panels and decorated with bas-reliefs of mythological subjects. The iconography of the sculptural system is extremely clear: the myths of the ancient world expressed the triumph of the public political virtues of the Serenissima, and the allegory of the state as the embodiment of justice was accompanied by those of the dominions and realms which belonged to her. The original meaning of the work, of the programme as assigned to Sansovino, was discussed soon afterwards by his son Francesco, who interpreted it at length in the *Arte Oratoria* of 1546[15] as the 'place of memory' (in the most literal sense), an exemplary case of architecture and sculpture put at the service of the public as *artes suadendi* (arts of persuasion).

The visual correspondence between the Loggetta and the Scala dei Giganti, the 'truly royal' staircase at whose sides Sansovino was to place the statues of Mercury and Neptune (1566) – the symbols of Venetian commercial and maritime power – now served to mark out a new triumphal r.oute between them, a veritable 'via sacra': the theme of the *forum romanum* was here reformulated quite unambiguously.

This concept undoubtedly lay behind the idea for the general remodelling of the Piazza mentioned by Francesco Sansovino as early as 1562. The facade of the Library was not to end at the corner adjoining the meat market, but was to 'surround the piazza', continuing as far as S. Geminiano, and then 'turn the corner . . . going all around as far as the hours' (Codussi's torre dell'Orologio).[16] Furthermore, the facade of S. Geminiano, built in 1557 to a plan by Sansovino and perhaps also based in part on a design for a church facade by Serlio, appears to have been conceived in architectural terms that were perfectly compatible with the idea of the great Marcian 'forum'. Although unrealized – except in part, and with different implications, in the late sixteenth century, in the form of the Procuratie Nuove – this bespeaks extraordinary perception and breadth if we bear in mind its probable coincidence in time with another important project, that of the extending of the Ducal palace beyond the rio di Palazzo, which was already under consideration in the last years of the dogeship of Andrea Gritti, according to the doge's biographers.[17]

The complete renewal of the Marcian area as a *forum romanum* with its mint, library, triumphal arch and *palatium* was of course never implemented. But the turning-point that occurred in Venetian architectural culture from Sansovino's works for the Piazza onwards was absolutely decisive. In this same context, too, the problem of the relations between magnificence and convenience, between function and formal dignity in public buildings also resurfaced, together with the closely related one of that between public and private grandeur.

Equally significantly in this context, Sansovino now simplified his style for the Fabbriche Nuove of the Rialto market, intended mainly to house shops and warehouses. He had received the commission for the project in 1554, but two years later stonemasons were still at work 'on its form, outline and measurements'.[18] Twenty-five ground-floor arches with smooth rustication in Istrian stone ran from the vegetable market to the fish market, for the unloading of goods arriving from the Grand Canal on to which they opened. The requisite sense of dignity was given to the buildings by the use of superimposed Doric and Ionic orders above the arcading, and of aedicules around the windows.

But it was also clear that Sansovino intended to limit expenditure, keeping the tone moderate and restrained without actually falling into the vernacular: this is evident both in the restricting of the use of Istrian stone in the facades on the two upper storeys to the architectural elements alone – on walls of plastered brick – and in the reduction of the Doric frieze to a mere 'framework'. The triglyphs are not grooved, while the guttae are replaced by a sort of continuous fillet, which could be executed more quickly and cheaply. Something similar occurred in villa Garzoni at Pontecasale, and in the facade of the landing-place for the Bucintoro at the Arsenal; and this general tendency was reflected in the functionalist approach adopted by the Senate in 1550 for the architecture of fortresses and fortified towns.[19]

The severe features of the long building planned as the facade of Europe's 'foremost market place'[20] on the Grand Canal (a role which view-painting was so clearly to emphasize) therefore demonstrated an

Andrea Palladio (from Jacopo Sansovino?),
design for the facade of the Scuola Grande della
Misericordia. Vicenza, museo Civico.

unwavering concern for the 'good of the
dominion', a visible 'demonstration' of the
circumspect use of public funds, rather than
pointless ostentation in those places designated for the exercise of prudent trading.

A triumphal classicism, however, was
still very much in evidence in the Scuola
Grande della Misericordia (built from 1532
onwards), described as 'most formidable
and marvellous', and 'strong and massive',
even though it was never completed.[21]
While keeping closely to the pattern normally adopted by the confraternities for the
functional organization of their spaces (and
although he was to some degree restricted
by what had already been built),[22]
Sansovino here set out to make use of a
grandiose and rhetorical style. He was in
fact reinterpreting the colonnaded ground-
floor hall as a classical basilican space,
divided into three aisles by two rows of
paired Corinthian columns. He repeated
this rhythm on the internal walls, and
declared it again on the strongly articulated
outer ones. The use of vaulting, suggested
by the architect and rejected by the Scuola,
would have given this powerfully unitary
building even greater consistency; the
external scheme (never realized, but known
to us from a famous drawing in the Museo
Civico at Vicenza),[23] with its fluted columns,
niches with statues and large windows
framed by colonnettes – spirally fluted in the
upper order – and divided up horizontally
by a powerful entablature, would have given
it a sustained aristocratic opulence that was
clearly to have been paradigmatic in intent.

Jacopo Sansovino, palazzo Dolfin
at Rialto, facade.

As it was, the great structure loomed in splendid isolation over the surrounding city fabric, set on what amounts to a sort of podium, with the campo in front of it raised on three steps above the *fondamenta* leading to it, and reached from the water by a *riva* conceived as a broad staircase. In fact, this aristocratic tone was suited neither to the confraternity itself, nor to the public functions performed by the Scuole Grandi in general. Sansovino's idea was presented in precisely these terms by his son Francesco, while he himself was still alive: the Misericordia was 'a deathless work, and worthy of this Dominion by virtue of its excessive beauty'.[24]

Sansovino's attitudes towards his commissions from private individuals seem to have been equally complex, if in some ways different. After the failure of his first project, his activity in this area consisted essentially of three palazzi: palazzo Dolfin at S. Salvador, palazzo Corner della Ca' Grande at S. Maurizio, and palazzo Moro at S. Girolamo. The first are two of the four 'modern' palazzi which sixteenth-century literature regarded as being 'the principal ones' on the Grand Canal; clearly, in both cases Sansovino's purpose was to present forms which would enable privately commissioned works to conform to the official language of the *renovatio urbis*. After Codussi's Ca' Loredan Vendramin Calergi, palazzo Dolfin laid claims to being the first palazzo in Venice to be built in accordance with the correct rules of architecture.[25]

As we know from contemporary sources, the functional organization of the building –

designed for Giovanni Dolfin, a nobleman engaged in shipping and trade – was clearly derived from the traditional Venetian *casa-fondaco*. Apart from being the master's residence, it included large storerooms on the ground floor and groups of rooms for rent on the mezzanine and some parts of the first floor; the portico over the canal allowed public traffic to pass along the *riva*, but also provided mooring for one of the ferries serving the Rialto area, on regular payment of an agreed rent. Sansovino resolved the needs connected to these particular functions – in fact, far from uncommon[26] – by means of a sequence of high Doric arches, similar to those of the nearby Fabbriche Nuove, but less severe. Following correct usage, he designed an Ionic first floor and a Corinthian second floor above the portico, and dignified the whole by the series of lions' head telamones on the crowning frieze, all perfectly in keeping with his reinterpretation of the courtyard traditionally to be found behind the 'casa da stazio' (later altered): with galleries on all sides, it made a deliberate show of imitating 'the Roman custom'.[27] In fact, however, not only were the various functions distributed overall according to the pattern typical of the Venetian merchant's house; the layout of the facade, too, thoroughly respected the conventional tripartite division, with the *saloni* running the depth of the main block corresponding to two high four-light windows opening over the Grand Canal. Here the laws of good architecture were called upon to correct and discipline ordinary usage, but without this latter being overwhelmed by them. This same respect for the norms, together with learned references to classical Roman architecture, were firmly and energetically asserted at Ca' Corner at S. Maurizio, which was already under consideration during these same years, though it was not actually begun until 1545. The formal language of the facade overlooking the canal – which, 'with its double columns, its Ionic order above and smooth rustication with its noble archways below, strikes the beholder as full of majesty'[28] – set the building apart from its context, making it a fitting vehicle for the celebration of those who had commissioned it, with their aristocratic origins, vast trading empire and estates, and eminent position in the government and ecclesiastical hierarchy of the republic.

Here, the triple arcade, approached by the waterside staircase, the ground-floor loggia leading into the vaulted *androne* and the large courtyard 'alla romana', all marked a much more overt move away from the Venetian palazzo of the early Renaissance. This was further underlined by both the virtual abandonment of the usual tripartite division of the facade (though a trace of it remains, on the two upper floors, in the slightly closer positioning of the three central windows in relation to the two on either side), and by the rich and stately display of architectural decor. In this way, Ca' Corner broke with the past, to assert the primacy of the Antique in the noble dwelling as well, 'with beauties and ornaments in the Roman style': in its polemical, aristocratic isolation, it radically altered the landscape of the last stretch of the Grand Canal towards the canal di San Marco, and its implications were immediately understood: 'it descries the lagoons, because of its great height, and in its turn may be descried from them'.[29]

In fact, there were specific reasons for this unusual formal magnificence. Here, the architect of San Marco was using the device defined in Francesco's short treatise on rhetoric (1546) as the demonstrative and laudative genre. The meaning of palazzo Corner was stated 'by way of statues', to use another concept specifically employed by Francesco, in this case through the iconographical system of bas-reliefs on the two *piani nobili* of the facade. The cuirasses, shields, war trumpets and armour in bas-relief serve as 'reminders'[30] linked to the proud humanistic reinterpretation of the greatness of the clan: Ca' Corner was now seen as the *domus* of the *gens Cornelia* from which Sansovino's clients claimed direct descent, in particular from the Scipioni, who were great *condottieri*, but also innovators in matters of Roman culture. This exceptional display of 'Roman' features was intended both as *nobilitatis theatrum* (theatre of nobility) and *magnificentiae exemplar* (example of magnificence).[31]

If Ca' Corner was conceived as the ultimate demonstration of the relation between the stylistic resources of the new architecture and patrician patronage, in Ca' Moro Sansovino found himself facing the

radically opposite task of asserting the primacy of the serviceable and the moderate.

Situated on an outlying site in the *sestiere* of Cannaregio, this work had such a far-reaching effect on the layout of the surrounding area that it was actually referred to, in the seventeenth and eighteenth centuries, as the 'Isola [island] of Ca' Moro at S. Girolamo'. Here, shortly before 1544, Leonardo Moro, a senator who had recently inherited a considerable mercantile fortune, embarked on an extensive building programme which was not finished until the middle of the century: it included two large 'case da stazio', a group of middle-range and slightly grander dwellings, and several more modest ones, about twenty in all. However, these took the form not simply of a series of repeated elements, but of a unitary complex – left partially unfinished – built 'almost with the appearance of a great castle':[32] namely, a large block on a rectangular plan, organized around a big courtyard, with buildings at the corners – two small palazzi with facades articulated with three superimposed windows corresponding to the rooms running the depth of the building – bounding a row of terraced elements interrupted by a small crenellated entrance leading to the inner courtyard. Although the overall arrangement was innovative, the structural solutions themselves were in many ways surprisingly traditional, an evident return to the more austere type of popular housing, a harking back to that ancestral 'parsimony' which was an important component in sixteenth-

above
Jacopo Sansovino, Ca' Moro at S. Girolamo.

right
Palazzo Gritti at S. Francesco della Vigna.

right
Sixteenth-century terraced houses in corte Nova near S. Giustina.

below right
Houses on Corte Paludo, sixteenth-century development at the eastern end of the *sestiere* of Castello.

century Venetian myth.[33] There can be no doubt that here Leonardo Moro was making a conscious, even Utopian stand as a private patron by moving away from the central areas (he had left the house he had inherited from his uncle at S. Agostino, and also abandoned the idea of living at S. Felice). It was widely felt that patrician clients commissioning new buildings should now commit themselves, through investment in real estate, to what we might call the 'perfecting' of the urban form, and the defining of marginal areas of the city's fabric.

What Sansovino was being asked to prove here was therefore the reverse of what he had previously achieved: namely, that architecture could rationalize vernacular practices and traditions, that it was fully able to deliver the 'convenient and serviceable' which, together with eloquence of form, was also part of the role accorded to it by Vitruvian culture. All in all, he was being asked to put himself at the service of the programmes of renewal that now took in the entire urban space. This development should be seen, to some degree, as related to the dawning idea of an overall plan for the city, which dates from just a few years later; but it was also linked to the patriciate's newfound interest in building in outlying areas, as exemplified in the stately and austere residence of doge Gritti next to the church of S. Francesco della Vigna, in a secluded and popular district, near the noisy timber stores on the muddy shores of north-west Venice and the walls of the Arsenal. That Sansovino agreed to be

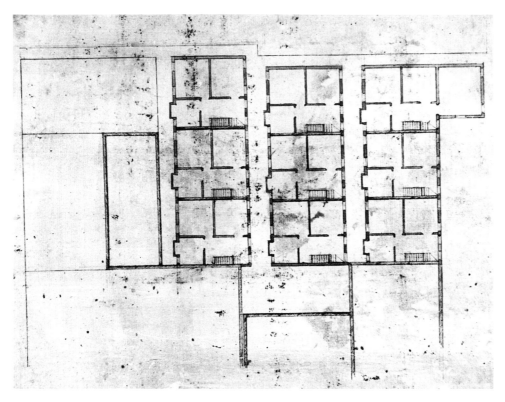

Three parallel rows of terraced housing. Venice, Archivio di stato.

involved in this undertaking is also clear evidence less of his openness to all manner of commissions, than of his conviction concerning the flexibility and relevance of the instruments of planning: it amounted to an enquiry into the minimal limits of the architect's rules and techniques, with a view to applying them over the whole range of unsolved problems and situations. These were also the decades when intensive solutions were being worked out in the field of popular building, with the elaboration of multi-storey blocks, the introduction of double staircases and so on, so as to improve the distributive plans and perfect the use of symmetry. In 1547 the Scuola di S. Rocco organized a competition for a group of rented dwellings (the 'case di Castelforte'), won by Scarpagnino, the *proto al Sal* who had rebuilt the Rialto. This was also very probably the period when Sebastiano Serlio was in Venice embarking upon his studies of various types of popular building, subsequently brought together in the sixth book of his treatise, then left unpublished. Sansovino's attitude clearly reflected the mood of the moment and the requirements of a particularly active clientele.

His work on the completion of the church of S. Geminiano, already mentioned, was not an isolated example of his interest in religious architecture. His official position as *proto* of San Marco involved not just responsibility for the fabric of the basilica itself, but also for the abbeys, hospitals and pious places under ducal patronage. Apart from an important group of built works, this interest produced sixty or so designs for churches, known to Vasari, but lost after the architect's death.[34] In his religious buildings for Venice, Sansovino clearly took various traditional elements into consideration, though reinterpreting them in his own way. For S. Martino di Castello, for example, he used a Greek cross plan of the Veneto-Byzantine type found in the small parish churches in central areas, and which had also been widely used in the early Renaissance period. Similarly, for the completion of S. Fantin he used a domed chancel with apses which bore some resemblance to works built in the city between the late fifteenth and early sixteenth centuries; the layout of the monks' choir behind the altar in S. Francesco della Vigna revealed the influence of the older Franciscan church of S. Giobbe. But what is even clearer is that Sansovino set out to inaugurate a 'modern' style of religious architecture in Venice – which was to bear particular fruit from the late sixteenth century and over the following one – marked by a newfound formal austerity also in keeping with the wishes of those who commissioned it.

Sansovino's chief experiment in this direction was the church of S. Francesco della Vigna, whose first stone was laid on 15 August 1534 with a public ceremony in honour of the feast of the Assumption, in the presence of doge Andrea Gritti. The rebuilding of S. Francesco was closely bound up with the doge's policy of renewal, and

Jacopo Sansovino, S. Francesco della Vigna, interior.

Jacopo Sansovino, S. Martino di Castello, facade.

with the Observant Friars' rigorist aspirations and propaganda for moral reform. A first model probably envisaged a church on a domed Latin cross; but Sansovino himself soon abandoned the idea of the dome, and settled for a harmoniously devised unitary space, with the single broad nave assuming paramount importance. In the well-known memorandum of 1535, countersigned by Titian and Serlio among others, Francesco Zorzi interpreted and defended the 'perfectly gauged' new solutions and proportions of the definitive plan on the basis of Platonist theories.[35] If the outward representation of harmony was the burden of the architectural idea, this was achieved through a deliberately spare and rigorous style, with Tuscan echoes (there are obvious parallels with Cronaca's severe church of S. Salvatore al Monte) and a very sober Doric order, appropriate to the ascetic virtues of the saint.

In S. Francesco, the nave has a series of five family chapels running down each side; it is distinguished from them by a difference in floor level, with a strip of three steps running around its perimeter and that of the transept, inscribing a second *crux commissa* within the Latin one. This was probably a symbolic allusion to perfection, to the sign of the just in Ezekiel's vision, and to the sign of salvation in St. Jerome. The church's architectural unity, which Francesco Zorzi himself had suggested when he stressed the need for a correlation between facade and interior (with 'the facade enabling us to read the form of the

Jacopo Sansovino, S. Martino di Castello, interior.

Jacopo Sansovino, Ca' di Dio.

building and its proportions, in order that all shall be rightly proportioned within and without'),[36] was nonetheless compromised because Sansovino had left the site by October 1561[37] and, as we shall see, the facade was built by Palladio.

The monastic complex of S. Francesco della Vigna was situated near the Arsenal and the surrounding port areas, and the church was extensively damaged when a powder-magazine in the public dockyard exploded in 1569. Sansovino was also commissioned to build another church (from 1553) in the nearby parish of S. Martino where the Arsenal stood. He designed it on a free Greek cross plan, similar to those which had long been characteristic of the parish churches of Venice, but in particular of S. Giacomo di Rialto, regarded as the first church to be built in the city. Moreover, here he abandoned not only the Byzantine-inspired solution of the domed ceiling, but also the erudite use of overtly classicizing forms. S. Martino was a further experiment in severity: its spatial configuration, consistent with the traditionalism of the popular area of the Arsenal and its skilled workers, was matched by a directness of style, simple and austere, a conscious renunciation of persuasive display. During this same period it was also decreed that the architecture of the Arsenal should observe the utmost restraint; it was to abstain from 'that grandeur imparted by copious use of marble, and that magnificence which the ancients used in their buildings, because they [the Venetians] have such excellence in other public buildings'.[38] Where a loftier tone was called for, as on the facade of the *squero* (covered landing stage) of the Bucintoro (1555), the architectural order would be simplified, as at the Fabbriche Nuove at Rialto. That these decisions were in accordance with a specific policy is evident from the comparable simplification of the facade of the Ca' di Dio (1544 onwards), originally a hospice for pilgrims to the Holy Land, and subsequently a refuge for needy women. The minimal formal concessions represented by the *Serliane* are easily explained: together with the nearby block of biscuit bakehouses and their annexes, the hospice formed the frontage of the buildings of the island of S. Martino di Castello – mostly publicly-owned – on to the canal di San Marco, between the rio dell'Arsenale and that of S. Giovanni in Bragora. For similar reasons, again to a plan by Sansovino, a small Corinthian doorway (1570), commissioned by Tommaso Rangone, was incorporated into the long bare facade of the monastero del Sepolcro, situated not far away and also overlooking the lagoon.

The rebuilding of the church of S. Zulian – originally on a triple-naved basilican plan – continued this same tendency in a central area of the city, on the Mercerie linking San Marco with Rialto. The space of the interior has neither architectural orders nor side chapels; the sanctuary, rectangular in plan and roofed with cross-vaulting, is flanked by two chapels with high arches supporting winged figures of angels. Altogether, the

space is far more reminiscent of a *sala di devozione* (assembly hall) in a Scuola Grande than of the usual interior of a parish church; it has a vaguely evangelical, or 'community' feel to it. Its simplicity proved of great importance for later Venetian religious architecture.

The exterior, too, which had been built earlier, left its mark upon Venetian Renaissance architecture by establishing the concept of the 'facade as memorial'. But here, since S. Zulian had been built as a celebratory building, the opulence associated with such works inevitably resurfaces. The tripartite scheme of Sansovino's facade, completed in 1559, reflected the original basilican structure of the church; the aisles were lit by windows and the nave was lit by the *Serliana* in the tympanum, the equivalent of the oculus of a medieval church. The basic framework of corner pilaster strips and a crowning pediment here also included a central section topped by a broken arched tympanum, containing eulogizing inscriptions and the bronze statue of the patron set in the arch of the portal between two pairs of elaborate fluted Doric columns. The figure of Tommaso Rangone, on a low sarcophagus, is seated nobly amidst a neat array of volumes, some open, some closed, and a terrestrial and celestial sphere and further eulogizing inscriptions in the three languages of ancient learning, Greek, Latin and Hebrew. The architectural and sculptural decoration as a whole is a clear allusion to the immortality ensured to men of culture, to the well-worn theme of glory as

Jacopo Sansovino, portal of the monastery of S. Sepolcro.

right
Jacopo Sansovino, S. Zulian, facade.

below
S. Zulian, the pediment.

a reward for virtue stemming no less from letters and learning than from arms and official rank, as discussed by Jacopo Sansovino in his *L'arte oratoria* of a few years earlier.[39] This topic was particularly well-suited not only to Rangone himself, but also to the church's council of maintenance, all of whom, unusually enough, were practitioners of the liberal arts: they included Tommaso Giunta, Gerolamo Surian, the son of another famous doctor, and Melchiorre Sessa, a publisher and bookseller whose shop was called 'la Gatta'.

In the context of Sansovino's religious architecture, special mention should also be made of his church of the Ospedale degli Incurabili (1565), demolished in 1831 but known through various graphic sources: its longitudinal plan, oval at the ends, was the first example in Venice of a space conceived specifically in terms of its acoustics, since it had been designed for the giving of choral concerts by the orphan girls for whom the institution cared.

During these same years, when Sansovino was becoming established in Venice, Sebastiano Serlio arrived there after the sack of Rome; he was to leave the city more than a decade later for the court of Francis I of Valois, where he assumed the role the Serenissima would never grant him. Yet Serlio did in fact play an active role in Venetian architectural culture during a crucial decade of the century: between 1528, when, together with Agostino de Musi, he asked for sole printing rights to a group of engravings intended to 'give assistance in

Agostino Veneziano and Sebastiano Serlio,
illustrations of the architectural orders.
Vienna, Albertina.

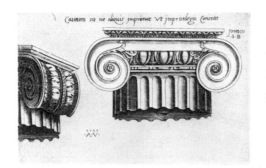

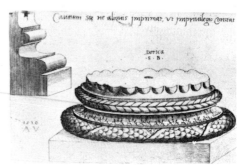

Sebastiano Serlio, drawings of facades for palazzi
'in the Venetian manner', from the fourth book of
the treatise.

discerning the various orders, that is, Tuscan, Doric, Ionic, Corinthian and composite',[40] and 1537, when his *Regole generali di architettura* were published, he was engaged in writing a series of widely-circulated treatises codifying the rules of Antiquity. If nothing or very little remains of his activity as an architect – and if the information concerning it is extremely fragmentary and contradictory – it can at least be said that his energies were largely devoted to an area of publishing that was particularly important for Venice's role in the Renaissance. Francesco Marcolini, his partner in this venture, was an unusually lively and eye-catching figure, a publisher, engineer and friend of Daniele Barbaro and Nicolò Zen, as well as the author of the project for the bridge at Murano, built in 1545 and technically approved by Sansovino himself.[41] In other words, Serlio's activity testified to a flourishing debate in Venice on the norms and institutions of architecture which, starting from the commentary on Vitruvius by fra' Giocondo published in 1511, and followed by the two editions of the commentary on him by Barbaro (1556 and 1567), was to continue with the *Quattro Libri* by Palladio (1570), and the *Idea dell' architettura universale* by Scamozzi (1615), not to mention other works of varying quality and subject matter, both published and unpublished.

Here Serlio appears to have advocated a middle way, maintaining that the features specific to Venice's architectural culture could to some degree be made compatible

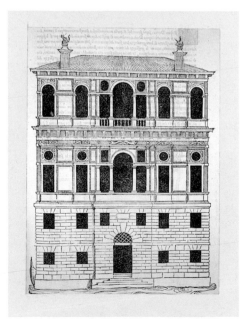

with the classical rules. As he stresses on several occasions, Venice built in her own particular way: courtyards and gardens were rarely found adjoining aristocratic residences, forms and structures were characterized by certain 'vices' and 'liberties'. The numerous windows – excessive if seen in terms of the classical canons – were echoed by a correspondingly large number of balconies overlooking the canals, for coolness in summer and for viewing the constant processions and regattas. These facts, to Serlio's regret, gave rise to solutions which ran counter to the accepted rules of utility and decorum. However, as we have said, as an architect and treatise-writer he sought a middle way, with suggestions for the rationalizing of building traditions ('to do such things with some logic'),[42] while at the same time observing the 'classical style in building'. He therefore looked at possible adjustments to the characteristics of Venetian houses, while approving their spatial and functional organization. His most interesting suggestion – which was to have a broad following – concerned the external frontage of the large rooms spanning the depth of the palazzo. Their three-light windows were to become two tall, narrow, architraved side openings, flanking a broader, arched central one, like the classical examples found, for instance, in the palace of Diocletian at Split: *Serliane*, in other words, as widely used from the mid-sixteenth century for the Venetian 'casa da stazio', the palazzo for 'the Venetian gentleman'. His studies were also to exert

above
Francesco Zen and Sebastiano Serlio, Ca' Zeno at
the Crociferi, general view.

below
Ca' Zeno, detail of a three-light window.

considerable influence on the Venetian
architecture of the sixteenth and seventeenth centuries.

The compromises, trade-offs and
uncertainties of Venetian culture in the
1530s were further reflected in the palazzo
designed for his own family by the nobleman Francesco Zen, a friend of Serlio's, a
patron of Marcolini's and extremely knowledgeable about architecture and antiquities.
Here, partly for reasons of family self-celebration, he and his architect tried combining sober Renaissance forms with elements
deriving from the Veneto-Byzantine lexicon
and the enduring Venetian interest in the
Levant. This experiment met with no
favour; but it did have a highly significant
bearing upon the first studies on the earliest
Venetian architecture, on the grandeur and
severity of the buildings of the age of the tribunes later to be carried out by Francesco's
nephew, Nicolò Zen.[43]

By the time Sansovino was engaged in
his projects for the Marcian area, the programmes for the renewal of the *forma urbis*
had become so all-embracing as to require
the summoning of another extremely
important architect, Michele Sanmicheli.
He had already been working as an engineer
for the Serenissima for some time, and on
14 April 1535 the Council of Ten assigned
him the twofold post of engineer in charge
of fortresses and of *lidi* (work on the shoreline). His intensive activity on the mainland, in Dalmatia and the Graeco-Venetian
Levant, in close though not always untrou-
bled collaboration with Francesco Maria

della Rovere, duke of Urbino, heir to the military tradition of the Montefeltro family and captain general of the Venetian army, does not concern us here, except to note that in this context Sanmicheli seems to have been active less as a 'war architect' – to use Serlio's expression – than as an expert *de re aedificatoria* who gave structural and technical form to the defensive programmes of the 'capo da guerra' (military leader). He was also expected to give suitable architectural form to the sovereign authority and protective presence of the state in specifically designated places such as city gates, this being an essential element in a programme of *renovatio securitatis* (renewal of defences) pursued at vast expense after the crisis of the wars of the League of Cambrai and the Holy League, and in the face of imperial and Ottoman pressure.

For Venice herself, Sanmicheli elaborated an overall plan for the defence of the lagoons on behalf of the Council of Ten, subdividing the programme into two specific projects: one for the fortification of the harbour centre of Chioggia, in the southern lagoon, and the other for the reinforcement of the defences of the Due Castelli, the fortification of the harbour mouth at S. Nicolò, and the subsequent radical rebuilding of the fortress of S. Andrea, one of the most important works of military architecture to be built in Europe in the sixteenth century.

As a work of fortification, the 'castle' of S. Andrea was a genuine anomaly: the fact that its facade was fortified only on the side

overlooking the sea, and not on that over the internal waters of the lagoon and towards the city, was the outcome of a compromise between two separate sets of requirements, those of defence and those of political image. These were discussed at length by the Council of Ten, and there is extensive documentation concerning them.

From a functional point of view, the 'castle' was the result of Francesco Maria della Rovere's advice carefully to weigh up 'the prejudice that might derive from seeing these two fortresses put up in a city with a reputation for freedom such as this one has'.[44] The rebuilding of the 'two Castles' in conventional terms might in fact have been interpreted technically as the incorporation of a citadel – viewed as a potential 'opportunity for tyranny' as long ago as Aristotle - into a city which had been celebrated as the seat of liberty since the times of Petrarch. The (harbour castle) castello 'da mar' of S. Andrea – like the opposite bastions of S. Nicolò – was therefore built using a design combining the 'fortress which fulfils the needs of war' with the 'defencelessness which befits a Republic in times of peace', modifying the original layout so that the facade towards the city might remain unfortified. Sanmicheli was entirely responsible for the sensational achievement of laying the foundations on the lagoon bed, with the technical assistance of the Arsenal, (celebrated by Vasari), and the architecture of the facade overlooking the sea, all in rusticated Istrian stone, conceived as a semi-circular bastion with a triple-arched

gateway in the centre, and side curtains fortified at water level by arched embrasures with keystones with lions' heads, at once a war machine and an image to strike awe in the beholder.

It was these publicly-commissioned works that introduced Sanmicheli to his first Venetian patrons: apart from various consultancies and partial works, he designed two of the greatest private palazzi of the High Renaissance, Ca' Corner at S. Polo and Ca' Grimani at S. Luca. Each in their own way, these two buildings addressed the same problems posed by Jacopo Sansovino in Ca' Dolfin and Ca' Corner at S. Maurizio; indeed they did so in terms of overt competition, as Francesco Sansovino was perfectly aware.

In both buildings Sanmicheli applied himself to the classic problem of the 'oblique site'. But while Ca' Corner used a solution that might be regarded as typical for the Venetian aristocratic Renaissance dwelling, Ca' Grimani was presented incontrovertibly as a model of magnificence *all'antica*, indeed as a pioneering demonstration of what the private patron could now aspire to: a 'mighty structure' put up in 'emulation' of Sansovino's Ca' Grande,[45] but following a different interpretation of classical grandeur.

Ca' Corner at S. Polo (designed around 1550), on two storeys above a rusticated ground floor overlooking rio di S. Polo, retained the traditional tripartite division of the facade and corresponding internal distribution. But, as in Sansovino's buildings,

here too the original family courtyard
annexed to the 'casa da stazio' was transformed into one connected exclusively with
the palazzo, preceded by an atrium reached
from campo S. Polo through a portal very
similar, according to Temanza, to that of the
atrium of the Pellegrini chapel at Verona.
The relative sobriety of the building designed
by Sanmicheli for Giovanni Corner was
duly noted, above all for its moderate use of
marble and Istrian stone: all in all, it seems
clear that Sanmicheli considered it as a sort
of prototype for a clientele of senatorial rank.
It also tallied largely with Serlio's views,
and indeed here Sanmicheli appears to
have based himself quite closely on one of
Serlio's drawings for a facade 'in the
Venetian style' published in the fourth book
(1537); he also used the *Serliana* on the two
upper floors in place of the multi-light windows corresponding to the *saloni*. These
choices might also have been influenced by
the fact that the Corner family of S. Polo
may have owned certain drawings by Serlio
– possibly supplied soon after the palazzo
was burned down – and by the close family
relations linking them to other close friends
of Serlio's, for instance Francesco Zen.[46]

Sanmicheli's interpretation of the aristocratic dwelling for the Grimani at S. Luca, on
the Grand Canal, was completely different,
and strongly aristocratic. Commissioned
between 1556 and 1557, it was completed
only in 1575, with the addition of a third
floor not envisaged in the original plan
(which had already been modified in
certain quite important details by 1566).

Michele Sanmicheli, facade of the fortress of S. Andrea.

Palazzo Grimani at S. Maria Formosa, facade
overlooking rio S. Severo.

The hypothesis concerning Sanmicheli's involvement in another more or less contemporary work of great architecture, formulated several times from the second half of the eighteenth century, namely the renovation of Ca' Grimani at S. Maria Formosa, does not seem acceptable. At all events, this palazzo certainly represented an important step in the process of the return to the Antique for mid-sixteenth-century Venice. The facade on to rio di S. Severo, built between 1559 and 1569, was architecturally restrained, relatively in keeping with Venetian custom with its superimposed four-light windows and asymmetrical layout; it was also partly conditioned by pre-existing structures. Here stone was used with manifest parsimony; only the water entrance was treated with a solemn rustication, repeated less emphatically at the corners. The pronounced monumentality of the land entrance, on the other hand, was more unusual, a prelude to the grandiose courtyard; the dedicatory inscription to the tutelary god of the city, *genio urbis*, held the key to the reading of this exceptional 'place of memory' for those who entered it. The inner side of the great 'da terra' doorway already had Michelangelesque features; this, and the architraved porticoes, Greek and Roman antiquities and colossal statues, introduced the visitor into the antiquarian collections of cardinal Giovanni Grimani (d. 1593), later bequeathed to the republic. In terms of architecture and decoration, the two *piani nobili*, each with its own independent access, are very different in tone. The severe one occupied by Vettore may even have been designed to suggestions by Sansovino, *proto* of the Ducal chapel, with whom Vettore often worked in his capacity as procurator of San Marco. The elaborate ornamentation of Giovanni's residence, on the other hand, drew upon a repertoire inspired by the spirit of Rome, and those who worked on it included Giovanni da Udine, Camillo Mantovano, Francesco Salviati and, later, Federico Zuccari. The ideal centre of this residence was the 'studio delle antichità', a richly decorated square room with coffered domical vault-ing and a cross-vaulted lantern.

The disparity of tone between the two 'case da stazio' which co-existed in the same building should not be seen as deriv ing from any radical difference of opinion between the brothers Vincenzo and Giovanni, indeed the former seems to have been per-sonally responsible for overseeing the works and interests of the cardinal during his long absences from the city.[49] Its reasons become clear if we consider the use made of his residence by Giovanni Grimani: the *domus mirifica* which Muzio Sforza records as having been built according to the architec-tural ideas of the man who commissioned it (even if this does not solve the numerous problems of attribution) was in fact the Venetian *domus* of the patriarch of Aquileia, *Venetiae caput et mater*,[50] the forebear of modern Venice, and from here Giovanni issued innumerable official acts. The 'Roman' magnificence and grandeur

of the architecture and collection of anti-quities were therefore commensurate with the dignity of the patriarchate 'long held by the Grimani family' almost as though by birthright,[51] and also with memories of the greatness of ancient Aquileia, the original legitimizing source for the return to the Antique currently under way in the Serenissima. The remains of this same magnificence, coming to light around the patriarchal basilica, had been referred to by Giovanni Candido when he urged Domenico Grimani – Giovanni's predecessor in this same see – to look to their *renovatio*.[52]

As we see, there was no lack of cultural energy in mid-sixteenth-century Venice. Programmes for public buildings were forging ahead, and various private indi-viduals were outdoing each other in works of self-celebration. Projects for renewal now affected the entire length and breadth of the urban space.

The first overall planning act for the city dates from 1557, elaborated on the basis of a long series of precedents by Cristoforo Sabbadino, an engineer with the Savi ed Esecutori sopra le Acque. First and fore-most, the plan envisaged the ringing of the entire city with a continuous embankment – *fondamenta* – in Istrian stone. Now that a firm boundary had been drawn between city space and lagoon space, the areas of marshy shallows which were to be included within the new perimeter might be put to two different uses: they might either be reclaimed, with the filling in of almost ninety thousand square *passi*,

producing new building land to be offered for sale in response to pressure for the urbanization of the outlying stretches; or they might be used for the formation of three artificial basins, to be obtained by excavating so many pre-existing 'sacche' (indentations),[53] serving as terminals for river-lagoon transport from the territories of Padua, Vicenza, Treviso and Friuli. Another lengthy series of sites, obtained by draining the lagoon shore of the Giudecca over 100,000 square *passi*, was earmarked for private naval dockyards.

Essentially, what this grand plan was doing was to establish a threshold for the city's expansion outwards, at the same time containing and delimiting the pressure on to the spaces of the lagoon, with the aim of producing a stable and firmly controlled balance between land and sea. It also went some way towards meeting the demand for urban growth at a time when there was a serious 'housing shortage',[54] since its pur-pose was to create possibilities for property investment in the marginal districts. In fact, in its turn Sabbadino's plan was linked to the programmes for large-scale territorial development elaborated by the Serenissima at this same time, and assigned mainly to the *provveditori sopra i beni inculti* (body concerned with agriculture), set up definitively in 1556, and engaged in the first great reclamation programme for the territory of Monselice from 1557. In other words, the urban space, the shores of the lagoon, and the vast agricultural hinterland, now all became the objects of an overall

programme. Sabbadino's plan, and the territorial projects promoted by the magis-tracy, were not only complementary, but should be seen as one single overarching scheme to accomplish the humanistic idea of the perfect city-republic, an 'image of the earth . . . in the midst of the ocean sea', 'between two elements suspended' in per-fect equilibrium. Carried to perfection, like a completed work of art, expanded just as much as the outward pull demanded – 'whence assorted persons are seen here, different in mien, in custom and in tongue'[55] – rational in its functioning, set between land now once more as fertile as in the age of gold, and the sea beneath her own dominion, the *forma urbis* was to be a fitting mirror of the republic's own perfection.

There can be no doubt that this concerted planning activity was directly related to the publication in 1556 of Barbaro's commen-tary on the *Ten Books* of Vitruvius, which was linked in its turn to a whole series of further works exploring the instruments and limits of the *res aedificatoria*: Barbaro's volume announced the forthcoming *Libro delle fortificazioni* by Giovan Jacopo Leonardi. But it also announced that 'a book will soon be appearing concerning private houses, written and illustrated by Palladio'.[56] For his part, Barbaro, the editor of the commentary on Vitruvius, was also engaged on works of mechanics and gnomonics, mentioned by Doni.[57] Thus the programmes under way were given theo-retical underpinning by intense debate on the nature and resources of architecture,

Cristoforo Sabbadino, plan for Venice, 1557.
Venice, Archivio di stato.

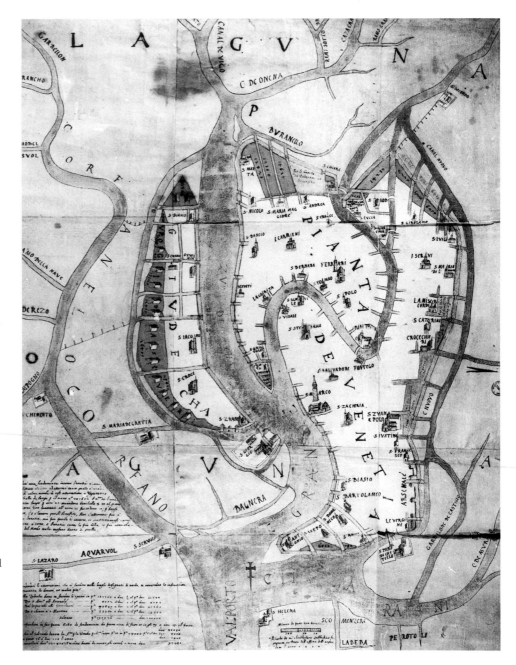

though not without calls for prudence and a cautious assessment of the nature of the relations between *res publica* and *res aedificatoria*.

Between 1557 and 1558, Francesco Marcolini published two successive editions of a history of the origins of Venice by a well-known nobleman and politician, Nicolò Zen, a friend of Barbaro's and a fellow student in Vitruvian studies.[58] Here Zen elaborated a sort of fable concerning the true relations between the hallowed Venice of the earliest times – sole fount of all legitimation – and the Antique. Amidst all the countless physical and spiritual *ruine et inondationi* caused by the corruption and fall of the empire and of Roman civilization – according to Zen – the earliest Venice of the lagoon, the descendant of the righteous Rome of the republic and not of the tyrannical Rome of the empire, had been the 'ark of the ancient seed', the only touchstone that could truly legitimate, censure, foster or condemn the multifarious forms of return to the ancient world. In Venice too, at a very early date, certain powerful men, private patrons, had begun to build 'superb palazzi and churches', though these had been abandoned once people became ensnared by the false promises of a foreign prince. Those austere members of the nobility, who had remained the true 'seed of the Antique', had freedom as their supreme goal, resolving 'to abandon the custom of building palaces and magnificent habitations . . . in order to attain greater equality and parity; . . . so as not to be obliged to overwhelm one another; . . . so that all habitations might be equal, of the same size and with similar decoration, as we still see today'.[59] The Venice of the earliest times had therefore foresworn immoderate demonstrations of private pomp. Thus it was not rank provincial ignorance which had prevented the private citizens of early Venice from decking out their palazzi in Roman-style grandiosity, but sheer native-born austerity.

In a word, while Ca' Corner was being built at S. Maurizio, and the foundations of Ca' Grimani were being laid at S. Luca – but also while Barbaro was offering the public his own interested interpretation of the foundations of ancient architecture – the authoritative voice of Nicolò Zen could be heard calling for a brake to be put on the private commissioning of works of family self-celebration: any display of magnificence was the exclusive prerogative of the state. This stance stung Francesco Sansovino into elaborating an opposing legitimizing theory – no doubt on his father's account – which also emerges from a passage in Vasari, but which was finally made explicit in the *Venetia nobilissima* of 1581.[60] Thus positive austerity, rather than mere prudence, was once more the order of the day in private architecture; not only was it widely adhered to, but, at a later date, it found expression in commissions of paradigmatic importance, such as the building of doge Leonardo Donà's palazzo on the Fondamente Nuove (1610), of which we shall say more later.

It was the debate on Vitruvius, and collaboration with Daniele Barbaro, which enabled Palladio's ideas on the architectural reinstatement of the Antique to find a foothold in mid-sixteenth-century Venice: this was an acceptance which was in some way problematical, disputed and hard-won. In 1554 Andrea Palladio took part unsuccessfully in the competition for the post of *proto al Sal*, and it was not until 28 September 1570 that he succeeded Sansovino as architect of the Serenissima. His plans for the Rialto bridge were rejected, and he was never given much scope in the sphere of public architecture, even if he was called upon several times to give opinions and consultations, and if Jacopo Contarini was to ask him for a project for arms and artillery depots at the Arsenal, which were never implemented. Furthermore, although he designed various aristocratic city dwellings, Palladio was never to see any of them become reality: instead, that same patrician clientele gave him commissions for villas on the Mainland, then in the throes of a radical agricultural transformation.

In fact, Palladio's task in Venice was to be the renovation of her great religious architecture – and hence of her image of public *pietas*, as we shall see – and here he tested and codified his main ideas for the reinstatement of classical greatness. Nor is it any coincidence that the patriarch Vincenzo Diedo's invitation to design the facade of S. Pietro di Castello (1558) – completed much later, probably not in accordance with the original plan – appears to

have been brokered and vouched for by Daniele and Marcantonio Barbaro: Palladio was now seen as the potentially suitable interpreter of a later, more mature phase of the transformation under way in Venetian architectural culture, consistent with the recent upsurge in Vitruvian studies. Indeed, it was these same studies which lay at the root of the unexpected solution elaborated by Palladio in 1560–1 for the convent complex of the Lateran branch of the Augustinian Regular Canons at the Convento della Carità, swayed as they were by the influence of 'Romanizing' circles. Here the functions of a convent, namely, of an institution with specifically medieval origins, were distributed within the space of a grandiose reconstruction of the 'house of the Ancients', extensively illustrated in the second of his *Quattro Libri*. Much of Palladio's building was badly damaged by fire in 1630, but the overall conception is known to us: the entrance next to the church was treated as a tall, imposing Corinthian atrium, at the sides of whose arcades two *tablina* housed the sacristy and chapter-house, from which an oval staircase led to the upper storeys. This entrance space led into the cloisters, interpreted as a peristyle with three superimposed orders – Doric, Ionic and Corinthian – while the spacious rectangular refectory was situated behind the arm facing the atrium. Palladio's concern for architectural 'truth' is evident in the Doric frieze, with its bucrania, paterae and festoons, but no alternating triglyphs because, as Temanza observed,

Andrea Palladio, cloister of the convent of the Carità.

Andrea Palladio, refectory in the monastery of
S. Giorgio Maggiore.

Andrea Palladio, facade of the church of S. Francesco della Vigna.

the corresponding ceiling did not have beams, but vaulting. Palladio also sought to combine grandiosity of style with a judicious eye to the congregation's economic resources, using costly Istrian stone only for the bases and capitals of the columns, the imposts of the arches of the staircases, and door and window frames, as Vasari's commentary on the work was quick to observe. The careful adaptation of techniques to the particular nature of the Venetian subsoil was clearly reflected in the idea of having the cellars placed beneath the refectory, 'built in the manner customarily employed for cisterns, to prevent the water seeping in'.[61]

Palladio's project for the refectory of S. Giorgio Maggiore (1560–2) has certain similarities with the building of the Carità. A little later – the project for S. Pietro di Castello having been put into abeyance because of the death of the patriarch Vincenzo Diedo – the new commission for the facade of S. Francesco della Vigna, on which Sansovino was no longer working, finally gave Palladio an opportunity to design a work of architecture that was not tucked away in some secluded corner of a monastic complex, but was visible to the city at large.

It was Giovanni Grimani who invited Palladio to redesign both the facade and corresponding inner wall of S. Francesco, though the latter was never built; he also tied its execution by his heirs in with ownership of the palazzo in S. Maria Formosa in case of his death.[62] By 1565 work was already under way on the facade, conceived as a juxtaposition of two orders: the front of a prostyle temple – with a major order corresponding to the nave, and four half-columns supporting the entablature and pediment – was superimposed upon a wall surface with six smaller half-columns and two pilaster strips, also supporting an entablature, and two half-pediments on the two side wings. This device was undoubtedly intended as an overt piece of 'ancient' triumphalism contrasting with Sansovino's austere space behind it; indeed, as a polemical statement explained by Palladio's convictions concerning the architecture of Christian churches, in open disagreement with those who, while 'guided by the best intentions', could not 'but be blamed somewhat . . . for not having also tried to build them according to that finer and more noble form which our state requires'. This statement was duly parried by the disdainful silence of Jacopo's son concerning Palladio's involvement at S. Francesco, a silence which was only later made good by seventeenth-century additions to *Venetia città nobilissima*.[63]

Furthermore, the bas-relief with an eagle and the motto *renovabitur* in the roundel in the centre of the tympanum may well provide the key to the implications of Palladio's work. If the inscription and the emblem undoubtedly allude to the call for renewal of psalm 104, and if the eagle is the symbol of Christ and Divine Wisdom, it is also the emblem both of John the Evangelist – the patron saint of the cardinal who commissioned the work – and of Grimani's patriarchal see of Aquileia. Thus in S. Francesco della Vigna – the place where St. Mark had had a famous vision on his way from Aquileia to Rome, according to Venetian legend – cardinal Grimani, the incumbent, in Venice's name, of the most ancient patriarchal see founded by the evangelist, was proclaiming and sanctioning the triumphal return to, and transcending of, the 'true' form of the Antique in Christian architecture through the work of Palladio.[64]

The idea put forward in S. Francesco reached full maturity in the Benedictine church of S. Giorgio Maggiore. After having made preliminary studies, Palladio was working on a wooden model of it as early as the end of 1565. The Serenissima had recently acknowledged the resolutions of the Council of Trent (22 July 1564), and Palladio's new church was a key example of an architectural space specifically conceived in terms of the revitalized liturgical and devotional forms they advocated. Looking back to the early Christian basilicas where, in Palladio's own words, 'the choir was fittingly placed around the altar, and the remaining space was left free for the congregation',[65] the choir at S. Giorgio was situated behind the high altar, separate from but communicating with the main body of the church, whose space was thus available for use by the worshipping public. The high altar accordingly stood on steps, with the side ones clearly subordinated to it. Palladio designed the church as a vast

Andrea Palladio, S. Giorgio Maggiore, facade.

rectangular space crossed by a transept ending in apses, and roofed with a high dome. The nave is separated from the two aisles by piers with composite half-columns on high pedestals, and the aisles themselves have Corinthian half-columns without pedestals, forming a solemn *all'antica* basilican space, as Palladio himself described it. The chancel is treated as an extension of the nave; an opening divided into three by two pairs of Corinthian columns leads from it into the monks' choir in the apse, lit by windows with pediments which are alternately triangular and curved, interpolated by niches with statues. The classical solemnity of the interior is echoed on the facade, which is treated with the typically Palladian scheme of a classical temple front with columns and tympana (another idea by Palladio for a free-standing pronaos in front of the church was never realized).

The facade was completed much later, between 1601 and 1611. In 1609, possibly at Palladio's own request, doge Leonardo Donà ordered the pulling down of some buildings which still bordered the space in front of it, partially obscuring its view; as a result, the architecture of S. Giorgio was fully to perform its function of defining the expanse of lagoon in front of piazza San Marco as an 'embellished piazza' – of water.

Palladio's new church now clearly constituted an architectural symbol deliberately conceived in terms of the dignity of its site and the ducal rituals associated with it: as the point of arrival of one of the main

Andrea Palladio, S. Giorgio Maggiore, nave seen from the entrance.

'triumphal progresses' taken by the doge and Signoria, S. Giorgio Maggiore was a new embodiment of public *pietas*. Palladio's style was therefore inevitably called upon to give architectural form to the city's triumph over death when, with the terrible plague of 1576, a decision was taken to build a church to Christ the Redeemer, another site for impressive new state rituals.

Palladio made two designs for this votive church: a first one 'in a round form', particularly well-received by Marcantonio Barbaro since it would have 'caused the dignity of the republic to shine forth the better',[66] and a second one on a longitudinal plan. The definitive choice in favour of the latter was made by the Senate on 15 February 1577. The first stone was laid on 3 May, and in July the first of the doge's triumphal progresses to the site was arranged, though work continued until 1588, and the church was not consecrated until 1592. Looking out over the waters of the Giudecca canal, the facade of the Redentore is set on a high base which raises it above the *riva*, with a broad staircase leading to the portal, framed between two half-columns supporting the pediment. Once again, this facade took up the theme of the *all'antica* pronaos: the central section, corresponding to the nave, takes the form of a series of overlapping temple fronts. At the two sides, the Corinthian wings and their half-pediments on half-pilasters are equivalent in depth to the six side chapels on the outside. In the interior, these open on to the aisles through tall arches between pairs of gigantic

Corinthian half-columns, with two super-imposed niches with statues between them, punctuating the ceremonial progress towards the altar. The presbytery, raised on two steps and entered through an imposing triumphal arch, opens out at the two sides into a transept with apses, and ends in a colonnaded semi-circular exedra with the deep choir of the Capuchin monks beyond.

The altar with the great bronze crucifix by Gerolamo Campagna, the focal point from the liturgical point of view, is placed at the precise centre of the crossing, with its triumphant light-filled dome, *pars celestis* of the architectural organism. The 'rectangular form' chosen by the Senate was treated by Palladio as a Latin cross plan which was highly unusual in that it was articulated by means of a triconch presbytery, a solution rare in religious architecture, though found in the repertoire of early Byzantium and not unknown in medieval Europe, and which Palladio had reinstated from among his erudite lexicon of forms with perfect awareness of the classical origins of the idea and of its recent reworkings in Renaissance architecture.

It was probably no coincidence that the choice of the Giudecca – an outlying site – for a building of such importance (S. Vidal, on the Grand Canal, had also been suggested, as had the monastero della Croce) should have been put forward by members of the patriciate such as Leonardo Donà, whose choice of an out-of-the-way site will be discussed in due course. Together with the two other Palladian buildings of

above
L. Grandis, plan of the Redentore. Venice, museo Correr.

below
Andrea Palladio, facade of the church of the Zitelle.

S. Giorgio Maggiore and the Zitelle, the Redentore, by drawing attention to itself from across the waters in front of the Piazza, now extended and established the confines of the city with a powerful visual metaphor.

Apart from the uncertainties, delays and conflicts that inevitably dogged the great projects of the second half of the sixteenth century, their implementation was further bedevilled by a dramatic combination of years of war and plague, which shifted political standpoints, swallowed up a huge portion of Venice's economic and technical resources, and drastically reduced the available work force.

Taken despite those inauspicious circumstances, the decision to build the Redentore was in fact a statement of intent, as well as something of an exception at a period when many proposed projects were being halted in mid-course.

The works undertaken to celebrate the battle of Lepanto were equally untypical, limited though they were: namely, the rearrangement of the fifteenth-century gateway to the Arsenal, with a specially devised iconographical scheme, carried out while Marcantonio Barbaro was one of the *provveditori*,[67] and the layout of the Scuola del Rosario at SS Giovanni e Paolo.

In fact, after the signing of the peace between Venice and the Turks in 1573, a large part of Venice's energies was being channelled into the resumption of vast works of military architecture in the Levant – in Crete, Corfu and elsewhere, and sometimes of crucial importance for the layout

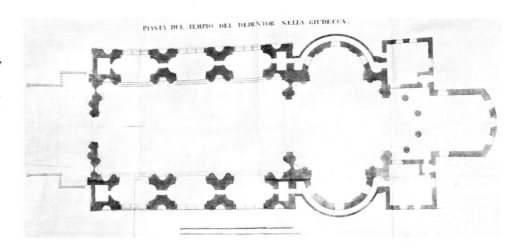

PIANTA DEL TEMPIO DEL REDENTOR NELLA GIUDECCA.

of the main urban centres – designed to act as newly-forged instruments for the reasserting of control by the 'stato da mar'. Similar undertakings occurred in Dalmatia, and work also now resumed in some places on the mainland itself.

As far as Venice was concerned, after some years of stasis, activity began again with the further enlargement of the dock-yards and military installations of the Arsenal (darsena delle Galeazze, the Galleass dockyard, 1581–5) and the long-planned radical rebuilding of the Corderie della Tana (rope factories), followed by the building of the arms depots and their annexes. The new Corderie, whose rebuild-ing was approved on 9 May 1579, was by far the most significant work undertaken in the Arsenal during the second half of the six-teenth century. The building 'of the Tana' was 910 Venetian feet long (c. 316 metres, a length dictated by the process of throwing, for the making of hawsers) and divided horizontally into three aisles by two rows of brick columns. The side sections had originally had wooden lofts for storing the hemp, linked by small balustraded bridges, also in wood, running across the central section. The building's utter functionality – studied by Colbert's envoys during the years when he was reorganizing the French navy – was expressed through the extreme simplification of the Tuscan order (the columns 'have none of the features of the normal architectural orders, yet they may be said to have something of the Tuscan manner', as Temanza commented),[68] the

prevalent use of brick, and the total lack of any decorative elements, in accordance with the instructions for its rebuilding passed by the Collegio in 1579, which also specified the design of the 'solid and unadorned' capitals, the articulation of the outer wall surfaces with two simple strips of Istrian stone and their crowning with a brick cornice. This functionality was confirmed and indeed accentuated by subsequent decisions taken in July 1584.[69]

The architecture of the Corderie was not the result of a unitary plan, but of the modification, when work was already under way – 'without destroying or altering any important aspect already built' – of the original officially approved project. In 1584, the vaulting originally planned for the ground-floor areas was criticized, and abandoned, in favour of absolute con-structional rigour, and the primacy of the *commodo et servitio* (convenient and serviceable) over *apparentia* (outward appearance),[70] which was apparently seen as having been too much in evidence in the first model. If a number of pointers tend to confirm the involvement of Antonio da Ponte, to whom Temanza attributed it prob-ably on a documentary basis, it also seems certain that other 'intendenti' also made their contributions, undoubtedly including Marc'Antonio Barbaro, who was *provvedi-tore all'Arsenale* between 1583 and 1585. The only work with claims to formal dis-tinction built in this context in the second half of the sixteenth century is also to be attributed to da Ponte and his circle, and

certainly not to Sanmicheli, if only for reasons of chronology: namely, the great rusticated portal triumphally marking the entrance to the Serenissima's arms depots, which might now be visited by sovereigns and diplomats, and which may be dated with certainty from 1591.

There is also information to suggest that the priority given to work on the state dockyards, and their architectural austerity, derived in part from the personal involve-ment of doge Nicolò da Ponte (1578–85). His dogeship also saw a simultaneous rekindling of interest in various aspects of the unfinished earlier programmes, largely translated into concrete decisions during the following dogeship of Pasquale Cicogna (1585–95), whom several Venetian sources present as the promoter of another positive *renovatio urbis* in the sixteenth century.[71]

From the early 1580s, attention centred mainly on the area of Piazza San Marco: the layout of the Piazza was now to be adapted to the norms of 'true' architecture, 'with dignified buildings, similar to those already there',[72] based on Sansovino's idea for its unitary reorganization already mentioned. A first model by Vincenzo Scamozzi for the Procuratie Nuove on the south side, basically in keeping with Sansovino's Library, was chosen from among others in 1582. Here too new designs were produced by Scamozzi himself, when work was already under way; the superimposition of a third Corinthian order on Sansovino's two-storey scheme, with architraved windows beneath alter-nating arched and triangular pediments,

Arsenal, portal of the Squero del Bucintoro.

Portal of the Stradal Campagna.

Arsenal, Corderie della Tana (Rope factories).

Anon., drawing of the Corderie della Tana
(Rope factories), seventeenth century. Paris,
Bibliothèque Nationale.

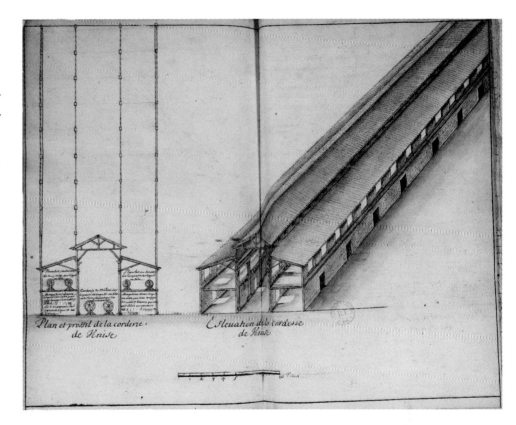

Plan et proffil de la corderie
de Venise

Eleuation de la corderie
de Venise

gave the facade of the Procuratie the requisite monumentality and grandiosity. Its relationship with the architecture of the Library, however, proved more controversial, and Scamozzi elaborated a 'correct' version of Sansovino's Ionic frieze and cornice.

Internally, Scamozzi had treated the houses of the procurators of San Marco in an intentionally original fashion: they were organized around courtyards with three orders of loggias on their short sides, and high pilaster strips along the long ones. For these houses, 'of our own invention and order', Scamozzi brought his own personal interpretation of the peculiarities of the Venetian house into play, claiming to have reintroduced 'the mode of dwelling typical of the ancient Greeks', restrained and inward-looking 'for greater *gravitas*' and political circumspection.[73]

The sensitive decisions concerning the Procuratie Nuove were made bearing the whole Marcian area closely in mind, together with its articulations and mutual relations with the surrounding space. In September 1594 a second wooden model of the entire area was being prepared, including the Ducal palace, the Piazza and Piazzetta, the Mint, the Granaries of Torranova, the Frezzeria and the Procuratie Vecchie up to the torre dell' Orologio and S. Basso, 'with the specific situations, lengths and widths of said squares, houses and buildings, and their height'.[74] It was therefore a supremely well-conceived instrument not only for evaluating the forms of the new buildings

below
Vincenzo Scamozzi(?), project for the facade of a
new Ducal palace (?), Chatsworth, Devonshire
Collection.

and the consequences of their incorporation into the Piazza, but also for reflection as to the extent, and limitations, to be given to any further pressure for renewal that might be inspired by the debates and initiatives under way. This was also the intellectual background to the famous drawing of the new Ducal palace[75] (now in Chatsworth), with its resemblances to Scamozzi's three-storey Procuratie. This design was undoubtedly inspired by the discussions following the serious fire of 1577, and the caustic comments on the 'flaws and failings' of the medieval palace advanced by Palladio. But it also owed something to the further serious criticism of the building made by Scamozzi, who had dubbed it 'extremely distorted and ugly',[76] publishing his adverse remarks unrepentantly in his *Idea dell'architettura universale*. The design put forward in the Chatsworth drawing was, of course, never implemented; but it gives the impression, confirmed by other information, of being part of a triumphally all-inclusive programme for the redefinition of the Marcian space in terms of the 'true architecture'. Moreover, it seems highly likely that Scamozzi's equally adverse criticism of the fourteenth-century Granaries of Terranova, near Sansovino's Mint, and his suggestions concerning them,[77] were tantamount to a proposal for their rebuilding, which would have completed the classicizing 'face-lift' of the frontage of the entire group of public buildings overlooking the 'basin of San Marco'. In fact, Scamozzi did receive a commission for another highly

emblematic work in the area of the Piazza, a sort of seal appended to all that had already been built there. In 1591 he was asked to lay out the antechamber of the Library for the exhibition of the antiquities donated to the state by cardinal Giovanni Grimani: the result was a severe and lucid piece of architecture, which redefined the space of Sansovino's Library, overlooking the Piazza with three large windows, which had previously housed the Marcian School of humanities. It was cardinal Giovanni himself who suggested the alternating of Ionic aedicules with pediments and niches 'in the Greek style' between Corinthian pilaster strips,[78] and he supervised the work in person until a few days before his death, on 3 October 1593. At his request, the public 'statuary' was to become one of the focal points in the presentation of the image of the Serenissima, 'in order that foreigners, after having seen the Arsenal and the other marvels of the city, might also see these antiquities set out in a public place'.[79] Here, then, Scamozzi's rigorously erudite language was merged with Grimani's classicizing line inspired by the idea of *renovation aquileiensis*.

Despite persisting periods of alternating activity and stasis, differences of opinion and rival schemes, from the 1580s here too attitudes became more incisive, with further important decisions concerning the complex of public buildings around San Marco, including those for the definitive transfer of the prisons from the ground floor of the Ducal palace, and the building

of a new prison complex on the other side of the canal, on a site which had twice been mooted as suitable for a new ducal residence between the fifteenth and sixteenth century. This choice was undoubtedly also dependent upon specifically Vitruvian considerations, recently reiterated by Palladio in his Quattro Libri.[80] But in fact the New Prisons, under construction from 1591, were built to a design by Antonio da Ponte, who was advised by the Council of Ten to take into account the suggestions of a convict serving a life sentence, one Zaccaria Briani.

The plan for this relatively uncommon theme paid close attention not only to security, but also to a series of functional problems, including ventilation, wells for water and piping for waste. The finished building was a complex consisting of the prison proper, set around a courtyard, with a small chapel for the use of the prisoners and an aerial bridge over the canal (the so called Bridge of Sighs); its outer walls were clad in powerfully expressive rusticated ashlar. The façade overlooking the waters of the Marcian basin, used for functions related to prison business, was conceived in autonomous though naturally compatible formal terms: as the headquarters of the magistracy of the Signori di Notte al Criminal, it required a solemn, awe-inspiring style, evocative of the state's powers of enforcement and repression, a sort of ideal pendant to that adopted by Sansovino for the 'prison and fortress' of gold, the Mint, which stood on an equivalent site at the other side of the Piazza and Library. The prison, too, would

Vincenzo Scamozzi, study for the juncture between the
Procuratie Nuove and Sansovino's Library. Florence, Uffizi.

have daunting rusticated walls, but articulated and distinguished by means of the symbolic language of the orders: the wall of the first floor, which housed the magistrates, had seven large windows opening up above the seven rusticated arches of the ground-floor portico. Their frames were unadorned, but they were topped by curved or triangular pediments, set between Doric half-columns, supporting an elaborate cornice with a frieze punctuated by corbels. The rooms behind had a cycle of paintings by Domenico Tintoretto, Palma Giovane, L'Aliense and Pietro Malombra, depicting the themes of Justice and Punishment, Truth and Envy, and the Crimes and Virtues.[81]

The recurrent controversies that hindered work on the Piazza were matched by a parallel and contemporary series of disputes and decisions concerning the problem of the stone bridge at Rialto. After complex discussion lasting the whole century, and the shelving of Palladio's plans – Roman in inspiration, and appropriate to a heroic model of Venice as a 'mother of many other cities'[82] – and after Scamozzi's views and project had been rejected, it was the model by the *proto al Sal*, Antonio da Ponte, which finally won the day. A bridge with a single four-centred span was a far cry from the classical solemnity of Palladio's proposals, but not entirely incompatible with early iconography;[83] da Ponte's model had a double row of shops, linked at the top, in the middle of the bridge, by two arches with rusticated Doric pillars and pediments. The foundation stone was

laid on 9 June 1588, with assorted ceremonies and public rejoicing. The definitive
replacement of the earlier wooden structure,
with its drawbridge to allow vessels to pass
through, has more than once been interpreted as a sign that the waters of the Grand
Canal were no longer used for shipping
(in fact this already appears to have been
largely the case by the end of the fifteenth
century). Perhaps more relevantly, the
new bridge now reinforced the continuity
between the commercial areas and
structures from the Piazza to the Rialto,
confirming their unitary nature and stressing their centrality. With its shops and
storerooms 'for various goods', the bridge
thus represented a focal point in the highly
symbolic system of commercial itineraries
and points for the sale of spices (the
'Speziaria' at S. Bortolomio) and of gold
(Ruga degli Oresi at Rialto, on the opposite
bank of the canal).

In other words, it proclaimed the image
of the city's commercial vitality along a
whole stretch of the Grand Canal (the previous wooden bridge had been described as
being 'so full of shops and wayfarers . . . that
every day seems to be a jubilee'),[84] and the
technical feat of its great single arch served
as a modern metaphor for the *miraculosissima civitas*: 'A great ornament to the city
and . . . a marvel for bystanders to behold'.

Meanwhile, as the two great focal points
of the space of the city-republic were being
conclusively defined, and other important
buildings were going up in the Arsenal,
consideration was also being given to a

left
Andrea Palladio, project for the Rialto bridge.
Vicenza, museo Civico.

below left
Vincenzo Scamozzi, project for the Rialto bridge.
London, RIBA.

opposite
Antonio da Ponte, Rialto bridge.

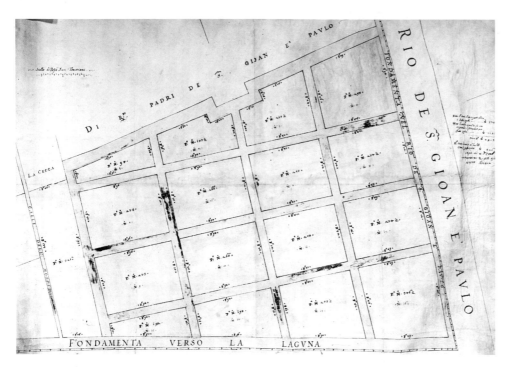

PADRI DE S. GIOAN E PAVLO

DI

LA CECCA

RIO DE S. GIOAN E PAVLO

FONDAMENTA VERSO LA LAGVNA

Project for the division of the area around the Fondamente
Nuove into lots, 1594. Venice, Archivio di stato.

resumption of Sabbadino's town plan of
1557. After private individuals had been
required to shore up various stretches of
riva, and *fondamente* had been built at
public expense along the canals and
lagoon of the Chiovere di S. Girolamo
(1586–9),[85] decisions for the building of the
Fondamente Nuove were taken between
1588 and 1590, that is, for the implementation of one part of Sabbadino's plan. In 1590
work began on the regularizing of about a
kilometre of the northern strip of the areas
between S. Giustina and S. Felice, in the
sestieri of Castello and Cannaregio. In 1594
it was decided to divide the newly-available
building land to the north of the Dominican
convent of Sti Giovanni e Paolo into lots
and, six years later, also the long adjacent
expanse as far as the then monastery of the
Crociferi (Crutched Friars), now of the
Jesuits. Lastly, in 1607, Tommaso Contin
drew up the plan for the filling in of Sacca
della Misericordia, never carried out in all
probability because of the general suspen-
sion of work caused by the plague of 1630.
As expected, this public work gave a considerable fillip to building in the area, both
of rented middle-to-upper-bracket housing,
and of owner-occupied dwellings, each on
occasions with premises for commercial
activities both indoors and out. The original
idea of creating moorings for ferries and
barges was abandoned, and a large public
charitable institution was now to be incorporated into the new urban fabric: this was
the Ospedale dei Mendicanti, which had
been under discussion in the Senate since

right
The complex of S. Lazzaro dei Mendicanti.

below right
The Quartier dei Soldati (barracks) at S. Nicolò di Lido, portal.

1594–5. Situated right next to the other large charitable institution of the Scuola Grande di S. Marco, the new complex was to house the city's homeless and destitute. It was also designed to purge the city of its 'mendicant hordes',[86] sweeping the newly embellished 'piazzas' clean of the more drastic casualties of late sixteenth-century life, with its serious famines on the mainland, and mass exodus of peasants who came literally to die in the *calli* of the Serenissima. Of the various projects put forward for the Ospizio dei Mendicanti at the Fondamente Nuove – a first temporary structure was inaugurated on 20 February 1601 – the one finally accepted was by Vincenzo Scamozzi, though he did not supervise the work in person.

A complex organism around two large four-sided cloisters, with a church on a longitudinal plan running between them, now came to occupy one portion of the recently created lots at the Fondamente Nuove, with its main facade overlooking the rio dei Mendicanti, and its north flank along the Fondamente themselves.

The buildings put up in this area, probably at least in part by the various *proti* who succeeded one another in its layout, marked another important turning-point: despite its longstanding popularity as an instrument for urbanization, further elaborated and refined in the early Renaissance (and despite the continuing presence of misleading place-names) the grouping of popular dwellings around courtyards here seems to have been finally abandoned.

In view of the fact that work had now resumed on the overall design for the city, in parallel with the formal and functional modifications to the three great focal points – San Marco, the Rialto and the Arsenal – it seems clear that the late sixteenth-century programmes had been devised to take methodical and coherent action over the entire range of urban amenities. This is strongly implied by the virtual coinciding, in time, between these works and the start of work on other state-funded undertakings, and the public support for important privately-funded buildings. The year 1589 saw the rebuilding of the Granaries of S. Biagio, near the Arsenal, together with the partial reconstruction of the biscuit bakehouses. To lessen the risk of fire, the *provveditori al Sal* had the internal staircases of the upper floors of the Fontego dei Tedeschi rebuilt in stone (1586–7). Loans were issued to fund work on the new building of the Purgo, undertaken at Santa Croce by the Guild of wool merchants, as a result of the upturn in the city's wool industry (1591).[87] At S. Nicolò del Lido some of the poverty-stricken immigrants who had poured into the city were now employed on the huge task of laying the ground for the fortress, the works of infrastructure for the street system within it, and the building of the Quartiere Grande (soldiers' barracks), discussed in some detail by Scamozzi in his theoretical writings and one of the most remarkable architectural complexes of its kind in contemporary Europe (1591–5).[88] During this same period the first stone

of the new fortified city of Palma (now Palmanova), on the eastern borders of the 'stato da terra', is also recorded as having been laid (1593).

Meanwhile, in the city itself, public *pietas* was finding expression in resumption of work on the Redentore and financing for the convent of the Capuchins; in the modest but significant work of restoration at S. Giacomo di Rialto by the *Provveditori al Sal*; but above all in backing provided for the renovation of the church and convent of S. Nicola da Tolentino (30 March 1594), a devotional centre of acknowledged and growing importance in the area of the city where the newly buoyant wool industry was centred. Significantly enough, the work was commissioned from Vincenzo Scamozzi, a rigorious interpreter of the language of public architecture.

If some sense of impending loss of status for the Serenissima was undoubtedly looming, it is also clear that the decades between the two terrible plagues of 1576 and 1630 were characterized by a powerful drive to perfect the form and self-image which the city-state had been tirelessly elaborating for herself – amidst conflict and resistance, but also with heartfelt support – in the middle of the century, when her standing as a new republican Rome was taking on physical form in the eyes of the world. A remarkable series of commemorative medals – in honour of the barracks on the Lido, the fortress of Palmanova, the churches of the Ascensione, the Redentore and S. Pietro di Castello, struck during the dogeship of

Pasquale Cicogna – emphasized the continuing value and significance attributed to this policy of great public works.

In this context, private patronage too took on a new lease of life. As we have said, during these same years Francesco Sansovino was devising a historical legitimization for private architectural magnificence. If a noble updating of tradition – in the antithetical terms of austerity and ornament – was being pursued by the Contarini degli Scrigni with the building of the palazzo on the Grand Canal, by Scamozzi, and by the Balbi with their 'casa da stazio' at S. Tomà, attributed by Temanza to Alessandro Vittoria, it is clear that the longstanding conflict between the two alternatives – between a display of 'Roman' grandeur and republican moderation – had flared up once again between the end of the sixteenth and the first years of the seventeenth century. Around 1592 Scamozzi was designing a magnificent palazzo for Federico Corner on the Grand Canal at S. Maurizio, near Sansovino's Ca' Granda. Although it was never built, because of Corner's death, the project was nonetheless significant for its pursuit of monumentality, its striving worthily to perpetuate the memory of the man who had commissioned it. It was noteworthy not only for its vast size, its courtyard, loggias and gardens, and the expedients used to enhance the grandeur of the ceremonial entrance from the Canal, with the high triumphal entrance 'da mar'; but even more so for its blending of private and public languages, suggested by

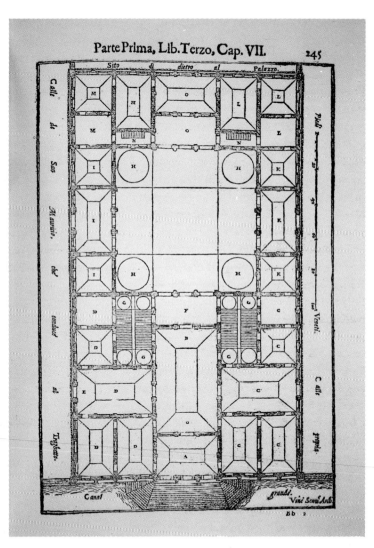

The fortress of Palmanova, plan, seventeenth century.
Venice, Biblioteca nazionale marciana.

Vincenzo Scamozzi, ground plan of the palazzo designed for Federico
Corner, from the *Idea dell'architettura universale*, 1615.

Scamozzi through echoes, on the facade, of the architecture of the Procuratie Nuove.

Such attitudes were repudiated soon afterwards by the private residence built for himself by doge Leonardo Donà (1606–12). That a doge should have chosen the peripheral area of the Fondamente Nuove for his new 'casa da stazio' during his years in high office was not without significance. Equally telling was his choice of a capable *proto* rather than a famous architect, and the fact that his residence then took on the unassuming architectural shape criticized by his own relatives 'as not having the form of a palace'.[89] Its main facade over the rio dei Santi Apostoli is extremely simple, a vast area of plastered wall, framed by corner rustication and a tall base, also rusticated (further extended to the buildings annexed to it, used for commercial purposes), and a severe *Serliana* with a Tuscan order. The Istrian stone is completely unadorned, and the second facade on to the Fondamente Nuove is even more restrained, with a large *Serliana* with pillars rather than the columns which define the central opening in the one on the main facade.

The private residence of the doge who had urged the demolition of the buildings that continued to impede the view of Palladio's facade of S. Giorgio Maggiore from the Piazza, and who was to be buried there, thus set an example encouraging other aristocratic patrons to commission buildings of a severity which, throughout the sixteenth century, had been typical of the palazzi of doge Andrea Gritti, the ambassador Pietro Zen and Leonardo Moro, and which Nicolò Zen had interpreted in the form of an apologue.

Doge Donà made a further gesture of austerity by using the open space adjacent to his property as a 'timber yard', with a storage shed on rusticated Istrian stone pillars: this was another way of emphasizing the distinction between what was proper to institutions, which required the magnificence of the classical style, and what was admissible and appropriate for wealthy private individuals, whose duty was to engage in public initiatives which would 'create the city', bringing the *forma urbis* to due perfection.

1 M. Sanudo, *I diarii, op. cit.*

2 F. Yates, *Astraea – the Imperial Theme in the Sixteenth Century*, London 1975.

3 V. Pellegrino, *De privilegiis, op. cit.*, p. 358.

4 'Venetiis architecturae sculpturaeque intermortuum decus primum excitavit': F. Sansovino and G. Martinioni, *Venetia, op. cit.*, p. 111.

5 G. Vasari, *Le vite, op. cit.*, VII, p. 501.

6 A.S.V., Senato Terra, reg. 28, f. 166.

7 M. Sanudo, *I diarii, op. cit.*, LVII, col. 151.

8 *Il Forestiere illuminato, op. cit.*, p. 57.

9 F. Sansovino, *Delle cose notabili che sono in Venetia, op. cit.*, pp. 23–4; G. Vasari, *Le vite, op. cit.*, VII, pp. 504–5; P. Contarini, *Argo vulgar, op. cit.*, p. a iii.

10 V. Fausto, *Orationes quinque*, Venice 1551, p. 14; A. Palladio, *I quattro libri dell'architettura*, Venice 1570, I, p. 5.

11 S. Serlio, *Tutte l'opere, op. cit.*, pp. 153–4.

12 F. Sansovino, *Delle cose, op. cit.*, p. 23; F. Sansovino and G. Martinioni, *Venetia, op. cit.*, p. 309.

13 A. Palladio, *I quattro libri, op. cit.*, I, p. 5.

14 See *Bessarione e l'umanesimo*, Venice exhibition catalogue, Naples 1994 and bibliography.

15 F. Sansovino, *L'arte oratoria*, Venice 1546, p. 52.

16 F. Sansovino, *Delle cose, op. cit.*, p. 21; F. Sansovino and G. Martinioni, *Venetia, op. cit.*, p. 309.

17 N. Barbarigo, *Vita di Andrea Gritti doge di Venezia*, Venice 1793, pp. 103–4.

18 A.S.V., Notarile, Atti V. Maffei, b. 8110, 1556, doc. 2 May, f. 422.

19 A.S.V., Senato Terra, reg. 37, f. 63v, 18.5.1550.

20 F. Sansovino and G. Martinioni, *Venetia, op. cit.*, p. 364.

21 F. Sansovino, *Delle cose, op. cit.*, p. 24.

22 See also the previous chapter.

23 Museo Civico, Vicenza, drawing D. 18.

24 F. Sansovino, *Delle cose, op. cit.*, p. 24; F. Sansovino and G. Martinioni, *Venetia, op. cit.*, p. 286.

25 *Ibid.*, p. 388.

26 Other examples of porticoed *rive* used as loading and unloading points beneath *case da
stazio* are still visible, such as at the *traghetto*
at Murano (San Canciano) and the one at
San Felice, neither of which is any longer in
operation.

27 F. Sansovino and G. Martinioni, *Venetia,
op. cit.*, p. 388.

28 *Ibid.*

29 *Ibid.*

30 Here the expression from Francesco
Sansovino's *L'arte oratoria, op. cit.*, p. 52, is
used intentionally: 'We may say that they are,
as it were, places of memory.'

31 G. A. Oliva, *Ioanni Cornelio, Praetori
Praefectoque Optimo et Humanissimo*, Venice
1567.

32 F. Sansovino and G. Martinioni, *Venetia,
op. cit.*, p. 387.

33 *Ibid.*, p. 382.

34 G. Vasari, *Le vite, op. cit.*, VII, p. 507.

35 'Memorandum' of Francesco Zorzi, 1.4.1535,
in A. Foscari and M. Tafuri, *L'armonia e i
conflitti. La chiesa de San Francesco della
Vigna nella Venezia del Cinquecento*, Turin
1983, pp. 208–11.

36 *Ibid.*

37 A.S.V., Notarile, Atti V. Maffei, b. 8131,
26.10.1561, f. 551v and enclosures ff.
533v–534r; doc. 1.12.1561, f. 666v.

38 D. Barbaro, *I dieci libri dell'architettura di M.
Vitruvio tradutti et commentati*, Venice 1556,
p. 163.

39 F. Sansovino, *L'arte oratoria, op. cit.*, p. 48.

40 A.S.V., Senato Terra, reg. 25, f. 70r.

41 B.N.M.V., mss. it. cl. VII, 518 (=7884), f. 41r;
S. Casali, *Annali della tipografia veneziana
di Francesco Marcolini da Forlì*, Forlì 1811;
V. Fontana, 'Tecnica, scienza e architettura',
in *Architettura e utopia nella Venezia del
Cinquecento*, catalogue of the Venice exhibition, Milan 1980, p. 190.

left
Alessandro Vittoria, palazzo Balbi on
the Grand Canal.

below
Palazzo Donà at the Fondamente Nuove.

42 S. Serlio, *Tutte l'opere, op. cit.*, pp. 177–8.

43 N. Zeno, *Dell'origine, op. cit.*, p. 29.

44 A.S.V., Consiglio dei Dieci, Secreta, reg. 4, doc. 9.11.1536, ff. 131 *et seq.*

45 F. Sansovino, *Delle cose, op. cit.*, p. 28.

46 There appear to have been close family ties between the Corner, the Zen, to whom Serlio was particularly close, and the Priuli, with whom he stayed during this period in Venice; see also A.S.V., M. Barbaro, *Arbori de'Patrizi, op. cit.*, and the present writer's *Dall'arabico a Venezia, op. cit., passim.*

47 T. Temanza, *Vite dei più celebri architetti e scultori veneziani che fiorirono nel secolo XVI*, Venice 1778, pp. 667–8.

48 *Ibid.*; A. Avena, *L'Arco dei Gavi ricostruito dal Commune di Verona*, Verona 1932, p. 20.

49 Vincenzo Grimani, 'frater et locumtenens generalis . . . D. Joannis Grimani miseratione divina Patriarche Aquileiensis': A.S.V., Notarile, Atti V. Maffei, b. 8105, 4.7.1555, f. 505r; procurator for building activities: *ibid.*, b. 8119, 1558, f. 486r. These are just two of the most significant among many other references.

50 For the patriarchal documents issued 'in nostro palatio apud S. Mariam Formosam Venetiis', see for example A.S.V., Notarile, Atti V. Maffei, b. 8104, 1554, ff. 42v, 45v, 72v; b. 8105, 1554, ff. 438r, 441r; b. 8114, 1557, ff. 2v, 26r, 116v, 117v, 122r, 138v, 170r, 174r, 175; b. 8116, 1558, ff. 31v, 32v, 136v, 137r; b. 8118, 1558, ff. 109r, 120r, 272r, 309r; b. 8145, 1565, ff. 26v–27v. For the *palazzo* itself, apart from the bibliography quoted at the end of this volume, see B.M.C.V., mss. P.D.C. 677/iv; A.S.V., Savi alle Decime, bb. 151, 143, 855; Notarile, Atti V. Maffei, bb. 8121–7, 8144. The present author is currently engaged in further study of the subject. For Muzio Sforza's evidence, see M. A. Michiel, *Notizia d'opera di disegno*, ed. G. Frizzoni, Bologna 1884, pp. 192–3.

51 Apart from the genealogies in A.S.V., M. Barbaro, *Arbori de'Patrizi, op. cit.*, see the *Orationi fatte al Ser.^{mo} Prencipe di Venetia Marino Grimani . . . accolte e postillate per Antonio Maria Consalvi*, Venice 1597.

52 G. Candido, *Commentariorum Aquileiensium libri octo, op. cit.*

53 *Sacca*: 'a broad stretch of canal', G. Boerio, *Dizionario del dialetto veneziano*, Venice 1856.

54 An expression found in stipulations of tithes made by owners of property in Venice in the sixteenth century.

55 M. A. Sabellico, *Del sito, op. cit.*, p. 43; F. Sansovino and G. Martinioni, *Venetia, op. cit.*, p. 4.

56 D. Barbaro, *I dieci libri, op. cit.*, p. 31.

57 A. F. Doni, *La seconda libraria*, Venice 1552, p. 86.

58 N. Zeno, *Dell'origine, op. cit.*

59 *Ibid.*, pp. 190–5.

60 G. Vasari, *Le vite, op. cit.*, VII, pp. 502–3; F. Sansovino and G. Martinioni, *Venetia, op. cit.*, p. 382.

61 A. Palladio, *I quattro libri, op. cit.*, II, p. 29.

62 A.S.V., Notarile, Atti V. Maffei.

63 A. Palladio, *I quattro libri, op. cit.*, IV, p. 3; F. Sansovino and G. Martinioni, *Venetia, op. cit.*, p. 52.

64 See again A. Palladio, *I quattro libri, op. cit.*, IV, p. 3.

65 *Ibid.*, IV, p. 10.

66 Cited in G. G. Zorzi, *Le chiese e i ponti di Andrea Palladio*, Vicenza 1966, p. 321.

67 A.S.V., Segretario alle Voci, Pregadi, reg. 5, f. 24, 1.7.1583; 30.6.1585.

68 T. Temanza, *Vite, op. cit.*, p. 506.

69 A.S.V., Collegio, Notatori, reg. 43, f. 191, 12.5.1579: Patroni e Provveditori all'Arsenal, b. 17; Senato Mar, filza (file) 17, 17.7.1584.

70 *Ibid.*

71 F. Sansovino and G. Martinioni, *Venetia, op. cit.*, p. 626; E. Piccolomini, *Oratio in funere Paschalis Ciconiae*, Venice 1595; E. Piccolomini, *De laudibus Paschalis Ciconiae . . . oratio altera*, Venice 1597; *Il Forestiere illuminato, op. cit.*, pp. 199–200.

72 F. Sansovino and G. Martinioni, *Venetia, op. cit.*, p. 619.

73 V. Scamozzi, *Dell'idea, op. cit.*, part I, pp. 242–3.

74 In F. Barbieri, *Vincenzo Scamozzi*, Vicenza 1952, pp. 128, 154.

75 Trustees of the Chatsworth Settlement.

76 V. Scamozzi, *Dell'idea, op. cit.*, part I, p. 58.

77 *Ibid.*, part I, p. 176.

78 T. Temanza, *Vite, op. cit.*, p. 438.

79 A.S.V., Proc. de Supra, b. 68, proc. 171, fasc. 3/1.

80 A. Palladio, *I quattro libri, op. cit.*, III, p. 31.

81 A. M. Zanetti, *Descrizione di tutte le pubbliche pitture della città di Venezia*, Venice 1733, p. 148.

82 A. Palladio, *I quattro libri, op. cit.*, III, p. 25.

83 See T. L. Donaldson, *Architectura Numismatica*, Chicago 1966 (reprint of the work published in London in 1859), nn. LXII–LXIII, pp. 241–3.

84 A. Calmo, *Le lettere*, ed. V. Rossi, Turin 1888.

85 A.S.V., Santo Terra, regg. 56–60, 1586–90; especially: reg. 57, f. 206v, 7.11.1587; reg. 59, ff. 46v–47r, 22.5.1585.

86 *Ibid.*, Maggior Consiglio, deliberazioni (resolutions), reg. 32, f. 101, 17.9.1595.

87 A.S.V., Senato Terra, regg. 56 (1585–6) to 65 (1595), *passim.*

88 *Ibid.*, regg. 61–5 (1591–5), filza (file) 138; Provveditori alle Fortezze, b. 68.

89 Quoted in M. Tafuri, *Venice, op. cit.*, p. 188.

BAROQUE VENICE: THE AGE OF BALDASSARE LONGHENA

THE seventeenth century was the age of Venice's triumph over death, with the last great plague in her history; it saw the final elaboration of the myth of her endurance over time, her political clash with papal Rome, and her adamant assertion of autonomy vis-à-vis the Church; lastly, it saw the Serenissima locked in ferocious military engagement with the Ottoman empire, the loss of Crete, but also the brief reconquest of Morea, and the illusion at least of the retaining, indeed of the partial regeneration, of the 'stato da mar'.

Just as the sixteenth century had ended in a sense triumphally for Venice, with the creation of the myth of Lepanto and the heroic virtues of a proud aristocracy of naval commanders – Venier, Barbarigo and others – so the seventeenth ended with the creation of the myth of the hero of the Peloponnese, Francesco Morosini, made doge in 1688, and with the perpetuation, in the eyes of many, of the Renaissance myths of Venetian greatness.

Architecturally speaking, during the seventeenth century such myths were expressed in terms of the great publicly-commissioned works built in the city; and here the field was dominated by one man and his works, namely Baldassare Longhena, *proto* of San Marco like Jacopo Sansovino before him, and his church of the Salute.

The original vow to dedicate a new church to the Virgin dates from 22 October 1630, when the plague was still raging; this church was to be visited by the doge, in perpetuity, on the occasion of the ending of the terrible epidemic, proclaimed a little more than one year later, on 28 November 1631.

The choice of site fell upon the church of the Trinità, near the Dogana da mar (maritime customs house), then served by the Somascans. A random set of circumstances caused the laying of the first stone, originally planned for 25 March 1631 (and indeed duly celebrated at San Marco on that date) to be delayed until the following 1 April, when it took place in the absence of the doge, Niccolò Contarini, who was on his death bed.

In the meantime, after a temporary wooden church had been built on a cruciform plan,[1] a committee was examining the eleven projects presented; in June, it chose the one by the young Longhena, in preference to the model made by Antonio Smeraldi, the son of Francesco, known as Fracao, in collaboration with Giovanni Battista Rubertini.

The decision in favour of Longhena seems to have been based on a variety of reasons. At the age of a little over thirty, Longhena had already given proof of his talents with the rebuilding of the cathedral at Chioggia, an important event in early seventeenth-century Venice, since it proved to be crucial to the re-establishment of good relations between the republic and the Vatican.

The decision to rebuild this cathedral was taken on 14 September 1629; it was to be based on a Palladian model, a version of S. Pietro di Castello, an episcopal type deriving formally from sixteenth-century tradition, with the exception of the roofing

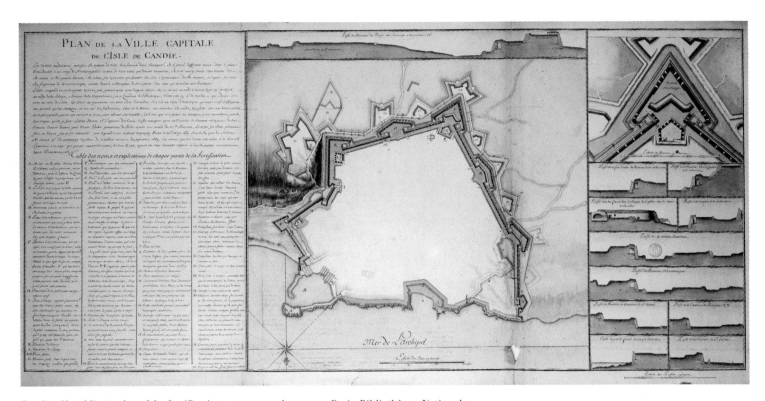

Candia (Heraklion), plan of the fortifications, seventeenth century. Paris, Bibliothèque Nationale.

of the nave. Here Longhena's sensitivity to
the surrounding urban fabric had proved
conclusive. The *soprintendenti* (supervisors)
had originally decided to rebuild the pre-
existing cathedral, which would have
allowed for a partial and more economical
reuse of the foundations, but here the young
architect's opinion had prevailed: 'it was
better to have the church facing on to the
Piazza, as indeed was recommended by
the *proto*, Signor Baldissera *quondam*
Melchisedec'.

Despite the adverse judgment of the
podestà Pietro Contarini, who saw the
building as 'a concept so vast and cumbersome that bringing it into being will be no
simple undertaking, since, truth to toll, the
decision was taken purely upon the basis
of the attractive appearance of the model'
(1629),[2] work had in fact proceeded thanks
partly to a generous papal contribution,
requested by the republic itself. In 1625
Urban VIII had agreed a grant of two hundred thousand *scudi* for ten years, drawing
on the Jesuits' original revenues in the
Veneto, with the revealing proviso that the
overseeing of the building, originally secu-
lar, should now become a joint affair, with
the involvement of the bishop. This initial
incident caused Longhena to be identified
as the author of a building which symbolized the settling of the disagreements with
the Holy See.

Shortly afterwards, with the decision
in his favour made on 13 June 1631, work
began on the most important architectural
undertaking in seventeenth-century

The seventeenth-century customs house and the church of
S. Maria della Salute by Baldassarre Longhena.

Venice, and one of the most momentous
in the whole panorama of the European
Baroque.

The implications which the republic
wanted its second great votive church to
convey were unambiguous, as was the set
of instructions given to its architect. First
and foremost, it was stressed that the church
was to be the visual symbol of the rebirth
of the city-state. It was no accident that the
date chosen for the ceremony marking the
start of work on the church should have
been 25 March, the Annunciation. *Unde
origo inde salus* – whence the origin, thence
the salvation and health – was inscribed in
the floor at the centre of the main body of
the building, in reference to its symbolic
meaning as a symbol of rebirth. The church
was not to proclaim merely the triumph
over the recent crisis, but also to embody
the vigour of this resurgence and prefigure
the city's sempiternal fortune. Hence the
request for pomp and magnificence, for the
'majesty of a great and famous structure', in
complete contrast with the specifications
formulated in 1576 for the Redentore, which
had prescribed only the sobriety and sub-
stantiality appropriate for a 'godly church'.[3]

The republic required the architect to
design a church which the eye could take in
at a glance right from the entrance, with the
lighting being evenly diffused accordingly:
this too was in marked contrast with the
Redentore, where the varying quality of the
light helped to distinguish the three main
spaces of nave, transept and choir. But no
direct preference was expressed concern-

240

Baldassarre Longhena, S. Maria della Salute, nave.

Salute, internal view of the main dome.

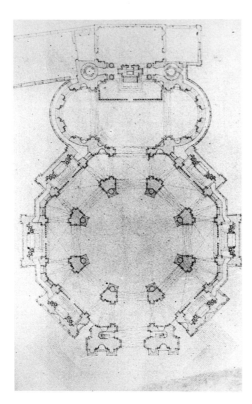

P. Paroni, plan of S. Maria della Salute.
Venice, museo Correr.

ing the nature of the plan, whether longitudinal or central. The Senate restricted itself to pointing briefly to the potential advantages of both types, while observing that a circular form would be an absolute novelty for the city. Longhena duly elaborated a church 'in forma di rotunda' (in the form of a rotunda), stressing its innovative aspects. 'Desired by so many', he claimed, the new church on a central plan would come to be seen as an extraordinary novelty, complementary to Palladio's church of some fifty years earlier, and hence as another great opportunity to bring Venetian architecture up to date. Inevitably, Longhena therefore came to be referred to by some as the 'new Palladio' (1644).[4]

The physical and technical conditions of its site gave this undertaking quite exceptional importance: the celebrated laying of almost one million two hundred thousand piles of oak, elm and larch required a concerted process of organization, and supplies, which constituted the much-vaunted testbed for the equally challenging resumption of work at the Arsenal dockyards, which also came up against the problem of technical resources.[5]

The building's symbolic allusions were highly complex. Longhena interpreted its circular form in such a way as to emphasize its similarity with the form of a crown, which he himself linked to the cult of the Virgin; in Christian iconography it is a symbol of victory, a promise of life eternal, readily transposable to ideas of renascence and regeneration such as had accompanied

the debates concerning the votive church. These ideas had also proved perfectly consonant with Longhena's choice of an octagonal plan for the central body: like an early Christian baptismal font, the octagon was to evoke the 'eighth day' of creation, presented as a geometrical configuration of the number of the new beginning through resurrection. In this way, the glorification of the Virgin, and a fresh start for Venice, were jointly represented in the geometry of the architectural forms. There were other evident parallels, too: for example the church of the Salute, on its high podium, preceded by a grandiose flight of fifteen steps, alludes to the temple of Solomon (although Longhena's project originally envisaged only thirteen, implying the subsequent involvement of some expert in Christian symbolism).

In point of fact, the reference to the temple of Solomon is evident in more ways than one. Nor is it coincidental: at the end of the sixteenth century a psalm had been composed hailing Venice – the bastion against the Turks – as 'an earthly New Jerusalem, established by God on high as a safe haven and tabernacle for His chosen people'.[6]

Furthermore, the great domed church symbolizing the Serenissima's resurgence in the seventeenth century – a fittingly high-flown tribute to her destiny – inevitably appeared as a reprise, an expanded evocation, of that first, so much more modest dome, a metaphorical reiteration of the venerable emblem of emergent Venice still to be seen at S. Giacomo di Rialto.

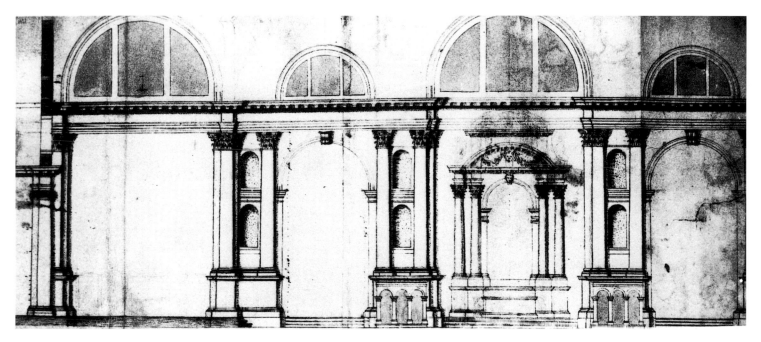

Church of the Scalzi, longitudinal section.
Venice, museo Correr.

right
Vincenzo Coronelli, plan of the church of
S. Maria del Pianto, seventeenth century.

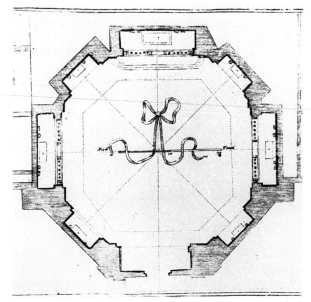

As we have said, the main body of the Salute is octagonal in plan, consisting of a central space roofed with a dome and lantern (buttressed from the outside by scrolls and supported on eight pilasters), with a broad ambulatory running around it. The main dome was a source of great and justifiable pride: in terms of statics, Longhena claimed that it had been treated in a totally unprecedented way, unknown to architects either classical or modern, and that it was based on supports so solid that they could hold a new Rialto bridge.[7]

Six chapels open off the ambulatory, as does the chancel, situated directly opposite the main door, with apses at the two ends on the Palladian pattern. The sanctuary too is roofed with a smaller dome, and separated from the rectangular choir by a high vault supported on great columns of Greek marble from Pola, Roman remains and emblems of magnificence reborn. All in all, the Salute is a complex architectural structure, whose functioning was conceived in terms of the solemn ceremonial to be enacted within it; a space of liturgical comings and goings connected to the ducal rituals culminating in the sanctuary, a distinct and autonomous space characterized by its side apses and smaller dome.

On the exterior, the main facade on the side of the octagon overlooking the canal rises on a high base; it has three intercolumniations formed by four composite columns, framing two superimposed niches with statues at the sides, and the main ceremonial entrance in the centre,

'most majestic and commodious'.[8] The two 'secret' side-doors were intended by Longhena to be used by the congregation, which would thus enter the church through their separate entrances. The main facade is flanked by two lesser ones, though more distinctive than the four others corresponding to the free sides of the basic geometrical figure, which are treated in a far more restrained way.

The forms displayed at the Salute might be described as in some sense similar to the rousing style of Monteverdi, a brilliantly theatrical statement which left its mark on the whole urban landscape around it. Not by chance did one contemporary observer – a member of the order of the Somascans to whom the church had been entrusted (in competition with the Jesuits, among others) – see it as 'built like an amphitheatre' (1644), that is, as an architectural symbol of urban greatness.[9]

There has been much debate as to the sources of Longhena's plan, and the models which might have contributed to the design of the Salute. There is certainly no lack of resemblances, affinities and influences, apart from those we have already mentioned. Briefly, these range from pictorial and graphic models such as the centrally-planned churches in works by Perugino, Raphael and Carpaccio, and the engravings of the *Hypnerotomachia Polyphili* (1499, with subsequent re-editions) depicting the temple of Venus, to an idea from the *Libro* by Mario Labacco (1558) which in turn derives from the plan for S. Giovanni dei

Fiorentini by Antonio da Sangallo; they extend backwards over time to works built in late antiquity, the Byzantine and Renaissance periods and, more particularly, to the rich vein of studies on the central plan carried out during the Renaissance itself.

But there are also similarities in layout with the church of the Madonna della Campagna at Verona – another votive church dedicated to the Virgin, designed by Sanmicheli in the year of his death (1559) – which also had a domed main body on a central plan, circular on the outside and octagonal internally, with a choir roofed with a smaller dome on a Greek cross plan with short transversal arms ending in apses.

While work was under way on the church of S. Maria del Pianto (1646–58), now unquestionably attributable to Francesco Contin – a sort of smaller scale and greatly inferior reworking of the Salute – Longhena agreed to design another work of considerable interest, though far less authoritative and compelling than the Salute: this was the church of S. Maria di Nazareth, belonging to the Discalced Carmelites who had settled in the city as recently as 1633, and in their definitive headquarters only sixteen years later. Basing himself on schemes elaborated during the course of the second half of the previous century and reworked by Vincenzo Scamozzi, in particular S. Lazzaro dei Mendicanti, which has various affinities with the Scalzi, Longhena here produced a plan with an aisleless nave and two large protruding side chapels, flanked

by two other small intercommunicating ones
set between double Corinthian columns.
The result suggests a Greek cross plan with
a chancel annexed to it: on a square plan,
and roofed with a dome, it stands on a level
higher than that of the nave, and is reached
through a large triumphal arch. Following
various Renaissance examples, the apsed
choir, for use by the monastic community,
stands beyond the colonnade around the
high altar.

At first sight, the general layout – which
influenced the designs of several other
churches built before the end of the seventeenth century – appears as a more taut and
dramatic reworking of certain sixteenth-
century features. But the ultimate overall
effect is quite different: the opulent varie-
gated marbles, with their strong, dark tones,
the richly glowing gilded capitals of the
Corinthian pillars with festoons suspended
between them, and the prevalently purple
stone cladding of the walls of the nave, all
create an atmosphere of lavish devotional
intensity which is unusual in Venetian religious architecture. Here the influence of
the Roman and Spanish Carmelite order –
reformed by St. Teresa of Avila and St.
John of the Cross – may have played a part,
together with the church's proximity to the
Spanish embassy; important Spanish families living in the city, such as the Suarez,
the Fonseca and others, were buried in the
church in large, ground-level tombs.

The facade of the Scalzi is not by
Longhena, who seems to have left the worksite around 1670, but was commissioned

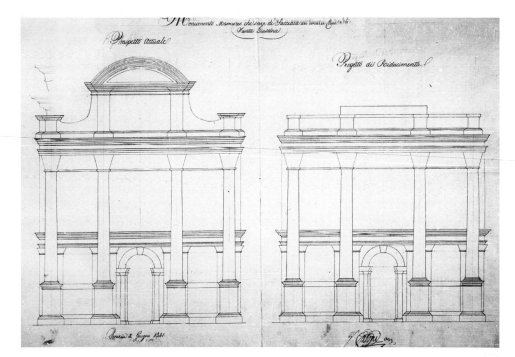

by the church's benefactor, Gerolamo Cavazza, from Giuseppe Sardi, an extremely active figure in seventeenth-century Venice.

But Longhena did design two important facades for the churches of S. Giustina and the Ospedaletto. According to Martinioni, the former was built from 1640 onwards, though arrangements for the facade to extend further forward than the previous one had already been made on 9 January 1636.[10] Built with funds from a bequest by Gerolamo Soranzo, Cavaliere and Procurator of San Marco, it drew upon the theme of the commemorative facade which had been devised in the sixteenth century, and which seems to have come back into fashion during this period. In fact, the great Gothic church of SS Giovanni e Paolo was also completed around this date, following the model of the monument to Francesco Maria della Rovere, duke of Urbino, put up in the Ducal palace in the early seventeenth century, to designs briefly outlined in the will of Domenico Trevisan (25 November 1637).

The facade of S. Giustina, as we now see it, bears the mark of alterations carried out by Giovanni Casoni in 1841 in order to adapt the building to its new use as a 'School for the education of seamen'.[11] But the detailed drawing done on that occasion enables us to form a very reliable idea of the appearance of the topmost portion of the building, reproduced rather sketchily in various eighteenth-century engravings. Originally, the central section of the tripartite facade was topped by an attic storey with a curved pediment (not unlike the facade of the church of the Misericordia), connected to the bases of two allegorical statues at the sides. Overall, the debt to Palladian syntax – partly filtered as always through Scamozzi – is extremely clear, not only in the expedient of the intersecting orders (the giant Corinthian pseudo-colonnade runs through an entablature on Ionic pilasters, with a Doric doorway opening in its centre with angels leaning on the arch, in its turn supporting the sarcophagi of the three benefactors), but also in the evident reference to various ideas for funerary monuments elaborated by Palladio, including the project for the Grimani tombs envisaged for the west wall of the nearby church of S. Francesco della Vigna. Here, though contained within the unbending triumphal severity suggested by the colonnade, the language is far more intense and robust, full of protrusions and richer in chiaroscuro, as we see in the recessed panels and bean-shaped ovals on the bases, for example, and the broken curved pediments above the two side tombs of the Soranzo, or the carving of the cornices of the small windows above the third tomb in the centre of the facade.

Yet even this did not approach the lavish array of figures and ornaments, and use of light and shade, deployed on the elaborate and theatrical facade at the nearby Ospedaletto, overlooking the Barbaria delle Tole, the crowded street of the timber merchants, where it was Longhena who replaced Sardi, also around 1670. Apart from the top section, the tripartite scheme used here is not unlike that found in other works by Longhena. But never before had such sculptural excess been superimposed upon, indeed taken precedence over, the actual structure, swamping the forceful Venetian colourist tradition along with it. In technical terms, this was a virtuoso demonstration of the expressive potentialities of what was defined at the time as 'lavorar d'intaglio', working by carving, typical of the stonemason's art. Now even the supports became plastic devices, with Ionic pilasters tapering towards the base, laden with festoons and decorated with monstrous *telamones*, half animal, half human, derived from *all'antica* herms, and anguished Atlantes on the upper order. The facade of the Ospedaletto has evident links with the almost contemporary monument in the Frari to doge Giovanni Pesaro (1658–9), certainly the most conspicuous piece of funerary architecture of the Venetian seventeenth century, as the French ambassador to the Serenissima noted in a letter of 1669.[12] A typical example of iconographic rhetoric, the second order of this mausoleum is framed by four Ionic columns between which the doge looms up theatrically from a tomb supported by devilish figures, also standing on gigantic black Atlantes. Here, however, the grandeur of the doge himself, immortalized in his public attire, had called for the retaining of more dignified classical conventions and stately rhythms, at least in the upper colonnade. It was this same ducal family – doge Pesaro and his nephew Leonardo – who had offered Longhena the opportunity to create the most important work of civil architecture of the Venetian seventeenth century, Ca' Pesaro on the Grand Canal.

This was certainly not Longhena's first Venetian palazzo, though doubts concerning its attribution and chronology still persist. The first group of palazzi which can be ascribed to him (which includes Ca' Giustinian-Lolin at S. Vidal and palazzo Widmann at S. Canciano) are still essentially derived from the styles current in the decades between the late sixteenth century and the early seventeenth, in particular from Scamozzi's dry classicism, and formulae adapted from Vittoria; they certainly do not include any innovations to the usual distributive pattern of the aristocratic 'casa da stazio' established during the course of the previous century.

Longhena therefore detached himself only gradually from the more recent tendencies, by now followed somewhat wearily; this development was visible at palazzo da Lezze, by the Scuola Grande della Misericordia, but found an opportunity for fuller expression in the extraordinary commission from the Pesaro family for the radical transformation of their great property in the district of S. Maria Mater Domini, overlooking the Grand Canal and completed in the second half of the sixteenth century with the acquisition of 'a house with two towers' from the Contarini and another residence from the Morosini. As early as 1652 Giovanni Pesaro's will expressed an intention to enlarge and

embellish the family house. Seven years later, his nephew Leonardo emerges as assiduously engaged in the overseeing of the work, which continued until 1682, the year of the death of both client and architect. Building had then ceased, with the facade having been completed up to the first floor (as proved, for example, by a view by Carlevarijs dating from 1703), until Francesco Pesaro put matters into the hands of Antonio Gaspari, who had the facade completed by 1710.[13]

The large aristocratic buildings by Longhena have rightly been described as intentionally harking back to those of Sansovino.[14] In fact, his return to the models of the mature Renaissance was significantly more complex, as well as more elaborate on the expressive level. There is no doubt that, for Ca' Pesaro, Longhena also looked to Codussi's Ca' Loredan Vendramin, not far away on the other side of the canal, imitating its paired columns to frame the large windows of the *saloni* on the facade (as Sanmicheli had also done at palazzo Grimani at S. Luca), so as to re-establish the tripartite structure of the facade which Sansovino's palazzo Corner at S. Maurizio had basically not respected, and also to intensify the sequence of windows at the two sides. From Ca' Loredan Vendramin he had also taken the idea of incorporating sculptural ornaments in the narrow area of wall space between the paired columns, as well as the use of fluted ones. References to the work of Codussi would have been even closer, if one of the ideas for the top part of

Baldassarre Longhena and Antonio Gaspari, Ca'
Pesaro, facade on the Grand Canal.

Baldassarre Longhena and Giorgio Massari, Ca'
Bon Rezzonico, facade.

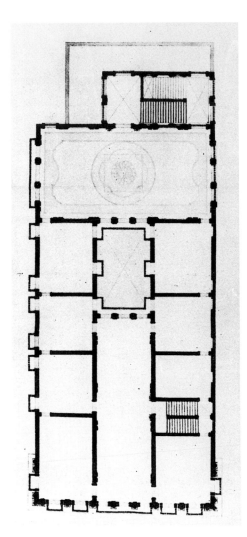

G. A. Battisti, plan of the *piano nobile* of Ca' Bon-Rezzonico, 1770. Venice, museo Correr.

the facade of Ca' Pesaro had in fact been executed: known to us from graphic evidence, it consisted of a frieze with eagles with spread wings, alternating with cartouches. The diamond-shaped rustication of the ground floor, on the other hand, unusually forceful in design, has obvious similarities with that executed at the start of work on Ca' del Duca, which Longhena must certainly have studied with care when working on the nearby Ca' Giustinian Lolin; particularly since Ca' del Duca, like Ca' Pesaro, extends further into the waters of the Grand Canal than the facades of the adjacent palazzi, so that its aggressive rustication is also visible on the sides. In short, Ca' Pesaro seems to have been conceived as a sort of compendium – centred on an interpretation of Sansovino – of various of the 'very greatest of all the palazzi' as identified by the guide book by Jacopo's son, a very popular and widely-read work in seventeenth-century Venice;[15] but at the same time it was also a courageous stylistic step forwards in its three-dimensional monumentality and supreme opulence (which was to be vehemently criticized, in the following century, by the purist Visentini).

In fact, if compared to palazzo Donà dalle Rose on the Fondamente Nuove, another private residence commissioned by a doge, Ca' Pesaro is telling evidence of the changes that had occurred in Venetian society over just half a century, and more particularly of the resumption of those leanings towards a self-celebratory monumentality which one section of the culture

of the second half of the sixteenth century had attempted to legitimize, countering the myths of the city's early parsimony and equality with others concerning the growing mercantile fortune of her private citizens, which had underlain the greatness of the city-state.[16] The theatricality of Longhena's building also had its *raison d'être* in the social and political outlook of the Pesaro themselves: a member of a fabulously wealthy patrician family, which claimed 'kingly and august' descent, doge Giovanni was passionately committed to the struggle with the Turks for control of Crete, and to a policy of 'kingly greatheartedness' in the Mediterranean in general, at a moment of Venetian military success in the Levant.[17]

Giovanni Pesaro's keen support for the Jesuits' return to the states of the Serenissima, and the subsequent protection he extended to them when they did so, had led him to espouse the 'Rome-oriented' line which had characterized the main works of Sansovino.

An old patrician family, that of Filippo Bon – appointed procurator of San Marco in 1660 and related to the Soranzo family – was responsible for the second great palazzo by Longhena on the Grand Canal which took on the name of Ca' Rezzonico after its later owners had it completed by Giorgio Massari, in the eighteenth century.

The first phase of the work can reliably be dated around 1666–7, and by 1697 Filippo Bon was already talking of the 'great building of the palazzo' whose ground and first floor were now standing.[18] Here

Longhena followed Sansovinian models more closely than in Ca' Pesaro, with another free interpretation of Ca' Corner at S. Maurizio (the Corner family was also related to the Bon). But its liberties and variants on the basic theme proved to be highly significant. The design and rhythm of the stately first *piano nobile* – which Massari was faithfully to repeat in the second – were also inspired by those of the Marcian Library (via the Procuratie Nuove, which Longhena was completing during this same period) and thus by examples of public architecture.

The great ground floor rustication, too, moves away from the example of palazzo Corner: by making it heavier and more emphatic, Longhena treated it rather along the lines of Sanmicheli's models, as a fortress or city gate; he also replaced the three great arches of the waterside entrance with three architraved openings, more like those of the Palladian palazzo Antonini at Udine, or – at a later date, in all probability – those at villa Tron di Dolo on the Brenta, subsequently destroyed.

Longhena's Ca' Bon-Rezzonico was thus a deliberate statement of intent, confirming a return to the architecture of the mid-sixteenth century, in the Sansovinian mould, but in a version whose magnificence was more forceful, if at the same time more controlled, than the somewhat intense and hyperbolic Ca' Pesaro.

The building of these two palazzi for powerful old patrician families coincided with three other developments: a change in

the make-up of the Venetian nobility, with numerous new admissions made possible by wealth; the rapprochement with Rome; and the disastrous military involvement in the Levant. The Turkish takeover of Crete – a Venetian possession for five centuries – dealt the most cutting blow to the pride of the republic and its aristocracy. Longhena was therefore called upon architecturally to interpret their stubborn desire for visible grandeur, in confirmation and support of the longstanding myths.

The seventeenth century also saw the layout of one of the city's focal points, the campo S. Salvador linking the Mercerie to the Speziaria. Here the Lugano-born architect Giuseppe Sardi, who was appointed *proto* to the procuratoria of San Marco in 1689, was commissioned to complete the unfinished facades of the Scuola Grande di S. Teodoro and the church of S. Salvador. The answer to the problems left unsolved in the late sixteenth century now came from a private individual, a very wealthy bourgeois merchant, Jacopo Galli, who had left generous bequests for both. Essentially, at S. Teodoro Sardi took up the scheme elaborated by Jacopo Sansovino for the facade of the church of S. Geminiano, imitated more closely here than in the facade of the Scuola di S. Fantin (on a model by Antonio Contin, modified by his relative Tommaso, 1600),[19] which also derived from it. The new facade of S. Salvador, which dated from some years later and was completed during the 1660s, wisely abandoned any attempt at reflecting the

architectural structure of the interior by Spavento and Tullio Lombardo, and indeed any reference to the original projects; instead, it repeated the pattern of the Scuola in a monumental key, replacing the Sansovinian twinned columns in the lower order with powerful Corinthian columns on high bases in the Palladian style, and adding sculptural elements to the upper order of the facade, following suggestions from Longhena. Also thanks to a bequest from Galli, by 1673 Sardi had completed the facade of the church of S. Lazzaro dei Mendicanti, begun between 1601 and 1631 to a project by Scamozzi. Here he kept even closer to the Palladian model, and the facade quotes blatantly from the nearby S. Francesco della Vigna (possibly also recalling the original model by Scamozzi).

Sardi did indeed oscillate in his allegiance to the great architects of the past: in S. Lazzaro, where he had recently designed the funerary monument to Tommaso Alvise Mocenigo (1654–64), standing between the vestibule and the church proper, he had again adopted a Sansovinian scheme for the outer side, reminiscent of that of the Loggetta, using costly African marble (normally used in Venice for the so-called 'altars of the crucifix' and in connection with the cult of the dead).

But he had crowned its inner side with a semi-apsed structure framed by twinned columns and flanked by obelisks, supporting a statue in the middle of the upper order to the glorious and immortal 'capitano da mar', the stately and imperious Mocenigo,

the hero of the war with Crete, for whom contemporary writers of panegyrics had coined the title *Maris Mars*, the Mars of the Sea, and *Terrae Terror*, the terror of the land. Here we already sense Sardi moving towards a Venetian version of the Baroque, as can be seen in two other works of some importance, the facades of the Scalzi and S. Maria del Giglio.

As we have said, in the Scalzi Sardi took over from Longhena. The general scheme of the new facade – financed by Gerolamo Cavazza, a local nobleman – derived directly from sixteenth-century tradition. It has two orders of twinned Corinthian columns, framing the portal and wall surfaces with niches and statues, with five intercolumniations on the lower order and three on the upper. This latter is linked to the wings by elaborate volutes and topped by a triangular pediment with a second curved one inscribed within it, giving emphasis to the median section of the upper order. Less directly, Sardi was also looking back to Sansovino's design for S. Geminiano. But, as we already sense in the Mocenigo monument, here the whole is treated in a style which is bombastic rather than eloquent, with much reliance placed upon the 'graceful company of columns, statues and carvings',[20] in an even more brazen imitation of the manner of Longhena. This influence is found again with undimmed relish in the facade of S. Maria Zobenigo, one of the most intricate of the seventeenth-century versions of the commemorative facade, where the

above
Giuseppe Sardi, facade of the Scalzi.

left
Antonio and Tommaso Contin, Scuola di
S. Fantin, facade.

A. Canaletto – A. Visentini, campo of S. Salvador
with the church and Scuola Grande of S. Teodoro.
Venice, museo Correr.

iconographical rhetoric of family celebration becomes even more turgid and declamatory. The facade of this parish church – very close to San Marco – is emblazoned with the self-glorificatory symbols of one of the branches of the Barbaro family, that of Antonio who, on his return from the post of ambassador in Rome, had been granted 'absolute control' over the facade by the chapter of the church, enabling him to turn it into a funerary monument to himself and his relatives, following an iconographical programme enclosed with his will of 3 October 1678.[21] Designs for this monument, commissioned by Barbaro from Giuseppe Sardi with several meaningful references to his work on the Mocenigo monument at S. Lazzaro dei Mendicanti, had already figured among his notarial deeds.

The extremely precise iconographical programme set out the subjects of the statues and reliefs in meticulous detail: the facade was to include a life-size statue of Antonio Barbaro, armed and wearing general's honours and flanked by statues of Honour and Virtue, Fame and Wisdom, beneath the family coat-of-arms and other allegorical figures alluding to glory and virtue. Then there were to be trophies of war by land and sea, scenes of naval battles, and views of the cities where he had held public office. The lower order was to incorporate statues of his brothers Giovan Maria and Carlo attired as *Savi agli Ordini*, of Francesco wearing the robes of envoy with the Venetian fleet and of Marino in senator's garb. The triumphal programme thus laid

Giuseppe Sardi, palazzo Savorgnan, facade over
the canal of Cannaregio.

particular (and to some degree unwar-
ranted) emphasis on the family's seafaring
and military virtues;[22] here Giuseppe Sardi
repeated the scheme used for S. Maria degli
Scalzi, with a double order of twinned
columns with intercolumniations with
niches, the portal, and the statue and tomb
of the benefactor and his coat-of-arms. Its
main distinction from the earlier work was
another nod in the direction of Longhena,
since the attic storey with the curved pediment was taken from the facade of S.
Giustina. Like the Scalzi, S. Maria del Giglio
is strongly three-dimensional and full of
contrasts of light and shade, though over-
loaded with eulogistic allusions. Sardi's
unfinished palazzo Flangini at S. Geremia –
attributed to him by an extremely reliable
source, namely Tommaso Temanza's
Zibaldone – also reveals his indebtedness
to Longhena; freely derived from palazzo
da Lezze, it too is characterized by an
excess of sculptural decoration.

Built some time between 1660 and 1680
for a client originally from Corfu, who had
recently joined the ranks of the Venetian
patriciate, Ca' Flangini in its turn became
the model for an important late seventeenth-
century palazzo, an architectural emblem
of the fledgling Venetian nobility newly
received into the aristocracy by virtue of
their wealth, since the Serenissima was
now in dire straits as a result of the Cretan
wars. This was the nearby palazzo Labia,
also situated in the *contrada* of S. Geremia,
where the canal of Cannaregio runs into
the Grand Canal, a site often portrayed in

seventeenth-century Venetian view-painting. There seems no reason not to accept the original attribution of the work to Andrea Cominelli, particularly since it has now been confirmed by the Labia family archive.[23] Originally from a family of Bergamo stonecutters already well established in Venice by the early seventeenth century, Cominelli had spent a long period as *proto* to the Carmelite nuns of St. Teresa.

Giuseppe Sardi's oscillating allegiances and pursuit of variants are further exemplified at the nearby Ca' Savorgnan, where elements of Longhena's vocabulary appear side by side with a revival of the late sixteenth-century type of facade with superimposed *Serliane*.

As we have said, with the new work at S. Salvador the Baroque age made its mark on the layout of one of the focal points of the city space just to the north of the Marcian complex; similar modifications were also made to the route leading to the Piazza from the west. Together with the church of S. Maria del Giglio, the parish church of S. Moisè was rebuilt in the seventeenth century. It occupied one of the oldest sites in the city, very near San Marco; the rebuilding in its present form seems to have been linked to the great plague and the ensuing wave of anguished religiosity. The first stone was laid in 1632, though the facade was built considerably later, between 1668 and 1683. The interior followed the sixteenth-century tradition, Sansovinian in origin, of the single nave ending in one main chapel and two smaller rectangular apses. On the exterior,

four fluted and ringed Corinthian columns on huge bases divide the lower order of the facade into three parts, its decoration centred around the funerary portraits of the benefactors. S. Moisè, in fact, was yet another reworking of the commemorative facade, commissioned and financed by the Venetian-Cypriot Fini family which had recently entered the nobility, and by Vincenzo in particular, who had been made a procurator of San Marco in 1687. His bust stands on a truncated obelisk, a symbol of immortality, carried on camels – possibly an allusion to the origins of the family's fortunes as traders in the Levant – together with allegories of Virtue, Modesty, Honour and Excellence. Above, in the centre of a second order divided into three by pilasters with four statues of Virtues in front of them, as in S. Salvador, is a wide thermal window supporting cumbersome figures of Sybils and a winged Fame. The attic storey, topped by a pediment and linked to the outer wings by two half tympana, holds the family coat-of-arms, beneath protecting prophets and Old Testament figures placed on the crowning pediment.

Pompous and contrived as it is, the fussy sculptural-architectural scheme clearly derives from Longhena's design – also commemorative in origin – for S. Maria dei Derelitti, the Ospedaletto, taking it to lengths that were unacceptable even in its own cultural context; nineteenth-century critics were not slow to describe it as 'the height of architectural folly', and in a sense it marked the beginning of the end for one

Palazzo Flangini, facade over the Grand Canal.

above
Palazzo Labia, detail of the facade on to campo
S. Geremia, portal.

right
Alessandro Tremignon, church of S. Moisè, facade.

Facade of the Scuola (synagogue) Spagnola or
Ponentina on the *campiello* of the Ghetto Vecchio.

Facade of the Scuola Levantina in the Ghetto
Vecchio.

particular line of Venetian seventeenth-century architecture. The man responsible for the rebuilding of S. Moisè turns out to have been the brother of the curate of the church: Alessandro Tremignon is now less of an enigma than he was, and is known to have had close ties with the official circles of the Venetian magistracies. At first *sotto-proto* to the *provveditori di comun* – who dealt with numerous aspects of town-planning – and for a time also an engineer with the *sopraconsoli dei mercanti*, from 2 June 1677 he took over the supervising of works at the Arsenal as *proto alle fabbriche*, and is also mentioned on several occasions as active in the Ghetto, where intense building activity was under way during this period.

The two important examples of synagogue architecture built in Venice during the seventeenth century were also linked to the circle and style of Longhena. Most of the work on the Scuola Spagnola, or Ponentina, a radical rebuilding and extension of the pre-existing late sixteenth-century Sephardic synagogue, was completed by the spring of 1657.

In point of fact, this was the first example of 'purpose-built' architecture in the history of the Venetian ghetto, even though here too there are signs of its having been cobbled together from spaces originally intended for other uses. The facade is treated extremely modestly and lucidly, its only point of formal distinction being the careful proportioning between wall surface and windows in the upper part. In fact, it resembles certain

examples of good residential building, such as the houses for the Greek community built between 1658 and 1660 under Longhena's supervision. On the exterior, only the soberly decorated doorway leading to the ground-floor atrium suggests the care that has gone into the rooms inside. The architectural framework of the dignified meeting room, arranged on the axis marked by the *aron* (ark) and *tebam* at either end, consists of a series of Ionic pilaster strips whose bases rest on the low backs of the outermost wooden seats around the walls, and whose tops support a powerful entablature; this in its turn makes a show of supporting the elaborate balustraded women's gallery running all around the upper part of the room, with two straight stretches down the long sides, and semi-circular ones on the short sides. Between the pilaster strips are large windows whose cornices have polychrome decoration and sturdy keystones; the elaborate panelled design of the ceiling is reminiscent of that of Ca' Pesaro and S. Nicolò dei Greci. Though it renounced all claim to self-declaration on the facade over the *campiello*, the community served by the Ponentina had clearly opted for a certain formal opulence reflecting current taste for the interior. The ark – the *aron* – which may date from slightly later, is a virtual copy of the high altar in Longhena's Vendramin chapel, even if the present writer does not believe it to be autograph.

Work had been under way on the rebuilding of the Sephardic Levantine

synagogue, opposite the Ponentina – also sixteenth-century in origin – since about 1683, to be completed by the first years of the eighteenth century; and here the tendency towards an outwardly autonomous architectural form was further developed. In a stroke of great originality, the Scuola Levantina broke resolutely away from the introspective pattern of Venetian synagogues, with the two disengaged faces on to the *campiello* and main *calle* of the Ghetto Vecchio being given a quite distinctive formal identity. Both have projecting panelling bordered horizontally by bands of Istrian stone, and, vertically, with rectangular cornices at the level of the synagogue proper, with oval oculi above. The entrances are framed by sober portals in Istrian stone with polychrome roundels, while a low band of smooth rustication makes a suitable base for the strongly articulated facades. All in all, therefore, the exterior is treated in a manner very similar to that adopted by many sixteenth-century palazzi, in particular to that used by Longhena for the collegio Flangini, serving the Greek community. Inside, the main room, and the *aron*, are almost identical to those of the Scuola Ponentina, while the *tebam*, with its dramatic Solomonic columns, was clearly influenced by the more exuberant and bombastic type of Venetian Baroque decoration. Bearing all this in mind, Tremignon might well have been the architect, and indeed he is documented as having worked in the Ghetto.

Thus the seventeenth century saw the emergence of an autonomous type of

Frontage of the Ghetto Novissimo on rio degli Ormesini.

synagogue architecture in Venice which essentially reworked contemporary tendencies to its own ends; and this same responsiveness to current trends determined the architectural choices made for the layout of the Ghetto Novissimo from 1633 onwards.

The new facade of the Ghetto overlooking the rio di S. Girolamo thus followed the line taken by contemporary Venetian middle-to-upper-bracket residential building, with *piani nobili* organized axially on the traditional *saloni* spanning the depth of the building, registered architecturally on the exterior by severe Doric three-light windows. The complex may well have been designed by Pietro Bettinelli, *proto* to the *provveditori al Sal* and documented as supervisor of the work in question. At all events it seems clear that the buildings put up as part of the extension of the Ghetto Novissimo should be seen as part of the rational revision and clarification of the traditional building types which had gained momentum in the second half of the sixteenth century.

Nor should this seem surprising, since the overall trends in Venetian building between the seventeenth and the first part of the eighteenth centuries can be summarized as essentially endorsing the repertoire of solutions elaborated during the early Renaissance. After the spurt of building activity around the Fondamente Nuove at the beginning of the century, and after the Sabbadino plan had been stalled in part because of the plague which had devastated the city and put a halt to the need for expansion, seventeenth-century initiatives consisted largely of replacing older buildings. In middle-to-upper-range housing, such buildings had carefully designed facades characterized by bands of Istrian stone and *Serliane*, while the more modest dwellings – where the older distributive plan persisted – now had single-or two-light architraved windows. It was only in the early eighteenth century that the last significant innovation in popular residential building began to emerge, namely the introduction of the communal staircase; the internal distributive functions of the 'portego' remained unchanged.

During the late-Baroque period, despite the persistence of traditional features and the widespread adoption of Longhena's style, certain less familiar elements now began to gain a foothold: Roman in provenance, they were associated more or less directly with the Jesuits' return to the city.

An important part in this dawning tendency was played by the Carmelite fra' Giuseppe Pozzo, the brother of the famous Jesuit architect Andrea, a painter and creator of sacred Baroque decor whose designs were widely circulated through two volumes of engravings published in 1685.

Giuseppe Pozzo was the third architect to be called upon to work on the church of the Scalzi, where he concentrated on three focal points – the altars of the two large median chapels and the high altar – in order to transform Longhena's space into a positive theatre of devotion.

Abandoning Longhena's known suggestions for the project, Pozzo's high altar made intensely dramatic use of the motif of the twisted column (used for the *tebam* of the nearby Levantine synagogue during this same period), the symbol of the sanctity of God's temple, juxtaposing it here with the triumphal apparition of the Saviour and the mystic ecstasy of St. Teresa of Avila and John of the Cross, represented in prayer in the colonnade. The ebullient altars of the Ruzini and Manin chapels have very similar features, and are clearly derived from the *Prospettive de' pittori et architetti* by Andrea Pozzo.

Significantly, it was thanks to the Manin – the aristocratic family which had tried to purchase one of the two main palazzi of Baroque Venice, Ca' Bon-Rezzonico, and of which the last doge of Venice was a member – that the Carmelite Pozzo put in an appearance in the new church of the Jesuits, which had been under construction since 1715. Here too his contribution was that of a specialist in theatrically devout architectural creations, particularly vital in this context because the Jesuits were currently insisting that no other Venetian church could command such a throng of worshippers and penitents.[24]

For S. Maria Assunta dei Gesuiti, Pozzo produced a more extreme version of the idea already formulated for the Scalzi: here, ten twisted columns support a heavy tile-covered dome, in a lively interplay between concave and convex, a triumph of light and glittering gilding. Antonio Visentini was to

Giuseppe Pozzo, high altar in the Scalzi.

Domenico Rossi, church of the Gesuiti, presbytery
with the altar by Giuseppe Pozzo.

attack Giuseppe's work as well as Andrea's. However, between the end of the seventeenth and the beginning of the eighteenth centuries, Giuseppe Pozzo had clearly been very successful in giving expression to the requirements of a powerful body of patrons.

The Manin had also provided generous support for the complete rebuilding of the church of S. Maria Assunta dei Gesuiti, which marked the order's definitive reinstatement in the Serenissima, and had endorsed its new role as educators of an important section of the nobility and haute bourgeoisie. Backed up by their own wealthy protectors, the Jesuits had no cause to renounce their own traditions, nor had they particularly exerted themselves to acknowledge those of Venice: the architect Domenico Rossi – a nephew of Sardi's – had turned resolutely to the canonic type of Jesuit ecclesiastical architecture derived from Vignola's Roman model, with its facade by Giacomo Della Porta, in both ground plan and facade.

The riotous exterior, all protrusions, recesses, scooped niches and dramatic sculptural decoration, is matched, in the interior, by a particularly lavish display of late-Baroque elegance: this is 'made beautiful and opulent in style'[25] by having the wall surfaces encrusted with white and verd antique marble, inlaid with brocade designs simulating heavy hangings, and gathered into sumptuous flounces over the parapet of the pulpit in order that the place where the sermon was given might have a richness corresponding to that of the words

of salvation issuing from it to the throng. Giuseppe Pozzo's altar was thus a fittingly spectacular device with which to conclude Rossi's exuberantly decorated space.

The propensities shown by Domenico Rossi and the Carmelite Giuseppe Pozzo at the Gesuiti did not go entirely unheeded: for example, in his design for the facade of S. Stae (1709), their contemporary Giacomo Gaspari too showed that he appreciated the contributions of the Roman Baroque. But the scene in early eighteenth-century Venice was already a hotbed of conflict, as we shall see.

In the meantime, public patronage had confirmed its attitude of traditional detachment from such leanings, giving proof of a return to relative moderation in such limited undertakings as it did engage in. In fact, this mood ushered in the end of the seventeenth century in Venice with several initiatives which were little more than symbolic, closely linked to the temporary reconquest of the Peloponnese by doge Francesco Morosini (1688–94), which was presented to public opinion as the Serenissima's return to maritime greatness.

When work on the Salute and S. Maria del Pianto was concluded in a fittingly emblematic way with their consecration in 1687 – the year of the conquest of Patras, Lepanto, Rumelia and the gulf of Corinth – the deliberate change of iconographical programme for the sculptures of the former had already been completed. The statue of the Virgin placed on the lantern of the main dome was now given the insignia and uni-

form of a 'Capitano da mar' (Admiral of the Venetian Navy), while St. Mark, his gaze directed towards the Ducal palace, was placed on the second dome in the guise of the helmsman of the metaphorical vessel the church had now become. From the end of 1670, moreover, the Cretan icon of the *Mesopanditissa* had been placed on its high altar, having been brought from the cathedral of Heraklion (Crete) on Francesco Morosini's own flagship. The church built to celebrate the indestructibility of Venice, her triumph over death, was now rededicated as a temple to the divinely-granted invincibility of her own navy. This was further alluded to by way of a celebratory updating of the portal and campo in front of the newly reorganized Arsenal shipyards.

Modifications to the official site of the 'sea' and 'land' entrances to the public shipyards had actually begun in 1685 with the dismantling and rebuilding of the church of the Madonna dell'Arsenale (subsequently demolished in 1809), together with its colonnades, loggia and terrace, in order to make space for the widening of the seaward approach: the features of the watergate were thus established, to be taken up soon afterwards by view-painters as a typical celebratory motif. Between 1692 and 1694 Alessandro Tremignon, the new *proto alle fabbriche*, had a section of the ground raised in front of the fifteenth-century portal; the small bridge over the canal was rebuilt, and a terrace was created on a rusticated base, decorated by Giovan Antonio Comino with a group of statues – Neptune and Mars,

Justice and Plenty – drawn from the time-honoured repertoire of Venetian military and political allegories. The paving of the campo in front of it was redesigned, and a bronze socket was placed there for a flag-pole with the Marcian ensign; its decorative iconography showed the apotheosis of Francesco Morosini, depicted triumphantly as a new Neptune, greeted by tritons to the sound of conches and accompanied by the angels of Peace and Faith. The celebration of the hero of the Peloponnese was taken up again in the ornamental motifs of the bronze doors, bearing the doge's family insignia and the trophies of victory.

But the short-lived reconquest of a part of the 'stato da mar' was celebrated more emphatically, and specifically, by the placing of the antique marble lions on two tall pedestals to either side of the balustrade: three of them had been brought back from Greece by Morosini himself, while the fourth – the nearest to rio dell' Arsenale – was placed there in 1716 in celebration of the reconquest of Corfu, besieged by the Turks in the last conflict ever to be waged between Venice and the Ottoman empire.

The official historiography of the Serenissima explained this latest use of *spolia* in the creation of the public image of the city-state as 'endowing Venice – where so many ancient fragments of the triumphal spoils of Constantinople and Greece may be seen – with others also from Athens, and in particular with examples linked to the banner of the Republic' (namely the lion).[26]

The turn of the century was thus officially marked by the positioning of yet further symbols denoting continuity, and the completion of a new scenic device at the very hub of maritime power. During this same period, the bird's-eye view of the city published by Stefano Scolari celebrated Venice as the 'the hobbler of time, the tamer of years, the conqueror of centuries':[27] in other words, as intent as ever on pursuing that deep-rooted desire to 'freeze' history which had been typical of Byzantine civilization.[28]

However, while the city was engaging in a temporary (and financially relatively modest) return to the rhetorical use of the arts, the real thrust of her planning and building activities, and indeed of her financial commitments, lay elsewhere: namely, in the fortification of the isthmus of Corinth, and the vast process of redesigning the defences of the city and harbour of Corfu. Spanning several decades of the eighteenth century, this military architecture was to make the island – the new capital of what remained of the Venetian 'stato da mar' – a 'model of the art' in the eyes of contemporary Europe.[29]

Seventeenth-century portal of the Arsenal with one of the lions brought from Greece by Francesco Morosini.

1 B.N.M.V., ms. lat. III, 172 (=2276), *Caeremoniale rituum sacrorum ecclesiae Sancti Marci Venetiarum*, pp. 1–2.

2 A.S.V., Senato, III, Secreta, filza (file) 92, Rome, P. Contarini, 1.3.1625; *ibid.*, Collegio, V, Secreta, rel., b. 39, n. 16, Chioggia, P. Contarini.

3 Quoted in A. Niero, 'I templi del Redentore e della Salute: motivazioni teologiche', in *Venezia e la peste. 1348–1797*, exhibition catalogue, Venice 1978, pp. 294–8.

4 See M. Muraro, 'Il tempio votivo di Santa Maria della Salute in un poema del Seicento', in *Ateneo Veneto*, vol. 11, 1973, pp. 87–119.

5 For the state of the Arsenal during the late sixteenth and early seventeenth centuries, see A.S.V., Collegio, V, Secreta, b. 57, rel. 1 to rel. 6 (1595–1636).

6 'Velut Nova Hierusalem in terris – statuit te (Dominus) in tutum refugium et tabernaculum electis suis': R. Benedetti, *Ad urbem Venetiarum tempore belli adversus turcas. Psalmus*, n.p., n.d. [Venice 1571].

7 G. A. Moschini, *La chiesa e il seminario di Santa Maria della Salute in Venezia*, Venice 1842, from B. Longhena's contract.

8 *Ibid.*

9 See note 4.

10 1635 m.v. The senate authorized the façade's 'coming forward' from the previous one by about two feet: B.M.C.V., mss. Gradenigo 37; cod. Cicogna 2258; cod. Cicogna 3235.

11 Kriegsarchiv, Vienna, Marinesammlung; cod. Cic. 3361/VI.7a, letters from A. Fadiga to G. Casoni, 1842.

12 Ministère des Affaires Etrangères, Paris, Correspondance Politique, Venice, vol. 90, f. 59.

13 A.S.V., Archivio Pesaro, b. 42, f. LI/I; b. 86, f. CXXII, p. mo, n. 1, f. 25; Giudici del Piovego, Terminazioni, b. 15v, 5.1.1718 m.v.

14 R. Wittkower, *Art and Architecture in Italy. 1600–1750*, Harmondsworth 1973, 3rd edn, pp. 299–300.

15 F. Sansovino and G. Martinioni, *Venetia, op. cit.*, p. 'principalissimi palazzi'.

16 *Ibid.*, p. 388.

17 A.S.V., M. Barbaro, *Arbori de'Patrizi, op. cit.*; G. Zabarella, *Il Carosio, overo origine regia et augusta della Serenissima fameglia Pesari di Venetia*, Padua 1659.

18 A.S.V., Giudici del Piovego, b. 22, 31.5.1649; Notarile, Testamenti, Atti Zon, b. 1232 f. 131r;

Dieci Savi sopra le Decime, Condizioni, b. 242, 1716; B.M.C.V., mss. P.D.C. 2219/11, 2227/IV.

19 A.S.V. San Fantin, b. 2, compendio, f. 94.

20 *Il Forestiere illuminato, op. cit.*, p. 218.

21 A.S.V., Notarile, Testamenti, Atti D. Garzoni Paolini, b. 487/48.

22 G. Benzoni, 'Barbaro, Antonio', in *Dizionario Biografico degli Italiani*, vol. 1VI, Rome 1964, pp. 86–9.

23 A.S.V., Archivio Labia, b. 1, f. 53.

24 A.S.V., Notarile, Testamenti, Atti Zon, b. 1281, f. 131r; Archivio Romano Società di Gesù, Venice, p. 266, 1714 *et seq.*

25 *Il Forestiere illuminato, op. cit.*, p. 199.

26 P. Garzoni, *Historia della Repubblica di Venezia in tempo della Sacra Lega contro Maometto IV . . .*, Venice 1720, pp. 217–18.

27 See the caption transcribed in J. Schulz, *Printed Plans and Panoramic Views of Venice (1486–1797)*, Florence 1970, p. 74.

28 The image referring to Byzantium is from J. Meyendorff, *La teologia bizantina*, Genoa 1984, p. 69.

29 E. Bacchion, *Il dominio veneto su Corfù (1386–1797)*, Venice 1956, pp. 191–200.

THE EIGHTEENTH CENTURY: ANTI-BAROQUE POLEMICS, 'STIL VENEZIANO' AND INNOVATION

As we have said, the architectural culture of the early eighteenth century was riven with tensions and conflicting tendencies.

Two almost contemporaneous events of some importance – the competition for the church of S. Stae on the Grand Canal, and the initial commission for the building of the church of S. Maria del Rosario (the Gesuati) on the Zattere – allow us to gauge the terms of the emergent anti-Baroque polemic. The case of the parish church of S. Stae was in many ways the first to stimul-ate a burst of competitiveness and a show of public interest, as implied by the wide-spread circulation of the engravings of the twelve projects, presented by at least six different architects, by the famous cartographer and engraver Vincenzo Coronelli. The medieval church of S. Stae had already been partially rebuilt, possibly in the late sixteenth century, and then again in the seventeenth, its original orientation having been altered so that its facade faced dramatically on to the Grand Canal. The architect, possibly also the author of one of the unsuccessful projects for the facade,[1] had turned somewhat conventionally to the type of aisleless church that had been widespread in the sixteenth century, with three chapels per side and the apsidal area treated as a chancel on a rect-angular plan, not unlike that of S. Pietro di Castello. In 1709, requesting to be buried without undue pomp in the parish church of his *contrada*, doge Alvise II Mocenigo had left a generous bequest for the building of the facade. After Antonio Gaspari's pretentious project for the facade of S. Vidal

(1700), which was never built, and which was to have served as a sort of memorial to the heroic values of doge Francesco Morosini, S. Stae marked a turning-point of considerable importance, that of the abandoning of the tradition of the commemorative facade, by now two centuries old. Given the extremely modest and restrained presence of the portraits of the Contarini doge and dogaressa in two niches of the neo-Palladian facade designed later by Andrea Tirali (1734–7), also for S. Vidal, such facades might now be said to have been phased out entirely.

In short, one type of relationship between patron and architect – which the Baroque age, with its specific leanings, had favoured and reinforced – now fell into decline. Equally interesting in this context were the designs that had been excluded, particularly the one by Lorenzo Boschetti, who had graduated from Padua in 1704 in civil and canon law, and who had been *viceproto* to the *magistrato dei Savi ed Esecutori sopra le acque* (body of Wise men and officials concerning with the Waters) since 15 May 1703. He had proposed a less portentous version of the scheme for the Scalzi facade designed by Sardi, with overtones reminiscent of Vignola. Even more symptomatic was the exclusion of Giovan Giacomo Gaspari, the son and collaborator of Antonio who was completing the nearby palazzo for the influential Pesaro family, also in 1709. Faithful to his father's proclivities, the young Gaspari's plan, like several others presented, was decidedly Baroque in tone,

Domenico Rossi, church of S. Stae, facade.

with a bold play of convex and concave surfaces, and a dramatic flight of steps sweeping up from the *riva*: a theatrical project bearing the stamp of Rome, with its plethora of sculptures on the crowning broken pediment. Perhaps the architect's failure was offset by a commission to build the Scuola dei Battiloro (1711) next to the church, its facade gracefully embellished by motifs very similar to those of his projects engraved by Coronelli. But S. Stae was destined to have the facade designed by Domenico Rossi, though with none of the 'Roman' features which the Jesuits were to require of him shortly afterwards for the facade of S. Maria Assunta, or the opulent decoration made possible there by funding from the Manin family.

However, S. Stae was not entirely lacking in Baroque elements, for example the broken pediment above the portal, the intricate scroll supporting its central section and the sculptures above it. But the decorative scheme is generally restrained, and the overall composition owes much to the influence of Palladio, filtered through the facades of S. Pietro di Castello and S. Lazzaro dei Mendicanti, with its four giant Corinthian half-columns on high bases and crowning triangular pediment. Its 'august form', as contemporary sources promptly described it,[2] marked an eloquent return to Venetian tradition, probably welcomed and indeed specified by the clients themselves, the Mocenigo of S. Stae, and consonant with what we know of the personality of Alvise II, the namesake of doge Alvise I Mocenigo

(1570–7) who had commissioned the church of the Redentore.

A few years later, around 1715, the suggested rebuilding of the church of the Dominicans on the Zattere, which had formerly belonged to the order of the Poveri Gesuati, provided the opportunity for an even more radical stance. Here the monks had called in a well-known mathematician and theorist, Andrea Musalo from Crete, to work on the project. He was a physicist, writer and practising architect who had been engaged by the Senate in 1697 to teach nautical science as it became accepted that work in the Arsenal should be underpinned by theoretical knowledge.

Musalo's project for S. Maria del Rosario was known to Tommaso Temanza, who left a fairly exact description of it: it was to have been an aisleless church with two shallow chapels and two pulpits, ending in a domed presbytery. But in other ways it was to be a highly innovative building, stripped of decorative superstructures and devoid of any reference to the architectural orders: 'The idea of this temple', as Temanza stressed, 'was based upon a particular method of his, and was to be without columns, capitals or anything at all that goes with Greek architecture. And, truth to tell, had it been executed, it would have brought no little credit to architecture and the city both.'[3]

The stark manner of Musalo's projected building, with its rejection of any superfluous classical elements, was to have been a complete and deliberate antithesis to the theatrical Jesuit church of S. Maria Assunta. Its unconventional design was intimately linked with the rigorist and pro-Jansenist leanings of the Dominican community on the Zattere, which championed a return to the severe morals of the times of the evangelists and Church fathers,[4] and which also had ties with influential cultural circles in Venice (as we see from the bequest to the order of his famous library by Apostolo Zeno, who founded the Accademia degli Animosi in 1691 and was a collector of antiquities and an active advocate of anti-Baroque ideas).[5]

There can be no doubt that the failure to implement Musalo's project – as a result of his death, of political pressure from the Council of Ten and despite the efforts of his pupils – heralded a lull in a potential process of innovation. But it is equally certain that both these, and other less progressive supporters of the anti-Baroque stance taken by Musalo – who himself always preached a return to the rigid system of Scamozzian rules as a safeguard against excess and extravagance – did not go unheeded in the architectural culture of eighteenth-century Venice, thanks in part to an important group of pupils and fellow-debaters, including Andrea Tirali, *proto alle acque* and subsequently also *proto della Procuratoria di Supra*; Giovanni Scalfurotto, architect and *proto all'Arsenale*; and Tommaso Temanza, architect and *proto alle acque*. Further linked by family ties, this dynasty of professional experts exerted an out-and-out hegemony in eighteenth-century Venice.

Andrea Tirali, pronaos of the church of S. Nicolò da Tolentino.

Andrea Tirali in particular was quick to sense the drift of the tendencies emerging at the end of the first decade of the eighteenth century: lacking any professional education, and cantankerous on the worksite, he nonetheless attended the study sessions and discussions held by the patrician Niccolò Duodo (a descendant of the clients of Vincenzo Scamozzi) and also, significantly, by Andrea Musalo.

Tirali had done years of service for various public bodies, and between 1706 and 1711 he was called upon to complete Scamozzi's church of S. Nicola da Tolentino ('i Tolentini'), whose facade had been left unfinished despite the involvement of Longhena himself, who had designed the exquisite tabernacle in the form of a small temple on the high altar. Tirali worked on various solutions, possibly bearing at least some relationship to the one originally envisaged by Scamozzi; one of his designs has fairly close parallels with Scamozzi's project for the facade of S. Vincenzo in Vicenza. But the one actually built was distinctly innovative: the building is preceded by a classical temple front, a true hexastyle pronaos, whose fluted Corinthian columns support a triangular pediment. The oval window in the tympanum, and certain details of execution, hint at a residue of late-Baroque sensibility; but the predominant tone is that of an *all'antica* classicism interpreted through the eyes of Palladio, who had done studies for a similar type of facade. The underlying severity, minimal decoration and recourse to the rules, run deliberately counter to the pursuit of theatrical artificiality being engaged in elsewhere. At the Tolentini, Andrea Tirali broke sharply with his own highly dramatic precedent, the Valier monument at SS Giovanni e Paolo (1700–8), the last Baroque funerary monument to a doge, and much admired by Johann Bernhard Fischer von Erlach.

Tirali took the same direction for another church facade designed towards the end of his life, that of S. Vidal, a reworking of Palladio's scheme for S. Francesco della Vigna (which at an earlier stage was also used as a model for the Tolentini). He followed a similar course, though taken to greater lengths, in his great aristocratic palazzi, for instance palazzo Diedo at S. Fosca and palazzo Priuli at S. Geremia. The former was built in the second decade of the century in a less weighty style than the one proposed in a first documented draft; although it was designed for an important patrician family, its architectural decoration was highly restrained, forgoing the use of columns on the facade, and articulated horizontally by two string-courses derived from a late sixteenth-century model, with a third under the roof. The three-light windows of the *piano nobile* are intended as a nod in the direction of the traditional tripartite facade; this was achieved here by giving the central windows and the entrance unusual prominence, suggesting a median axis of symmetry for the facade. Ca' Diedo therefore now looked back to the vein of formal severity for the Venetian patrician house which had been interrupted during the early seventeenth century after doge Donà's palazzo on the Fondamente Nuove.

Situated next to the recently-built Baroque palazzi of the Labia and Savorgnan, and built shortly after them, Palazzo Priuli was a more extreme version of the same theme, designed as what seems to be an overt tribute to the ideas of Musalo. In the year work began on this palazzo (1724–31), the lively *Giornale d'Italia* discussed Musalo in a long article based on information provided by Pietro Antonio and Giovanni Filippini. The Priuli were a noble family which played an important part in Venetian political life, yet the facade of the palazzo had neither carving, columns nor arches, except in the two portals, framed by rectangular cornices; the severe surfaces in smooth Istrian stone were punctuated solely by moulded architraves based on Scamozzian models.

In its unbending rigour, this building was clearly making a bid to be taken as a paradigm, a polemical statement not only in relation to the nearby works by Cominelli and Sardi, but also, indeed prevalently, as a reproach to another recent architectural event, the building of Domenico Rossi's Ca' Corner della Regina at S. Cassiano. Begun in 1723, this was one of the very last examples of an imposing palazzo to be built on the Grand Canal, though Rossi's first extremely grandiose project was subsequently toned down to produce a relatively sober and unfussy work, generally classicizing in tone and certainly clearly at variance with

left
Andrea Tirali, facade of palazzo
Diedo at S. Fosca.

below
Palazzo Priuli-Manfrin on the
Fondamenta di Cannaregio.

Longhena's posturings at nearby Ca'
Pesaro, with which it inevitably came
to be compared.

Nonetheless, Ca' Corner undoubtedly
made use of a good part of the sixteenth-
century 'Roman' repertoire. The palazzo
is generically neo-Sansovinian in tone: the
ground-floor rustication reappears, as do
columns – Ionic and Corinthian, twinned
and superimposed to frame the central five-
light windows (which moreover do not
correspond to the narrower *salone* running
the depth of the building) and the upper
part of the facade.

At the end of the first quarter of the eighteenth century, two different and mutually
antagonistic attitudes therefore coexisted
in civil architecture commissioned by
patrician clients, a recrudescence, to some
degree, of the old sixteenth-century conflict
between the champions of Republican
severity and the supporters of 'alla romana'
grandeur.

Palazzo Priuli, significantly enough,
kept very closely to the line systematically
adopted by the Serenissima in the extensive
series of undertakings she was currently
engaged in virtually throughout her states
'da terra e da mar'. During this same period,
there was a growing call for austerity in
public architecture: for buildings 'designed
purely for convenience and utility, not for
pomp and circumstance', such as the new
merchants' lazaretto in Split (1730), which
was still an extremely active port of call
on the Balkan trade routes from Istanbul.
There was a general desire to 'limit

Domenico Rossi, Ca' Corner della Regina, facade over the Grand Canal.

expenditure', and many public works were accused of 'needless ostentation'.[6]

All in all, the architecture of palazzo Priuli may be seen as embodying a model for a new congruence between private attitudes and the needs of the state. In the second quarter of the eighteenth century, Venice was engaged in two exceptionally taxing operations: the planning and building of the 'murazzi' (dams) protecting the lagoon against the sea, and the modernizing of the already sophisticated defence system of the city of Corfu using the most up-to-date techniques.

Reaction to the Venetian late-Baroque was therefore twofold; of these two strands, however, the more highly regarded, and hence widespread, was what might be described as the *neocinquecentista*, as pursued by the man who was possibly the most successful architect in Venice in the decades around the middle of the eighteenth century, Giorgio Massari.

It was Massari who took on the rebuilding of the Dominican church of the Gesuati after Musalo's death (1724–43; last work done in 1756). Abandoning the innovative rigour of the earlier project, here he designed a work which was a happy combination of overt reminiscences of two others: bearing in mind the precedent established for S. Stae by Domenico Rossi, he derived the facade from the central section of S. Giorgio Maggiore, carefully avoiding any signs of Baroque fussiness, though he did place four niches with statues of the cardinal virtues in the intercolumniations, and an oval

Giorgio Massari, church of the Gesuati, facade.

View of the interior of the Gesuati looking towards the presbytery.

Giorgio Massari, ceiling of the church of the Pietà.

window in the tympanum, similar to the one in Tirali's Tolentini. References to the Redentore, which stands virtually opposite, are equally evident in the aisle-less interior, with its three interconnected chapels and domed chancel behind the high altar, with its side apses. Here, at all events, commitment to sobriety was subtly tempered: the ceiling has the typical swell of the late-Baroque, with cornices framing frescos by Giambattista Tiepolo.

Massari was also to rework Palladian themes for the facade of S. Marcuola (unfinished), for the Pietà – built only in 1906, to his plans in the Museo Civico – and, in a highly simplified version, for the Catecumeni (1727).

In fact, however, this did not amount so much to a single-minded adherence to one single model, as to an informed selection from among the wealth of examples offered by Venice's High Renaissance architectural culture, which in reality Longhena too had made his own, albeit very freely, discreetly and independently. At the church of S. Maria della Visitazione (la Pietà, 1745), where concerts were given by the young orphan girls for whom the institution cared, Massari used a vestibule similar to that designed by Scamozzi for S. Lazzaro dei Mendicanti, in order to create an acoustic buffer between the crowded, noisy riva degli Schiavoni and the large inner space of the church-cum-concert hall. He also studied and improved upon the acoustic solution adopted by Sansovino for the now vanished church of the Incurabili.

The church of the Pietà has a rectangular plan with rounded corners, so that the sound vibrations would 'flow' and not 'break', or 'echo'. The altars are placed at the four corners of the rectangle in which the space is inscribed, but all projections were deliberately kept to a minimum, for acoustic reasons. The church was roofed with a 'smooth and gentle vault', rather than with beams, as in Sansovino's church.[7]

On occasions, Massari's interest in the Renaissance past could yield surprising results, inspiring him, for example, to use scrupulously careful reproductions of the Codussian two-light window in an extensive restoration of the Scuola Grande di S. Giovanni Evangelista. Bernardo Maccaruzzi did something similar in his work on the facade of the church of S. Rocco (1761–71), reproducing the architectural features of the adjacent Scuola Grande, with the evident intention of giving a unified appearance to the *campiello*, where public ceremonies were held.

Massari's palazzo Grassi – begun around 1748 – has a central courtyard with a Doric colonnade and late-Baroque decoration which moves away from such Renaissance inspiration, but its dignified facade is a positive patch work of classicizing Venetian quotations, based on the by now canonic Sansovinian scheme, though also including various elements from Scamozzi's palazzo Contarini 'dagli Scrigni', from palazzo Coccina-Tiepolo by Giovan Giacomo de' Grigis and more particularly from palazzo Mocenigo 'Casa Nova' at S. Samuele.

Project for the complex of the Pietà. Venice, museo Correr.

Bernardino Maccaruzzi, church of S. Rocco, facade.

This same basic Sansovinian scheme was adopted both by Lorenzo Boschetti's project (1749) for the unfinished palazzo Venier dei Leoni, and in the slightly later wooden model for it by Domenico Rizzi.

Less extensive, but of considerable interest, was the work of another architect active mainly in the service of public bodies at around the same time, namely Giovanni Scalfurotto, the 'beloved disciple' of Andrea Musalo. In 1711 he had been made *proto* of the buildings at the Arsenal, and had supervised various works for the wealthy Widmann family during the years that followed. He built one of his most important works inside the Arsenal itself, the great timber depots and sawmills called the 'tezon alle seghe' (hangar of the sawmills), later known as the 'officina degli Squadratori' (Squaring shop). Work on this building proceeded by fits and starts, both because of various technical difficulties, and because the architect was involved in a court case (though subsequently acquitted), but it was certainly carried out over the period between 1737 and 1745. The building's partial demolition and heavy-handed alteration during the second half of the nineteenth century have made any reading of it impossible in its original form; but plans presented to the Senate while the work was already in progress give us a reliable idea of the general approach. The 'superb building of the sawmills',[8] as a French observer described it, had an imposing facade 148 metres long, punctuated by thirteen tall arches: since the architectural orders were

not to be used, references to the architecture of late Antiquity, and the structural rigour of sixteenth-century works such as Sansovino's Misericordia, found expression through the use of circular windows at the ends, powerfully articulated wall surfaces, and a rustic-ated base, now no longer visible, probably because of a rise in the level of the ground in relatively recent times.

Whereas Scalfurotto had successfully executed an ambitious work of architecture within the Arsenal with his 'tezon alle seghe', he was less fortunate with his complex for the armoury (then a museum of antique weaponry and a gathering point for official visits to the Arsenal, as well as a depot for war material), for which he had drawn up an interesting plan between 1728 and 1734, with ground-floor storerooms and rooms on the upper floor organized around a vast courtyard with massive arcading.

His best-known work, however, was of quite another kind, namely, the rebuilding of the church of S. Simeon Piccolo, commissioned as early as 1718–19. It was the first church in Venice to be built on a circular plan, with a deep free-standing portico. It stands high on the majestic flight of steps that lead up to it from the bank of the Grand Canal, its Corinthian pronaos supporting a great triangular pediment. The main body of the building – on a circular plan, as already mentioned, with two protruding side wings reaching as far as the architrave of the pronaos, and a double order of columns and pilasters in its interior – is roofed by a stilted dome with a lantern. The

above
Giorgio Massari, palazzo Grassi,
facade.

below
Palazzo Venier dei Leoni, unfinished.

above
Facade of the end section of the 'Tezon alle seghe'
by Giovanni Scalfurotto, 1739. Venice, Archivio
di stato.

below
Giovan Maria Maffioletti, bird's-eye view of the
Arsenal, 1798. Trieste, Biblioteca civica.

chancel is raised on three steps above the
circular nave, with apses to the two sides,
also roofed with a small dome. The architectural scheme is complex and rich in allusions. It has sometimes been described as
a Venetian pantheon; in fact, it is more a
distant suggestion of it, repeated by heart
(though Scalfurotto did visit Rome in 1710),
a rereading on a minor scale, filtered in part
through Palladio's *tempietto* at Maser. It
was also, of course, a tribute to Longhena
at the Salute, as implied by its layout in two
sections, by the ground plan of the chancel,
and by the juxtaposition and structure of
the two domes. In short, by developing the
message implicit in Tirali's pronaos for the
Tolentini, Scalfurotto's S. Simeon Piccolo
was deliberately perpetuating the lesson of
Palladio and later interpretations of it. This
may also explain the church's immediate
popularity, and Canaletto was to place it
at the centre of one of his imaginary
urban landscapes.

Thus the move forward from the anti-
Baroque polemic to a first, moderate change
of course, had already essentially been
taken by the end of the first half of the eighteenth century, though other factors apart
from those already mentioned also played,
or were to play, a central role.

Here it should be borne in mind that
the first part of the eighteenth century, in
Venice, was the age of the practical man:
Rossi was an 'unlettered man', Tirali was
almost illiterate, although he was highly
intelligent and in friendly contact with
Musalo and Duodo.

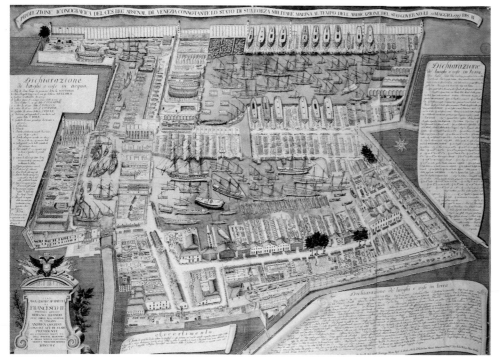

Giovanni Scalfurotto, church of S. Simeon
Piccolo, facade.

Concern for rigour, sobriety and the
rules in general was inevitably linked to
the revitalization of the Serenissima's great
university centre, the Studio at Padua, as
well as to the pressing need for a systemiza-
tion of the various branches of technical
and constructional expertise, and to the
lively discussions on art and history now
taking place in the main intellectual
centres of her states.

It was not until the late seventeenth century that the Studio at Padua awarded a first
chair to a follower of Galileo, Geminiano
Montanari.[9] This appointment implied a
shrewd eye for the potential scientific control such a figure might exert over planning
activities on a territorial scale, of the kind
the Venetian magistracies had already been
engaged in in Venice proper for some time.
Montanari responded by an attempt at
giving Venice a territorial policy modelled
on that of Colbert and the works of Vauban,
starting with the opening of a navigable
canal running from Muscoli to Palmanova,
and then to Udine, 'with an eye to the great
advantages to trade with Germany deriving
from such navigation'; he also drafted a
treatise, *Dell'ingegniere civile* (of the civil
engineer), completed shortly before 1680
(though never published), and provided the
engineers of the *magistrato alle acque* with
advanced instruments such as the dioptric
level (1680). But from 1720 the main public
technical bodies – those for which almost all
the eighteenth-century Venetian architects
of any importance worked permanently
as *proti* – were already being supervised

(and, in part, instructed) by the 'public mathematician', who was also constantly called upon to give his opinion on the main building works promoted by the state.

Bernardino Zendrini, who was responsible for overseeing the *magistrato dei Savi sopra le Acque*, belonged to the second generation of experts who believed that 'hydraulic architecture' should be reduced to an experimental science by means of the Galilean approach embarked on at Padua: that planning expertise should be scientifically based, but also aware of its own processes and history. Around 1726, Zendrini had also reorganized the archive of this magistracy, using it as the basis for his important *Storia delle Acque venete* (History of the waters of Venice). Together with his engineering treatise *Leggi e fenomeni delle acque correnti* (Laws and phenomena of running water), published in 1741, this formed the educational mainstay of the officials of the *Savi alle acque*, who included Tommaso Temanza and Matteo Lucchesi.

The education and practice of the corps of Venetian military engineers, too, was put on a sound technical and mathematical footing, on the basis of proposals by Giovanni Maria von Schulenburg, who had been responsible for the design of the new fortifications of Corfu.

Venetian military engineers had also recently gained a first-hand knowledge of Greek architecture, albeit for reasons of war: Filippo Verneda, who had been particularly active on the great late seventeenth-century worksites, had organized a scrupulous survey of the Acropolis, and had brought together architectural descriptions of the monuments of Athens (1687), subsequently used in part by Coronelli for the maps he printed at his works near the convent of S. Maria dei Frari. These events sparked off a marked upturn of interest in the ancient world which was to be explored in contemporary studies.

Schulenburg's project brought together the combined experience of some of the most forward-looking engineers at the Arsenal, including the Alberghetti, descendants of long-established dynasties which had had direct dealings with Tartaglia and Galileo, and who then became foreign fellows of various international scientific bodies, including the Royal Society in London.

Such developments should be seen in relation to the attention now being paid to military and also civil architecture in the courses given in the faculty of mathematics at the University of Padua. A course on the principles of military architecture, the first after Galileo's own teaching, was given by Giovanni Poleni in the academic year 1729–30 and repeated several times between 1737 and 1756,[10] that is, from the years when the first company of engineers was set up, to be extensively involved in various planning and map-making activities in Dalmatia and the Levant. But an even greater novelty occurred with the introduction, by the same faculty, of discussion of matters concerning civil architecture, beginning, in all likelihood, with the courses of 1755–6 ('architecturae militaris doctrinam nec non architecturae civilis mathematica principia explicabit', theory of military architecture and mathematical principles of civil architecture) and of the following year, partly repeated later by Simone Stratico.

In Poleni's opinion, the necessary review of the architect's instruments was to be carried out 'iuxta textum Vitruvii et mentem Neutoni', according to the text of Vitruvius and the mind of Newton. The new disciplinary definition of the 'mechanics of architecture' therefore went hand in hand with a thorough and demanding reassessment, both critical and scientific, of Vitruvius and the Vitruvian tradition, implying a distinct move away from the total, and stated, lack of interest in the classical text evinced by the architectural culture of Musalo and his teaching (as witness Temanza). The *Exercitationes vitruvianae* published by Poleni (1739–41) now came to constitute a further point of reference for the changes under way.

Another was the process of revision being carried out by Venetian antiquarian culture itself, partly through a re-examination of the history of classical architecture, far from neutral on the practical front.

Architecture was also a 'profession requiring knowledge and science' for the Veronese Scipione Maffei; a friend of Zendrini and Poleni, he was one of the most active figures in the study of antiquity in Venice, as well as one of the most committed to 'regularity and reason' in architecture, as against the last ramblings of the Baroque.

Fortifications of Corfu, anon. Eighteenth-century painting. Venice, museo Navale.

At the heart of his concerns was the return to a distinction between the public and private uses of the grandiose in architecture – a recurrent theme, as we have seen – a distinction currently blurred 'by corruption'; he also championed some hypothetical form of public building control to be implemented, on the Roman pattern, through a 'magistracy composed of intendants ... in every well-run city ... to whose scrutiny ... everything that would be visible on the streets, or to the public gaze, was to be exposed' (1738), a proposal not unlike those about to be formulated in the French political press. A similar interest in the norms and forms of the classical city were at the root of his *Degli anfiteatri* (Of amphitheatres) (1728); while contact with the circles mentioned above inspired his *Ragionamento degli Itali primitivi* (Discourse on the early Italic peoples), in which he told his readers to 'open their minds ... to a third category [of antiquity], to consider that host of venerable and inscrutable monuments ... namely, the Italic or Etruscan'. This was a 'category' of antiquity distinguished by a sublimity of style – 'a wildness, and magnificence ... which they possess to a supreme degree', a claim foreshadowed by Maffei in 1727, when he wrote: 'it is my opinion that they [the Etruscans] achieved more in architecture ... and the Greeks rather less ... than is believed'.[11] Such reflections were also at the root of comparable interests shown by Matteo Lucchesi and his nephew and one-time pupil, Giovanni Battista Piranesi.

They were equally crucial to the thinking both of the chief figures in Venetian architectural debates in the mid-eighteenth century, and to the new institutions inspired and fostered by such debate over the last decades of the century.

We see this particularly clearly in the case of fra' Carlo Lodoli (1690–1761), an architectural theorist rather than a practising architect, the son of Bernardo, public prosecutor at the Arsenal, nephew of the engineers and mathematicians Sigismondo and Giust'Emilio Alberghetti and brother of Giovan Battista, military engineer to the Serenissima, all of whom worked on various projects and map-making enterprises in Dalmatia, Albania and Greece: a family network of some importance, and one which instantly defines the circles where Lodoli was educated. Scipione Maffei himself boasted of having brought him 'out of his lair'. An antivitruvian, critical of the classical models and of Palladio, Lodoli was a Galilean in his thinking and scientific training: 'He had me know that it was most unlikely that the corollaries of the scientific principles that Galileo had discovered in mechanics, would differ much from those which he himself had discovered in architecture,' as Memmo remarked, while Algarotti characterized him as 'a philosopher from whom Vitruvius' doctrine has all the more to fear, in that his own imagination is so fertile'.[12]

Though inspired by Musalo's radical and functionalist stance, Lodoli was more extreme: for him, in a work of architecture, 'philosophical reason admits as ornament only such things as happen to be functional to it', as Gian Rinaldo Carli summarized his views in a little-known work.[13]

At one point Lodoli was regarded with some suspicion by certain government circles, and he frequented the Venetian salon of the consul John Smith at the SS Apostoli, where new ideas on such matters were freely debated. But it is also true that he enjoyed the support of cultured and influential politicians, from Andrea Memmo senior to Andrea Domenico Querini, Nicolò and Andrea Tron, the Giustinian family, who held open house in calle delle Acque, Lorenzo and Ferigo Tiepolo, and the doges Ruzzini, Pisani and Grimani.

Thus his views, though not circulated in printed form until 1786 and 1833–4, with the publication of an account of them by his pupil Andrea Memmo junior, in his *Elementi di architettura lodoliana* (Elements of Lodolian architecture), gained currency in the meantime through the school he had opened for young patricians in 1720, which encouraged a degree of progressive thinking and made its mark on educated circles and patrons in the middle of the century. Its pupils included front-ranking figures in the world of European culture, for instance Girolamo Zulian, who championed Canova from his early years. He was also a well-known collector, and promoter of the great map of Padua by Giovanni Valle; during his years as ambassador at Constantinople, he had collected drawings of the antiquities of Troas and Greece, as well as 'outstanding architectural pieces . . . [and] stupendous statues'.[14] His interests clearly pointed the way towards the age of Neoclassicism.

This was also the background to the activity of Tommaso Temanza, though he had little involvement with salons and was closer to scientific and technical circles. He was a typical figure among the Venetian architects active in the decades immediatly after the middle of the century: *proto alla laguna* from 1742, Temanza was also a writer on the history of architecture and the city. Known as an intellectual – his contemporaries described him as a 'man of letters and talented mathematician' – with connections with the controversial Dominican circles of the Gesuati, where opposition to the more excessive developments of the Venetian Baroque had first found open expression,[15] he set himself equally firmly against the hegemony of the 'unlettered' men of action who had dominated the first decades of the eighteenth century (and, in his view, much of the seventeenth too, with a consequent decline in rigour and correctness of style).

Modelling himself on Vasari, in 1778 Temanza published a collection of *Vite dei più celebri architetti e scultori veneziani che fiorirono nel secolo XVI* (Lives of the most famous Venetian architects and sculptors who flourished in the XVI century) and, three years later, the *Antica pianta dell'inclita città di Venezia* (ancient map of the illustrious city of Venice), which reproduced the parchment plan from the fourteenth-century Marcian manuscript of the

Chronologia Magna and thus initiated a series of studies on the development of the city. Here Temanza was reflecting the views of both Zendrini, with whom he also collaborated, and Maffei, whose suggestions for the revitalization of university studies in the Serenissima had included the assertion that 'as to learning, its very history already constitutes a large part of it'.[16] By proposing a systematic reinterpretation of the history of Venetian Renaissance architecture, Temanza's *Lives* implicitly summed up contemporary tendencies, and suggested an equally systematic and critical review of them in a search for rules and principles which could be measured with the criteria of the 'scientific logic' and the 'philosophic logic' of art.

Temanza did not build much, mainly because of his time-consuming public duties. His architectural ideas were presented most coherently in the small church of S. Maria Maddalena, built after a revealing series of events involving first the better-known Massari, and then his replacement by the very pupil of Musalo whom Massari had replaced at the Gesuati: another symptom of the changing times.

The surest judgment on Temanza's model was put forward by marchese Giovanni Poleni, to whom the design had been submitted in August 1760: 'He gave his unstinting approval, casting aside any doubt as to the execution of such a well-conceived, judicious and masterly plan.'

Work on the church began on 8 May 1763, and ended as late as 1790. The resulting

'temple with a hexagonal and circular shape' was one of the most significant works of architecture produced during the second half of the eighteenth century in Venice, or indeed anywhere in contemporary Europe. Its 'scientific architect', as the parish records refer to Temanza, was here returning to problems that had already been broached in the Tolentini and S. Simeon Piccolo, opening up direct and pointed dialogue with this latter church in particular, by Temanza's uncle Scalfurotto.

Circular in plan externally and hexagonal internally, its walls articulated by deep niches framed by pairs of columns, the main body of this church too was inspired by the model of the Pantheon; but now it was interpreted more correctly by the elimination of the Palladian element of the protruding wings, and the use of a dome with a double calotte, here much closer to the classical model. As in S. Simeon Piccolo, the chancel takes the form of a lesser space with a dome and apses, opening off the main one. But at the Maddalena this is done in such a way as to conceal the second small dome on the outside, that is, emphasizing the unity of the architectural organism rather than the contrived play of its parts.

Like the Pantheon, the interior of the Maddalena includes a display of rare marbles: Greek marble for the altar, with a carved architrave and tympanum, and half-columns of flecked ash-grey oriental marble in the choir. However, Temanza demonstrated his independence in his treatment of the temple pronaos, replacing

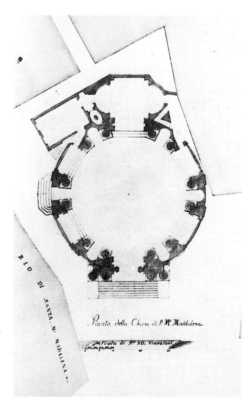

above
Plan of the church of the Maddalena by Tommaso Temanza. Venice, museo Correr.

right
Church of the Maddalena.

the Corinthian portico – incompatible with the space in front of the building – with a pediment supported by four Ionic half-columns. In its austerity and compositional rigour, the Maddalena thus firmly reasserted the need, in the Venice of the second half of the eighteenth century, for unremitting recourse to the classical language of architecture, generated and regulated by the 'exact and universal' rules of geometry: a goal unswervingly pursued by Temanza himself, always a scrupulously painstaking overseer of his work down to the last detail.

Apart from solving the specific problems of the site – that is, after having 'proved' the primacy of geometry and rationality in establishing the nexus between architecture and urban space – Temanza had also clearly intended the severe structural logic of the Maddalena to be offset by the haphazard articulation of volumes and planes of the traditional buildings around it, and by the stratification of traditional practices they suggested.

Work on the church was continued, after Temanza's death, by one of his most famous pupils, Giannantonio Selva, who did a measured drawing of the main chapel prior to designing its balustrade, thereby creating an emblematic link between the building of S. Maria Maddalena and the advent of Neoclassicism.[17]

'Mattietto', or Matteo Lucchesi (1705–76), whose archaeological interests have already been referred to, was a close friend and contemporary of Temanza's: they both frequented the studio of Giovanni

Tommaso Temanza, project for the Casino Zenobio. Venice, museo Correr.

Scalfurotto, the courses at Padua given by Poleni and Zendrini (1724–9), and the Veronese circle of G. B. Recanati, where 'fine debates' on architecture were regularly held. The author of an impulsive pamphlet attacking Maffei on the subject of the Tuscan entablature,[18] Lucchesi too joined the engineers of the *magistrato alle acque*, becoming *proto alla laguna* in 1737, and then *proto ai lidi e ai fiumi*. As with Temanza, these demanding public commitments, in particular his involvement in the Murazzi, may explain his limited architectural output. His main contributions were two works in Friuli (the rebuilding of the castle of Polcenigo in 1738, and the plan of the Monte di Pietà of S. Daniele dating from twenty years later), and two works in Venice: the design and partial realization of the church of S. Giovanni Novo, and the little music room for the Ospedaletto dei Derelitti at SS Giovanni e Paolo, where he was *proto* from 1751.

In this latter work, whose design dates from 1771 but which was executed only in 1776, Lucchesi inevitably bore in mind not only the precedent of the Pietà, but also specific information concerning the acoustics of concert halls provided by his two Paduan masters. The former kitchen serving the young girls of the Ospedaletto was now transformed into a little auditorium on an oval plan, its walls devoid of protrusions in so far as this was possible, and decorated exclusively by paintings by Guarana and Agostino Mengozzo Colonna, son of the better-known Girolamo.

Lucchesi is known to have been active on S. Giovanni Novo from 1749 to 1759, leaving the site before the work had been completed (as indeed it never was); nonetheless, the church is an important example of the more established tendencies in mid-century Venice. Neopalladian in design, it was vividly described by Moschini as a sort of *Redentore redento* (Redeemer redeemed) – though in fact it seems to have been far closer in plan to recent religious buildings such as S. Stae or the Gesuati – and a heartfelt answer to the suggestion voiced by Massari, now elderly and successful, that architects should 'imitate, as best they may . . . those works which are most highly esteemed, while diligently eschewing their defects'.[19]

Antonio Visentini (1688–1782) was another architect and viewpainter who built little owing to his involvement in two other areas: as a versatile and highly productive engraver, documented from 1717, and later as a teacher. His work in the former capacity ranged from the *Iconography of the Ducal Basilica of the Evangelist Saint Mark* to his well-known views of the city and its lagoon, and numerous plates for printed books, a sphere of activity closely linked to Canaletto's viewpainting. He also put together the volumes of drawings making up the *Admiranda urbis Venetae* for the English consul John Smith, a treasure-house of works of Venetian architecture, though their dogmatic and pedantic observer sometimes purged them of the 'errors' he perceived in them. Another contribution to the spread of the image and

myth of the glories of Venice was made by an architect-engineer, Giorgio Fossati, the author of a large bird's-eye view of the city (1743) where the urban scene was visually expanded so that its architecture appeared more monumental, its spaces broader and its buildings denser, creating a particularly graphic image of a great metropolis.

In his capacity as viewpainter, Visentini was also one of the founders of the Accademia; he taught architecture there from 1761, producing numerous works on the subject, some published, some in manuscript, but all revealing a deep indebtedness to Palladio, and a commitment to an architectural purism by which he hoped to purge Venetian culture of some of its more deeply-rooted idiosyncrasies. They also show him to have been a remorseless opponent of the 'follies of Piranesi . . . pure flights of fancy engaged in by one who seeks absurdly to magnify whatever he has cast his gaze upon', in the name of a 'truthful and well-regulated'[20] knowledge of Antiquity (the subject of the famous painting he presented to the Accademia in 1777). Visentini designed a villa at Mogliano for John Smith, and a small palazzo on the Grand Canal (1751), later completed by Selva. His third work of any importance, probably datable around the 1760s, was the design for another work on the Grand Canal, palazzo Coletti Giusti, next to Ca' d'Oro. These latter works were modest in tone, the former in particular being intended as demonstrations of 'virtuous architecture'.

Antonio Visentini, palazzo belonging to consul Smith,
subsequently Mangili-Valmarana on the Grand Canal.

In the palazzetto for Smith, Visentini
used elements of a classical language
clearly derived from Palladio, arranged
on the facade so as to give emphasis to the
central window of the *piano nobile*, in a
deliberate move away from the tripartite
system and continuous rhythm of multi-
light windows typical of the 'stil veneziano',
yet not without similarities, for example, to
the nearby palazzo Civran at S. Giovanni
Crisostomo. Here, Visentini was therefore
proffering a rearrangement of the layout of
the facade of the noble Venetian house, continued in palazzo Coletti Giusti, which also
had two distinctive parallel balconies on the
piani nobili and niches with statues on the
lower order, treated as a nymphaeum facing out over the waters of the Grand Canal.

The move towards rigour and rationality,
the desire to recast Venetian architectural
culture which can be sensed in Temanza
and Visentini, occurred in parallel with a
further standardizing of the training of
Venetian architects and engineers, and of
the teaching of related disciplines, which
took place soon after the middle of the
century. This radical revision led first to
the setting up of the Accademia, which
was opened in 1751 as a school of drawing,
painting and sculpture, with courses in civil
and military architecture, at the orders of
one of Lodoli's fellow debaters, doge Pietro
Grimani (1741–52). The idea derived from
a project devised with Giovan Francesco
Morosini as early as 1724, when Grimani
had been Riformatore of the studio at
Padua: its aim, clearly generated by a

Antonio Visentini, palazzo Coletti-Giusti on the Grand Canal.

climate of international competitiveness, was to 'demonstrate to outsiders that the liberal arts of sculpture, painting and architecture in this city are being raised from the decline into which they have presently sunk'.[21] Soon afterwards the engineering studies at the Veneto Militar Collegio of Verona were reorganized (1764), modelled in some ways on the French 'Ecole des Ponts et Chaussées' and 'Ecole de Mezières'; partly through research undertaken by the Venetian embassy in Paris. The first course in the 'Practice of civil architecture' was then opened at the University of Padua (1771) and a five-year course in 'physical and mathematical studies relating to naval architecture' was inaugurated at the Arsenal in Venice, under the auspices of the Paduan chair of mathematics, physics and naval architecture, held at the time by Simone Stratico. By no means insular or stagnant, this was the background to the last important architectural event in eighteenth-century Venice: the building of the great new theatre of the Fenice.

This was an innovative undertaking in itself: firstly, the preliminaries (1787–9) to the setting up of what was to become Venice's main centre for musical performances required a special waiving of the current legislation, and, secondly, the theatre was to be sited right in the centre of the city, directly behind the Piazza. This entailed an ambitious architectural programme with far-reaching consequences, which would also necessitate giving a new configuration to one side of campo S. Fantin, which already had two good buildings, the church of the same name and the Scuola of S. Maria della Giustizia.

Contemporaries were fully aware of the momentousness of the decision: 'It was found surprising that a capital city formed of magnificent public and private buildings, many of which were excellent examples of sound architecture by renowned masters of the 'bel secolo', a city which had been the first to give public performances of musical works, and which had always had more theatres than any other, should never have thought to build a single one among them that might compete with her other buildings.' The allusion to regeneration implicit in the emblem adopted for the new theatre ('the two meanings embracing both the uniqueness and the rebirth of the fabulous bird')[22] was therefore not merely a play on words. The choice of site, and the commissioning of the work, was influenced by one of the partners in the undertaking with very specific cultural views, namely Andrea Memmo who, as the main heir to Lodoli's theories, had published a well-known summary of them at that same period. The choice of architect, too, was perfectly log-ical in the circumstances: after various debates and wranglings, a complex project by Giannantonio Selva was selected. His first important work, it was extremely sensitively designed in terms both of the urban complex and of its own carefully calculated volumes (subsequently altered), with the elaboration of a style which was subtly gauged so as to reflect the building's import-

ance and implications. The back facade, overlooking the new canal dug specially to allow direct access from the water, with its ground-level order of five rusticated arches, and its upper wall surface soberly articulated with three windows with tympana, was a reworking – rigorously correct from the point of view of grammar, geometry and proportion – of certain problems already presented by certain sixteenth-century buildings (for instance Sansovino's palazzo Dolfin Manin, and the Fabbriche Nuove at Rialto). The main feature of the facade over the square was a strictly functional Corinthian portico framed by simplified pillars, raised above the campo on an austere and simple flight of steps; only the central section had any decoration, in the form of carefully balanced niches with statues of Music and Dance, and bas-relief panels with Tragedy and Comedy, as an external statement of the building's function. The side sections had no ornament at all, which was tantamount to a declaration of adherence to the values of Neoclassicism. The

architect, Giannantonio Selva, had been a pupil of Temanza and had trained at the Accademia, but he had also travelled widely throughout Italy, France, England, Holland and Austria; his friends included Canova and Quarenghi, and he was championed by followers of Lodoli such as Girolamo Zulian and Andrea Memmo.

Inaugurated in 1792, the Fenice epitomized, indeed transcended, the more advanced tendencies present in the Venice of the second half of the eighteenth century: a confirmation that she was well abreast of international trends, and a symbol of an intellectual vitality among the elite that persisted within the Serenissima until the very end.

Giannantonio Selva, wooden model of the Fenice theatre. Venice, teatro La Fenice.

1 Coronelli attributes two projects to a certain *Gio. Gralis* and a *Gio. Gratij*, the spelling of whose surnames is uncertain.

2 *Il Forestiere illuminato, op. cit.*, p. 264.

3 T. Temanza, *Zibaldon*, ed. N. Ivanoff, Venice and Rome 1963, pp. 26–7.

4 V. A. Vecchi, *Correnti religiose nel Sei–Settecento veneto*, Florence 1962, and *La chiesa di Venezia nel Settecento*, ed. B. Bertoli, Venice 1993 and bibliography.

5 F. Corner, *Notizie storiche, op. cit.*, p. 444.

6 On the *palazzo* Priuli see V. Farinazi, 'Interni e architettura nel primo Settecento veneziano: Palazzo Priuli Manfrina Cannaregio', in *Venezia Arte*, vol. 6, 1992, pp. 53–66; B.M.C.V., mss. Donà 327/III.

7 Quoted in E. Bassi, *Architettura del Sei e Settecento a Venezia*, Naples 1962, p. 319.

8 Archives Historiques de l'Etat Major de l'Armée, Vincennes, Plans et projets, Italie, 1376 (1775–1800).

9 G. Montanari, *La livella diottrica*, Venice 1780; A. Favaro, 'I successori di Galileo nello Studio di Padova fino alla caduta della Reppublica', in *Nuovo Archivio Veneto*, vol. 33, 1917, pp. 56–182; M. L. Soppelsa, *Genesi del metodo galileiano e tramonto dell'aristotelismo nella Scuola di Padova*, Padua 1974, and 'Le scienze teoriche e sperimentali tra Sei e Settecento', in *Storia della cultura veneta*, vol. V/II, Vicenza 1986, pp. 271–345.

10 Apart from the works cited in the previous note, see L. Guadagnino Lenci, 'Per Giovanni Poleni. Note e appunti per una revisione critica', in *Atti dell'I.V.S.L.A.*, vol. 134, 1976–7, pp. 547–78; *Giovanni Poleni: idraulico, matematico, architetto, filologo. 1683–1761. Atti della giornata di studi*, ed. M. L. Soppelsa, Padua 1988.

11 S. Maffei, *Osservazioni letterarie*, III, Verona 1738, and 'Ragionamento sopra gl'Itali Primitivi . . .', in *Istoria Diplomatica che serve d'introduzione all'arte critica in tal materia*, Mantua 1727.

12 F. Algarotti, *Saggi*, ed. G. Da Pozzo, Bari 1963, p. 31.

13 G. R. Carli, *Della antichità italiche*, I, Milan 1788, p. 202.

14 B.M.C.V., mss. Cicogna 3165/7.

15 Interestingly enough, in his *Vite* (*op. cit.*) Temanza tries to prove that the Venetian Renaissance had its origins in the work of two Dominicans, fra Giovanni Giocondo and fra Francesco Colonna.

16 S. Brugi, 'Un parere di Scipione Maffei intorno allo Studio di Padova sui principi del Settecento', in *Atti dell'I.V.S.L.A.*, vol. 49, 1909–10.

17 This account of the rebuilding of the Maddalena is based on the records of the Council of Maintenance now in the Archivio parrochiale (parish archive) of San Marcuola.

18 M. Lucchesi, *Riflessioni sulla pretesa scoperta del sopraornato toscano*, Venice 1730.

19 A. Memmo, *Elementi dell'architettura lodoliana*, vol. I, Rome 1786, p. 4.

20 Quoted in E. Bassi, *Architettura, op. cit.*, pp. 367–8.

21 Letter of 12.12.1724, in E. Bassi, *La regia Accademia di Belle Arti di Venezia*, Florence 1941, pp. 131–2.

22 Quoted in N. Mangini, *Teatri di Venezia*, Milan 1974, p. 171.

ARCHITECTURE AND THE CONTEMPORARY CITY

THE end of the republic, with Venice's incorporation into the political orbit of Napoleon and then, less briefly, that of the Habsburgs, inevitably brought with it a number of more or less radical changes during the early nineteenth century, but also, more specifically, a deep shift in the models underlying the interpretation, organization and workings of her urban structures.

Between 1796 and 1813 the government of the Napoleonic kingdom of Italy embarked upon a systematic review of the instruments serving for a knowledge of the city, and the means of acting upon it, ranging from a general administrative overhaul to the setting up of the *Commissione all'ornato* and the introduction of a plot-by-plot land registry. The ensuing great 'exact' cartographic representation of Venice in fact amounted to an annexation and commandeering of the urban space which, by its very nature, tended to homogenize the age-old quirks embedded there, at a time, moreover, when people were fully aware that one kind of history was ousting another.

The territory thus explored, partly through a series of missions (one for the surveying of the lagoon, led by captain Denaix, 1809–11, one carried out by the Génie militaire which gave rise to the *Atlas de Venise* now at Vincennes, one for the Commission Maillot, carried out by the French navy) was regarded not so much as an immutable space with its own rules, but rather as a physical area to be modified by completely new strategies, within the orbit of large-scale planning policies which were

quite unlike the codes which had preceded them.

In this context, the perplexity admitted to in 1797 by Pierre Alexandre Forfait – a naval engineer shortly to become a minister of the French republic – is extremely revealing: for the Venetians, he observed, 'the usefulness of roads and quays, even in a city, remains a vexed question'.[1] This was the start of a puzzling process of comparison between the city's urban structure, with its own logic and manner of functioning, and the geometry-based rationality underlying the culture of the new institutions. As is well known, the early years of the nineteenth century saw the dawn of a long process of normalization, which was to leave its mark on a broad swath of pre-existing urban activities and inter-relations.

A series of Napoleonic measures now redefined the interaction between religion and the city: these included the transfer of the seat of the patriarchate from the outlying island of S. Pietro di Castello to the basilica of San Marco (1807), bolstering the centrality of the Piazza; the amalgamation of numerous smaller parishes, with the removal of their activities to certain of the large monastic churches, and the suppression of others, as well as of various religious centres and confraternities. These steps not only transformed the old Venetian system of *contrade* and the network of social relations between large and small *Scuole*; they also freed sites and buildings for the introduction into the city of new and previously alien activities. The widespread military

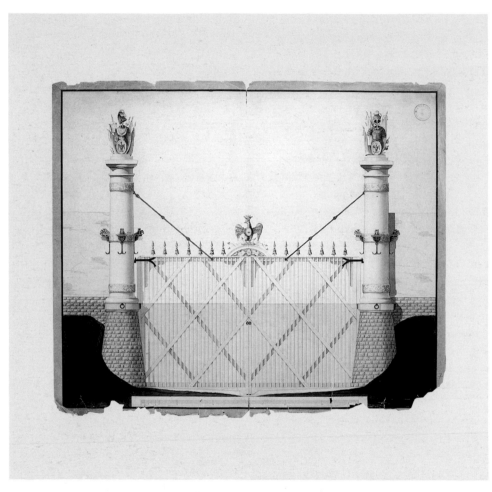

Andrea Salvini, project for the new maritime gate
of the Arsenal (never built). Trieste, Biblioteca civica.

appropriation of buildings belonging to suppressed religious guilds, too, now began to constitute something more than a simple change of use, albeit on a large scale: one of the underlying principles of Venetian town-planning, laid down over the course of the modern period, was now being overturned: briefly, a system for the quartering of sea-going troops was now being put into place around the Arsenal, occupying a group of nearby convent buildings. The army was definitively assigned twenty-nine complexes throughout the city and surrounding islands. The thinking behind this was to distribute the infantry around the edges of the city, and to set up a logistical infrastructure with the use of depot complexes already in existence (such as those of S. Biagio and the Riva del Megio) and of the sixteenth-century hospital of S. Lazzaro dei Mendicanti as a military hospital, with the annexation of the monastery of SS Giovanni e Paolo. The fourteenth-century granaries of Terranova (subsequently demolished) were now used as barracks for the royal guard, and the cloisters of S. Salvador as the headquarters of the Engineers.

A hitherto unknown military 'geometry' – largely perpetuated and strengthened in the Austrian period – was now inscribed within the city space, stretching outwards to include the nearby islands. Alterations to the main fortified buildings and sites, and innovations carried out by the French *Génie* between 1806 and 1813, also produced a thorough reordering of lagoon and

Porta Nuova at the Arsenal, built to a project by
Lessan. To the right, the neo-Gothic tower at
the entrance to the dry-docks built in the late
nineteenth century.

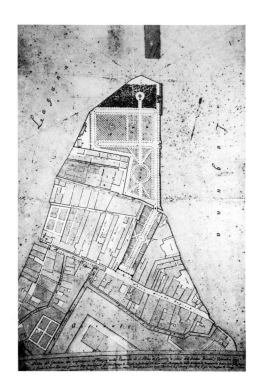

Giannantonio Selva, project for the public gardens and via Eugenia at Castello. Venice, museo Correr.

coastal defences, with the building of the fortifications of Marghera, discussed as early as 1805 by the first Austrian government, and actually begun between 1807 and 1808. This was the start of a rapid, and very noticeable, escalation in the military use of the lagoon (intensified both by the Habsburg government and, from 1871, by the kingdom of Italy), with numerous and important works of military architecture, designed to control internal navigation (lagoon redoubts and batteries), the lesser harbour mouths (the forts of S. Erasmo and Treporti), and the seaward front of the Lido (forts of Quattro Fontane and Malamocco).

In parallel, complementary work on the reorganization of the dockyards and port facilities was also begun at the end of the first decade of the nineteenth century. Here the French aim was to develop the maritime port vis-à-vis nearby Trieste, so as to restore Venice to her pre-eminent position on the communication routes between the Adriatic and the eastern Mediterranean. The first new work in the Arsenal began between 1809 and 1811, including the opening of the porta Nuova to the northeast of the darsena Novissima (new basin), and a canal linking it with the port of Malamocco, to be made deeper by means of the new dike at Alberoni (where work was broken off in 1813 and resumed in 1827). There is an important study by Andrea Salvini for a new dry-dock (never built), which was to have been situated near the new seaward entrance, where the great refitting basins were to be realized in the

second half of the century, but the project was never implemented. Nonetheless, though still linked to it topographically, in functional terms the Arsenal was now detached from the basin of San Marco, which was used almost exclusively as a mercantile harbour.

During this same period the French navy also built an important work inside the Arsenal itself: this was the tower of Porta Nuova, designed by Lessan, technically modelled on the masthouse at Copenhagen, but with certain formal resemblances to the towers at the old medieval entrance from rio della Madonna, such as the large pointed rusticated windows. This stylistic compromise was all the more significant when seen in relation to an alternative project put forward by the director of naval constructions, Salvini, which was firmly imperial and Neoclassical in tone.

Meanwhile, in the basin of San Marco, the use of the suppressed Benedictine monastery of S. Giorgio Maggiore as a free port area had necessitated the building of a new artificial wet-dock, closed in by a slender dike and overlooked at its end by two lighthouse towers designed by Giuseppe Mezzani and Romeo Venturelli (1810–11): these took the form of small polygonal buildings in smooth rusticated Istrian stone, topped by open lanterns, modelled on the type of fortified lighthouse that was canonic at the time. These innovating tendencies, and their controversial relations with the past, were registered particularly clearly at the edges of the city, at Castello,

The Napoleonic wing, piazza San Marco.

Lorenzo Santi, Coffee House on the Molo di San Marco.

where they proceeded in parallel with the internal restructuring of the Arsenal. The 'Strada Eugenia' (the present-day via Garibaldi) was now being opened up not far from the outer walls of the shipyard: designed by Giannantonio Selva in 1808, it entailed the filling in of rio di Castello and its transformation into 'the most beautiful street in Venice, both because it runs so straight' – extending into the open space of the waters of the basin to end, visually, at the Dogana da Mar – 'and for its ample breadth',[2] since it included not only the canal, but also the *fondamenta* to the sides. This was a first, clear pointer to the shift in town-planning culture referred to above. A direct offshoot of this street, both topographically and ideologically, was the second important work by Selva, the Giardini Pubblici (Public Gardens) (1810), created by means of extensive demolition, and originally part of a more complex plan. Laid out 'all'italiana', the gardens were to have included a romantic little Ionic temple on a circular plan, 'in the midst of the wood', on the Motta di S. Antonio. The overtones of this undertaking were multifarious, but it was clearly designed 'for the people' in a working-class suburb entirely dependent on the nearby naval installations, and intended as an innovative political gesture indicating an interest in some 'two thousand citizens whose lives had been entirely devoted to this labour and this living'.

The creation of the Giardini Pubblici aroused various controversies, some of a social nature, since 'vast crowds were drawn, particularly on feast days . . . by the entertainments and other things to be seen and heard there, so that these streets became impassable to modest, decent persons of sound morals'.[3]

But the search for some architectural form of embodiment for the new institutional order, and its tendencies, was at its most intense in the area around San Marco. The main proposed alterations to what had been the heart of the *ancien régime* were set out in Antolini's plan for the layout of the Procuratie Nuove as a royal palace: decided upon in 1807, after a chain of complex and controversial events, this ultimately led to the demolition of the large fourteenth-century granaries of Terranova, in order to make room for the Royal Gardens. This was followed by the demolition of Sansovino's church of S. Geminiano and the adjacent section of the Procuratie Vecchie, to be replaced by the Ala Napoleonica (Napoleonic wing) by Giuseppe Maria Soli and Lorenzo Santi, closing in the Piazza to the west. In point of fact, the impact of these innovations proved to be limited in terms of architectural inventiveness. Soli looked to the Sansovinian-Scamozzian model of the first two orders of the Procuratie Nuove, extending it along the side opposite San Marco, crowning it with a long attic storey decorated with bas-reliefs to conceal the vault of the ballroom, and also to mediate visually between the differing height of the New and Old Procuratie. Oddly enough, his solution had obvious affinities with the sixteenth-century idea, documented by Francesco

Sansovino, for 'surrounding the piazza' following the architectural model of Jacopo's Library. Moreover, Giovanni Antonio Antolini's project for the facade of the Royal palace overlooking the lagoon had taken on something of the assertiveness of Sansovino's classicism, proposing a replica (never built) of the Zecca to the west of the Molo. A degree of compromise between architecture and city was therefore already at work in Neoclassical Venice, amidst a welter of controversy and unconcealed conflict.

Greater autonomy was shown by the facade to the back of the Napoleonic wing, with its giant Ionic order above the ground-floor rustication, and its crowning statues. Together with the facade of the Corpo di Guardia in front of it – by Santi and Giovan Alvise Pigazzi – this stretch of calle Larga dell'Ascensione thus became a perfect microcosm of Neoclassical taste. Lorenzo Santi was also responsible for one of the most graceful examples of Neoclassical architecture, annexed to the Napoleonic complex of the Royal palace: this was the domed garden pavilion of the coffee house (built 1815–17), which Selvatico accused of looking like 'a model, or a child's plaything',[4] on account of the disparity between the vigorous use of the Greek Doric order – however careful, and largely successful – and the general scale of the building.

Significantly enough, at the point where the nearby calle Vallaresso runs into the Grand Canal, we find an example of Selva's Neoclassicism in one of the few privately

commissioned works dating from this period, the facade of palazzetto Erizzo (now Hotel Monaco): with its ground floor in rusticated Istrian stone, the layout of its facade – largely indifferent to longstanding Venetian tradition – and its very simple windows with their triangular pediments on the first *piano nobile* and the centre of the second, it is a severe version, stripped of all direct Palladian reference, of the facade of the house for the consul John Smith designed by Visentini in the middle of the eighteenth century, whose top floor was added some thirty years later by Selva himself. Moreover, it continued to be taken as a model followed more or less closely over several subsequent decades.

Naturally enough, the climate in the early nineteenth century as described above did not lend itself to the building of works of religious architecture in the city, though David Rossi restructured the interior of the church of S. Polo with the incorporation of architraved Ionic colonnades running between the nave and aisles. More importantly, Giannantonio Selva did in fact build two churches, both completed by Antonio Diedo: S. Maurizio, a parish church not far from San Marco, rebuilt from 1806, and the outlying church of the Nome del Gesù (1815–34). The former, intentionally reminiscent of the demolished S. Geminiano, took the form of a domed Greek cross, though the facade is completely independent of the Renaissance model. It has a severe facing of Istrian stone crowned by a triangular pediment, with reliefs from the

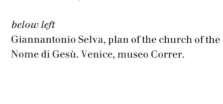

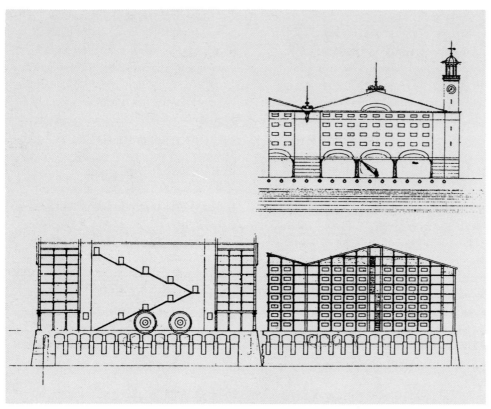

left
Giuseppe Jappelli, project for a warehouse on the Zattere. Padua, museo Civico.

below left
Giannantonio Selva, plan of the church of the Nome di Gesù. Venice, museo Correr.

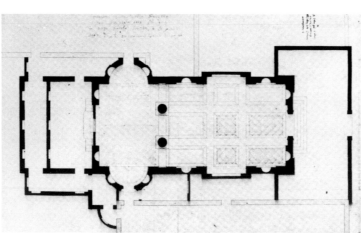

above
Giannantonio Selva, church of S. Maurizio, facade.

left
Lorenzo Santi, palazzo Patriarcale, facade.

Giovanni Casoni, Corpo di Guardia at the Arsenal.

life of the soldier-martyr St. Maurice and the Theban legion he commanded at the time of Maximianus, and is articulated by two panels with bas-reliefs, a large semi-circular window on a powerful cornice (interrupted centrally so as to suggest a tripartite division of the vast wall surface) and a pedimented Ionic portal, flanked by two window-aedicules. All in all, this too was an innovative work, combining rigorous though simplified allusions to sixteenth-century classicism with a scrupulous use of archaeological learning. Though with a different emphasis, these factors reappeared in the fine church of the Nome di Gesù, whose facade is more lively than that of S. Maurizio, partly because of its smaller dimensions and the side pilaster strips which support the pediment. It is notable above all for the unusual treatment of the chancel, with apses at the two ends, roofed with crosswise barrel vaulting and separated off from the body of the church by two Ionic columns, in a manner not dissimilar to that found in certain works of English Palladianism.

Thus the architectural transformations to the Piazza had also triggered off an important clutch of works in adjacent areas. But activity in the Marcian area itself ended only several decades later, with one conclusive building, also by Santi, the palazzo Patriarcale (1836–50). Backed up against the north side of the basilica – once ducal, now a cathedral – it closed in the piazzetta dei Leoncini with one final innovative addition to the by now highly

right
John Ruskin, *Corner of the Basilica of San Marco.*
London, Tate Gallery.

below right
Lodovico Cadorin, palazzina Marioni-Mainella,
facade over the Grand Canal.

stratified appearance of a particularly sensitive urban site. An emblem of the patriarchate's new role in city affairs, it was built
at a time when the Venetian church was
poised to regain its former authority, following the steps taken by patriarch Pyrker
(1821–8) with the Viennese court for the
promoting of an upturn in the Venetian
economy, and the efforts of patriarch
Monico to obtain greater freedom of ecclesiastical action. The solemnly declamatory
tone of the facade is therefore not surprising:
the building stands on a high base supporting the six giant Corinthian pillars – their
capitals interpolated with classical festoons
beneath an attic floor with windows and
ornate metopes decorated with sacred motifs
in strong relief (and an open book bearing
the signature of the architect). Here a stately,
if hardly pioneering, Neoclassicism was used
to confer a special dignity upon an autonomous work of completion for the Piazza: the
numerous unsuccessful projects included
some clearly deriving from Palladianism,
and others from a Sansovinian classicism,
but also an interesting – and early – proposal
for a return to the style and decoration
typical of the Lombardi.

A continuation in many ways of the
programme outlined in the Napoleonic
years, the Austrian government's policy for
the city was still centred essentially upon
transforming the canal system, in part, into
a pedestrian one; on strengthening the maritime military base of the Arsenal; and on
works of fortification for the lagoon. The
building of the railway bridge linking

Venice with the mainland (to a project by
Tommaso Meduna and Luigi Duodo, 1841–6)
was its most radical contribution to the city's
infrastructure, in terms of psychological
impact, if not immediately in social and
economic ones: now Venice was no longer
marooned on her lagoon, and the myth of
her hallowed island status was shattered.
The building of the railway station had
necessitated the demolition of the Palladian
church of S. Lucia; seen in conjunction with
the construction of fortified works within
the city itself (the batteria del Ponte, 1846;
the forte della Stazione, 1861), the filling in
of various canals, the building of cast-iron
bridges – including the two main ones over
the Grand Canal, at the Accademia and the
Scalzi (1854 and 1858, by Alfred E. Neville,
demolished in 1934) – and the installation
of a system of gas lighting, the general
impact of this epoch-making event, and its
potential repercussions on the city fabric
as a whole, become increasingly clear.

This was also the background for other
works of public architecture, characterized
by a general Neoclassical decorum, from
the Doric pillars of the facade on the rio Terra
dell'Archivio di Stato (also by Lorenzo
Santi), housed in the former monastery
of the Frari from 1815, to the sturdy neo-
cinquecentismo of the Salt Storehouses
near the Salute by Giovanni Alvise Pigazzi
(c. 1830) – similar in approach to that
adopted by G. Mezzani for the depots
overlooking the basin for the free port of
S. Giorgio – and the sedate, subdued facade,
minimally decorated with a triangular

Palazzo Cavalli Franchetti on the Grand Canal.

tympanum, of the slaughterhouse at
S. Giobbe, by Giuseppe Salvadori. In tandem with the railway bridge, this latter
was intended to become part of the new
'ordered' facade, overlooking the railway,
of the somewhat ragged westernmost edges
of the urban fabric, where the canal of
Cannaregio ran into the lagoon, replacing
a rambling older area of mixed residential
and charitable buildings, and premises
used by artisans and small factories. The
Greek Doric, on the other hand, had been
used for the formal treatment of the buildings put up at the Arsenal: these included
the galleries for the maritime depots in the
country (1824, now demolished), and the
severe tetrastyle facade of the Corpo di
Guardia built in 1832 after various changes
in plan. This latter work – like the galleries,
by Giovanni Casoni, in charge of building
work in the dockyards and on various
buildings in the city belonging to the navy –
similar in tone to several academic projects
dating from the Napoleonic era, and situated
next to the facade of the treasury of Naval
Warfare (almost certainly also by Casoni,
influenced by Selva), was a visual declaration of the Austrian military presence in the
city, one on which much of the Venetian
economy depended in its current somewhat
parlous state.

   'Venice, it must be admitted, is in her
second childhood. Venice will be great
again,' wrote the Chamber of Commerce
in 1845. Her model and objectives, now
vigorously reasserted, were to be those of a
capital city, 'called upon by nature herself

303

to be a centre of communications with all states near and far', an international market place for passing trade.[5]

This striving for recovery – which, in the 1840s, was anticipated as being lengthy and hard-won – together with various strains of nostalgia and romantic stirrings, such as had stimulated Byron's dramatic outpourings[6] and Ruskin's passionate involvement around this same time, now inspired a yearning to return, architecturally, to the Venice of the Middle Ages and early Renaissance, through the use of styles typical of her age of greatness and mercantile expansion. Apart from his Neoclassical works, Giovanni Alvise Pigazzi also engaged in exercises in the neo-Gothic and Lombardesque; at the end of the 1840s the Gothic revival found expression in the palazzetto on Campo S. Fantin by Giovan Battista Meduna (1846), a more or less exact recreation of the traditional tripartite facade in its symmetrical fifteenth-century version, with superimposed three-light windows, single-light side windows framed between slender twisted columns, and cladding in dentilled panels of precious marble.

This same mood inspired the caffé Florian, under the porticoes of the Procuratie Nuove on piazza San Marco, a smart society meeting-place, but also the headquarters of the rebels in the years of revolution of 1848-9. The refurbishing of its interior in 1858, by Lodovico Cadorin (who also restored the caffé Quadri at the beginning of the following year) was sophisticated,

elegant and thoroughly eclectic, with certain eighteenth-century touches, largely in keeping with the ori-ginal name, 'Venezia Trionfante'(Venice Triumphant). Also in 1858, Cadorin looked to Lombardesque models for the facade of the small palazzo Marioni, visible from the Grand Canal, making extensive use of decorative features in brick, which were not unknown in the city, despite being inconsistent with Venetian early Renaissance sources of inspiration. The municipality was now in the process of acquiring the old thirteenth-century palazzo of Fontego dei Turchi, restored by Federico Berchet from 1861 (the part overlooking the Grand Canal being completed in 1869). Radically restructured and 'hypervenetianized',[7] it was opened as the home of the civic art collections in 1869. In its turn, the Fontego became a model, whether direct or indirect, for a determined reinstatement of the 'Byzantine style', and for a concomitant rapid spread of architectural decoration in the form of salvaged paterae, marble slabs and cornices, but also, far more frequently, of imitations, with the widespread mass production of thousands of medieval sculptural fakes, mostly in Nanto or Costoza stone, a phenomenon which reached its peak in the early twentieth century, leading to the 'Venetianization' of much of the building on the Venetian hinterland, Friuli and Istria.[8] This was the start of a widely-felt revivalist mood which continued throughout the nineteenth century and the first decades of the twentieth.

Meduna too had experimented with the fifteenth-century Gothic in his renovation of palazzo Giovanelli at S. Fosca (1847–8), and Camillo Boito had reorganized the interiors of palazzo Cavalli Franchetti at the Accademia in a neo-medieval style. If the Gothicizing structures of the cemetery of S. Michele, by Annibale Forcellini (1871–2), and those enclosing the new wet-docks at the Arsenal, were less distinctly 'Venetian', some aspects of SS Giovanni e Paolo were nonetheless reproduced on a smaller scale in the little chapel at S. Vio, by Pividor, who had also made various drawings for a possible completion of the facade of the Dominican church. Then came the elegant neo-Gothic flourishes of the early twentieth century, and the flowery decadent line followed by Giorgio Franchetti for the monumental restoration of his palazzo Ca' d'Oro. Here aestheticism and nostalgia mingled with the myth of lost craftsmanship, restored to Venetian culture in a famous study by Agostino Sagredo. In short, at Ca' d'Oro, 'after heinous processes of demolition, stolid restoration and irreverent industrialized tampering, Giorgio Franchetti was the first person in Venice to attempt . . . a restoration that truly followed the dictates of art'. It is not hard to fathom the implications of his wish to have the Venus of Cyrene placed in the open-air atrium overlooking the Grand Canal, on the encrusted marble flooring he himself had designed on the Marcian model: they reflected the hallowed, if decadent, idea of a Venice-Venus reborn in art from the waves. With the

Iron bridge at the Ghetto Novo on rio degli Ormesini.

Via XXII Marzo.

renewed use of old materials such as those contained in the 'box belonging to an old house-painter, with its burnt red earth, the sort that comes from the Murano factories which make mirrors, unrivalled in quality and unobtainable', and with the collaboration of the architect Forlati, who 'already associated the study of architecture with the practice of old working methods, and surrounded himself with fine craftsmen who set aside all concept of haste and teamwork, and sought to work free hand, on their own', such a rebirth would be seen as expressing the quintessence of a 'grieving Venice', and at the same time as an 'undaunted quest for her original beauty'.[9]

A new wave of drastic transformations affecting whole swathes of the urban fabric also occurred immediately after Venice's union with the kingdom of Italy: numerous alterations to the street system and works of slum clearance culminated in the plan of 1891, with the opening up of campo Manin; the demolition of the church of S. Paternian and some of the adjacent buildings; the creation of the Orseolo basin just to the north of the Piazza; and the opening of via Vittorio Emanuele II (Strada Nuova), via XXII Marzo, calle Larga Giacinto Gallina and via II Aprile. Meanwhile, the city's hotel system was growing (for instance with the Hotel Londres et Beau Rivage, the classically-inspired section by Carlo Ruffini and the neo-Renaissance one by Giovanni Fuin, 1855–67); the commercial port of S. Basilio and the stazione Marittima were built; the Arsenal was further extended and industry was

encouraged to move to outlying areas; whilst the enlarged gardens of Castello hosted the first international Biennale in 1895.

The ensuing city-wide surge of building activity, by no means restricted to the areas mentioned above, was particularly favourable to the spread of an eclecticism which found its most interesting expression, as far as the Gothic revival was concerned, in the Fish Market at Rialto (1907), designed by the painter Cesare Laurenti and the architect Domenico Rupolo as an elegant loggia on a fourteenth/fifteenth-century model overlooking the Grand Canal; in the original, and in some sense irreverent and ironic, facade of the house designed for himself by Mario De Maria (*Marius pictor*, 1910–13), which drew freely upon architectural and decorative features of the Ducal palace; and in several buildings by Giuseppe Berti, for instance the palazzetto Stern (1909–12), also on the Grand Canal, with its neo-Byzantine interior and display of 'antique' fragments, whether genuine or exhibited as such, and large Gothicizing side window reminiscent of that of the De Maria house.

A contemporary parade of Veneto-Byzantine revivalist virtuosity was provided by another artist's house, that of Giulio Torres on the Fondamenta del Gaffaro (1905–7): a treasury of scrupulously accurate quotations (the facade is a virtual copy of that of a fine medieval house with a workshop and a multi-light window with cusped arches on the nearby campo S. Margherita), it is an inspired combination

right
Hotel Londres et Beau Rivage (left-hand part by
Carlo Ruffini, neo-Lombardesque right-hand
part by Giovanni Fuin).

below right
Mario De Maria and Bartolomeo Bezzi, palazzo
Pro Arte at the Biennale, 1895.

Rialto market, with the Pescheria by Cesare
Laurenti and Domenico Rupolo on the right.

Giuseppe Berti, palazzetto Stern on the Grand Canal.

of the use of colour (with its minute fresco decoration) and a strikingly conceived play of volumes, with generous corner windows, set in a shady garden overlooking the green waters of the canal in front of it. But the medievalizing jugglings so popular at the time might also be deployed in unexpected ways: together with the usual repertoire of pseudo-thirteenth-century sculptures and panels, Giulio Alessandri applied various clumsy Romanesque and Byzantinizing features to the out-of-scale volumes of the massive complex of apartments running around two sides of the Corte dell'Alboro (Case Nardi, 1905–14). Distortions sometimes verged on the absurd, as with the great medievalizing portal with its huge cusped arch and crenellated wall built in calle dei Botteri to surround the space in front of Titian's house.

A further list of comparable works would be lengthy and tedious (it might also include mock-Renaissance buildings on key sites, such as the rebuilding, by Consiglio Fano, of Ca' Ruzzini, the so-called Fondaco dei Persiani near Rialto). There were also sensational examples of large church facades being completed 'in period', sometimes to 'original' designs, ranging from S. Geremia near the station (1871) to the Pietà on riva degli Schiavoni (1906) and S. Silvestro near the Rialto market (1909).

A parallel route was also taken, from the late nineteenth century onwards, in popular building, with the involvement of a number of architects including Francesco Marsich, Francesco Balduin, Giovanni Sardi,

Ernest Wullekopf, Mulino Stucky (ex-flour mill) on the Giudecca.

above
Giovanni Sardi, Hotel Excelsior on the Lido.

below
Francesco Marsich, Hotel des Bains on the Lido.

Consiglio Fano and, later, Ambrogio Narduzzi, Paolo Bertanza and others. After a series of variations on local building practices and types (Campo S. Ternita, 1867–8), here too historicist allusions and picture-sque inflections now prevailed.

Exceptions were few and far between: they include the palazzetto for commercial use by Guido Costante Sullam (1908–10), overlooking the recently opened Orseolo basin, where the problem of the building's incorporation into a focal point just two steps away from San Marco was solved by using a facade with simple, clear geometrical lines framing Ionic windows on the *piano nobile*, which have something of the delicate freedom of Art Nouveau.

Other *sui generis* examples – though still in the historicist vein – were generated by the brief and doomed attempt to industrialize certain outlying areas, particularly the Giudecca; here references completely alien to the city's architectural culture were introduced, in particular in the massive, turreted Mulino Stucky opposite the stazione Marittima of S. Basilio (1897–1920), by Ernest Wullekopf, with its northern Gothic features typical of the great Hanseatic ports; Consiglio Fano and Ugo Vigevano, too, looked to the south German Gothic in the nearby Dreher brewery (whose interior has recently been restructured by Giuseppe Gambirasio for Erp housing).

Despite a degree of protest at the destruction of the Lido seashore, urbanization proceeded rapidly, with numerous transformations occurring as early as the

Guido Costante Sullam, villa Monplaisir on the Lido.

last decades of the nineteenth century, when the main built-up nucleus moved from around the fortified complex and monastery of S. Nicolo to the area around S. Maria Elisabetta. Midway between nostalgia and modernity, the Moorish bulk of the beachside Hotel Excelsior, with its domes and minarets by Giovanni Sardi (1898–1908), and the more retiring eclecticism of the Hotel des Bains by Francesco Marsanich (1905–9) – both indicative of the growth of a well-heeled, blue-blooded tourism – were part of the revivalist wave which also swept the new seaside centre and its tree-lined avenues, while villa Monplaisir by Giulio C. Sullam (1906) was a more cultured, forward-looking and inventive version of the popular Art Nouveau style in a context where restrictions and conditionings were far fewer than in the city centre.

But the overall picture was still changing rapidly. As it became clear that any future for the island of Venice as a port and industrial centre was unlikely to bear fruit, at the beginning of the century the idea of a 'New Venice' – a 'greater Venice' – gained ground, giving rise to various plans which were partially implemented between 1917 and 1924. These, it was hoped, would rescue the city from her dilemma of becoming either a superb necropolis, or the object of brutal modernization, and focused essentially on the resumption of her role as a great port-of-call, and the installation of new life-giving industrial activities, within a framework which would radically revise the functioning of her entire, extended municipal territory.

These initiatives found an echo in D'Annunzio's images of Venice as a 'pregnant' city, productive, dynamic and aggressive, with San Marco becoming the 'Wild Beast', accoutred with wings and crouched in readiness for the 'great leap forwards'. Her waters might be 'troubled', but they could still act as a powerful source of inspiration for forceful and energetic minds.[10]

In this way, Venice's thorny relationship with history – experienced by the nineteenth century as the memory-cum-destiny of a vanished mercantile wealth – now tended to blur into anticipations of the imperial destinies of Fascist Italy.

This led to the building of the new port, and of the new industrial zone and working-class districts of Marghera, the plans for which were presented at the Fiera campionaria at Padua in 1932, in the pavilion of the Società del porto industriale di Venezia (Company of the new industrial port of Venice), which was built in silver aluminium made and worked by the new industrial installations to a project by Brenno Del Giudice. The city was now linked to them by means of a canal which was presented as a 'broad and modern variant' of the traditional Venetian trading route. The stretch of motorway between Padua and Venice was built, and the goodsyard at Mestre was extended; Mestre itself, which was merged with the municipality of Venice in 1926 together with other smaller places, was destined for unlimited expansion as a modern outcrop of the city of Venice, linked to the industrial zone and

residential districts of Marghera by means of a flyover. This unification of the 'two shores of greater Venice', island and hinterland, was further achieved by the new road bridge across the lagoon (1932–3) and the opening of a canal near the Venice head, intended as a rapid link with the stretch of the Grand Canal flowing into the basin of San Marco. This 'wider Venice' thus 'embraced two cities', the one ancient and immortal, the other supposedly a hotbed of activity.

An 'untouched gem of ancient art, set in the vibrant steel of modernity'[11] was the image coined by one of the men of the hour, with the addition of quite specific suggestions: the old Venice, revitalized as a new 'city', a business and service centre, home to political and cultural bodies, was to remain inviolate within an outer ring of healthy yet controlled activity. In a way, this implied the bolstering of some tendencies which had already emerged *in nuce* with the plan of 1891, and which the exact rebuilding of the campanile of San Marco after its collapse in 1902, 'where it was and as it was', had graphically exemplified.

In point of fact, no sooner had decisions concerning the industrial port been taken, than the new municipal Commissione all'ornato, which included the historian Carlo Lorenzetti and the architect Duilio Torres, found itself confronting the question in terms of its own working criteria, namely: 'Jealously to preserve everything in Venice which pertains to art', according to the basic principle enshrined in the report drafted by Torres himself.

The accompanying set of directions, whether consequential or complementary, were intended on the one hand to put a stop to architectural revivals in general, and neo-medievalisms in particular, to halt the spread of 'fakes', and the use of concrete as a material for ornament (to be replaced, if at all, by brick, soft rock or artificial stone); on the other, should any large-scale intervention prove necessary, they suggested drawing upon 'inspiration' from the 'pure' sources of Italian architecture, while confessing themselves perplexed as to the feasibility of building 'any very modern construction adjacent to an old one'. At the same time, while maintaining that 'the character of a city does not derive exclusively from its chief buildings or monuments . . . but rather from the sum total of all its ordinary buildings, and in particular from the houses lived in by the mass of the people' – and hence essentially calling for it to be protected – they nonetheless did not intend to endorse 'any exaggerated preservation of old and inconvenient houses, or walls, or other insignificant constructions purely in the name of art'.[12] Lastly, for the more modest dwellings on new developments, they proposed the imitation of popular building types dating from 'recent periods characterized by good architecture', with facades with harmoniously grouped round-headed arches, and suggestions for an increase in green city space and extremely generalized proposals for the Lido and Marghera. This document clearly covered a wide range of topics, but was

riddled with ambiguities and hard to implement, as was reflected to some extent by the
architectural achievements of the twenties
and thirties.

The road bridge (ponte Littorio, now
ponte della Libertà, to a design by the
engineers Vittorio Fantucci and Eugenio
Miozzi) was inaugurated on 25 April 1933.
Although its repercussions were more
intrusive than those of the railway bridge,
since it brought motor traffic straight on to
the island itself – albeit to a peripheral area
– structurally speaking its appearance was
deliberately reassuring. Thus it went some
way towards dispelling the dread image of
a Venice 'with her Grand Canal filled in
and traversed by the noisy bustle of electric
carriages, her buildings ringing to the roar
of motor cars and swathed in billowing
fumes'.[13] In fact, it was doubly unthreaten-
ing, both as a replica, or rather 'twin', of the
nineteenth-century railway bridge – by
now an accepted part of the urban image –
and in terms of the materials used, brick
and Istrian stone. The impact of its entry
into the city was tactfully marked with
tall piers with the neo-cinquecentesque
Marcian 'Lion of Traù,' recalling the official
rhetoric of the great public works of the
past, and the enduring importance, for the
city, of her points of linkage and communication. Nor was it any accident that the
official press should have presented the
work, at its inauguration, as 'safeguarding'
the hallowed needs of the new Venice.

But attitudes changed completely
when it came to the layout of the Piazzale

Brenno Del Guidice, Fire Station.

Casa del Farmacista on the Lido.

adjacent to the city bridgehead: here the obvious demands of modernization were expressed through the abandoning of all stylistic compomise, with the sober but aggressive rationalism of the multi-storey car park (Eugenio Miozzi et al., 1931–4), trumpeted by the press as the largest in the world, another symbol of Venetian superiority. Here, in line with the general approach mentioned above, two provisos had been stipulated concerning the work's incorporation into the city: that its height should be limited, so as not to clash with the 'general appearance of the city';[14] and that the old frontage on to the Grand Canal should be preserved in its entirety, this being the only 'characteristically Venetian' part of the pre-existing pattern of the area. Here the stated aim was to conceal the sight of motorized traffic in all directions; in fact, the partial demolition of the building curtain gave the 'Ina garage' an unexpectedly stark role as backdrop to the western end of the Grand Canal, thus highlighting the ambiguities and contradictions inherent in such an approach. Affirmation and denial, imitation and innovation, emphasis and concealment instantly came together in the first head-on encounter between Venice and modern architecture.

The same line was followed for other related works in the heart of the urban fabric: the ponte degli Scalzi (Eugenio Miozzi, 1931–2), 'a slender marble ribbon' replacing the old Habsburg station bridge, and constituting an integral part of the layout of the new ponte Littorio, built in the traditional Istrian stone, was a highly simplified version of the sixteenth-century model of the Rialto bridge, without the shops. The bridges designed to span rio Nuovo at Ca' Foscari and S. Margherita, too, were evocative rationalizations of traditional Venetian practice; the latter provided the opportunity to straighten out the bank of campo S. Pantalon, and to give it two quays 'alla romana'.

The winning project at the 1933 competition for a new bridge at the Accademia, by Duilio Torres in collaboration with Ottorino Briazza, with sculptures by Antonio Maraini, was never built; the 'temporary' solution in wood, given permanent status by the restoration of 1983–4, is by Miozzi. However, one new project to be built between 1932 and 1934 was the large Fire Station, beside one of Miozzi's two bridges. The building was situated at the delicate juncture where rio Nuovo runs into the Grand Canal, and the architect, Brenno Del Giudice, approached the problem of the incorporation of the 'modern' into the urban fabric in a direct and uncompromising manner. A lecturer at the Scuola superiore di architettura di Venezia from 1927–36, here he set aside the elegant late-Baroque of his earlier works, such as the Casa del Farmacista on the Lido, in favour of the unbending eloquence of the official idiom, although once more reworked with concessions dictated by the context: these ranged from the powerful neo-secentesque rustication of the basement, at water level, to the grouping of the double order of windows of the facade overlooking the *rio* into multi-light clusters, the long first-storey balustrade, the horizontal strips dividing up the facade, the corner rustications, and the massive arches of the four deep 'cavane' (moorings), with their Baroque-style keystones. Often regarded as the first uncompromisingly modern work to be built in Venice, the Fire Station does nonetheless exhibit certain unmistakable signs of continuity with the past, however superficial.

A similar approach was adopted during this same period for work on the long stretch of *riva* of the basin of San Marco; which was now being extended and laid out afresh to create a new pedestrian link between the Piazza and the eastern area of the city, towards the Arsenal, the Gardens and the Biennale; in 1933 work began on a long new wharf (riva dell'Impero, now riva dei Sette Martiri), opened in 1937.

Now it was Duilio Torres's turn to update Renaissance models (ponte delle Guglie) in his two designs for the ponte dell'Arsenale at S. Biagio, and the ponte di S. Domenico on rio di S. Giuseppe.

A series of developments was also simultaneously under way both at the outermost point of the area of Castello, and along the lagoonside area of the Lido, which was now being prepared for incorporation into the 'greater Venice' as its eastern zone, middle-class in its social structure and economically dependent mainly on tourism. The main components of this process at Castello were the reinforcing of the maritime military system, and various housing developments, together with improvements to the infrastructure for the Biennale. On the Lido, the promotion of an exclusive type of tourism now required the building of yet another means of access, in the form of the airport.

One of the purposes of the new layout of the riva was to link the city centre with the district of Vittorio Emanuele, built as a new development to the north of the gardens of S. Elena and bounded by the Parco della Rimembranza, with a general plan and individual buildings by Bertanza, Gusso and others (1924-7).

This provided the opportunity for a belated, but extensive, diverse, and once again reassuring use of the more eclectic repertoire of 'Venetian' styles. An 'austere and impressive ... classicizing style', on the other hand, was adopted for the technical and naval Istituto Paolo Sarpi, by the engineer Cicogna (1926). More innovative proposals in the sphere of popular housing had been set aside, for instance those by A. Narduzzi for the Giudecca (1920), which had a slight Austro-German flavour.

Shortly afterwards, when work on the riva dell'Impero was almost completed, the projected 'Scuola marinara' (sailing school) by Mansutti-Miozzo, at the tip of the island of S. Elena, was altered to become a naval college (1936). The completion of the various works of reorganization at the Arsenal was celebrated with the laying out of the piazzale dell'Impero, backing on to the Bucintoro dockyard, with its neo-medieval tower of the Campanella, rebuilt to a

Piazzale dell'Imperio and torre della Campanella at the Arsenal.

Bird's-eye view of the complex of the Casino and
palazzo del Cinema by E. Miozzi, on the Lido.

project by M. E. Ponzo of the Naval
Engineers, with *soprintendente* Forlati as
consultant. Both episodes proved significant for relations between architecture
and the city: in the naval college, the
modernism fostered by the Fascist regime
(together with a mosaic cycle based on
imperial Roman and Mussolinian iconography) was curbed, indeed 'sacrificed', in
terms of the height of the building, to the
'demands of the landscape';[15] in the second
case, the rebuilding of the tower, presented
as a symbolic reference to the work of the
medieval guilds, and passing for a faithful
reproduction of the fourteenth-century
building, the fruit of careful iconographic
documentation, was made possible by the
demolition of three *squeri* which were gen-
uinely late-medieval in layout. Thus in the
city itself, it seems reasonable to conclude
that there was no innovation without compromises of varying degrees of success,
together with the deliberate, and suitably
judged, use of 'characteristic' forms and
styles, as well as out-and-out 'fakes'. The
truly modern was destined to find expression elsewhere: in the enclosed, autonomous areas of the exhibition centre of
the Biennale and its expansion towards
S. Elena, and in those of the Lido, in a
sense related to it.

It was in fact the Biennale which thus
afforded an opportunity for Duilio Torres
to demonstrate his 'rigid twentieth-century
classicism' in the Italian pavilion, as in the
'extremely modern' Venice pavilion of the
decorative arts (1932 and 1938), which

Palazzo del Cinema.

were next to well-known works such as the Austrian pavilion by Joseph Hoffmann (1934). But the Biennale buildings were really tantamount to a sort of 'collection' of works which were destined to be subsequently added to virtually until the present day.

On the Lido, the architecture of the sanatoria and welfare institutions showed a receptiveness to modernity: Duilio Torres's lucidly functionalist Istituto Elioterapico (1922–3) made overt allusions to middle European precedents; the later Principi di Piemonte, a seaside colony at Alberoni, by Daniele Calabi (with Antonio Salce, 1936–7) drew both upon the rationalist mood, with its awareness of *l'esprit moderne*, which Calabi had encountered in his recent stay in Paris, but also upon a distinctive and recurrent feature of the collective spaces of the Veneto, that of the portico. During this same period, also at the Lido, the newly-established Mostra del Cinema (film festival) came to represent the second fixed point in a trio of cultural venues, the other two being the Biennale and the project for the artistic and theatrical centre at S. Giorgio (1939), promoted by Antonio Maraini, and designed by Brenno Del Giudice with the collaboration of Marino Meo.

The outcome of these developments was a further reinforcing of the international nexus already existing between the recently modernized Hotel Excelsior, the nearby palazzo del Cinema (L. Quagliata, 1937) and the adjacent palazzo del Casino (Miozzi and Quagliata, 1936), stripped bare of any stylistic reference by virtue of its utterly modernist functionalism. Connections between Venice and the Lido were now becoming rapidly closer and stronger. They were to be interpreted in two different ways in the two most important works, in this context, of the twenties and thirties: the church of S. Maria della Vittoria, and the Lido airport.

Originally conceived as a church dedicated to the Nicopeia, the icon from Constantinople housed on her own altar in San Marco, S. Maria della Vittoria was built following a vow made in 1918, in the great Venetian tradition of votive undertakings; the plan, by Giuseppe Torres, was exhibited at the first Roman Biennale, presented by the architect as a deeply symbolic work, the outcome of his search for a style stripped of all servile imitation, yet not incompatible with tradition. Indeed, the first version to be approved was a basically classicizing concept for a circular domed church set in a circular portico and approached by a tall flight of steps, with equally classically-inspired ornaments and sculptures; it was subsequently modernized with the simplification and paring down – surprising for an architect who had designed the house on rio del Gaffaro some ten years earlier – of its lines and surfaces, entirely eliminating all decorative and sculptural additions. But the original aims remained unchanged, namely to create an echo of the distant outline of the Salute, at the opposite side of the lagoon space in front of it, towards which the axis of its flight of steps was oriented, in an emblematic gesture making the Lido an integral part of a 'greater Venice' in the urban landscape of the basin of San Marco. In point of fact, in terms of interaction with the lagoon, these aims remained largely unmet, and Torres's attempt at image-making found itself actually addressing the bourgeois inhabitants of the Lido itself.

The purpose underlying the building of the new airport was quite different. The idea of Venice as an 'air port' developed in parallel to that of Venice as an industrial port; the idea of the Lido airport grew from the seeds of two small military installations at the Idroscalo (seaplane base) of S. Andrea, and the G. Nicelli airport on the Lido, taking shape in 1926 with the inauguration of the first regular air services. The airport itself was opened in 1934, a strongly horizontal building, with a spiral staircase, a terrace-gallery for the public during air displays, an iron and glass tower in the centre and wide rectangular windows, its facade clad in dark red stoneware (designed by the aeronautical department of Padua, and Santabarbara, in collaboration with Emmer, engineers). The first airport entirely built and equipped in Italy – according to the publicity of the time – it presented an avant-garde image of the 'ultra-modern' vitality of the age-old Serenissima, furthered by the scrupulous attention lavished upon the layout and decoration of its interior, which also flaunted the most up-to-the-minute lines and materials, including steel and rubber, together

Giuseppe Torres, votive church of S. Maria della Vittoria on the Lido.

with marble, glass, silk, mosaic and expensive varieties of wood. The decor and furnishings were designed by the painter Neri Pasinetti, with 'aeropitture' (aerial paintings) in the lobby by Tato (Guglielmo Sansoni) – a signatory in 1929 of the Manifesto of Futurist 'aeropitture' – and others, including Venini for the stained glass.

The general layout of all the interiors, offices included, had been carried out under the auspices of the 'Gruppo arti decorative' formed a few years earlier, in 1930, in reaction both to the mock eighteenth-century furnishing now more in vogue than ever, and the spread of Art Nouveau. Offering its services as interior designers of spaces which would be 'highly modern variants of Venetian tradition', the group had one representative for each branch of interior design (including stage design, from 1934 onwards): among them were Venini for glassware and lamps, Checchin for glassware and crystal, Neri Pasinetti for decoration, Cecolin for iron and metalwork, A. Chiggiato for Fortuny fabrics, Rosa for goldsmithery and Crovato for screens, and they worked in collaboration with various architects, including Virgilio Vallot, Brenno Del Giudice and Duilio Torres. The group was involved in a number of pioneering enterprises, from the Acnil passenger office and the bar at its seaside building on the Lido, to the district office in palazzo Corner della Ca' Granda, the Hotel Excelsior and several rooms at La Fenice and Ca' Giustinian at S. Moisè, which they turned into a typical Venetian *ritrovo* (meeting-place). They also designed furnishings for the Breda ship-yards, for the new motorboats on the direct line between Venice and the Lido, and certain projects for private individuals.

Their work was always culturally highly intelligent, with a preference for local materials.[16] The examples mentioned above are far from exhaustive, but typically forward-looking, and here, as in all their work, the group restricted themselves to the creation of interiors.

The *Progetto di massima per il piano di risanamento di Venezia insulare* (general plan for the reorganization of the island of Venice), mooted in 1939 by the municipality and drawn up by the chief engineer, Eugenio Miozzi, was never implemented, and the postwar panorama was marked by highly contradictory tendencies and initiatives. But the general picture was far from static, and a number of works were built, including several on particularly sensitive sites, from the extension to Hotel Danieli on riva degli Schiavoni (V. Vallot, 1946–8) and Hotel Bauer at S. Moisè (M. Meo, 1949–54) to the headquarters of the Società adriatica di navigazione on via XXII Marzo (A. Scattolin, 1957–9), the new railway station (P. Perilli and Ufficio tecnico, engineering department, 1952–5), the rebuilding of the palazzetto Foscari on the Grand Canal (M. Meo, 1951–4) and the large block of flats on riva dei Sette Martiri (C. Cristofoli and M. Pavanini, 1952–4). All in all – apart from numerous cases of works whose effects were highly negative for the townscape in general – this period produced little of interest in terms either of general plans or individual buildings. The Biennale, however, continued to be more fertile terrain: it now included works by Gerrit Thomas Rietveld (Dutch pavilion, 1954) and Alvar Aalto (Finnish pavilion, 1956).

Nevertheless, these same years also saw the rejection of Frank Lloyd Wright's project (1953) for the palazzina Masieri at the 'volta del Canal', opposite Ca' Foscari, despite the fact that it demonstrated that it was possible to avoid being derivative, while still remaining sensitive to the surrounding fabric.

It is worth noting that this project had been opposed by a figure as eminent as

Marino Meo, Hotel Bauer at S. Moisè.

Duilio Torres (who taught at the Istituto superiore di architettura until 1952), but was regarded as potentially furthering the acceptance of a more incisive architecture – 'whose close-knit chromatic vibrancy could have given the city a valuable lesson in environmental enrichment' – by Giuseppe Samonà, the architect of one of the few authoritative additions to the urban scene during those years, and a key figure in the revitalization of the Venice School of architecture. 'Various and ambiguous' shades of resistance thus came to the fore, following the blanket assertion that 'the whole environment was comprehensively inviolable', as Samonà himself wrote.[17] These same objections resurfaced, with slightly different arguments, in the face of the two projects by great contemporary architects: the hospital by Le Corbusier, to be built on the site of the slaughterhouse at S. Giobbe (1964) – a reworking of the cityscape which would have made an extremely forceful contribution to what was now the main entrance to the city, that is, from the mainland; and the project by Louis Kahn (1968–9) for the palazzo dei Congressi (conference centre) and exhibition hall at the Biennale. This latter too would have made an impact on an urban scale, since, among other things, its monumentality would have redefined the relation between this 'palace of the meeting of minds' and the image of the city by giving new shape to the presence of the Biennale on the *riva*.

These unbuilt projects therefore amounted to so many messages unreceived.

Frank Lloyd Wright, project for the
'Masieri memorial' on the Grand Canal.

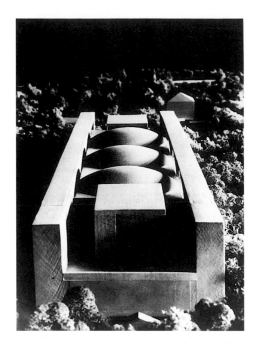

above
Louis Kahn, relief model of the palazzo dei Congressi in the Biennale gardens.

above right
Le Corbusier, hospital at S. Giobbe, view of the relief model from above.

below right
Oscar Niemeyer, sketch of an idea for the ponte dell' Accademia.

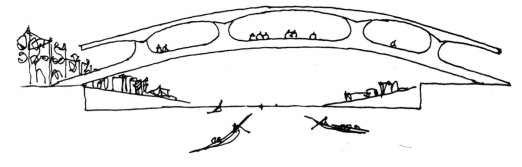

Giuseppe Samonà and Egle R. Trincanato,
building for Inail offices at S. Simeon Piccolo.

At least as many projects were put forward by Italian architects over these same years, from the 'Wrightian' casa Taddei by Carlo Scarpa on rio Terrà dei Catecumeni (1957) to the S. Giuliano project by the Quaroni group, which would have radically altered the relations between the two shores of the lagoon, and the Novissime project for the district of Tronchetto, by Samonà and associates, with its Utopian proposal for the demolition of the bridge, the elimination of the eyesore of the harbour infrastructure, and a return to the pre-nineteenth-century limits of the western edges of the city 'now shaped afresh by means of an architectural control of space ideally in accordance with the sensibilities of our time'.[18]

In fact, the relationship between Venice and new architecture had already been broached in a different way in two noteworthy examples, though not the most sensitive in terms of site. The first was the Inail headquarters – at right-angles to the Grand Canal, tucked away beside S. Simeon Piccolo, but also an extension of a recently built area cobbling together various old-established working spaces – by G. Samonà and E. R. Trincanato (1955–8). Samonà described his work as 'a series of continuously vibrating icons which repudiates any basic difference between solid and void . . . a continuity [which] tries to avoid the temptation of allusions to the iconographical tradition of the city, while structurally retaining the city's relatively small proportions in its single parts'.[19] A reference not to the forms, but to the basic principles

Ignazio Gardella, apartment block on the Zattere.

Pier Luigi Nervi and Angelo Scattolin, Cassa di Risparmio (savings bank) at S. Luca.

of Venetian architecture, is indeed perfectly apparent here.

For his houses on the Zattere – originally a peripheral area, characterized by utilitarian and commercial buildings, and public assistance services, and only more recently by residential building – Gardella once more deliberately turned to dialogue with the basic and distinctive features of Venetian architectural culture. Essentially, here he was proposing a sophisticated model that would enable contemporary architecture to participate in the last possible definition of the image of the city; the meticulously observed spatial and visual articulations are his own individual version of a sensitivity to the pre-existing environment originated by Rogers, as has already been observed.

Meanwhile, one last important building was going up in the city centre, between campo Manin and campo S. Luca, with the replacing of the neo-Renaissance building (1883–1906) for the offices of the Cassa di Risparmio, in an area that had been the object of a late nineteenth-century development (engineer C. Fano and others). The new building, by Pier Luigi Nervi and Angelo Scattolin, was notable for a display of extremely modern technology. In the preliminary project, the facades had been covered with one single outer skin, so as to 'form a lucid volume defined by extensive continuous surfaces, allowing one chromatic value to predominate';[20] but the definitive version – arrived at after a somewhat convoluted process involving various commissions – despite its apparent neutrality, nonetheless paid lip service to tradition through the uninterrupted double order of windows on the facades, set above the long strip of stone, and the solid-void relation between the upper part of the facade and the glassed-in base.

The urban development scheme for Venice, drawn up in 1959 and approved definitively three years later, earmarked most of the city as untouchable; the international campaigns for its protection included the famous contribution by the 'Corriere dell'Unesco' (1968), comparing the Venice in Peril appeal after the disastrous flood of 1966 with that for the Egyptian temples at Philae, in Nubia, flooded by the waters of the Nile. Clearly, the 'rallying call for conservation'[21] of the urban environment was now being reasserted. Briefly, then, in the early 1960s realistic opportunities for contemporary architecture in Venice seemed to be offered either by internal spaces, or by distinctly peripheral ones, topographically 'external' or self-contained.

In point of fact, Scarpa's two most significant Venetian works, the Olivetti showroom in the Procuratie Vecchie (1957–8), and the new design for the ground floor of palazzo Querini at S. Maria Formosa, the headquarters of the Querini Stampalia Foundation, fit into the first of these two categories only superficially, since in both cases the key to his thinking, the ultimate aim towards which his typical instruments – namely light, colours, materials, a subtle and sensitive use of texture, and a sophisticated statement of structural values – were jointly brought to bear, was in fact the figurative negation of the external-internal boundary. Thus the Olivetti showroom is a space 'on the piazza', open to inspection from the outside as a demonstration of the expressive potentialities of a degree of formal autonomy, while his work at the Querini Stampalia hinged on the establishing of a twofold relationship with the city and its waterways by diverting the unruffled waters of the canal in front of the palazzo into the entrance hall, and extend-

ing the architect's formal attention to the little access bridge, with its simple lines and archaizing use of wood over the steel structure, as it crosses the *rio* to end at the *riva* of the *campiello* in front of it.

Another important and roughly contemporary building on the Lido was the studio-house designed for himself by the architect Daniele Calabi (1961–3), clearly a key work, in its spareness and its relation to its site, in the pursuit of 'integrity in building'[22] which was his hallmark. But the problem here apparently thrust off to the edges of the city and lagoon environment remained that of the ideal relations to be established between project and setting, project and history and project and image (and myth) of the city, in the midst of differing and antithetical approaches to the 'problem of Venice': essentially, whether to contrive her survival in splendid isolation, or to redefine her role and future through a different frame-work of urban and territorial relations.

By and large, the history of these problems might be interpreted as that of the relations between Iuav, Venice's school of architecture, and the city itself, stemming in part from the stance taken by Giuseppe Samonà himself in his introductory lectures of 1948 and 1953, which asserted the need for a study of Venice in order to plan for her current requirements. The presence in the school of some of the most noteworthy post-war figures (Albini, Astengo, Belgioioso, Calabi, De Carlo, Piccinato, Samonà, Trincanato and Zevi; Muratori remained

alone in the attitude he adopted) also implied commitment to a less provincial position, and a lively and well-informed debate on the building of the future city, particularly evident between the end of the fifties and the early sixties, including several of the episodes already mentioned.

These were also years of physical and metaphorical renewal for Iuav, with the move to a site that was in some ways emblematic of the institution itself, namely Scamozzi's convent of the Tolentini, after a 'modernizing' restoration between 1960 and 1964 by Daniele Calabi (completed in 1968 under the supervision of M. Bacci), itself a formative event for ideas of restoration between the end of the fifties and the beginning of the sixties.

Despite assorted difficulties – not least of which was the relationship with the city's public institutions, and various shifts in local political balances – debate and research concerning the instruments for the refining, and implementing, of the school's cherished ideas nonetheless persisted throughout the seventies.

It is true that even in 1978, in presenting the 'problem' of Venice, Carlo Aymonimo could still talk of a 'state of impotence in both planning and architecture';[23] but it is also true that Iuav had intensified its efforts to dispel this same situation.

This was the background for a whole range of analytical studies and planning hypotheses (which also attracted suggestions from many protagonists in the field of architectural and town-planning research),

Carlo Scarpa, interior of the Olivetti showrooms.

Part of the ground-floor layout at Ca' Querini Stampalia.

Daniele Calabi, studio-house on the Lido.

Luciano Semerani and Gigetta Tamaro,
in-patient wards in the ospedale civile.

as well as for a clutch of works of public building, mainly residential.

A case apart – which should be considered in the somewhat complex framework of the Venice hospital as a whole – was the building of the in-patient department of the civil hospital at SS Giovanni e Paolo (Luciano Semerani and Gigetta Tamaro), conceived as a repeatable module roofed with barrel vaulting, with a semi-circular pediment over a central oculus or square, reminiscent both of the top section of the Scuola Grande di San Marco (which forms part of this same hospital), and the barrel vaulting of the nearby church of the Miracoli; it also made use of the traditional polychrome marbles for its cladding, and trachyte – traditional for Venetian paving – for the floors in the tall arcades which frame the view of the apse and transept of the church of Sti Giovanni e Paolo to the south.

The picture presented by publicly-owned residential building is more complex. For his new district of low cost housing at Mazzorbo, Giancarlo de Carlo and collaborators (1979–86) deliberately chose to follow the local building texture, basing themselves on a meticulous interpretation of the codes governing the clustering of public spaces, and of the configuration of the houses themselves, giving fresh life to deeply entrenched habits in buildings whose relationship with the traditional lexicon was most imaginatively reworked.

Similar reflection on the basic features of Venetian architecture, structural analogy with the island's industrial building, and a

reinterpretation of pedestrian systems and public spaces which respected the morphology of the area, was followed by Gino Valle in his starkly simple complex on the Giudecca, built on the site of a cement works (1980–6). The complex is conceived as a sequence of four-storey 'towers' aligned along two canals, a 'carpet' dipping from four to two storeys, and two-storey terrace houses, overlooking the projected course of a new canal.

In the district of the former Saffa company in Cannaregio, Vittorio Gregotti and associates (1981–9) knitted up the previously discontinuous and fraying mesh of what was still an outlying area, between S. Geremia and S. Giobbe, architecturally emphasizing the system of spaces and circuits around the new blocks without seeking any particular sanction. The complex is presented as an example of industrialized building, and references to the structural and organizational practices of the past are kept to a minimum, for instance with the functional retaining of the *altane* (wooden roof platforms), long regarded as characteristic.[24]

The residential complex at Sacca Fisola (Fregnan area, 1982–9; Iginio Cappai, Pietro Mainardis and Valeriano Pastor) is organized around a courtyard space: its facades, with their horizontal bands of white stones, and its long sequence of windows and dormer windows once again refer back to features of bourgeois Venetian building, while the ground-floor 'cavane' (moorings) emphasize the relation between the dwelling and

above
Giuseppe Gambirasio, residential structuring of
the Breweries on the Giudecca, cross section.

below
Gregotti Associati, residential complex in the
Saffa district at S. Giobbe.

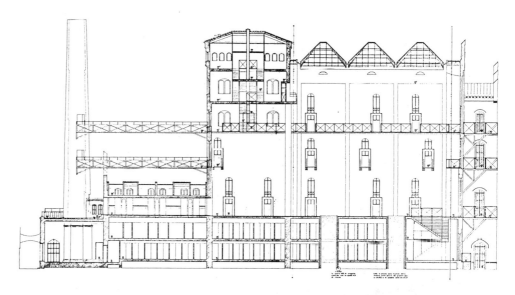

the lagoon, whose waters are brought into
the building *à pilotis*, following any number of long-established models (the layout
of berths in shipyards, the waterside *squeri*
of the Arsenal, and so on). Here again, the
aim was to give a subtly updated and
structurally rigorous variant of Venetian
architectural tradition.

The building complex at Sacca S.
Girolamo (F. Bortoluzzi and Ufficio urban-
istico comunale, municipal town-planning
department, 1987–90), on the other hand,
makes far more explicit play with its sur-
roundings: situated opposite the S. Giobbe
slaughter-house, and hence a crucial presence in the city's image as seen from the
bridge with the mainland, it seems to derive
directly from features of the large popular
fifteenth- to seventeenth-century complex
of the Marinarezza and other traditional
features, with occasional somewhat
'stagy' touches.

From 1980, Wullekopf's Dreher brewery
afforded Giuseppe Gambirasio an opportunity to address the problem of adapting
disused industrial buildings for residential
purposes, investigating the relationship
between architecture and the legacy of
'industrial archaeology', between the
scrupulously restored architectural shell
and the dynamics of internal transformation. Here the interior was, as it were,
redesigned as an exterior, as a central
arcade, street or *calle* roofed with skylights
(partly inspired by undertakings such as
the adaptation of Fondaco dei Tedeschi,
realized from 1938 to 1941) 'overlooked

above
Franco Bortoluzzi and Ufficio urbanistica comunale (municipal town-planning department), residential complex at Sacca S. Girolamo.

right
Valeriano Pastor, study for a residential complex near the 'ice factory' on the Giudecca.

by the new internal facades and galleries leading to accommodation on one or more levels';[25] the observer is informed of the changes in use that have occurred by means of relatively minor indications – the *altane* leading to the arcade, the glass 'lanterns' in the roof, or the 'iron bridges' leading to the emergency staircase.

Nearby, a similar problem was tackled from 1989 onwards by Valeriano Pastor, for the residential building to be incorporated into the remains of the early twentieth-century 'ice-making plant' on the Giudecca, though here the pre-existing structure was in a state of advanced deterioration. In this case, the system of dwellings was accommodated within the original (and technically unusual) surrounding walls, so that the new fabric was layered into what remained of the old, following a layout which echoed the system of *calli* and *rughe* perpendicular to the *fondamenta* which is typical of the area, though the new building fabric – in unfaced brick – is kept formally and technically distinct from the old.[26]

With this series of multifarious experiments, the myths of the origins have been shaken off; the features common to much of the best and most recent architecture therefore seem to lie in their overtly experimental nature, their stated value as built reflections, proposed as model undertakings: that is, as architectural attempts to launch a process of cultural renewal.

1 Archives Historiques de l'Etat Major de l'Armée, Vincennes, Plans et projets, Italie, 1376 (1775–1800).

2 Quoted in G. Romanelli, *Venezia Ottocento*, Rome 1977, p. 55.

3 Archivio patriarcale di Venezia, Archivio segreto, various ff., 1815–16. Note for October 1816.

4 Quoted in *Venezia nell'età di Canova*, exhibition catalogue, Venice 1978, p. 185.

5 A.S.V., Cam. di comm. (chamber of commerce) (1845), tit. IV, b. 162, f. 14.

6 L. Pellegrini, 'L'"Ode su Venezia" di Lord Byron, in *Ateneo Veneto*, vol. 130, 1939; M. Meneghetti, *Lord Byron a Venezia*, Venice 1960.

7 The expression is used by M. Tafuri, in M. Caccari, M. Tafuri and F. Dal Co, 'Il mito di Venezia', in *Rassegna*, 22 June 1985, p. 8.

8 A. Rizzi, *Scultura esterna a Venezia*, Venice 1987, pp. 87–95.

9 G. Fogolari, 'Giorgio Franchetti e la Ca' d'Oro', in *La Regia Galleria Giorgio Franchetti alla Ca' d'Oro*, Venice 1929, pp. 5–45.

10 G. Damerini, 'Gabriele d'Annunzio e Venezia', in *Le Tre Venezie*, vol. 13, no. 4, 1938, pp. 86–99.

11 A. Fradeletto, *Venezia antica e nuova*, Turin 1921, p. 241.

12 'Le nuove costruzioni e la Commissione all'Ornato', in *Rivista Mensile della città di Venezia*, vol. I, 1922, pp. 20–5. For earlier calls to 'debar fakes and copies' see M. Ongaro, *L'architettura moderna a Venezia*, Venice 1912.

13 A. Fradeletto, *Venezia antica, op. cit.*, p. 240.

14 E. Miozzi, 'Come fu progettata e realizzata la nuova comunicazione', in *Rivista di Venezia*, vol. 12, no. 4, 1933, pp. 189–215.

15 O. L. Passarella, 'Il Collegio Navale di Venezia', in *Le Tre Venezie*, vol. 12, no. 12, 1937, pp. 396–9.

16 E. Zorzi, 'Una importante iniziativa veneziana nel campo dell'arredamento: il "Gruppo arti decorative"', in *Le Tre Venezie*, vol. 14, nos. 7–8, 1939, pp. 237–48.

17 G. Samonà, 'I progetti di archittetura per Venezia', in *Progetto Venezia. Ricerche e sperimentazioni sull'area veneziana*, exhibition catalogue, Venice 1980, pp. 145–58.

18 *Ibid.*

19 *Ibid.*

20 *Cassa di Risparmio di Venezia. La nuova sede*, Verona 1975.

21 See note 17.

22 M. Dalla Costa, 'La casa-studio al Lido di Venezia', in *Daniele Calabi. Architetture e progetti, 1932–1964*, exhibition catalogue, Venice 1992, p. 148.

23 C. Aymonino, 'Il "caso" Venezia', *Casabella*, vol. 42, no. 436, 1978, pp. 10–11.

24 F. Sansovino and G. Martinioni, *Venetia, op. cit.*, p. 282.

25 Quoted from the shortened text of the *Relazione al progetto* (project report).

26 See the *Relazione descrittiva* (descriptive report) concerning this project.

left
Iginio Cappai, Pietro Mainardis, Valeriano Pastor, residential complex at Sacca Fisola, general view.

below left
Massimo Scolari, *Wings on the Fondamenta della Tana.* Sculpture for the V Mostra internazionale di architettura – Biennale di Venezia (international architecture exhibition), 1991, now in the Iuav headquarters in the ex-cotton factory at S. Marta.

Select bibliography

GRADO

1957

G. Brusin, 'Aquileia e Grado', in *Storia di Venezia*, vol. II, Venice, pp. 481–594

G. Brusin and P. L. Zovatto, *Monumenti paleocristiani di Aquileia e Grado*, Udine

1971

P. L. Zovatto, *Grado, antichi monumenti*, Bologna

1973

G. Bovini, *Grado paleocristiana*, Bologna

1974–5

M. Mirabella Roberti, 'Il Castrum di Grado', in *Aquileia Nostra*, vols. 45–6

1980

D. Gioseffi, 'I pavimenti musivi del vescovo Elia', in *Grado nella storia e nell'arte*, Udine

G. Marchesan Chinese, 'La basilica di Piazza della Vittoria a Grado' in *Grado nella storia e nell'arte*, Udine

M. Mirabella Roberti, 'Impianto urbano e architettura di Grado Vecchia', in *Grado nella storia e nell'arte*, Udine

M. Pozzetto, 'Ipotesi sui presupposti teorici delle architetture eliane di Grado', in *Grado nella storia e nell'arte*, Udine

HERACLEA

1984

P. L. Tozzi and M. Harari, *Eraclea Veneta. Immagine di una città sepolta*, Parma

MURANO

1861

C. Boito, *Relazione sul progetto di restauro per la basilica de S. Maria e Donato in Murano*, Milan

1903

H. Ratgens, *San Donato zu Murano und Ähnliche Venezianischen Bauten*, Berlin

1980

M. Perry, *La basilica dei Santi Maria e Donato di Murano*, Venice

1981

M. Vecchi, 'Murano: la zona del Battistero', in *Rivista di Archeologia*, vol. 5

TORCELLO

1749

F. Corner, *Ecclesiae Torcellanae*, Venice

1758

F. Corner, *Notizie storiche delle chiese e monasteri di Venezia e di Torcello*, Padua

1927

L. Conton, *Torcello, il suo estuario ed i suoi monumenti*, Venice

1939

G. Fiocco and F. Forlati, *Torcello*, Venice

1979

M. Vecchi, *Torcello. Ricerche e contributi*, Rome

1982

M. Vecchi, *Torcello. Nuove ricerche*, Rome

1984

R. Polacco, *La cattedrale di Torcello*, Treviso

VENICE

1 Urban cartography

1962

La pianta prospettica di Venezia del 1500 disegnata da Jacopo de' Barbari. Illustrata da Giuseppe Mazzariol e da Terisio Pignatti, Venice

1970

J. Schulz, *The Printed Plans and Panoramic Views of Venice (1486–1797)*, Florence

1982

G. Cassini, *Piante e vedute prospettiche di Venezia (1479–1855)*, with an interpretation by Egle R. Trincanato

G. Romanelli and S. Biadene, *Venezia. Piante e vedute. Catalogo del fondo a stampa del Museo Correr*, Venice

1989

Atlante di Venezia. La forma della città in scala 1:1000 nel fotopiano e nella carta numerica, ed. E. Salzano, Venice

1991

P. Falchetta, 'La misura dipinta. Rilettura tecnica e semantica della veduta di Venezia di Jacopo de Barbari', in *Ateneo Veneto*, vol. 188

2 Guides and descriptions of Venice

1565

F. Sansovino, *Delle cose notabili che sono in Venetia*, Venice

1581

F. Sansovino, *Venetia città nobilissima et singolare*, Venice

1587

G. Bardi, *Delle cose notabili della città di Venetia. Libri III*, Venice

1603

L. Goldioni, *Le cose meravigliose e notabili della Città di Venetia*, Venice

1663

F. Sansovino and G. Martinioni, *Venetia città nobilissima et singolare con aggiunta di tutte le cose notabili fatte et occorse dall'anno 1580 al presente 1663*, Venice

1666

N. Doglioni, *Le cose notabili de Venetia*, Venice

1667

V. Coronelli, *Guida de' forestieri sacro-profana*, Venice

1684

D. Martinelli, *Il ritratto di Venezia*, Venice

1745

Il Forestiere illuminato intorno le cose più rare e curiose, antiche e moderne, Venice

1815

G. Moschini, *Guida per la città di Venezia*, Venice

1838

A. Quadri, *Guide de Venise*, Venice

1852

P. Selvatico and V. Lazari, *Guida di Venezia e delle isole circonvicine*, Verona

1856

F. Zanotto, *Nuovissima guida di Venezia e delle isole della sua laguna*, Venice

1881

R. Fulin and P. Molmenti, *Guida artistica e storica di Venezia e delle isole circonvicine*, Venice

1953

M. Muraro, *Nuova guida di Venezia e delle sue isole*, Florence

1968

G. Piamonte, *Venezia vista dall'acqua*, Venice

1973

A. Salvadori, *101 architetture da vendere a Venezia*, Venice

1980

G. Bellavitis, *Itinerari per Venezia*, Rome

M. Sanudo il Giovane, *De origine, situ et magistratibus urbis Venetae ovvero La città di Venetia (1493–1530)*, ed. A. Caracciolo Aricò, Milan

1982

G. Lorenzetti, *Venice and its Lagoon*, tr. John Guthrie, Trieste

1985

M. A. Sabellico, *Del sito di Venezia Città (1502)*, ed. G. Meneghetti, Venice

1993

G. Zucconi, *Venezia. Guida all'architettura*, with an essay by D. Calabi, Venice

3 Building terminology

1988

E. Concina, *Pietre, parole, storia. Glossario della costruzione nelle fonti veneziane. Secoli XV–XVIII*, Venice

4 Historiographical and art-historical problems concerning the origins of the city

1797

G. Filiasi, *Memorie storiche de' Veneti primi e secondi*, Venice

1937

G. Marzemin, *Le origine romane di Venezia*, Venice

1978

S. Bettini, *Venezia, nascita di una città*, Milan

A. Carile and G. Fedalto, *Le origine di Venezia*, Bologna

1983

W. Dorigo, *Venezia Origini. Fondamenti, ipotesi, metodi*, Milan

1987

Da Aquileia a Venezia. Una mediazione tra l'Europa e l'Oriente dal II secolo a.C. al VI secolo d.C., Milan

1988

La 'Venetia' dall'antichità all'alto medioevo, Rome

1994

C. Azzara, *Venetiae. Determinazione di un'area regionale fra antichità e alto Medioevo*, Treviso

W. Dorigo, *Venezie sepolte nella terra del Piave*, Rome

5 Venice: development of the city

1959

S. Muratori, *Studi per una operante storia urbana di Venezia*, Rome

1971

E. Trincanato and U. Franzoi, *Venise au fil du temps*, Paris

1982

E. Concina, *Structure urbaine et fonctions des bâtiments, du XVIe au XIXe siècle. Une recherche à Venise*, Venice

1985

G. Bellavitis and G. D. Romanelli, *Venezia*, Rome and Bari

1988

G. D. Romanelli, *Venezia ottocento. L'architettura, l'urbanistica*, Venice

1989

E. Concina, *Venezia nell'età moderna. Struttura e funzioni*, Venice

1992

E. Crouzet-Pavan, *Espaces, pouvoirs et société à Venise à la fin du Moyen Age*, Rome

6 Works on the history of Venetian architecture

6.1 *General works*

1815–20

L. Cicognara, A. Diedo and G. A. Selva, *Le fabriche più cospicue di Venezia*, Venice

1847

P. Selvatico, *Sulla architettura e scultura in Venezia dal Medioevo sino ai nostri giorni*, Venice

1851–3

J. Ruskin, *The Stones of Venice*, London

1860

O. Mothes, *Geschichte der Baukunst und Bildhauerei Venedigs*, Leipzig

1980

D. Howard, *The Architectural History of Venice*, London

1985

Le Venezie possibile. Da Palladio e Le Corbusier, exhibition catalogue, Milan

6.2 *Medieval architecture*

1965

E. Bassi, 'L'architettura gotica a Venezia', in *Bollettino del C.I.S.A. Andrea Palladio*, vol. 7

1966

S. Bettini, 'L'architettura esarcale', in *Bollettino del C.I.S.A. Andrea Palladio*, vol. 7, no. 2

E. Grube, 'Elementi islamici nell'architettura veneta del medioevo', in *Bollettino del C.I.S.A. Andrea Palladio*, vol. 7, no. 2

G. Lorenzoni, 'L'architettura carolingiana e ottoniana nel Veneto', in *Bollettino del C.I.S.A. Andrea Palladio*, vol. 7, no. 2

1970

E. Arslan, *Venezia gotica. L'architettura civile gotica veneziana*, Venice

1976

W. Wolters, *La scultura veneziana gotica*, Venice

1983

G. Lorenzoni, 'Venezia medievale tra Oriente e Occidente', in *Storia dell'arte italiana*, vol. V, Turin

1985

X. Barral i Altet, *Les Mosaïques de pavement médiévales de Venise, Murano, Torcello*, Paris

1986

G. Lorenzoni, 'Sui problematici rapporti fra l'architettura veneziana e quella islamica', in *Venezia e l'Oriente Vicino*, Venice, pp. 101–10

1987
A. Rizzi, *Scultura esterna a Venezia*, Venice
1988
A. Rizzi, *I portali medievali di Venezia*, Venice
1991
D. Howard, 'Venice and Islam in the Middle Ages. Some observations on the question of architectural influence', in *Architectural History*, vol. 34, pp. 59–72

6.3 The Renaissance, architecture and architects
1778
T. Temanza, *Vite dei più celebri architetti e scultori veneziani che fiorirono nel secolo XVI*, Venice
1893
P. Paoletti, *L'architettura e la scultura del Rinascimento in Venezia*, Venice
1921
L. Serra, *Alessandro Vittoria*, Rome
1954
C. Semenzato, *L'architettura di Baldassare Longhena*, Padua
1960
Michele Sanmichele architetto veronese del Cinquecento, exhibition catalogue ed. P. Gazzola, Venice
1961
L. Angelini, *Bartolomeo Bono e Guglielmo d'Alzano architetti bergamaschi in Venezia*, Bergamo
F. Cessi, *Alessandro Vittoria, architetto e stuccatore*, Trento
1966
G. G. Zorzi, *Le chiese e i ponti di Andrea Palladio*, Vicenza
1969
M. Tafuri, *Jacopo Sansovino e l'architettura del '500 a Venezia*, Padua
1971
L. Puppi, *Michele Sanmicheli, architetto di Verona*, Padua
1972
Andrea Palladio, exhibition catalogue, Venice

1973
Palladio, exhibition catalogue, Milan
1975
D. Howard, *Jacopo Sansovino: Architecture and Patronage in Renaissance Venice*, New Haven and London
L. Puppi, *Andrea Palladio*, London
1977
J. Ackerman, *Palladio*, Harmondsworth
L. Puppi and L. Olivato, *Mauro Codussi e l'architettura veneziana del primo Rinascimento*, Milan
1978
A. K. Placzek, J. S. Ackerman and M. N. Rosenfeld, *Sebastiano Serlio on Domestic Architecture. The Sixteenth-century Manuscript of Book VI in the Avery Library of Columbia University*, Cambridge, Mass. and London
1980
Architettura e utopia nella Venezia del Cinquecento, exhibition catalogue, Milan
J. McAndrew, *Venetian Architecture of the Early Renaissance*, Cambridge, Mass. and London
1981
Palladio e Venezia, ed. L. Puppi, Florence
D. Lewis, 'Patterns of preference: patronage of sixteenth-century architects by the Venetian patriciate', in *Patronage in the Renaissance*, Princeton
1982
R. Lieberman, *Renaissance Architecture in Venice 1450–1550*, London
1983
A. Markham Schulz, *Antonio Rizzo, Sculptor and Architect*, Princeton
A. Markham Schulz, 'Giovanni Buora lapicida', in *Arte Lombarda*, vol. 65
1984
'Renovatio urbis'. Venezia nell'età del Gritti (1523–1538), ed. M. Tafuri, Rome
1986
N. Huse and W. Wolters, *Venezia. L'architettura del Rinascimento*, Venice

1989
M. Tafuri, *Venice and the Renaissance*, Cambridge, Mass. and London
1990
E. Concina, *Navis. L'umanesimo sul mare*, Turin
1993
V. Polli, *Mauro Codussi architetto bergamasco*, by E. Bassi, Bergamo
1994
E. Concina, *Dall'arabico a Venezia tra Rinascimento e Oriente*, Venice

6.4 From the Baroque age to Neoclassicism
1936
E. Bassi, *Giannantonio Selva architetto veneziano*, Padua
1955
E. Kaufmann, 'Piranesi, Algarotti et Lodoli. Une controverse dans la Venise du XVIII siecle', in *Gazette des Beaux-arts*, vol. 2
1962
E. Bassi, *Architettura del Sei e Settecento a Venezia*, Naples
1964
E. Kaufmann, Jr, 'Memmo's Lodoli', in *The Art Bulletin*, vol. 46
1967
D. Lewis, 'Notes on XVIII century Venetian architecture', in *Bollettino dei Musei Civici Veneziani*, vol. 12
1971
A. Massari, *Giorgio Massari architetto veneziano del Settecento*, Venice
1978
Venezia nell'età di Canova, 1780–1830, exhibition catalogue, Venice
G. Cristinelli, *Baldassare Longhena architetto del Seicento a Venezia*, Venice
1980
M. Brusatin, *Venezia del Settecento: stato, architettura, territorio*, Turin
1982
Longhena, exhibition catalogue ed. L. Puppi, Milan

1983
E. Bassi, 'Andrea Musalo', in *Piranesi tra Venezia e l'Europa*, ed. A. Bettagno, Florence
1989
P. Valle, *Tommaso Temanza e l'architettura civile*, Rome

6.5 Architecture in the nineteenth century
1977
G. Romanelli, *Venezia Ottocento. Materiali per una storia architettonica e urbanistica della città nel secolo XIX*, Rome
1983
Venezia nell'Ottocento. Immagini e mito, exhibition catalogue ed. G. Pavanello and G. Romanelli, Venice
R. Hewison, *Ruskin a Venezia*, Venice
1990
Archeologia industriale nel Veneto, ed. F. Mancuso, Milan

6.6 Architectural works, sites and urban structures from the Middle Ages to the nineteenth century

Arsenal:
1829
G. Casoni, *Guida per l'Arsenale di Venezia*, Venice
1868
C. Veludo, *Cenni storici sull'Arsenale di Venezia*, Venice
1877
F. Martini, *Progetti e lavori per riordinamento ed ingrandimento dell'Arsenale marittimo di Venezia*, Venice
1938
M. Nami Mocenigo, *L'Arsenale di Venezia*, Rome
1983
G. Bellavitis, *L'Arsenale di Venezia. Storia di una grande struttura urbana*, Venice
1984
E. Concina, *L'Arsenale della repubblica di Venezia. Tecniche e istituzioni dal medioevo all'età moderna*, Milan

1990
M. Marzari, *Progetti per l'Imperatore. Andrea Salvini ingegnere all'Arsenale. 1802–1817*, exhibition catalogue, Trieste
1991
E. Concina, 'La Casa dell'Arsenale', in *Storia di Venezia*, vol. XII, *Il mare*, ed. A. Tenenti and U. Tucci, Rome

Grand Canal and St Mark's Basin:
1815
A. Quadri and D. Moretti, *Il Canal Grande di Venezia. Rappresentato in tavole rilevate ed incise*, Venice
1932
G. Pavanello, 'La riva degli Schiavoni', in *La riviera di San Marco*, ed. by il Magistrato alle Acque, Venice
1950
L. Candida, *Il porto di Venezia*, with an introduction by G. Luzzatto, Naples
1989
E. Concina, 'Mercanti in crisi e "honor civitatis": struttura e lingua fra l'"arsenatus communis" e il "chanal de San Marcho". 1270–1370', in *Città portuali del Mediterraneo. Storia e archeologia*, ed. E. Poleggi, Genoa
E. Crouzet-Pavan, 'Le Port de Venise au XIVème et XVème siècles: faux-semblants, définitions, mutations', in *Città portuali del Mediterraneo. Storia e archeologia*, ed. E. Poleggi, Genoa
1991
D. Calabi, 'Canali, rive, approdi', in *Storia di Venezia*, vol. XII, *Il mare*, ed. A. Tenenti and U. Tucci, Rome

Houses and minor buildings:
1948
E. Trincanato, *Venezia minore*, Milan
1961
P. Maretto, *L'edilizia gotica veneziana*, Rome

G. Scattolini, *Contributo allo studio dell'architettura civile veneziana dal IX al XIII secolo. Le case-fondaco sul Canal Grande*, Venice
1984
G. Gianighian and P. Pavanini, *Dietro i palazzi. Tre secoli di architettura minore a Venezia. 1492–1803*, exhibition catalogue, Venice
1986
P. Maretto, *La casa veneziana nella storia della città dalle origine all'Ottocento*, Venice
1989
R. J. Goy, *Venetian Vernacular Architecture*, Cambridge
1993
W. Dorigo, *L'edilizia abitativa nella 'Civitas Rivoalti' e nella 'Civitas Veneciarum' (secoli XI–XIII)*, Venice

Churches, convents, monasteries and abbeys:
1749
F. Corner, *Ecclesiae Torcellanae*, Venice
F. Corner, *Ecclesiae Venetae*, Venice
1758
F. Corner, *Chiese e monasteri di Venezia e di Torcello*, Padua
1819–42
G. A. Moschini, *Ragguaglio delle cose notabili nella Chiesa e nel Seminario Patriarcale di S. Maria della Salute*, Venice
1822–3
G. B. Soravia, *Le chiese di Venezia*, Venice
1861
C. Boito, *Relazione sul progetto di restauro per la basilica di S. Maria e Donato in Murano*, Milan
1863
G. J. Fontana, *Venezia monumentale. I templi*, Venice
1888
La basilica di San Marco, ed. C. Boito, Venice
1889
Guida artistica di San Michele in Isola di Venezia, Venice
1890
C. A. Levi, *I campanile di Venezia*, Venice

1911

F. Apollonio, *La chiesa e il convento di Santo Stefano in Venezia*, Venice

1931

G. Fogolari, *I Frari e i Santi Giovanni e Paolo*, Milan

1946

S. Bettini, *L'architettura di S. Marco. Origine e significativo*, Padua

1950

G. Mariacher and T. Pignatti, *La Basilica di San Marco in Venezia*, Florence

1952

M. Brunetti, *Santa Maria del Giglio vulgo Zobenigo nell'arte e nella storia*, Venice

1957

A. Mazzuccato, *La Scuola Grande e la chiesa di San Rocco in Venezia*, Venice

1958

S. Tramontin, G. Scarpa and A. Niero, *L'Isola della Salute*, Venice

1959

S. Tramontin, *Santa Maria dei Miracoli*, Venice

1960

O. Demus, *The Church of San Marco in Venice*, Washington

1961

S. Tramontin, *S. Stae. La chiesa e la parrochia*, Venice

1962

S. Tramontin, *S. Maria Mater Domini*, Venice

R. Wittkower, 'Le chiese di Andrea Palladio e l'architettura barocca veneziana', in *Barocco europeo e barocco veneziano*, ed. V. Branca, Venice

1963

A. Alberti, *La chiesa di S. Maria del Riposo in Barbaria delle tole, a Venezia*, Venice

R. Wittkower, 'S. Maria della Salute', in *Saggi e Memorie di Storia dell'Arte*

1965

A. Niero, *La chiesa dei Carmini*, Venice

F. Zava Boccazzi, *La Basilica dei Santi Giovanni e Paolo*, Venice

1968

Ch. A. Isermeyr, 'Le chiese del Palladio in rapporto al culto', in *Bollettino del C.I.S.A. Andrea Palladio*

W. Timofiewitsch, *Die sakrale Architektur des Palladios*, Munich

1969

G. Damerini, *L'isola e il cenobio di San Giorgio Maggiore*, Florence

W. Timofiewitsch, *La chiesa del Redentore. Corpus palladianum. III*, Venice

1970

H. Dellwing, *Studien zur Baukunst der Bettelorden im Veneto*, Munich

A. Niero, 'Un progetto sconosciuto per la basilica della Salute e questioni iconografiche', in *Arte Veneta*

1971

A. Niero, *Chiesa di S. Maria della Salute*, Venice

W. Timofiewitsch, *The Chiesa del Redentore*, London

1972

M. Gemin, *La chiesa di Santa Maria della Salute e la Cabala di Paolo Sarpi*, Abano Terme

R. E. Lieberman, *The Church of Santa Maria dei Miracoli in Venice*, Ann Arbor, Mich.

1973

M. Muraro, 'Il tempio votivo di Santa Maria della Salute in un poema del Seicento', in *Ateneo Veneto*, vol. 11

1974

H. Dellwing, 'Die Kirche S. Zaccaria in Venedig. Eine ikonologische Studie', in *Zeitschrift für Kunstgeschichte*, vol. 37

1976

U. Franzoi and D. Di Stefano, *Le chiese di Venezia*, Venice

1977

J. S. Ackerman, 'Palladio e lo sviluppo della concezione delle chiese a Venezia', in *Bollettino del C.I.S.A. Andrea Palladio*

A. Clarke and Ph. Rylands, *The Church of the Madonna dell'Orto in Venice*, London

D. Howard, 'Le chiese di Jacopo Sansovino a Venezia', in *Bollettino del C.I.S.A. Andrea Palladio*

1978

A. Niero, *La chiesa di Santo Stefano in Venezia*, Venice

1979

D. Lewis, *The Late Baroque Churches of Venice*, New York and London

S. Tramontin, *San Zaccaria*, Venice

1980

A. Foscari, 'Accordo per la facciata della chiesa di San Pietro di Castello in Venezia', in *Ateneo Veneto*

Ch. A. Isermeyr, 'Il primo progetto del Palladio per S. Giorgio secondo il modello del 1565', in *Bollettino del C.I.S.A. Andrea Palladio*

W. Timofiewitsch, 'Delle chiese palladiane: alcune osservazioni in rapporto alle facciate', in *Bollettino del C.I.S.A. Andrea Palladio*

1981

F. W. Deichmann, *Corpus der Kapitellen der Kirche von San Marco zu Venedig*, Wiesbaden

1983

M. Dalla Costa, *La Basilica di San Marco e i restauri dell'Ottocento*, Venice

A. Foscari and M. Tafuri, *L'armonia e i conflitti. La chiesa di San Francesco della Vigna nella Venezia del '500*, Turin

1985

L. Moretti, *La chiesa della Madonna dell'Orto in Venezia*, Venice

G. M. Pilo, *La chiesa dello 'Spedaletto' in Venezia*, Venice

1986

R. Canova dal Zio, *Le chiese delle Tre Venezie anteriori al Mille*, Padua

B. Jestaz, *La Chapelle Zen à Saint-Marc de Venise. D'Antonio à Tullio Lombardo*, Stuttgart

1987

R. Polacco, 'Le colonne del ciborio di San Marco', in *Venezia Arti*

1988

W. Dorigo, 'Una nuova lettura delle sculture del portale centrale di San Marco', in *Venezia Arti*

E. Concina, 'Una fabbrica "in mezzo della città": la chiesa e il convento di San Salvador', in *Progetto San Salvador*, Venice, pp. 72–153

1989

R. Pellegriti, 'La chiesa dell'ospedale di San Lazzaro dei Mendicanti', in *Arte Veneta*

1990

AA. VV., *San Marco*, Milan

A. Niero, *La chiesa di San Giacomo dall'Orio*, Venice

J. Warren, 'The first church of San Marco in Venice', in *The Antiquaries Journal*, vol. 73

1991

R. Polacco, *San Marco. La basilica d'oro*, with contributions by G. Rossi Scarpa and J. Scarpa, Modena

G. Suitner, *Le Venezie*, vol. XII of *Italia Romanica*, Milan

1992

Basilica patriarcale in Venezia. San Marco. La cripta. La storia, la conservazione, Milan

I. Gatti, *S. Maria Gloriosa dei Frari. Storia di una presenza francescana a Venezia*, Venice

G. Goebel-Schilling, 'L'idea originaria e le proporzioni della chiesa di Santa Maria della Salute', in *Eidos*, vol. 10

1993

La basilica di San Marco. Arte e simbologia, ed. B. Bertoli, Venice

1994

M. De Min, 'Lo scavo archeologico nella chiesa di S. Lorenzo di Castello a Venezia', in *Studi di archeologia della X Regio in ricordo di Michele Tombolani*, ed. B. M. Scarfi, Rome

L. Salerni, *Repertorio delle opere d'arte e dell'arredo delle chiese e delle scuole di Venezia*, vol. I, *Dorsoduro. Giudecca. Santa Croce*, Vicenza

1995

Le scultore esterne di San Marco, Milan

Fondaci:

1860

A. Sagredo and F. Berchet, *Il Fondaco dei Turchi in Venezia*, Venice

1887

H. Simonsfeld, *Der Fondaco dei Tedeschi in Venedig*, Stuttgart

1941

M. Brunetti and M. Dazzi, *Il Fondaco nostro dei Tedeschi*, Venice

1991

D. Calabi, 'Magazzini, fondaci, dogane', in *Storia di Venezia*, vol. XII, *Il mare*, ed. A. Tenenti and U. Tucci, Rome

Fortresses and military architecture:

1906

G. Rusconi, 'Il Castello di S. Andrea del Lido', in *Nuovo Archivio Veneto*, vol. 12, no. 1

1978

P. Marchesi, *Il Forte di Sant'Andrea a Venezia*, Rome

1983

E. Concina, *La macchina territoriale. La progettazione della difesa nel '500 veneto*, Rome and Bari

1984

P. Marchesi, *Fortezze veneziane. 1508–1797*, Milan

1988

A. Morsiani, 'Le fortificazioni ottocentesche della piazzaforte marittima di Venezia', in *Castellum*

1991

P. Morachiello, 'Fortezze e lidi', in *Storia di Venezia*, vol. XII, *Il mare*, ed. A. Tenenti and U. Tucci, Rome

The Ghetto and synagogue architecture:

1964

R. Wischnitzer, *The Architecture of the European Synagogue*, Philadelphia

1978

D. Cassuto, *Ricerche sulle cinque sinagoghe (scuole) di Venezia*, Jerusalem

1985

C. H. Kinsky, *Synagogues of Europe: Architecture, History, Meaning*, New York

1987

U. Fortis, *Il Ghetto sulla laguna*, Venice

1991

E. Concina, D. Calabi and U. Camerino, *La città degli Ebrei. Il Ghetto di Venezia: architettura e urbanistica*, Venice

Hospitals and hospices:

1983

F. Semi, *Gli ospizi a Venezia*, Venice

1985

La memoria della salute. Venezia e il suo ospedale dal XVI al XX secolo, exhibition catalogue ed. N. E. Vanzan Marchini, Venice

1989

B. Aikema and D. Meijers, *Nel regno dei poveri. Arte e storia dei grandi ospedali in età moderna. 1474–1797*, Venice

Palazzi and public buildings:

1853

F. Zanotto, *Il Palazzo Ducale di Venezia*, Venice

1865

G. J. Fontana, *Venezia Monumentale. I Palazzi*, Venice

1868

G. B. Lorenzi, *Monumenti per servire alla storia del Palazzo Ducale di Venezia*, Venice

1879

G. Tassini, *Alcuni palazzi ed antichi edifici di Venezia storicamente illustrati*, Venice

1886

G. Boni, 'La Ca' d'Oro e le sue decorazioni policrome', in *Archivio Veneto*, vol. 31

B. Cecchetti, 'La facciate della Ca' d'Oro dello scalpello di Giovanni e Bartolomeo Buono', in *Archivio Veneto*, vol. 31

1906

L. Beltrami, *La Ca' del Duca sul Canal Grande ed altre reminiscenze sforzesche in Venezia*, Milan

1920
P. Paoletti, 'La Ca' d'Oro', in *Venezia. Studi di Arte e di Storia*, vol. 1
1936
G. Lorenzetti, *Ca' Rezzonico*, Venice
1950
G. Marachier, Il Palazzo Ducale di Venezia, Florence
1960
E. Bassi and E. R. Trincanato, *Il Palazzo Ducale nella storia e nell'arte di Venezia*, Milan
1965
G. Marachier, *Palazzo Vendramin Calergi*, Venice
1976
E. Bassi, *Palazzi di Venezia. Admiranda Urbis Venetae*, Venice
U. Franzoi, *Il Palazzo Ducale di Venezia*, Venice
D. Pincus, *The Arco Foscari. The Building of a Triumphal Gateway in Fifteenth Century Venice*, New York and London
1978
P. Lauritzen and A. Zielcke, *Palaces of Venice*, London
1982
F. Pedrocco, T. Pignatti and E. Martineli-Pedrocco, *Palazzo Labia a Venezia*, Venice
1983
P. C. Hamilton, 'The Palazzo dei Camerlenghi in Venice', in *Journal of the Society of Architectural Historians*, vol. 42
1984
V. Sgarbi, *Mito e storia di Giovanni Dario e del suo palazzo tra Oriente e Venezia*, Milan
1985
Palazzo Loredan e l'Istituto veneto di Scienze, Lettere ed Arti, Venice
1986
G. Romanelli and G. Pavanello, *Palazzo Grassi. Storia, architettura, decorazione dell'ultimo palazzo veneziano*, Venice
1987
M. Tarufi, 'Aggiunte al progetto sansoviniano per il palazzo di Vettor Grimani', in *Arte Veneta*, vol. 41

1990
U. Franzoi, T. Pignatti and W. Wolters, *Il Palazzo Ducale di Venezia*, Treviso
M. Gemin F. and Perocco R., *Ca' Vendramin Calergi*, Milan
1992
A. Manno, 'Pietre filosofali. I capitelli del Palazzo Ducale di Venezia: catalogo delle iscrizioni', in *Studi Veneziani*, n.s., vol. 23
1993
J. Schulz, 'The houses of the Dandolo: a family compound in medieval Venice', in *Journal of the Society of Architectural Historians*, vol. 51/4
R. J. Goy, *The House of Gold: the Contarini and the Ca' d'Oro, Building a Palace in Medieval Venice (1420–1440)*, Cambridge
G. A. Popescu and S. Zoppi, *Palazzo Papadopoli a Venezia*, Milan
G. D. Romanelli, *Ca' Corner della Ca' Granda: architettura e committenza nella Venezia del Cinquecento*, Venice
J. Schulz, 'The houses of the Dandolo: a family compound in medieval Venice', in *Journal of the Society of Architectural Historians*, vol. 52/4

Piazza San Marco:
1970
Piazza San Marco. L'architettura, la storia, le funzioni, Padua
1991
M. Agazzi, 'Platea Sancti Marci': i luoghi marciani dall'XI al XIII secolo, Venice
1992
Il Campanile di San Marco. Il crollo i la ricostruzione, exhibition catalogue, Milan
1992–3
J. Schulz, 'La piazza medievale di San Marco', in *Annali di Architettura*, vol. 4–5
1993
D. Howard, 'Ritual space in Renaissance Venice', in *Scroope. Cambridge Architecture Journal*

Rialto:
1934
R. Cessi and A. Alberti, *Rialto. L'isola, il ponte, il mercato*, Bologna
1987
D. Calabi and P. Morachiello, *Rialto. Le fabbriche e il ponte. 1514–1591*, Turin

Scuole:
1929
P. Paoletti, *La Scuola Grande di San Marco*, Venice
1978
PF. L. Sohm, 'The staircases of the Venetian Scuole Grande and Mauro Coducci', in *Architectura*, vol. 8, pp. 125–49
1981
Le Scuole di Venezia, ed. T. Pignatti, Milan
1985
U. Willmes, *Studien zur Scuola di San Rocco in Venedig*, Munich

Theatres:
1974
T. Mangini, *I teatri di Venezia*, Milan
1987
M. Brusatin and G. Pavanello, *Il Teatro La Fenice. I progetti, l'architettura, le decorazioni*, Venice

6.7 Contemporary architecture and projects in Venice
1899
C. Emo, *L'edilizia veneziana*, Venice
1912
M. Ongaro, *L'architettura moderna a Venezia*, Venice
1913
G. Sichea, *Ville del Lido a Venezia. Tracciato, particolari, sezioni, piante*, Turin
1921
A. Fradeletto, *Venezia antica e nuova*, Turin
1922
P. Donatelli, 'Le case popolari e la "Domus Civica"', in *Rivista Mensile della Città di Venezia*, vol. 1

D. Torres, 'Le nuove costruzioni e la Commissione all'ornato', in *Rivista Mensile della Città di Venezia*, vol. 1

1925

D. Torres, 'Urbanismo veneziano', in *Rivista Mensile della Città di Venezia*, vol. 3

G. Torres, 'Il nuovo tempio votivo del Lido', in *Rivista Mensile della Città di Venezia*, vol. 3

1928

P. Donatelli, *La casa a Venezia nell'opera del suo Istituto. Relazione*, Rome

A. Maraini, 'L'architettura e le arti decorative alla XVI Biennale veneziana', in *Architettura e Arti Decorative*, vol. 2, no. 2

1929

V. Ruffini, 'Venezia Porto Aereo', in *Rivista Mensile della Città di Venezia*, vol. 8

1931

E. Motta, 'I lavori del ponte in laguna e del Rio Nuovo in città', in *Rivista di Venezia*, vol. 10, no. 12

1932

'Lo sviluppo delle grandi opere in corso per l'avvenire di Venezia', in *Rivista di Venezia*, vol. 11, no. 2

1933

'I progetti per il nuovo ponte dell'Accademia', in *Rivista di Venezia*, vol. 12, no. 5

'La sistemazione della Riviera di San Marco', in *Rivista di Venezia*, vol. 12, no. 5

G. Damerini, 'Il Ponte del Littorio, salvaguardia dell'antica necessità della nuova Venezia', in *Rivista di Venezia*, vol. 12, no. 5

E. Miozzi, 'Come fu progettata e realizzata la nuova comunicazione', in *Rivista di Venezia*, vol. 12, no. 5

E. Miozzi, *Il ponte del Littorio*, Venice

1934

'L'opera del Comune nell'anno XII per rinnovamento e l'incremento di Venezia', in *Rivista di Venezia*, vol. 13, no. 10

U. Nebbia, 'Autorimessa a Venezia', in *Casabella*, vol. 83

1935

'Autorimessa a Venezia', in *Architettura*, no. 1

'La nuova stazione passeggeri dell'Aeroporto di Lido', in *Rivista di Venezia*, vol. 14, nos. 1–2

E. Miozzi, *Il nuovo Casino di Venezia*, Milan

1937

U. Dal Missier, 'Ripristino della "Torre della Campanella" nell'Arsenale di Venezia', in *Le Tre Venezie*, vol. 12, no. 6

E. Miozzi, *Dal ponte di Rialto al nuovo ponte degli Scalzi*, Rome

O. Passarella, 'La Riva dell'Impero', in *Le Tre Venezie*, vol. 12, no. 3–4

O. Passarella, 'Il Collegio Navale di Venezia', in *Le Tre Venezie*, vol. 12, no. 12

1939

'Mosaici di Guido Cadorin nel nuovo cinema San Marco', in *Le Tre Venezie*, vol. 14, nos. 11–12

'Il progetto di trasformazione dell'isola di S. Giorgio in un centro di vita artistica e teatrale', in *Le Tre Venezie*, vol. 14, nos. 7–8

E. Zorzi, 'Una importante iniziativa veneziana nel campo dell'arredamento: il "Gruppo arti decorative"', in *Le Tre Venezie*, vol. 14, nos. 7–8

1958

'Una casa riflessa dalla laguna veneziana', in *L'Architettura, Cronache e Storia*, vol. 37

G. Samonà, 'Una casa di Gardella a Venezia', in *Casabella continuità*, no. 220

1959

G. C. Argan, *Ignazio Gardella*, Milan

C. L. Ragghianti, 'La "crosera de piazza" di Carlo Scarpa', in *Zodiac*, vol. 4

1960

V. Gregotti, 'La nuova sede dell'Inail a Venezia di Giuseppe Samonà', in *Casabella continuità*, no. 244

1964

G. Mazzarariol, 'Un'opera di Carlo Scarpa: il riordino di un antico palazzo veneziano', in *Zodiac*

1969

P. Maretto, *Venezia. Architettura del XX secolo in Italia*, Genoa

1971

G. Mazziol, 'Le Corbusier e Venezia', in *Il fenomeno città nella vita e nella cultura d'oggi*, Florence

1972

G. D. Romanelli, 'Architetti e architetture a Venezia tra Otto e Novecento', in *Antichità Viva*, no. 5

1978

'Venezia: dibattito per una città', in *Casabella*, vol. 42, no. 436

1979

C. Magnani and P. A. Val, 'Vedere piccolo', in *Rassegna*, vol. 50

1980

10 immagini per Venezia, exhibition catalogue ed. F. Dal Co, Venice

Progetto Venezia. Ricerche e sperimentazioni sull'area veneziana, exhibition catalogue ed. G. Fabbri, Venice

1981

V. Gregotti, 'Megasegno in lagona', in *Domus*, no. 617

L. Semerani, 'La chiara formulazione: l'ospedale di Venezia', in *Gran Bazaar*, vol. 13

1983

Edilizia popolare a Venezia. Storia, politiche, realizzazioni dell'istituto Autonomo per le Case Popolari della Provincia di Venezia, ed. E. Barbiani, Milan

Venezia nuova. La politica della casa, 1893–1941, Venice

1984

'Una ristrutturazione a Venezia. I materiali del progetto', in *Casabella*, no. 503

F. Dal Co and G. Mazzariol, *Carlo Scarpa. 1906–1978*, Milan

1985

Progetto Arsenale. Studi e ricerche per l'Arsenale di Venezia, exhibition catalogue ed. P. Gennaro and G. Testi, Venice

'La riorganizzazione degli spazi', in *La memoria della salute. Venezia e il suo ospedale dal XVI al XX secolo*, exhibition catalogue ed. N. E. Vanzan Marchini, Venice

'Venezia città del moderno', in *Rassegna*, no. 22, special issue ed. C. Magnani and P. C. Val

C. Magnani, 'Il concorso dello IACP di Venezia per Campo di Marte alla Giudecca', in *Casabella*, no. 518

1986

Venice for Modern Man, Rome

Venezia restaurata, Milan

P. A. Croset, 'Un immenso appartamento collettivo', in *Casabella*, no. 528

P. A. Croset, 'Sul progetto di Valle alla Giudecca', in *Lotus International*, no. 51

M. De Michelis, 'Nuovi progetti alla Giudecca. Tipi, edificazione e morfologia dell'isola', in *Lotus International*, no. 51

1987

F. Irace, 'Nuovi quartieri in laguna', in *Abitare*, vol. 260

1988

M. Mulazzani, *I padglioni della Biennale. Venezia 1887–1988*, Milan

G. Pertot, *Venezia 'restaurata'. Centosettanta anni di interventi di restauro sugli edifici veneziani*, Milan

1989

E. Ranzani, 'Gregotti Associati. Quartiere residenziale area ex Saffa', in *Domus*, no. 704

1991

S. Polano, *Guida all'architettura italiana del Novecento*, Milan

1992

Daniele Calabi. Architetture e progetti, 1932–1964, exhibition catalogue, Venice

Ignazio Gardella. Progetti e architetture. 1933–1990, exhibition catalogue ed. F. Buzzi Ceriani, Venice

1993

Costruire a Venezia. Trent'anni di edilizia residenziale pubblica, Venice

1994

F. Tentori, *Imparare da Venezia. Il ruolo futuribile di alcuni progetti architettonici veneziani dei primi anni '60*, Rome

7 Venetian settlements in the Mediterranean

1925

M. Roberti, 'Ricerche intorno alla colonia veneziana in Costantinopoli nel sec. XI', in *Scritti storici in onore di Camillo Manfroni*, Padua

1973

J. Prawer, 'I Veneziani e le colonie veneziane nel Regno latino di Gerusalemme', in *Venezia e il Levante fino al secolo XV*, ed. A. Pertusi, vol. I, Florence

1988

E. Concina, 'Il quartiere veneziano di S. Giovanni d'Acri (1110–1291)', in *L'Italia e i paesi mediterranei*, Pisa

8 Venice and antiquarian culture

1900

C. A. Levi, *Le collezioni veneziane d'arte e d'antichità dal XIV secolo ai nostri giorni*, Venice

1926–7

P. Paschini, 'Le collezioni archeologiche dei prelati Grimani del Cinquecento', in *Rendiconti della Pontificia Accademia Romana di Archeologia*, vol. 5

1976

G. Billanovich, 'Tradizione classica e cristiana e scienza antiquaria', in *Storia della cultura veneta*, vol. I, Vicenza

1977

M. Perry, 'Saint Mark's trophies: legend, superstition and archaeology in Renaissance Venice', in *Journal of the Warburg and Courtauld Institutes*, vol. 40

1978

S. Will, *The Sculpture of Tullio Lombardo. Studies in Sources and Meaning*, New York and London

1979

D. Pincus, 'Tullio Lombardo as restorer of Antiquities: an aspect of fifteenth-century Venetian antiquarianism', in *Arte Veneta*, vol. 33

1990

I. Favaretto, *Arte antica e cultura antiquaria nelle collezioni venete al tempo della Serenissima*, Rome

1991

A. Sacconi, *L'avventura archeologica di Francesco Morosini ad Atene (1687–1688)*, Rome.

Index of names

Index of places and works